P

MW01076584

"No group of Americans has had such an important impact on our nation's development as Catholic nuns. The story of *Sisters* is the history of the development of the poor and immigrant in America and how they are able to survive. *Sisters* tells this history as well as any book I have ever read."
—Raymond L. Flynn, former U.S. ambassador to the Vatican and former mayor of Boston

"Like John Fialka, I owe an unpayable dept to the Catholic nuns who helped raise and educate us half a century ago. One cannot read *Sisters* without recalling the memories of those years and those wonderful, godly, and irreplaceable women."
.   —Pat Buchanan, syndicated columnist, television commentator, and former presidential candidate

"This fascinating study provides an overview of the enormous contribution Catholic nuns have made to the American educational, social, and cultural landscape."
—*Booklist*

"Fialka skillfully and entertainingly balances historical fact with journalistic prose in narrating these dramatic accounts of individual heroines and communities."
—*Library Journal*

"Fialka sprinkles his account with personal recollections and writes sympathetically of a group that has often been maligned and caricatured. Nuns will appreciate his treatment of their lives, as will Catholics pondering a church with diminishing numbers of the women who helped shape it."
—*Publishers Weekly*

"The stories Fialka tells of these strong and faith-filled women religious are engaging, told in a popular style that holds the attention of the reader.... As a journalist, Fialka knows how to tell a story well and these stories of fearless, dedicated, and spirited women, the heart of the book, provide the reader with interesting insights and details about the impact they have had on American culture."
—*National Catholic Reporter*

"Much of the book is a wonderful exercise in nostalgia; some of the stories brought tears to my eyes."
—Sister Mary Ann Cunningham, *Conscience*

ALSO BY JOHN J. FIALKA

Hotel Warriors: Covering the Gulf War

War by Other Means: Economic Espionage in America

SISTERS

Catholic Nuns and the Making of America

JOHN J. FIALKA

 ST. MARTIN'S GRIFFIN NEW YORK

www.stmartins.com

Title-page-spread photo courtesy of the Archives of the
Daughters of Charity, Emmitsburg, Maryland

Library of Congress Cataloging-in-Publication Data

Fialka, John J.
  Sisters : Catholic nuns and the making of America / John
J. Fialka.—1st. ed.
    p. cm.
  Includes bibliographical references (page 337) and index
(page 355).
  ISBN 13: 978-0-312-32596-1
  ISBN 10: 0-312-32596-7
  1. Nuns—United States—History. 2. Monasticism and reli-
gious orders for women—United States—History. 3. Monas-
tic and religious life of women—United States—History. 4.
Catholic Church—United States—History. 5. United
States—Church history. I. Title.

BX4220.U6 F53 2003
271'.90073—dc21   2002028137

P1

To Mildred Lense

(whom we knew as Sister Mary Winifred,

a high-school English teacher)

They seemed to us mere words on pages.

You helped us find the fun and hear their music.

CONTENTS

ACKNOWLEDGMENTS

I began thinking about the ingredients for this book eight years ago, started by what seemed to be a simple question from a colleague at the Washington bureau of the *Wall Street Journal,* Barbara Rosewicz. I had written an article about what was then a $2 billion shortfall in efforts to provide pension funds for Catholic sisters. My phone rang for weeks with people offering help: "Where do I send the check?"

It was a hard question. Catholic bishops, who were in many cases the sisters' employers, were then resisting the idea of taking up a new collection for the sisters' retirement needs. Barbara's question proved to be harder: Where have all the sisters gone? We both grew up in an age where Catholic hospitals and parochial schools were filled with nuns.

Histories of the Catholic Church were not much help. They seemed to have a common void about the activities of religious women. Catholic colleagues of mine often answered with a shrug. Then Frank Butler, a friend and founder of FADICA, a Washington-based group that represents Catholic donors and foundations, pointed me to the headquarters of the Sisters of Mercy, where the then-head of the order, Sister Doris Gottmoeller, had the patience to endure a great many questions.

I owe much to the order's archivists, Molly McMahon and Sister Paula Diann Marlin (cq), and to the archivists of other orders described in this book. They helped me dig through piles of books and pictures. Sisters Amy Hoey and Mary Ann Walsh were also helpful in guiding me through the rich history of the Sisters of Mercy. When my interest flagged, there was my agent, Ron Goldfarb, a supporter of Jewish causes in Washington, steadily prodding this cause on. The lives of these women told a good story, he said. It wasn't just a story for Catholics. If I wrote it, he and his hardworking assistant, Robbie Anna Hare, would sell it. My thanks to my editors at St. Martin's Press, particularly Michael Denneny and Diane Higgins, for their enthusiasm and good suggestions that shaped and enlarged *Sisters*. I'm also grateful to Nichole Argyres, who spent long hours at St. Martin's making sure the pieces fit together.

I thought I knew what the story was, but when I went to interview the first of my chosen "characters," Sister Mary Roberta, once the principal of my high school, I soon came to realize that, like many of her students, I really didn't know much about her life. We were too busy getting her to help with ours. My debt to her, to Sister Doris, to Sisters Sharon Burns, Mary Scullion, and the other religious women who opened a window to let an outsider peer into their world, is enormous.

PROLOGUE

A dusty Chevrolet pulls up in front of a diner in a one-stoplight town. A somber-looking family gets out to stretch after the long drive from the family farm. There is an obvious tension among them, and to break it, Lucille Frances Lyness, a seventeen-year-old with dark hair and bright, inquisitive eyes, rushes in and pours some nickels into the jukebox. As it starts to play some tinny-sounding waltzes, she reaches for her older brother Donald. They slowly circle the floor. The mood continues as another brother, her mother, and father look on glumly. Her father, Arthur Lyness, a big, well-muscled man, can barely conceal the ache of what is about to happen. This is his only surviving daughter and she has been the light of his life. This is her last dance. They are on the way to the convent where she will dedicate her life to serving God with the Sisters of Mercy. He knows he will rarely see her after she exchanges her dress for the order's voluminous black habit, for the order's visitation rules are very strict. So this is good-bye, but bringing himself to admit it is perhaps the hardest thing he has done in his whole life.

And Lyness thought he was used to hard times. An intellectually gifted man, he was taken from school in third grade because his immigrant family was desperately poor and needed an extra hand on the farm. He had raised five children in the Depression. Nothing seemed to shake his faith in himself or his faith in a just God, even after his first child, Mary, died in a senseless auto accident at the age of eight. In Lucille, he felt, the Lord had sent him a replacement. He had built a prosperous farm, toughing out the lean years and figuring out how to get the best market prices for his crops in the summers when you could almost hear the corn growing in the humid, flatland heat. His crops always filled him with a sense of wonder. To him they were beautiful because, no matter what he did, the results were always somewhat beyond his control. So he would take what came and work with it. "He'd say this is God's vineyard," Lucille would later recall. "The Lord would provide. His attitude was that it was an honor to be a farmer. Later I picked that up. If he felt that about farming, that's the way I would feel about being a teacher."

Arthur Lyness's currency was love, not money. When money was tight, as it often was, he always found enough to scatter good books and magazines about the house, which Lucille devoured. His four boys would sometimes be heard to complain that they knew more about the neighbor's chores than his own. He helped build the church in his farming community, Ryan, Iowa, which was not that unusual.

The American Catholic Church was built largely through the money and sweat—mostly sweat—of working-class immigrants. But now Lyness was steeling himself to make what might be considered the ultimate gift— his daughter. Daughters nurtured the Church's growth in America. As teachers and nurses, they asked little and gave all, adhering to strict codes of poverty, chastity and obedience.

In the Irish-German community around Ryan, both Protestants and Catholics knew this and respected the nuns. Yet when one of the community's girls left for the convent, there was always this funereal ritual to endure. A man might go, but a woman's place was in the home having children. Arthur felt that, too, but when Lucille told him she would be a nun, they had worked it out. She must take a year of college first. If afterward she still felt that way, he would not stand in her way.

On the evening before the trip to Cedar Rapids, Arthur had taken his daughter around to the homes of his sisters and brothers for a round of good-byes. One of his sisters doubted how Lucille—a free spirit who had boyfriends, raced horses and loved barn dances—could possibly endure the drab life of the convent. A brother took aside Arthur to mutter: "How can you do this? I have seven girls and not one of them talks about being religious."

Arthur shrugged. "It's the work of God."

"You're just going to let her go?"

Arthur shrugged again. "God took the other one without asking me."

That night Lucille was packing her trunk upstairs when she heard the still-soft voice of her fifteen-year-old brother, Pat, confiding to their mother: "We'll all have to be real brave tomorrow, won't we?"

They tried. After the waltz and lunch, they climb back into the Chevrolet and drive to Mount Mercy College, a barnlike brick building situated on a hill in nearby Cedar Rapids, the county seat. As the family waits stiffly amid the dark, Victorian furniture in the convent's parlor, inside a transformation occurs. Lucille puts on a black dress and conceals her long hair with the black lace cap of the postulant, or beginner in the order. She goes to a chapel and reads a short prayer, promising to devote her life to God. When she returns to the parlor, the stiffness intensifies. The brothers sense that, somehow, she was no longer just their sister. "We visited for a while and then they went home," she later recalled. "Everybody was trying to keep the emotions down."

If this seems like a strange event, consider the fact that there have been at least four hundred thousand variations on this scene in the history of Catholic sisters in America. Lucille emerged with a new name, Sister Mary Roberta, and a larger family: the sisters who taught children and ran hospitals in Eastern Iowa. Arthur Lyness died quietly in 1961. He was sitting against a fence post, admiring a field of ripening corn. There were twenty sisters at his funeral.

As for his daughter, she taught for fifty-one years and has spent thirteen more helping the poor, the uneducated, the lonely and the sick. Shortly before she died, on December 4, 2002, she said she could not imagine a happier life.

SISTERS

I

SPIRITED WOMEN

ost of the histories of the Catholic Church in America have been written about men—the priests, bishops and cardinals credited with building the nation's largest church. But the reality was that if you were educated in a parochial school, nursed in a Catholic hospital or had other contact with a church institution, the face of the church you saw most often was a woman's. For every priest there were at least three sisters.

Their contributions to American culture are not small. They built the nation's largest private school and nonprofit hospital systems. They were the nation's first large network of female professionals in an age when the pervading sentiment was that a woman's place was in the home. They were America's first feminists, battling for the rights and opinions of women in a workplace where bishops sometimes regarded nuns as their subjects or, worse, part of their "turf." "They [nuns] were the Catholic serfs," writes Jay P. Dolan in his book *The American Catholic Experience.* "Obviously, all bishops and pastors did not act in this manner, but those that did were so numerous that this aspect of American Catholic history would constitute a book in itself," says Dolan.

Such a book would have to begin by describing a peculiarly American phenomenon: Long after 1790, when Catholic sisters began arriving here with their boxes of books and bolts of sturdy dark cloth, entering the convent gave a young woman a ticket for some of life's grand adventures. That may not square with the pious, submissive image of the nun in classic literature, but that image comes from Europe, where sisters were usually secluded in convents or monasteries. Those who worked outside the convent often settled into a life of unvaried routine. Orphanages, schools and hospitals were already there, facts on the ground, some even predating the Middle Ages.

America was very different. The nation's rapid economic growth and unprecedented religious freedom created a rough, sprawling void. It had few charitable institutions in settled areas. On the fast-moving frontier that beckoned beyond the Appalachians, there were often none. There were forests to cut, farms to plow, cities to build, mines to dig, rivers to explore. Though hospitals and schools are part of the glue that holds together communities, men often had little time and no money to build them. As for women, their place on this vast stage was supposed to be home, preparing meals, tidying up the house, raising children.

But there were exceptions. For some young, spirited women, like Lucille Lyness, the convent offered another pathway. As Catholics put it, they felt "the call" to serve God. For them, God's love and service to others became the centerpiece of their lives. Opting for convent life also offered some substantial side benefits. It was often the only way to a decent education for a woman.

Becoming a Catholic sister offered the curious a way out of a stifling, small community and a ticket to see the larger country, especially frontiers and other places where few women, aside from prostitutes, dared go alone. The nun's habit—then not too dissimilar from what ladies wore on the street in the early nineteenth century—was seen as a kind of badge, a license to do good works, and it was usually respected and welcomed. Ambitious women who had the skills and the stamina to build and run large institutions found the convent to be the first and, for a long time, the only outlet for their talents.

Vowing to live a life of celibacy, agreeing to obey male superiors and living on a few dollars a month might seem hopelessly anachronistic to many modern women—to some, downright un-American. But the vows created strong, disciplined, selfless organizations that adapted very well to the rigors of America.

Eventually some four hundred orders of religious women emerged in the United States. They created an odd paradox in a church where the prevailing attitudes were shaped and blessed by men. By 1906, when one Catholic newspaper soberly quoted a New York doctor who warned that "higher education was dangerous to a woman's health," educated women in the Catholic Church were well on their way to creating an empire of a size that existed nowhere else in the world: some eight hundred hospitals and ten thousand schools, colleges and universities.

At its peak, in the 1950s, the Catholic parochial school system contained 11 percent of America's students. The financial and managerial innovations of sisters made possible one out of every five hospital beds in the United States. Other demanding religions, the Shakers, the Quakers and the Mormons among them, have certainly left their benevolent mark on parts of America, but the work of Catholic sisters surrounds us.

Their rise is one of those seemingly improbable American adventure stories containing romance, the ever-present threat of danger, high drama, marvelously nutty moments, seemingly impossible dreams and a business plan that would daunt the most cocksure of modern entrepreneurs: The Lord Will Provide. Their ambition was to lift us all, and they did, giving a critical boost to waves of illiterate immigrants flocking to the young and predominantly Protestant nation. The soil of a country that built a strict separation between church and state was, for more than a century, the planet's most fertile ground for recruiting sisters.

Can there be romance in orders of nuns? They imported the tradition of great dreamers to our shores—the gentle Saint Francis and the stunning medieval poet and mystic Hildegard von Bingen—among them. Two of the homegrown American orders were founded by upper-class Protestant women, both deeply in love with husbands who left them. Elizabeth Ann Bayley Seton, founder of the Sisters of Charity, was the granddaughter of an Episcopal minister and the wife of William Seton, a New York merchant who died nearly bankrupt in Italy, leaving her with five children. (Her order is related to a French order that later sent to the United States sisters known as the Daughters of Charity.)

Sister Sabina, a maternity nurse at a Catholic hospital in Bismarck, North Dakota, 1916. (COURTESY OF ST. ALEXI MEDICAL CENTER, BISMARCK, NORTH DAKOTA)

Cornelia Augusta Peacock, later founder of the Sisters of the Holy Child Jesus, had crept away from her silk-stocking Philadelphia family to elope with a roguish charmer, an Episcopalian minister named Pierce Connelly. He took her to Europe in his restless quest to find the perfect faith. He found it in Italy: Roman Catholicism. He asked her to convert. When she had accomplished that, he revealed his next move.

His destiny, he confided to her, was not to be just an ordinary Catholic. He had great gifts that made him capable of becoming a cardinal—a pillar of the Church. To accomplish this, though, he explained to his stunned wife, he must begin by becoming a priest. That meant that their marriage—which had produced three children—had to be annulled. As a final way to tidy up their family situation and to give the appearance that she was secure, he suggested she go to a convent, seen in the early 1800s in Europe as a convenient refuge for gifted or overly ambitious women.

A dutiful wife, she did all that he asked. Then it was Pierce Connelly's turn to be stunned. In the convent, Cornelia founded her own religious order and later moved it to America. Pierce was so outraged that he became an Episcopalian again. Then he sued her in an English court, demanding to resume his rights as her husband, but to no avail. She was protected by American law and American bishops. She became a pillar of the Church. He was thrown out of court.

Danger was never a stranger to sisters. Many of the orders that formed in America had fled from the guillotines of the French Revolution, the state suppression of Bismarck's Kulturkampf or the savage results of Great Britain's penal laws imposed on Catholics in Ireland. Having known real tyranny, they did not back away from the relatively mild and often inept assaults of the "Nativists," the "Know Nothings" or the Ku Klux Klan.

Fired up by cheap liquor and anti-Catholic rhetoric, a mob burned down an academy run by Ursuline sisters in Charlestown, Massachusetts, in 1834, killing one sister. One rumor was that guns were stored there. What the mob found were sixty frightened girls, most from upper-class Protestant families, who were being schooled in the arts. "No firemen, policemen or citizens came to their aid," says one account of the blaze.

By the mid-nineteenth century, the huge influx of Catholic immigrants from Europe made Catholics the largest religious congregation in the United States, but attacks on Catholics continued. There were rioting and burning in Cincinnati, Louisville and Philadelphia. In Maine, a priest was tarred and feathered. Mrs. Sarah Worthington King Peter, a rich Episcopalian socialite from Cincinnati, was so outraged by all this hatred that she changed her lifestyle. Accustomed to importing objects of art from Europe, she volunteered to bring in members of the newest and—when it came to reaching out to the poor—the most aggressive of the European orders, the Sisters of Mercy from Ireland.

The event that finally disarmed the hot-tempered mobs and convinced the average American that Catholics could be trusted, even respected, was the Civil War. Twenty percent of the nurses for both sides were Catholic nuns. Some turned their convents into hospitals. Others took over disease-ridden public hospitals, such as a cholera-plagued Union facility at Indianapolis. The sisters' discipline and utter lack of fear of death kept them standing by beds of infected soldiers after local medical help fled.

Sisters carted the wounded off the smoke-wreathed, blood-slick fields at Shiloh, Antietam and Galveston. Soldiers saw them as part of their terrain. "My God, look at those women. What are they doing down there? They'll get killed," gasped one dying confederate at Galveston. "Oh those are the sisters," said his companion. "They are not afraid of anything."

On December 29, 1861, Sister Lucy Dosh, a twenty-two-year-old Daughter of Charity, collapsed and died, infected by typhus and bone-weary from working long hours at a makeshift field hospital set up in a factory at Paducah, Kentucky. That made her patients, Union and Confederate wounded lying side by side on bloody pallets, reflect on their situation: They had more in common than their pain.

In the quiet of the evenings Sister Lucy had often sung hymns to them. She had a sweet soprano voice that seemed to cut through the gloom. It would lift them up and take them home, if only for a few moments. They all looked forward to it. Now, quite suddenly, her song had ended. They declared a truce and formed an honor guard to take her body to the river.

The cadence was set by muffled drums. The guns fell silent as they accompanied her casket in a Navy boat up the Ohio River to Uniontown, Kentucky, where she was buried in the convent graveyard with her sisters. Her sacrifice and the soldiers' reflections about it became a theme that played over thousands of dinner tables after the war was over.

High drama? One of the missing elements in cowboy movies is nuns who, in the real Wild West, often hovered somewhere around the action. There was Sister Blandina Segale, a short, fiery Italian, the daughter of a Cincinnati fruit vender. As a fledgling Sister of Charity, she was told on the train as she headed west that "no virtuous woman is safe near a cowboy." She spent her life among cowboys, rustlers and "land sharks." She saved the souls of some and the lives of others. She taught their children to sing Mozart.

In Trinidad, Colorado, a small mining town where she built a school, she faced down a lynch mob with the local sheriff, who told her the mob couldn't be controlled. It was. Later a desperado she knew as Billy the Kid—probably the legendary brigand—threatened to scalp all of the

Sister Blandina Segale.
(COURTESY OF THE SISTERS OF
CHARITY OF CINCINNATI)

town's four doctors for failing to treat one of his wounded gunslingers. When he rode in with his gang, he found Sister Blandina quietly nursing the man after the rest of the town had abandoned him.

"It would give me great pleasure to be able to do you any favor," said the pink-cheeked killer. Sister Blandina said there was one thing. "The favor is granted," snapped the Kid, shaking her hand. She then asked him to "cancel" the scalping of the physicians. The Kid looked around, frowning. His henchmen frowned. Then the Kid grinned. "She is game!" he told his men. They grinned. The doctors kept their hair. Later on, the Kid performed horse tricks for his new friend, the nun.

Nutty moments? Humor was the drug that kept sisters going when courage began to ebb, for the Lord sometimes chose to provide for them in odd ways. In the early 1850s groups of "Know Nothings" appeared outside the convent of the Sisters of Mercy in Little Rock, Arkansas. Riled up by anti-immigrant propaganda, they prepared to torch the building. The sisters could only pray. There were few Catholics in the state, where Know Nothings dominated the politics.

But then the leaders of the mob, two brothers-in-law, began to argue over tactics. It grew more and more heated. Finally they drew guns and simultaneously fired. They were good shots. Two corpses were carted away, a sobering moment for the crowd. "It evidently had an influence on the dismemberment of the Know-Nothing party in the state," says one sister's laconic account. "There were no more anti-Catholic upheavals."

Sisters were, far and away, the biggest risk-takers of the Church, often taking out big mortgages to build schools and hospitals, gambling on a future that would rise above the shanties and mean streets where they worked. A fiery, twenty-six-year-old Sister of Mercy, Mother Mary Baptist Russell, built many of San Francisco's first charitable institutions that way. Care for the poor now and worry about the financing later, was her motto, causing one bishop to tut-tut that "her heart was bigger than her purse." When her purse failed her, she would smuggle linens out of her hospital to give to the poor. She once dragged out her own mattress. Her sisters put an end to that by writing "Rev. Mother" on her next one.

The cover story for Cornelia Augusta Peacock, the aforementioned superior of Sisters of the Holy Child Jesus and former wife of Pierce Connelly, was that she had a genius for evading financial hardship by prying money out of people at the last moment. "If you listen to the superior, instead of to facts, she will persuade you out of your senses," warned one donor. She told visitors not to worry, she had a gift. Money would always turn up from somewhere.

Father C. Carter, the bookkeeper for the diocese of Philadelphia, discovered that her gift was self-denial. She had created a community of teachers in Towanda, Pennsylvania who were determined to give help, never to seek it. They lived on thin pea soup during the winter and slept in a draughty, leaky old house using their habits, old cloaks and pieces of carpet for blankets. There were many days when they didn't know where their next meal was coming from. When Father Carter inquired, however, they refused to talk about it. "I got a smiling, evasive answer."

Sometimes the sisters' projects crashed, forcing the bishops to bail them out. But more often than seemed reasonable, they succeeded because nuns' work built bridges into the larger community. Merchants gave them groceries and lawyers and doctors donated their services because they felt sisters brought stability and civilizing gifts to the community. Railroad tycoons gave them lifetime passes because their hospitals offered the only decent care for railroad workers.

Even the Klan provided. In the early 1920s the knights of the bed sheets cooked up a scheme in Kokomo, Indiana to drive out the Sisters of St. Joseph, who ran the local hospital. The Klansmen founded a competitor, Howard County Hospital, and ran it successfully. Then one night a sick, disheveled man stumbled into their emergency room. He had no money, so Howard County threw him out. In those days, nuns didn't ask patients about money, so they welcomed him at St. Joseph's and healed him. He was J. Henry Fisse, Jr., a local real estate magnate and one of the Klan's major benefactors. He struck the Klan out of his will and substituted the sisters, who, later needing room to expand, used Fisse's money to buy Howard County Hospital.

Sisters built the first schools east of the Mississippi and moved west with the first settlers. Some may have lived lives of quiet piety, but many walked the streets, begging, cajoling good citizens to help them build hospitals, orphanages and schools. They worked long hours in the nation's immigrant ghettos teaching the often unruly sons and daughters of people who had never been educated. Because some of the nuns were nurses and others thought they were, they were often the community's main response to yellow fever, cholera, influenza and other plagues the cures for which were then a mystery.

Impossible dreams? Two Catholic sisters, Mother Mary Elizabeth Lange and Saint Katharine Drexel, created orders to help African Americans, and battled the racism within their own Church. One woman, a poor Creole immigrant from Haiti; the second, a Philadelphia socialite, the richest heiress in America, found a common mission. At a time in America when it was considered wrong, in some places illegal, to educate black people, they started the schools and colleges that helped create the beginnings of a black middle class.

Seen through the lens of the last thirty years, when the structure of many religious and fraternal groups has disintegrated, the bonds that held groups of sisters together on such seemingly impossible missions seem mysterious. A young Sister of Mercy, Sister Mary Francis, once wrote a friend that smallpox was a "truly horrible disease . . . so disgusting." Still, she volunteered to work many long hours in the "pest house," which is where small pox victims, often with puss oozing from sores over their entire bodies, were sent in San Francisco. How did she endure it? Her strength, she said, came from her fellow sisters. "I do know they are praying for me . . . I am two weeks here and I feel my strength keeping up."

And the sisters made sure the strength was passed on. In 1878 after becoming infected by yellow fever working in the hospitals of New Orleans, Mother Xavier McDermott quietly cleaned up her tiny cell in her convent, lay down on her cot and invited the younger nuns to watch her die. "Never until you lie on your death bed will you understand the grandeur of your vocation and the ineffable peace and joy that will bless your closing hours," she told them, "if you strive earnestly to live up to your rules and become perfect Sisters of Mercy."

In the parlance of our age, much of what these sisters did amounted to low pay, "burnout jobs." To be sure, some of them did fall by the way, but many refused to burn out, often serving careers of a half-century or longer. In the 1880s an Irish priest wrote to his first cousin that he was proud that she was about to become a Sister of Mercy in America. "I am only afraid you are not wild enough," he went on, "it requires considerable life and fun to bear up against hard work."

Fun, in the form of recreation periods, was part of the daily life of convents. One of the Mercies' favorite pastimes was making up nonsense rhymes. Mother Frances Warde, the order's founder in the United States, collected them. Following is one of her favorites, sent to her from a group of young disciples she'd sent to a tiny dot on the map next to the Missouri River:

> *Have you ever been in Omaha?*
> *Where mud is splashed from every mound*
> *To fill your eyes and ears and throat?*
> *Where all the steamers are aground*
> *And all the shanties are afloat?*
> *If not, take heed to what I say.*
> *You'll find it just as I have found it;*
> *And if it lies upon your way,*
> *For God's sake, go around it!*

For the Sisters of Mt. Carmel, an order in New Orleans that suffered from chronic shortages of money, relief was singing Irish songs on Sundays. The founder of the order, Mother Clare Coady, would read selections from the funny papers. Recreation time was an opportunity for younger sisters to bond with the order's elders. It may sound silly now, but such bonding held them together under hardships that few of us have ever experienced.

In February 1920, the order sent three volunteers to open a new elementary school in Westwego, a working-class suburb in New Orleans. Sister Bonaventure Monhollan, the youngest of the group, later recalled that on Mondays they rose at dawn and walked two and a half hours to reach the school. They had a cold lunch of jelly and cheese sandwiches. At night they went to a small cabin, rented with borrowed money, which had no cooking utensils. One night they looked in the larder to find only a small glass of jelly, one teaspoon and two slices of bread. "Well, I looked at the other two, then at the two slices of bread and said to myself, 'I am the youngster,' so I got up from the table, went to bed and cried myself to sleep."

After a time of struggle, sisters often had the satisfaction of standing back and looking at something they had created. Sometimes it was simple but necessary, such as the first sewer system in Joplin, Missouri. Other constructs were more heroic. A statue of Mother Joseph, a Sister of Providence, stands in National Statuary Hall in the U.S. Capitol, partly because she built the first hospitals and schools in the Northwest, literally. A coach maker's daughter who learned carpentry at an early age, she prowled construction sites with a saw in her hand and a hammer dangling from her belt. When her construction crews brushed aside her objections that they had built a chimney wrong, they returned the next day to see that it had been torn down and rebricked in the way she wanted. As one account put it: "There was no stranger sight around Ft. Vancouver [Washington] than Mother Joseph in her black habit bouncing on a high cross beam to test its strength or wriggling out from beneath the ground level where she had been inspecting a foundation."

She also had other ways of getting peoples' attention. Her begging tours through the mining and timber camps of the Old West were legendary. They lasted for months. Nearly everyone had heard of the nun who didn't take "no" for an answer. On a trip to Denver, bandits held up her stagecoach, forcing the passengers to line up and the coachman to unload their luggage at gunpoint. When Mother Joseph got out, she confronted the youngest bandit.

"My boy," said Mother Joseph, "please give me that black bag." The other passengers cringed.

The gunman hesitated. "Which one?" he said, finally.

She pointed at it. The two hundred dollars she'd collected went back to her hospital.

All of this, the striving for perfection, the grace and wit under fire, the intense staying power of orders of nuns may seem distant to us now, but in the 1930s it was an accepted part of our landscape, a piece of Americana to Catholics and non-Catholics alike.

On November 1, 1930, a stocky, black-bearded young man entered St. Vincent Hospital in Billings, Montana. He was in agony, holding his left arm, shattered in a car crash. Soon, he found himself being charmed by his nurse, a shy young nun, Sister Florence Cloonan. She was continually fretting over whether she had done enough for her patients, most of them a rough lot of cowboys and gamblers.

Her bearded patient was Ernest Hemingway. He later immortalized her as Sister Cecilia in the short story "The Gambler, the Nun, and the Radio." As she went from patient to patient, she would mutter things like: "When I was a girl it seemed so simple. I knew I would be a saint . . . Now it seems almost impossible." Then she would dash out to catch a moment of an epic struggle on the radio: The "Fighting Irish" of Notre Dame were on the gridiron. Hemingway's main character—a tough guy named Frazer—gets a nudge and a cynical wink from another patient, a Mexican who fancies himself a Marxist. "Is she a little crazy?" the Mexican whispers.

"Who?"

"That sister."

"No," Mr. Frazer said. "She is a fine woman of great intelligence and sympathy."

Later in the thirties another chance encounter took place at a hospital: Dr. Bob Smith, a physician recovering from alcoholism, met Sister Mary Ignatia Gavin at St. Thomas Hospital in Akron, Ohio. She was a frail, displaced music teacher. Her order, the Sisters of Charity of St. Augustine, had shifted her to hospital work after she had had a nervous breakdown. Dr. Smith was desperate for a hospital that would help with his idea that alcoholics might be sick.

While her superiors were against the idea, Sister Gavin was ready for an experiment. She began sneaking his patients into the hospital, hiding them at first in a room reserved for flower arrangement. The result of this collaboration was Alcoholics Anonymous, probably the most successful rehabilitation program in American history. The shy, bespectacled nun always made light of her role in this. "We're just like the Army, you know. We go where we are sent."

The fact that there have been more than four hundred religious orders in the United States and that they each had independent missions and creative ways of doing things fascinates sociologists because it represents a major difference between the Catholic Church and Protestant denominations. The Protestant movement in America has tended to grow in stairstep fashion with mainline organizations losing membership and new sects rising to attract new members. But the Catholic Church just continued to grow. Dr. Roger Finke, an associate professor of sociology at Purdue University, argues that the diverse groups of sisters and brothers within the Catholic Church perform the equivalent role of Protestant sects and that their innovations within the church have been "a source of revival and reform . . . for nearly two millennia."

One of the great ironies of the saga of Catholic sisters in America is that by the 1950s, when Hollywood began depicting nuns as near-magical creatures who prayed, sang, conquered and sometimes even flew, sisters were experiencing their first severe organizational crisis. The problem was that the explosive growth of the Catholic school, feeding off the post–World War II baby boom, had created an exhausting treadmill. Ill-prepared sisters worked eighty-hour weeks in overcrowded parochial schools for as little as five hundred dollars a year. While their orders continued to grow, the Church's demand for them grew faster. Rigid rules of bureaucracy began to dull the spirit in convents, taking away the creative opportunities of the frontier days and making the sisters' work a mere habit in a habit, not a license to do good works.

The 1950s cartoons of nuns as stern, old, ruler-wielding women itching to whack unruly youngsters remain funny, but they're mostly wrong.

Sister Ignatia Gavin. "We're just like the army, you know." (COURTESY OF THE ARCHIVES OF THE SISTERS OF CHARITY OF ST. AUGUSTINE, RICHFIELD, OHIO)

To be sure, parochial schools had some of that, but so did public schools where the culture of "spare the rod" did not take root until the 1960s. While some teachers reveled in this cruelty, most, I think, employed it because they knew—and we often didn't—that life has a series of blunt instruments to use on people who don't learn the lessons of the past. They are far more painful and lasting than the sting of a ruler.

For the most part, nuns were typically young women fired with faith and idealism but often saddled with classes of sixty or more pupils as the Catholic school system exploded. Educators are still probing what they managed to accomplish. There is the mysterious "Catholic

School Effect," which causes some students, particularly those from poor economic backgrounds, to regularly outperform their peers in public schools. The source of this magic, academics are finding, is not the ruler. It is love.

One of the other remarkable things about nuns is that they did all this while locked in a seemingly endless, often-losing battle of the sexes with Catholic bishops, many of whom were accustomed to treating them as subjects. Nuns versus bishops, perhaps the nation's oldest gender war, has endured for 150 years. It has served as a kind of creative tension that keeps the Church alive and resilient, although under the strain of the turbulent 1960s it became one of many reasons for the massive erosion of religious orders.

Here is an event that sociologists and historians still puzzle over: In 1968 there were 179,974 sisters—convents had filled to an all-time high. The following year the flow of young women into the sisterhood nearly stopped. It was as if someone had turned off a tap. The causes are many and complex. Underlying all of them was the fact that the nation was changing.

Membership in community-building groups was being replaced by a cynicism bred by the Vietnam War about government and all authority. Within convents, pressure was building to jettison convent rules that had gone unexamined for decades. In the outside world, professional opportunities for young women in business, law, medicine and the arts had begun to appear. For the first time many doors were opening for the woman who wanted something more.

One other cause: The all-male officialdom of the Catholic Church convened in Rome on October 11, 1962, to rewrite the rules of the Church. In Vatican II, the historic church council that droned on for three years. Theologians thrust and parried. Jesuits made nimble distinctions and cardinals pondered. But one voice was missing. Only one U.S. sister was allowed to observe the deliberations. She was Mary Luke Tobin, a Sister of Loretto for fifty-seven years and former elected head of the association that represents the leaders of most groups of religious women in the United States. She was given the same nonparticipant status as the council's Protestant observers.

Vatican II wrought changes that have proved to be healthy for the

Church, but two in particular posed unappreciated hazards for groups of religious women. One blurred the distinction between religious groups and lay Catholics. To some Catholics, it ended a tradition going back to the days of the persecutions of Christians in imperial Rome that gave a special status to religious organizations of sisters and brothers who sacrificed to help others. Meanwhile, another change required religious groups to review their basic rules to make them harmonious with the needs of the poor and "present-day physical and psychological conditions."

While the former change appears to have discouraged young women from starting careers as sisters, the latter amounted to a loophole that was exploited by a parade of players. They included flocks of well-meaning reformers, avant-garde theologians, psychotherapists and others called in to help groups of sisters decide how to adjust to the modern day. Many tended to view teaching and nursing as skills that were hopelessly outdated. They preached new causes: Ralph Nader, Cesar Chavez, the Sandinistas, ecofeminism and SANE.

Some sisters refocused their zeal against the Vietnam War or the military-industrial complex. Some went to jail. (Sister Tobin later accomplished both, visiting North Vietnam and then getting herself arrested in the rotunda of the U.S. Capitol for praying after closing time.) The visions of the reformers took nuns way, way beyond the needs of the local parish. As one sister put it, responding to a survey: "I dream of having all of us spending some time outside of the U.S., outside of the U.S. culture, with the poor and acquiring a global perspective and becoming global citizens rather than simply U.S. citizens."

Fittingly, perhaps, the most dramatic blowup occurred in Hollywood, home of "The Singing Nun," where in 1968 the six-hundred-member order of the Sisters of the Most Holy and Immaculate Heart of the Blessed Virgin Mary waged a tragic game of ecclesiastical chicken with James Francis Cardinal McIntyre. The IHMs were brimming with ideas for reform they felt were inspired by Vatican II, ranging from collective bargaining for teachers to the right to wear pedal pushers. The cardinal, on the other hand, tended to distill them into one supreme sin: The nuns were challenging his authority.

Four hundred IHM sisters asked to be dispensed from their vows, a move that ended their status as sisters. The cardinal complied, leaving a gaping hole in the Los Angeles parochial school system. While their situations were not as dramatic or as clear-cut as the IHMs, women in many other religious orders ventured down this same rocky road to "reform."

The most complete review of the resulting damage of "reforms" was done in the early 1990s by two Catholic psychologists, Father David Nygren and Sister Miriam Ukeritis, a Sister of St. Joseph. They polled more than ten thousand members of religious orders, nearly all women. What they found was that between 1962 and 1992, orders of sisters shrank by 42 percent. The orders had shut down 23 percent of their hospitals, 15 percent of their universities and colleges and 42 percent of their elementary schools.

Without young recruits, populations of sisters began to age rapidly in the 1970s. That introduced a new crisis, this time involving the Church's murky economics. In traditional convent life, the young sisters cared for the old. It was one reason why Catholic institutions had come so far with so little money. Part of what supported the nuns amounted to a barter of services. With the departures of young sisters and the abrupt decline in recruits to replace them, this system broke down.

Now cash was needed. While there are some "safety nets" for the poor in America, there were none for the poor embedded in the Catholic Church. Bishops had failed to set aside retirement money for sisters. While not technically in their care, many of them had served as their long-term, faithful employees. Catholics began scrambling to fill this gap in the 1980s, but the Church is still some $7 billion short of what it would take to give them all a decent retirement.

Of the younger sisters who remained, many took professional jobs as lawyers, probation workers, managers and hospital executives. They were sometimes depicted in the press as the "new nuns," fearless women pioneering yet another mission. But they were also preparing for an end. Their enlarged salaries were essential to pay the medical bills of older nuns, many of whom were suffering from Alzheimer's and other expensive diseases. These bills are formidable. There are now about 65,000 sisters in America. Their median age is sixty-nine.

The women who once applied their arts to opening institutions, now had to systematically close them: emotionally wrenching but necessary exercises that have left communities all across the United States with voids to fill. The buildings are still there, but they've been converted to businesses. The ethos of giving that made them peculiarly alive has ebbed away.

But the spirit still lingers. Politicians still ask why poor students in inner-city neighborhoods often do better in Catholic schools than in better-funded public ones. In many blighted communities, Catholic hospitals still stress the need to serve charity patients, to do community outreach and other care-spreading policies that do not gladden the hearts of insurance companies nor fatten the bottom line.

These hospitals, many of them founded by orders of sisters, constitute the largest source of free health care in the United States outside the federal government and they represent a long tradition of emergency care. It includes the chaos and the pain of nearly every American crisis, running from the War of 1812 to the war that began on September 11, 2001.

When the *Titanic* sank, in April 1912, rescue boats brought 174 injured survivors into New York Harbor. Of those, 117 were brought to St. Vincent's Hospital, run by the Sisters of Charity in Greenwich Village. On September 11, 2001, when two hijacked planes hit the World Trade Center towers, three hundred victims were brought to the nearest major hospital—St. Vincent's.

St. Vincent's is not the same. Once it had seventy sisters managing its operations. On the day the terrorists struck, it was down to three. But they pulled in thirty retired sisters and mobilized the hospital's staff to deal with the patients and to create a family crisis center that responded to calls from eleven thousand people looking for survivors amid the chaos.

Small things count in Catholic hospitals, and one of the points of the crisis center, according to Sister Miriam Kevin Phillips, a Sister of Charity and vice president of the system that runs St. Vincent's, was to make sure that all of these desperate callers "should hear a human voice and not get a voice mail or a roll-over. Our values state that we treat everyone with integrity, compassion and excellence."

The family crisis center went around the clock for ten days. "In some cases we had to order our employees to go home. I mean, in some cases they couldn't see straight, but they didn't want to leave." As in the case of the *Titanic,* St. Vincent's absorbed most of the costs.

As readers of this book will learn, there are many lesser American dramas involving sisters. An order of black nuns has made the "Catholic School Effect" flourish in the most blighted neighborhoods of Baltimore.

Innovative housing policies, begun by nuns, continue to lift the poor out of crack-savaged ghettos in Denver and are renewing the bombed-out landscape of inner-city Philadelphia. In places like Nashville, young women continue to be drawn to religious life, especially to conservative orders, which are enjoying a small resurgence. In sum, it has been a rough ride of late, but the life of religious orders of women goes on.

So who really built the largest church in America? Writers of some church histories suggest that it sprang out of uncultivated soil, guided by the somber, often infallible pronouncements of popes and the grand governance of cardinals who directed legions of obedient priests. But that is not, by any means, the whole story. Catholics may not know the rest, but we all know how the nuns would begin to tell it. They would say sit up straight. Keep your feet under your desks. Be quiet. And pay attention.

In the pages that follow I have tried to pay attention to the common elements of their experience in America. To describe the journeys of all four hundred orders of Catholic sisters would more nearly resemble a catalog or a database than a book. So with some excursions to sketch in the larger background, this book will follow the adventures of the Sisters of Mercy, the group that became the largest and most pervasive of those that belong to the Women of the Church.

2

"THE WALKIN' NUNS"

In the early 1780s, as American politicians in Philadelphia sparred over radical statements they wanted to put in the Constitution and as mobs in Paris edged toward a bloody revolution, James McAuley, a local contractor in Dublin, started his own small rebellion.

He invited a group of dirty street children into the wide hallway of his well-appointed house and proceeded to drill them in the rudiments of his religion. McAuley, a bright, industrious man, was Catholic. The fact that he had acquired some wealth and the respect of his Protestant clients was a radical statement all by itself. The act of teaching his religion went beyond that. It was a criminal act.

Our literature is rich in portraits of what it was like to be a Jew in Germany in the late 1930s or to be a black in America in the eighteenth and nineteenth centuries. To be a Catholic in Ireland in the latter part of the eighteenth century was not far from that, measured in pain, poverty and risk. But it is a story that many Irish Americans have tended to blot out of their literature and their memory in their rush to assimilate. It begins in

1695, after the English finally conquered all of Ireland. They developed a separate set of laws, called the Penal Laws, to deal with the people they defeated. The laws were intended to keep them defeated for generations. As laws go, it was an ambitious undertaking. Eighty percent of Ireland's population were Catholics.

The laws stripped Catholics of most of their property and gave them a second-class status so that a Protestant who fancied anything they might have retained, like a house or a horse, could use the courts to simply take it. Catholic education was forbidden. Catholics were not allowed to hold public office, to bear arms or to enter a profession. Priests were hunted, threatened with castration, jailed and sometimes executed.

The result was a nation where a man's typical career went from rags to rags. Apart from death, a woman rarely had anything to hope for, outside her religion, and the authorities were working to kill that. Ireland, to the European observer, was a place of mean streets and mud shanties; a land where a majority eked out a living tilling tiny, rented plots and where wealth was counted in potatoes or, for the most fortunate, pigs.

The poverty in Ireland was so abysmal that English radicals, like William Cobbett, used accounts of their visits to Ireland to tweak the consciences of London's political establishment. Here is Cobbett's account of the hovels in an Irish village: "They all consisted of mud walls, with a covering of rafters and straw. None of them so good as the place where you keep your little horse. . . . The floor, the bare ground. No fireplace, no chimney, the fire . . . made one side against the wall, and the smoke going out of a hole in the roof. No table, no chair. . . . Some stones for seats. No goods, but a pot and a shallow tub, for the pig and the family both to eat out of."

For the drafters of the Penal Laws, their final solution was more benign than the Nazi's. Their goal was simply to force all Catholics to become Protestants, but the laws that conveyed that message were not subtle. A Catholic who attempted to privately educate his children faced confiscation of his remaining property, but he could send them to state-sponsored schools, where the curriculum was designed to make them Protestants. Upon becoming a Protestant, the eldest son in a family gained the right to take over its management. Thus, he could dispose of his father's property against his will.

The end result was an even deeper poverty as Catholics shunned schools and took their religion into an underground that evolved as the way of life for most Irish. There were secret "penal walks" that led to guarded "mass fields" where Sunday services were celebrated. There were "hedge schools," a sporadic, floating system of outdoor education, usually held on high ground so the teacher could see his jailers coming.

Over time, a wide gap between the literate and the illiterate grew along religious lines. The social impacts of such gaps are profound and long-lasting. In 1861, more than thirty years after this near-serfdom had been lifted, a survey in Ulster showed that 29 percent of Catholics could read or write compared with 50 percent of members of the official Church of Ireland and 59 percent of Presbyterians.

The dim world created by the Penal Laws was described by Edmund Burke as the worst "contrivance for the impoverishment and degradation of the people . . . as ever proceeded from the perverted ingenuity of man."

The outrage of Burke, the eighteenth-century political philosopher, was shared by some sympathetic Irish Protestants. Some were conscience stricken by the poverty that surrounded their estates with endless slums and blighted the lives of the people they had to pass every day. Others became keenly aware that talented Irishmen came cheap and could do valuable professional work. So, as the century neared its end, the island's elite permitted some informal opportunities for a few lucky Catholics. If they had the right talents, they might "pass" through these legal barriers and enter the establishment. McAuley, an honest man who built solid, tasteful houses, had done that.

But openly inviting the Irish poor into his home for religious education was a brazen act that brought him close to the blunt edge of the law. His wife, Eleanor, a beautiful woman, was much more conventional. She prized above all the pleasures of middle-class life in Dublin and often argued with him about the teaching. It was wrong, she would insist, and "unbecoming to his character and position" to hold Sunday school for these smelly, sometimes unruly street children. Sometimes he escaped her weekly sermons by holding his classes out on the lawn.

Bold as it was, Mr. McAuley's dangerous experiment would have probably gone unnoticed by history were it not for a pair of brown, wide-set eyes that watched his every move. He had a five-year-old daughter, Catherine, and seeing her father teach was an experience that became etched in her mind. It is not clear how she was able to grasp the power of what her father was doing, but it seems indisputable that she did. The year she became five, he died, leaving Catherine to be raised in a Protestant society. The story of how she emerged from this background to found the Sisters of Mercy, a Catholic religious order that has founded more schools than any other religious order in the English-speaking world, seems straight out of the pages of a Charles Dickens novel. It is one of those uplifting stories about people rising out of the misery of the industrial age that Dickens, the social reformer, wished would happen. In Catherine McAuley's case, it did.

She grew into a bright, hopeful young woman with polished manners and a knack for diplomacy, but underneath all that she had the gift from her father: a quiet sense of outrage and the steely determination to make things change. As one of the hundreds of young women she later recruited put it, Catherine McAuley carried with her "the Celtic fire of her character, invariably controlled, but never extinguished."

Her mother took her to live with Protestant friends and relatives, where talk about the Catholic faith was forbidden. For a time she lived with an uncle, Owen Conway, an Army surgeon. Although a Catholic, he had also passed into the "Irish gentry." Unfortunately, his story was a much more familiar one than that of Catherine's father. Passing, for him, meant proving he could spend and party with the best of his new establishment neighbors. The upshot was bankruptcy, which was how Catherine was introduced to the life that was normal for most Irish. "Often after an entire day spent without food, they had nothing but a little bread at night."

Her mother died in 1796, when Catherine was eighteen. Her brother and sister did what many children of the Catholic "gentry" did to get a more secure foothold in the sweet life of Dublin: They became Protestants. The Dublin they knew was a kind of glittery bubble floating on a sea of human misery. Only 3 percent of Ireland's population lived there, but they rode in handsome carriages and were served by footmen. They clip-clopped down the city's wide brick streets, lined by Georgian-era town mansions where people lounged in rooms with twenty-foot ceilings and dined off of fine China. Dublin had very nearly the nation's entire inventory of substantial houses along with other rarities, such as schools, parks, universities and hospitals.

Catherine was more interested in the city's slums, neighborhoods where the servants lived and where, around 1790, the first Catholic schools in a century began to appear as the death grip of the Penal Laws finally began to ease. She became acquainted with priests as they emerged from the underground. Mass could now be held indoors, in shops on grimy side streets. She was particularly fascinated by one Dr. Betagh, who started a night school for boys in a cellar.

Then, in 1804, her life changed dramatically. A childless Quaker couple, Mr. and Mrs. William Callaghan, "adopted" Catherine McAuley, then twenty-six. She was what they wanted—a bright, well-read, capable woman who could help manage the affairs of their suburban mansion, called Coolock House.

The agreement that they made was that she could not practice her religion openly, but the rules were relaxed after Mr. Callaghan, a chemist, saw Catherine's deep involvement with the poor, an interest that he came to share. He let her collect the poor children of the neighborhood and hold school for them in a small house on the Callaghans' property called the lodge.

Catherine's job as manager of the household required her to be well dressed and she had the family carriage at her disposal to shop at the finer stores, but she sometimes used it to make detours into dingy back streets, like Liffey Street. There Catherine once encountered a scruffy, homeless woman, hopelessly senile, wandering aimlessly amid the squalor. Rather than see her dumped into the city's crowded, filthy asylum, Catherine took the woman back to Coolock House, where she tried to make her comfortable in surroundings that were a world away from Liffey Street.

As a contemporary recalled later, this was definitely a learning experience: "With the perversity of madness, she [the mad woman] from the first conceived an absolute hatred for her [McAuley]." She constantly swore at her and stole "everything she could lay her hands on, hiding those things she could not use, so that the inconvenience was equally great." Cautioning the servants not to tease the woman, Catherine cared for her for five years, until she died.

Word of McAuley's actions began to spread among the priests in the Catholic community, including Rev. Dr. Murray, the future bishop of Dublin, then serving a church on Liffey Street. As the men of that day might have put it, Catherine might be a member of the "unlearned sex," but she was no dilettante. Other ladies might give lip service or a few volunteer hours to the sometimes thankless job of helping the poor. Catherine McAuley stayed with it.

Mr. Callaghan was also impressed. Once, in a jocular way, he asked Catherine what she would do if he left her a sum of money in his will. She said she wouldn't know what to do with it. "Well I know what you would do," he said, laughing, "you would do a great deal of good with it at all events." He died on November 11, 1822, leaving "my kind and affectionate friend Miss Catherine McAuley" the bulk of his estate, which would be worth more than $1 million in today's dollars.

Now Catherine not only passed as gentry; she was rich. At age forty-two, in a society where twenty-year-old women were considered spinsters, she had suitors. "She lived in what is usually called good style, that is she kept a carriage, dressed well, went into society and sometimes gave parties at her house," says one biographer.

Instead of suitors, however, she preferred the company of priests. She told them she wanted to use her money for something lasting. The deliberations over what to do with her fortune narrowed down to a building that would serve as a parochial school and a home for servant girls. It didn't go up in Liffey Street, where the Catholics were. She was determined to build it next to the tall, brickfront Georgian town houses on Baggot Street, one of Dublin's fanciest neighborhoods.

It was a flashy, nouveau-riche move that her destitute uncle Owen Conway would have heartily applauded, only Catherine was not thinking of just showing off her money. She wanted the house to be like her father's hallway Sunday-school classes. Baggot Street was not just to be a school, but a political and religious statement. "If you would have a public institution be of service to the poor, place it in the neighborhood of the rich," advised one of her counselors, Rev. Michael Blake, the vicar general of the diocese of Dublin.

There was, of course, a great deal of fuss among the neighbors over the idea of the poor blighting the fine Baggot Street neighborhood, but Catherine secured the property and then hired lawyers to fend off the opposition. After that the rich lady's carriage became a fixture in the neighborhood. It was often seen parked a few blocks away, in front of the Kildare Street Society, one of the toniest, state-subsidized schools in Ireland.

She was interested in two things: the elements of a state-of-the-art education and, on a more parochial level, the names of the Catholic students in attendance. Rather than have Kildare's teachers turn them into Protestants, Catherine's strategy was to invite the students to finish their work at her school.

Catherine left many of the details of construction of the Baggot Street house to her priestly advisors, who, it turned out, also had their own agenda. She discovered what it was in 1827 as the building she would call the House of Mercy neared completion. Its design was strikingly similar to that of a convent.

At first she thought it was amusing. As one of her contemporaries put it, Catherine had "imbibed certain Protestant prejudices." She did not like the idea of taking vows, of becoming shut in a house that was cut off from the community. And she didn't want to become bound by what she felt to be the many stultifying rules of convents of her day, which were imposed by bishops. "She . . . told us that she never intended to establish a religious order."

The closest advisor among the priests she consulted, Rev. E. Armstrong, shared her dream, but seemed to sense that it would mean endless friction with the all-male bureaucracy of the Church. That year, before he died, he told her, in effect, to stick to her guns. "Place no trust or confidence in any man living, place all your trust and confidence in God alone."

To the more rebellious Irish, Catherine was now a symbol, a civil rights figure. Among the other Irish Catholics who "passed" was Daniel O'Connell, a French-educated lawyer who led the fight for repeal of the Penal Laws, which happened in 1829. When the house on Baggot Street opened, he made it a point to turn up at functions there.

O'Connell, a member of the English Parliament, was a legendary orator who knew how to make the Irish pulse pound. As the confetti descended upon London after news of the momentous victory over Napoleon at Waterloo, he snorted: "The scoundrels of society have now every triumph. The defeats and disasters are reserved for the friends of liberty."

He also understood what Catherine McAuley was all about. At a Christmas party for poor children at Baggot Street in 1828, he carved the roast beef and then sat next to an ugly, deformed little girl who was being shunned by her peers. He spent the evening waiting on her, telling her jokes and finally declaring "she was his favorite of all the little girls there."

By this time McAuley was no longer alone. Dozens of young women, many like her from "gentrified" backgrounds with some education—still a rarity for Catholic women—were coming to Baggot Street to volunteer. From an American viewpoint the most important of these was a cheery, beautiful redhead, Frances Warde, then seventeen.

Known as Fanny to her friends, Frances Warde lost her mother in her infancy. Her father, who raised her and educated her with private tutors, lost Belbrook House, the family's rural home, in 1819 when she was nine. A rich neighbor, Sir Robert Staples, fancied it as a splendid site for a school for Protestant boys. Thanks to the Penal Laws, he soon had title to it. Shattered by the move, Frances's father died five years later. The family was dispersed.

As she began to blossom into a young woman, Frances came to live with relatives in Dublin where she became acquainted with the same champagne-lubricated lifestyle that had been the ruination of Catherine McAuley's hapless uncle. "Balls, musical concerts and theater parties filled her days," writes Kathleen Healy, Warde's biographer. An early associate described her: "Tall, well proportioned with a dignity of bearing and ease of manner that characterized her to her last day. She could have graced a court."

But Frances had a hunger that needed much more than parties. A friend, Catherine McAuley's sixteen-year-old niece, brought her to Baggot Street where Warde volunteered to help teach school. Soon she was Catherine McAuley's secretary, organizing the daily functions of the house and following her on visits to the Kildare schools and to the local hospital, where they visited the sick.

McAuley, Warde and the other volunteers began working as a close-knit team. They began to call each other "sister" and developed a kind of uniform, a simple black dress. This was too much for many of the priests who envied McAuley's growing status among their parishioners. Either she was in the Church, they reasoned, or she wasn't. And if was she was working as a woman in the Catholic Church, she had to be in a recognized religious order and in a convent.

They ridiculed the house on Baggot Street as "Kitty's Folly." When it began drawing prominent Catholics like O'Connell, they tried another tack. Rev. Matthias Kelly, the priest of the parish serving Baggot Street, appeared at the house one day and told McAuley that the bishop had decided he would take it over and give it to a recognized group of nuns, the Sisters of Charity. After the shock of that had registered, he told her that she might be allowed to keep a small apartment in it for herself.

Rev. Kelly's sense of the mistress of Baggot Street was that she could be counted upon to be submissive to the archbishop and once she did that, her order would be "suppressed." It was a good reading of McAuley, for she went directly to the archbishop, who was then her previous acquaintance, Dr. Murray. She told him that if he wanted the house at Baggot Street, she would simply give it to him.

The bishop was astonished. He had never asked to have her house, but then he began to ponder. There was a problem; she was a round peg trying to fit into a church that had only square holes. "Really, Miss McAuley," he said in freezing tones, "I had no idea that a new order would start up in this manner."

A clever man who admired McAuley, the bishop negotiated a compromise. If she would agree to serve as a novice, or a beginner, in a traditional order, then he would help her with the paperwork and bureaucratic maneuvering to get the "Sisters of Mercy" to be recognized as an official order of the Church by the Vatican in Rome.

And so, in September 1830 Catherine McAuley and two of her volunteers presented themselves at the convent of the Presentation Sisters in Dublin and asked to be accepted in their novitiate, normally a testing ground for teenage prospects. For the fifty-two-year-old millionaire who had become used to running her own establishment, it was the equivalent of an army general submitting to marine boot camp.

She endured. "She often said it was so hard a struggle for her to remain on account of meeting there many things repugnant to her feelings," recalled Clare Moore, a contemporary. After fourteen months, she returned to the House of Mercy, bringing with her some of the new discipline and sense of decorum she'd acquired.

To the simple black dress she added a coif, a kind of starched, white cotton helmet that covered the hair and the sides of the face. There was a guimpe, a starched collar that concealed the shape of the breasts. Then a broad black belt from which hung a large rosary. From then on Warde and the other "sisters" in the House of Mercy would follow an Horarium, a rigid schedule of prayers, meals, work and recreation that had been the hallmark of Catholic monastic orders since the early Middle Ages.

They would take the vows of poverty, chastity and obedience that were followed by Catholic nuns. To this McAuley added a fourth, service to educate the poor and to help women, who, she felt, were the first victims of poverty and the last to be rescued.

Mercy nuns, she counseled her novices, must become accustomed to a life of self-sacrifice. Good works that involved risks or discomfort, she told them, were the most pleasing to God and most effective. As she would put it: "without the cross, the real progress cannot come."

Seen from another land and from a decidedly different age, that might seem an antiquated spiritual statement, even a cruel one to some Americans. Yet in our locker rooms and fitness centers, some of us apply it to our bodies daily without a thought. It is "no pain, no gain."

McAuley's young volunteers soon found themselves positions where the training came in handy. In 1832 when cholera broke out, Dublin invited the Sisters of Mercy into a hospital on Townsend Street where victims of the epidemic had been quarantined. No one else had volunteered.

McAuley, who had a strong dread of contagion, led her sisters there. They worked four-hour shifts amid people vomiting blood, dying of diarrhea, and suffering other repulsive agonies of the highly infectious disease that, then, had no cure. The nuns' faith and discipline kept them at it. As for McAuley, she "scarcely left the hospital."

The Irish had never seen anything like it. Catholic women, from the upper class, no less, risking their lives to help the poor. Bishops from other areas of Ireland began appearing regularly at Baggot house to beg McAuley to start another convent in their communities. She was eager to oblige them because she knew Dublin was a bubble; the countryside was where the real victims of the Penal Laws lived.

Warde and the other sisters who followed her later catalogued, in the vernacular, some of the remarks that met them on these missions:

A FAT WOMAN DRESSED IN RUFFLES: "Johnny . . . get up and go near the blessed nuns. Sure if ye only stand in their shadow, alanna, ye'll never get the sickness that's goin."

A MOTHER TO HER GRANDMOTHER: "Oh gran! Look at the tall wan on the outside. That's the great mother-abbess herself, that came from

Dublin sailin' all the way to Cork. Glory be to God! Isn't she a beauty all out?"

A YOUNG WOMAN TO HER CHILDREN WHO ARE FIGHTING: "Tim! Take yer curly head out of the light and be paicable, the walkin' nuns are comin' to yer sick aunty. Be quiet no, an I'll give ye apples an' sugar by the by. Oh! Here they are, ten thousand welcomes to the darlin's! Ah! Then, Davy, look out at the wan on the step, isn't she a divine creature all out?"

AN OLD LADY SELLING FRUIT: "I seen 'em sittin' down on the settee in Kitty Fagan's garret, and they spoke to the old woman like she was a queen, now, and they's the rale quality. An' thin they wint down on their binded knees, they did, and prayed for her an' for all of us, praise be to th Lord!"

As for Mr. O'Connell, the consummate politician, he used to pump up the enormous crowds he drew in the country by talking about Mother McAuley and her sisters: "Look at the fairest portion of creation, educated and possessing all the virtues that adorn and endear life, forsaking their homes and families and friends, entering a convent in the morning of their days. . . . Look at the Sisters of Mercy (hear, hear) wrapped in their long black robes. Thus they go forth, not for amusement or delight—No; they are hastening to the lone couch of some sick fellow-creature fast sinking into the grave, with none to comfort, none to soothe, they come with love and consolation and by their prayers bring down the blessings of God on the dying sinner, on themselves and on their country (great cheering). Oh! Such a country is too good to continue in slavery (immense cheering)."

As the center of all this attention, McAuley sometimes found it amusing. She mailed out copies of O'Connell's tub-thumpers to friends with the notation "As a test of my humility, I have [this speech] on my desk, to look at occasionally."

To be sure, she had her eccentricities, one of which was pennypinching. Her rationale was that the lifestyles of Mercy sisters should be no different from the poor they served. It did not set well with some of the daughters she had lured away from their gentrified families.

"The breakfast table was a trial to one's nerves," wrote Clare Moore, who lived in Baggot house. "Sugar of the very blackest and coarsest kind with no sugar spoon." Three of the sisters, she noted, came down with "virulent scurvy" from Baggot House's inadequate fare.

The first Sister of Mercy, Mother Catherine McAuley. (COURTESY OF THE MERCY INTERNATIONAL ASSOCIATION)

McAuley once wrote a verse instructing her sisters how to be good superiors, once they were assigned to one of the Mercies' new convents opening in the country:

You've 15 hours from 6 to 9.
Be mild and sweet in all your ways.
Now and again bestow some praise.
Avoid all solemn declaration.
All serious, close investigation.
Turn what you can into a jest
And with few words dismiss the rest.

As hard as she was on the young Mercies, McAuley always reserved the hardest burdens for herself. She always chose the "poorest and cheapest mode of travelling," frequently sleeping on the floors of new convents she was opening. When she served meals, the portions she left for herself were "very scanty."

The objective of her charity was the working poor, especially young women who came from the country to serve in the fine homes along Baggot Street. They often found themselves exploited and sometimes propositioned or raped by their new employers. McAuley offered them protection: a place to stay and a job that taught them marketable skills. "We will soon have a valuable laundry as the neighborhood is so good," she once wrote Warde.

Having an income stream from the laundry, she noted, freed her from daily fund-raising and helped stabilize her operations at Baggot Street. Her next goal was to replicate it. Her recruits followed her to every corner of Ireland, establishing thirteen more Houses of Mercy as people realized that the spirit of the Sisters of Mercy was something that they needed. Some of the Irish Church's hierarchy privately derided her because Catherine McAuley often left one convent, unfinished, to start the next one before all the details, including the financing, were fully in place. One bishop came to calling her the "Sister of Divine Providence," because her stock answer to all of these problems came from her unusually strong faith. The Lord would provide.

Another clergyman took a different tack, playing to the prevailing sentiments of the age. McAuley, he declared, had crossed into forbidden territory, to be occupied only by men. She had "ipso facto unsexed herself" by attempting to start an order on her own.

Despite all this, the Lord did provide, often in the form of generous donations from people who had maintained the Church in the old days, when it was still underground. Accustomed to stealth and subterfuge, they were happy to pass the torch to the "walkin' nuns," who came boldly through the community in uniform, prayed in the open and almost immediately started schools in communities that had seen none for generations.

In Tullamore, where McAuley formed her second convent, a doughty seventy-year-old named Constantine Molloy, Esq., bought a house and donated it to the Mercies for a hospital. "Con" Molloy was no effete country squire. His reputation came from the days when he and other young men "formed themselves into a body-guard, and taking their stand before the hovel that served for a chapel, threatened to shoot anyone who should dare to interrupt the sacred rites."

She also had faith that her other source of income, the dowries that accompanied her young recruits, would continue to come. When a priest told her that some areas would produce no novices, she told him that was nonsense and compared her approach to that of an army recruiting party with trim uniforms and stirring, military music. The "drum the fife and the cockade," she explained, "aroused new thoughts, new hopes and new projects and the recruiting party is soon followed by a new supply for the ranks."

With the few records we have we may never fully understand this woman's obvious charisma. She kept no diary and there are no known paintings of her. The likenesses that do appear—including her face on Ireland's last five-pound note before the conversion to the euro—were done after her death, taken from women who were thought to resemble Catherine McAuley. Somehow, she was a magnet that attracted many young women and girls, often a third of her age. Most came from comfortable homes, and yet were eager to take up the long hours and the near-poverty sustenance that came with being a "walkin' nun."

It seems clear that some were drawn by McAuley's sense of freedom: She made business deals and took risks, much like a man. There was a palpable, driving force behind McAuley that kept her order in a constant state of expansion. It may have been, in part, a fear that the opportunity to lift the Irish poor would be only temporary, that the English would soon crack down again. It may stem simply from the strength of her faith and her feeling that the human soul—despite the poverty of its surroundings—had incalculable value and beauty. She was going to use her new organization to reach as many souls as she could.

Whatever it was, it made her relentless. One sister recalled McAuley's reaction to her first steam engine as it chugged past a convent she had just opened in Booterstown. Why couldn't humans, she asked herself, somewhat wistfully, apply themselves "as unweariedly to the service of God?"

Attached to all of this was a large funny bone in the woman, who loved to make up nonsense rhymes and silly songs and then challenged others to beat her at it.

"We all loved her very dearly," one of her recruits from Limerick wrote in 1838, when McAuley was fifty-nine. "She would not allow a trace of loftiness or pretension and had nothing of the kind herself. I never saw any remarkable woman who was more free from everything that could suggest the idea of what the world calls a 'clever woman.'"

Whatever it was that she had, it was transferable. When Frances Warde left the Baggot Street house at age twenty-seven to become the "mother" of the new convent in Carlow, she was soon doing the things her mentor would have done. When the town prostitute, Poll, lay on her deathbed, Mother Warde sent her sisters to nurse her, an act which set tongues wagging in the more polite sectors of town.

Warde had had the misgivings of any young person being put in charge of people in situations that were complicated. "What shall I do if we be misunderstood or maligned?" she once asked McAuley. Her leader simply told her that, in that case, "I will come to you my darling."

But McAuley came to realize she couldn't come everywhere. On December 26, 1840, as the Vatican was completing the "rule" that made the Sisters of Mercy an official religious organization under the authority of the pope in church law, McAuley, now nearing sixty-three, wrote a letter from her fourteenth convent, in Birr.

"How many new beds have I rested in!" she remarked. "When I awake in the morning I ask myself where I am; and on the last two or three foundations (new convents) I could not recollect for some moments." The remarkable engine that drove McAuley was finally wearing down.

She died on November 11, 1841, in her house at Baggot Street. Most of the hierarchy of the Catholic Church in Ireland attended the funeral of the nun who had begun her career determined never to be one. By then what she had set in motion was far beyond the Emerald Isle. There was interest in England, Australia and Canada to have Houses of Mercy.

Her biggest legacy came two years later in the form of a tall, young American priest, Rev. Michael O'Connor, who knocked on the door of the convent in Carlow. He had just come from Rome, where he had been given the job of translating the Mercy "rule" into Latin.

The more he read, the more he sensed that "walking nuns" were what he needed for his next assignment. He had the dubious honor of being Pittsburgh's first Catholic bishop. At Carlow, he explained to the sisters that it was a hardship post on the American frontier. There would be few amenities. Catholics there were poor, a besieged minority often ridiculed and threatened by a politically strong group of bigots.

Nearly every Mercy in the convent wanted to go with him. That set off an uproar in Carlow. Relatives of the sisters objected that they would never see them again. Town fathers, who had just become accustomed to the many services of the sisters, were upset. The women told Father O'Connor that there was only one sister who could straighten out this mess.

Frances Warde, then in the process of starting up another convent, was summoned back to Carlow. She and O'Connor and the townspeople worked it out. There would be seven sisters boarding the ship to America. While this provoked more grief and even a day of mourning when the sisters made their farewells, there was no dissent on one point: The woman to lead the sisters to the New World would be McAuley's protégée, Frances Warde.

3
FANNY AND
HER "SWANS"

On November 10, 1843, the *Queen of the West,* a great three-masted schooner, set sail from Liverpool. Among her passengers were seven ladies. Six wore black cashmere dresses with white tuile caps trimmed in white. The seventh, a tall, attractive, outspoken woman, was dressed exactly like them except that her cap was trimmed in lilac.

This was the bishop of Carlow's idea of a disguise. He had had grim visions of the wild mob of bigots that would, doubtless, be waiting for them at the dock when they arrived in New York. He warned them that they should not display any religious insignia. There should be no evidence that they were Catholic nuns, arriving from Ireland.

Since most of the women were in their mid- to early twenties and they were the only women on the ship, they attracted plenty of attention, anyway. They strolled on deck and played literary games with a tall, well-built young man who carried himself with an air of confidence. He was Pittsburgh's new bishop, Michael O'Connor, and this was the beginning of his lifelong friendship and working relationship with the lady in the lilac cap: Frances Warde.

As he and other American bishops would soon learn, this woman was different. Catherine McAuley, the founder of the Sisters of Mercy, was usually deferential when it came to relations with her male superiors. Mother Warde had all the charm of McAuley and then some, but she was never accused of being submissive. Here was a lilac that also had thorns.

At one time or another during her pioneering forty years in America, Mother Frances Xavier Warde, as she was formally known, had dealings with almost the entire leadership of the Catholic Church. For the Church, this was morning in America. It was just beginning its spurt of rapid growth. Among religious women, whose pioneering resulted in schools, hospitals and colleges all across the country, Mother Warde's long career would stand as a benchmark. But the man strolling with her on the ship's deck, Bishop O'Connor, also set the standard for the men of the Church who would follow him. When sisters got into trouble they couldn't handle, he was there to provide support.

Seemingly mild mannered, he had not wanted to be a bishop and preside over the yahoos in America's backwoods. He had readily adapted to the intellectual life in Rome and yearned to become a Jesuit. For this vigorous young American with clear leadership potential, however, the bureaucracy in Rome had one answer: He was to be "a bishop first, a Jesuit afterwards."

So here he was, on his way to Pittsburgh with a cargo of nuns. He had picked them. While there was definitely no guidebook for what he was about to do, he had developed this theory that nuns were essential to build the community-based church he wanted. While the women were his wards, they were not his subjects. He treated them with respect. He assured them that while he lived, the bishop of Pittsburgh would always be there for the sisters, whether it be for Mother Warde or for other orders who became ensnared by the many traps that awaited them in the New World.

In America, Bishop O'Connor once saved Mother Warde's life, but her correspondence with him gives the feel of a woman who would not swoon in response. She had the mettle and power of someone who wished to be treated as a friend and an equal. "Now please write again," she once wrote him, "but not in a stiff cold style like your last or I will not promise that I will be so humble again."

When they arrived in New York, there were no mobs of anti-Catholics to be seen anywhere in the vicinity of the waterfront. Instead they were greeted by a swirl of priests in black, the entourage of the two prime U.S. Catholic leaders: the bishops of New York and Chicago. They were each eager to see Ireland's famed "walking nuns" and to make their pitch for Mercy contingents for their cities.

Chicago, in the form of Bishop-elect William Quarter, was first aboard. He reasoned that since this was the case, Mother Warde should send the first delegation of nuns from her convent in Pittsburgh to Chicago. Perhaps to his surprise, she readily agreed. It was not a frivolous gesture because Mother Warde, then thirty-three, intended to populate a good part of the United States with schools and hospitals staffed by Sisters of Mercy. Impossible? She had helped do it in Ireland.

For a woman of her day, she was well educated. She enjoyed the music of words and was a legendary raconteur. "The writer never knew any man or woman to exceed her in conversational powers," said Mother Austin Carroll, one of her most eloquent contemporaries. Mother Warde had read Sir Walter Scott and memorized a great deal of Byron. Another of her peers later commented that "she probably could not bound [define the borders of] Europe or work a sum in long division, but where is the other person in America or anywhere else who could converse like her and show such stores of general information?"

Bright as she and her colleagues were, Bishop O'Connor had second thoughts about his whole venture as they approached Pittsburgh. He was leading a group of seemingly delicate, mostly city-bred, middle-class, foreign women on a rough carriage ride over the ice-covered Alleghenies into one of the rawest parts of America. Pittsburgh was then more than 150 miles from the nearest railroad. Was he mad?

Raw was an understatement for what he found waiting for them in Pittsburgh. It was a city where some of the working class earned their living "running the river" as deck hands and stevedores serving the growing steamer and barge traffic where the Monongahela and the Allegheny joined to form the Ohio River. The residents called it Smoky City because an acrid haze often hung over it from the constant burning of coal for heating and for the town's major industry, which was making iron.

The streets were paved with mud, fragrantly laced with cow dung. Rush hour came when the cattle were driven through the city to slaughter. Charles Dickens, who visited Pittsburgh in 1842, left thoroughly underwhelmed by its charms. "Pittsburgh is like Birmingham in England, at least its townspeople say so. . . . It certainly has a great quantity of smoke hanging over it," he noted.

In Ireland, where Catholics were the great majority, the Mercies never had to go far to find someone in need of their help. In the diocese of Pittsburgh, three-quarters of the population were Protestants. There were twelve thousand Catholics, but they were spread all over the piney vastness of western Pennsylvania, where the bishop had but twelve priests.

But these *were* Mercies, women who were trained to believe that the harder their mission was, the more it was pleasing to God. Their expectations were shaped by McAuley's obsession with frugality. Moreover, they were led by McAuley's lieutenant, Mother Warde, an inveterate optimist who ruled by example and always praised her subordinates' talents to the heavens.

"All of Mother Frances' geese are swans," was the somewhat ironic word among her peers in Ireland. Of course, some stubbornly retained geeselike characteristics, but because they believed they were swans, they tended to soar over some of the obstacles in the muddy, smoke-filled outpost on the river that would become their first home in America.

Few in Pittsburgh had ever heard of Catholic nuns. Protestants looked upon them with suspicion and Catholics viewed them with coldness "and with fear that they would add to their burdens, without any advantage which they could understand," says one account. But from the first day Mother Warde got them involved with the community, making modifications as she went along to account for the differences in the new territory. Catholics may be scattered, but she had decided that the poor were her main interest, whether they were Catholics or not.

She took her "swans" on long walking tours of Pittsburgh and nearby Allegheny. First they went to the poorhouse. It was an old wooden house jammed with twenty to thirty occupants—men, women and children "Cleanliness was almost unknown in this ill-ventilated, miserable home; the inmates had a woe begone expression most distressing to see," was the way one sister later recalled it.

Their walks also included regular visits to the new penitentiary, a large stone structure just outside Allegheny. After a few sessions, the warden became alarmed when some of the inmates, who weren't Catholic, "expressed a desire to become Catholics after meeting Sister Frances." He devised a new rule saying that "gentlewomen who came for religious purposes" were not to visit with prisoners. Mother Warde found herself locked out of the lockup.

A regular feature of their walks was the homes of the sick. At first the occupants were shocked to open the door and find women speaking in strange accents, dressed in the bulky dark cloaks that McAuley and the Irish bishops had selected for discreet outdoor wear. But then there was a glimmer of recognition. "Oh! You are the Bishop's Sisters. Please, come in." Thanks to the hard-working, popular bishop, another threshold had been crossed and Mother Warde used this entrée to proliferate the Church's ties within the community.

The first Mercy convent in the United States was a four-story brick building on Penn Avenue at the corner of Irwin Alley in Pittsburgh. It had been partially furnished by local Catholic women and Mother Warde completed the furnishing with a chapel, using the money from the dowries of her sisters. She started a small school in the basement in September 1844. An academy for women followed in 1845, and in 1846 the Mercies began to branch into other fields, starting an orphanage.

As she was remembered by her younger sisters, Mother Warde insisted from the very beginning that teachers who used spankings or beatings to keep order in their classrooms were failures. This ran against the accepted teaching practices of the day, but she hated corporal punishment. "[S]he always insisted that any teacher worthy of the name would never find it necessary to resort to it."

As word of the Mercies spread, American women began asking to join the order. The first was Eliza Jane Tiernan, twenty-five, the daughter of a wealthy banker. She was received in an elaborate ceremony, parts of which date from the earliest days of the Catholic Church. Some contend that the inspiration for it is even older, stemming from the Vestal Virgins of ancient Rome. They were noblewomen who dedicated their lives to serve in the temples of the gods. If nothing else, Eliza Tiernan showed the Catholics in Pittsburgh that the Church had a special place for religious women.

First came the cross bearer, a tall girl dressed in purest white, then small girls dressed as angels and carrying garlands of white roses. Then, as this was to be a wedding ceremony, four bridesmaids appeared, young girls robed and veiled in white. Finally Miss Tiernan appeared between Mother Warde and her assistant, Sister Josephine Cullen. Following the ancient custom, Miss Tiernan appeared in a silk bridal gown with a long, flowing train. Her dark hair was held back "by a rich lace veil that swept the floor, while lilies of the valley clustered on her head and in her corsage."

The choir sang a Latin hymn, "O Gloriosa Virgine," because the tradition held that religious women were to be the brides of Christ. It was meant to legitimize their independent standing in the community and it also drove home the point that a young woman was committing her entire life to the works of the Church.

Mass began and Bishop O'Connor explained the significance of the vows that Miss Tiernan, the first American Mercy, was about to take. After the Mass was completed, she left the sanctuary and reappeared in a black habit. "Her long black hair had been cut off and her head was enveloped in the coif and veil of a Sister of Mercy."

She was given a thick silver wedding ring and a black and white Mercy cross that did not have the body of Christ on it. In the young Mercy tradition, the empty space on the cross was reserved for her. It signified that she was willing to take on a cross, a life of hardship to carry out her mission to help the poor. "A suppressed murmur ran through the congregation," when the new nun appeared, says one account.

Once Mother Warde had assured herself that American women were attracted to her order, she began thinking about the promise she had made to Bishop Quarter of Chicago. That, she decided, would be the place for her second convent, so she began preparations. The determination and strong faith of the youngest sister she had brought with her from Ireland, Margaret O'Brien, only twenty-three, had caught her eye. Mother Warde elevated her to "Mother O'Brien" and put her in charge of the four sisters who had volunteered to go to Chicago.

Mother Warde, an old hand at founding convents, led them. Her pioneering trips in Ireland rarely took more than a day. In America of 1846, the trip to Chicago took more than a week, a journey that required a river steamer, a lake steamer and two stagecoaches rumbling over the flat, dusty prairies. It's not clear what Bishop Quarter told them about his frontier outpost. In those days bishops were prone to exaggerate to get help. The first reactions of the nuns, taken later from their letters, make it clear that when they arrived on September 24, they knew that Chicago was something less than the Promised Land. They saw a town of small, jury-built wooden buildings perched like toys on the edge of an enormous lake. "It looked quite smart in the evening haze; its more stylish houses were of dead white with grass-green shutters. It seemed to the travelers as they gazed on the only beautiful object in view on this chill September evening—the waters of Lake Michigan stretching away to meet the sky on the distant horizon—that they had left not only home, but civilization behind them."

When he greeted the young women from Ireland, Bishop Quarter had the same misgivings that Bishop O'Connor had had in Pittsburgh. He showed them their convent, a small, slab-sided, unpainted cottage that they later described as a "sieve in summer and a shell in winter." It was all Quarter could afford and he wondered how long these delicate, citified women would cope with the rigors of a place that made Pittsburgh seem downright comfortable and Old Worldly.

As the bishop talked with Mother Warde in one room about the arrangements, Mother O'Brien and her nuns were exploring the rest of the house. He could hear them through the plank walls. First they were giggling, then there was a chorus of laughter. Quarter felt a little better after that. These were young women, full of the spirit of adventure. Maybe, he thought, they had a chance.

Mother Warde, who evidently shared the same concerns, lingered in Chicago. She set up the walking trips to town, visiting the sick and the jails. Then, in November, bad news arrived from Pittsburgh: Bishop O'Connor was struggling with a smallpox epidemic. Mother Warde began packing for the return trip. This, she knew, would have to be primarily overland. There were no more ferries because the lakes were beginning to freeze.

The Church's rule, stemming from the hangover of the Penal Laws in Ireland, was that nuns always had to travel in pairs. That way they could protect each other and provide witness in the event of any allegations of scandalous behavior. But Mother Warde was in a hurry; she convinced Bishop Quarter to waive the rule after she found an elderly, asthmatic priest who was traveling to Allegheny to visit a sick relative. They left in a hailstorm that distracted Mother Warde so much that she forgot to take the food basket that Mother O'Brien's sisters had carefully packed for her.

The Conestoga wagon took three days to reach Toledo, navigating roads that were often mere wagon ruts in the snow. Mother Warde spent two of the days without food. Although she was dressed in civilian clothes, she was not inconspicuous amid the rest of the passengers on the wagon, who were trappers and other frontiersmen with a natural tendency to gawk at the rare woman they happened to see. They appeared rough enough that Mother Warde preferred to remain in the wagon when it stopped at wayside taverns, where the men had coffee and whisky.

As the wagon jerked and bounced over the washboard roads, the old priest beside her was taken by frequent fits of coughing. "The poor mother, who at all times of her life was the pink of neatness and refinement, had her garments covered as with feathers from his frequent expectorations," describes one account of this journey, apparently taken from Mother Warde's letters.

At the time Ohio was still being hacked out of the vast forest that once covered it and there were long stretches through the dark woods on roads that probably followed ancient buffalo trails. One of Mother Warde's biographers says she found the trip to Toledo "mysterious and terrifying. The only sounds that she heard were the snoring of the passengers and the screeching of the prairie chickens. She [Mother Warde] wondered if she would ever get out of this vast, lonely desert alive."

In Toledo she found a hotel where a chambermaid gave her directions to church the following morning. It was a near blizzard and a coach driver refused to take her there, so Mother Warde stumbled through the stinging, drifting snow to get to Mass. Afterward the priest, Father Louis de Goesbriand, who had spotted her during communion, motioned her to visit him in the sacristy, the room where priests put on their vestments for Mass. He had, somehow, guessed that she was a nun. They had a pleasant chat.

Heading east again on the stagecoach, her spirits began to lift. Mother Warde found herself sitting next to a Protestant minister. He seemed rather stiff and full of himself until the wagon tipped into a deep ditch and the driver ordered him out with the other male passengers, leaving Mother Warde by herself for two hours. The men returned with some timbers and a team of oxen. After much prying and pulling, they brought the Conestoga back up on the road.

The minister resumed his seat, but found it harder to resume his dignity because he was now coated with mud. Mother Warde thought that was funny. "Oh! Sir," she exclaimed, "the next place we come to the people will think we threw you overboard." As they bumped along, he con-

*Mother Frances Warde
(from a painting).*
(COURTESY OF THE SISTERS
OF MERCY OF THE AMERICAS)

cluded it *was* funny and they laughed about it the rest of the way to San-dusky, where Mother Warde freshened up, using a basin "for general use" next to a horse trough.

On the next stage she met a Methodist minister, who began muttering about the "superstition and priestcraft" of Catholics. Mother Warde took him on and for the next hours the other passengers were amused to see the strange, solitary woman and the minister locked in a serious religious debate. While she enjoyed the exchange, by the time they pulled into Brownsville, Mother Warde found herself exhausted, too tired to eat. The fact that an iron bar had somehow become disengaged from the roof of the coach and had fallen on her head didn't help matters.

She took a midnight steamer on the Ohio and arrived on the wharf at Pittsburgh at three in the morning. There was no one to meet her and no coaches for hire. She staggered through the deserted streets to the con-vent, where it took a full thirty minutes of knocking and shouting for her nuns to discover that "Mother" was back. "When the sisters saw how ill she was," says the history of the Pittsburgh Mercies, "they summoned a doctor. For ten days she hovered between life and death."

House calls were the beginning and the end of medical treatment west of the Alleghenies in those days. It was Bishop O'Connor's longstanding dream to build Pittsburgh's first hospital, and he and the Mercies collaborated to turn a building the sisters had used as a convent and an academy into a hospital capable of handling 150 patients.

It opened on New Year's Day 1857, and it was no small feat in a Calvinist town where the "overriding faith," as one Pittsburgh history put it, was "in work and in the certainty of its rewards." Typical of many American histories, which give much more attention to buildings and bridges, the book notes simply that Pittsburgh's Mercy Hospital opened in 1847. That was five years before the city fathers arrived at the decision that they needed a board of health.

Who founded the hospital and who financed it? The history leaves these questions unanswered, as if it had simply sprung out of the ground. Ironically, the nuns' first patient was a sick sailor who had been brought up from the wharf. The sisters learned he was a Know Nothing who had been part of a mob that had earlier burned the Catholic cathedral in Philadelphia. He was admitted. Mother Warde shared Catherine McAuley's aversion to red tape. It was always better to offer assistance first and ask questions later, she would tell her nuns. The sailor met Mother Warde's sole admissions requirements: He was poor and he was sick.

During the following year, she concentrated on the hospital, which also saw an influx of soldiers returning with various diseases from the Mexican War. The community began to provide resources for the hospital, which was a fortuitous thing, because it was about to meet its most severe challenge. In the winter of 1847 a plague of "ship fever" broke out among the waves of Irish immigrants arriving in New York, Boston and Canada. It was a nightmare from Mother Warde's old world, the cold, dead hand of the Irish Penal Laws returning to haunt her.

The great potato famine had struck Ireland, a blight that wiped out the only reliable crop that the impoverished Irish had. Potatoes were among the few nutritious crops they could grow in sufficient quantity on the small plots of rented farmland that the laws had consigned them to. When the potato crop failed, landlords faced a dilemma. Their starving renters could no longer pay them, but they, the landlords, were forced to pay an annual rent for each tenant they kept on the land. Consulting shipping rates, some landlords discovered it was cheaper, in the long run, to ship their former tenants to the United States and Canada. Other Irish bought their own way out, desperate to escape the ravages of the famine.

In the mass exodus that followed, it is estimated that a million Irish emigrated, mostly to the United States, and another million died. Among those who emigrated, many arrived in so-called famine ships, where they had been jammed without adequate food, clothes, bedding or sanitary facilities for weeks.

The fare to Canada was the cheapest, so well over 100,000 Irish were shipped there. According to notes taken by doctors at the receiving point, Grosse Isle, an island in the St. Lawrence near Quebec, medical facilities were quickly overwhelmed by the arriving cargoes of misery. Here is an account of the arrival of the *Virginius,* which set sale from Liverpool in the spring of 1847 with 476 passengers, most of them Irish.

"Fever and dysentery cases came on board this vessel in Liverpool and deaths occurred before leaving the Mersey. . . . Yesterday it was found that 106 were ill of fever . . . and the large number of 158 had died on the passage . . . the few that were able to come on deck were ghastly yellow looking spectres, unshaven and hollow cheeked."

The ancestors of some of America's future elite—the families of Henry Ford and John F. Kennedy among them—staggered off ships in this condition. It is one part of their American experience that Irish tend to forget. We now know that "ship fever" was an especially virulent form of typhus. As some of the afflicted began to show up on the wharves of Pittsburgh, Mother Warde prepared an isolation ward in her hospital for the grim battle that she knew lay ahead.

The disease was spread by bacteria on the feces of body lice, but no one knew then how to deal with infectious diseases. Mother Warde and her nuns did what they had been trained to do during the cholera epidemics in Ireland: They worked night and day to keep their patients clean and comfortable. When there was nothing else they could do, they prayed over them.

They succeeded, but at a chilling price. Of nineteen typhoid patients, thirteen survived. In this effort, eight of Mother Warde's nurses died, including three of five nuns who ran the hospital. A fourth, Sister Elizabeth Tiernan, collapsed from exhaustion after weeks of night-long sessions, laboring over patients in the isolation ward. When she was lifted onto her hospital bed, she asked where Mother Warde was, because she was rarely absent from the hospital. Mother Warde, she was told, was also sick. "Don't disturb her," whispered Sister Tiernan. The first American Mercy, the one who became the bride of Christ in the festive and ancient church ceremony, had borne her cross with dignity. Sister Tiernan died on March 9, 1847. Much of Pittsburgh turned out for her funeral.

Her heroic example and that of the other Mercies "killed all bigotry against the nursing Sisters of Mercy among Pittsburgh residents," writes one of Mother Warde's biographers. It didn't totally annihilate bigotry, though. Just two years later Joe Barker, a street preacher, was arrested for starting a riot with one of his rousing anti-Catholic homilies. Upon conviction, he was thrown into jail. There, he was elected mayor of Pittsburgh.

But by then the Sisters of Mercy were a recognized fixture in the Smoky City as more women asked to join the order. Plans were laid for a bigger hospital and a new convent, but for several months the order was without a leader. Mother Warde's health was "completely shattered" by the experience, says one of her confidantes. Bishop O'Connor sensed the vacuum, quickly closed the schools and moved Mother Warde and the remaining sisters to his house near the cathedral for rest and recuperation.

Meanwhile he and his priests lived temporarily with parishioners. It was a small sacrifice to make, compared to what the nuns had been through. The priests were amazed to see how quickly these women, just two years off the boat, had moved into the heart of the community. Bishop O'Connor had sensed their power. Perhaps it was the bishop's male intuition that told him Mother Warde and her "swans" deserved the best care he could give them. Their American adventure had hardly begun.

4

MOTHER EXODUS

To the average Catholic, the face of America in the middle of the nineteenth century wore a mask of hatred. The flood of Catholic immigrants, led by the impoverished Irish, closely followed by Germans, was rapidly changing the demographics of the country—especially its cities.

With the immigrants came hundreds of orders of religious women who, like Mother Warde, seemed very foreign at first, parading in the streets in their distinctive habits. But they, too, were soon building institutions that gave them a following in the community and made them a political and social force. Following Bishop O'Connor's success, many other Catholic bishops had gone to Ireland seeking nuns. Women recruited from these trips started separate Mercy convents in New York, Little Rock and San Francisco.

The bishop of Cincinnati had his own special emissary for this purpose. She was Mrs. Sarah Worthington King Peter, a wealthy Episcopalian who was accustomed to taking grand shopping trips to Europe for the purpose of collecting objects of art. But she had become so outraged over acts of anti-Catholic bigotry that she volunteered to recruit and bring back eleven Mercies from Kinsale, Ireland. For a while, they operated out of her mansion. Mrs. Peter became so absorbed in helping them get a start in Cincinnati that, when she died, her heirs were surprised to find a Madonna by Botticelli that she had collected and put aside. It was sitting in her attic, still in its packing crate.

Importing sisters was an experiment that continued to work. By 1852 Catholic sisters had created 133 schools, mostly for women. Hospitals and orphanages were springing up everywhere.

During her long convalescence in Pittsburgh, Mother Warde liked to read letters about what her "swans" were doing, especially in Chicago, where they had bought a lake-front hotel and turned it into a hospital. It dealt with everyone, including trappers, horse rustlers and other men who had lead rough lives on the prairies and came back to the city to die.

The sisters were fascinated by one elderly patient, a man who was deliberately vague about his occupation. Fellow patients in his ward were frequently jolted awake when he would cry out, "Hands up, gentlemen!" in his sleep.

The hospital was run by a Dr. N.S. Davis, a man who had a stiff, slow way of speaking, but had gotten the Mercy philosophy down pat: He made the rich wait while he treated the poor. When wealthier patients tried to pull rank, they got a crisp, "Very well, take a chair, sir." When they persisted, pointing out that they were one of the city's growing class of prospering burghers or related to so-and-so in City Hall, the answer was raised eyebrows and feigned awe. "Oh! Well then, take two chairs, sir!"

Many working-class Americans didn't see a funny side to the new inroads being made by Catholics. They regarded them as a foreign invading force. The new immigrants were often uncouth. They were taking away jobs, beginning to push their way in politically, creating a velocity of change that made many Americans feel confused and uncomfortable.

Signs saying NO IRISH NEED APPLY were pasted up in shop windows. In 1849, New Yorkers saw the birth of the Order of the Star Spangled Banner, an anti-Catholic secret society, which later evolved into the American Party. When asked about their political aims, the members would often say, "I know nothing," a name which newspaper editorialists soon baptized them with.

But they had power, feeding from hatred that had already precipitated anti-Catholic riots in Cincinnati, Louisville, Albany and Philadelphia, where fifteen people were killed in 1844 as mobs burned two Catholic churches and a seminary. The rioters culminated with a celebratory bonfire made from five thousand books they found in the seminary's library.

Further fuel for the mobs came from various anti-Catholic tracts, many of which regarded nuns to be the most convenient targets because they stood out. People were curious about them. One popular tract was the "Awful Disclosures of Maria Monk," purported to be written by an escapee from a Montreal convent who described convents as being places with hidden tunnels and bizarre motives, where sisters committed infanticide and were sex slaves of priests.

"Rome's Traffic in Nuns" noted that nuns often beat themselves daily with steel-tipped whips and had early deaths from "diseases and lunacy." It went on: "They belong to the type which dreams dreams and sees visions. . . . A certain number would be certified as insane by any medical man who examined them."

Mother Warde was certainly aware of all this, but in 1849, as she regained her strength, she needed it to deal with a threat from a different direction. James Oliver Van de Velde, the new bishop of Chicago, had determined that the sisters in his territory had no right to hold property. He ordered the Mercies to turn over the deeds to their lucrative, lakefront land to him. Mother Warde reminded him that the Mercies were an order recognized by Rome. If he pressed the issue, she would withdraw the sisters. The bishop backed down.

The following year an odd thing happened. It is the custom of Mercies to hold periodic elections for their leaders, and in 1850, the most obvious candidate was Mother Warde, the order's American founder. But the vote resulted in a split, giving neither Mother Warde nor her assistant, Sister Josephine Cullen, a majority. So Bishop O'Connor stepped in and declared Cullen to be the new superior; Mother Warde was sent to teach at the local academy.

One of her biographers, Kathleen Healy, concluded in 1973 that this must have had something to do with Mother Warde's sparring with the bishops. She had not been "docile" enough. But the circumstances of Mother Warde's life suggest a simpler reason: She was bored. While Catholics in other cities were on the front lines in the battle against bigotry, Pittsburgh was too quiet. The woman craved action and she soon found it. In 1851 Bishop Bernard O'Reilly of Providence, Rhode Island, invited her to bring some sisters and start a convent. New England was the chief hotbed of Know Nothings. Mother Warde accepted.

She selected four sisters for the trip. Mother Warde was now forty. A colleague who met her in New York, on the way to Providence, remarked, "I did not know Mother Francis when I first saw her. She is greatly changed in appearance . . . quiet and subdued."

To avoid a mob scene, Bishop O'Reilly asked the sisters to wear nondescript clothes and he entered the city with them at night, taking them to a small house he had selected as a future convent and school. Things went badly, at first. Crowds mocked the women in the street. A young man, a Yale student, picked one sister up bodily and then dropped her to the ground to the laughter of his friends. Small boys threw mud at the sisters and marked chalk crosses on their habits when they took their long walks to visit jails and the sick.

A desperate request by Mother Warde to the Mercies in Ireland for more teachers brought Sister Mary Austin Carroll, a bright twenty-year-old who had just graduated from Ireland's new teacher-training program. She recalls the abuse extending into the evening, with sisters enduring a shower of glass during their recreation period as rocks crashed through the windows. The rock throwers were methodical in their efforts to drive out the sisters. Sister Carroll, a gifted writer, wrote it all down, remembering "one bright midnight [when] the glass of every window was completely shattered."

Through all this, Mother Warde flourished. The daily punishment brought her a steady stream of young women from as far away as Rochester and New York City who wanted to join the Mercies. Some Protestant leaders felt guilty about the mob actions and offered to help. One, a Mr. Stead, offered the Mercies a more substantial house with stone walls and a walled garden. They accepted.

Among the new recruits was Miss Rebecca Newell, a spinsterish woman from a well-known Puritan family. She was twenty-eight and became intrigued after teachers at the local high school told her how well educated Mother Warde was. At the time Mother Warde, who could be seen almost daily riding in her carriage in a plain blue suit and bonnet, was busy opening new schools and convents in Hartford and New Haven.

When Newell asked Mother Warde to instruct her in the Catholic faith, Newell's family retaliated by banishing her from the home. She went to Pennsylvania to live with an uncle, a minister. That experience apparently pushed her over the edge. Miss Newell reappeared at the convent and made formal application to become a member of the Sisters of Mercy.

Rumors soon spread throughout Providence that Miss Newell was being held in the convent against her will. The *Providence Journal* wrote that Newell had made the choice of her own free will "however unpleasant it may be to see a young lady of high intelligence and character forsake the religion of her fathers."

The editorial made no difference to the crowds forming in front of the convent. This was the excuse they had been waiting for. "Unlock your prison and free the beautiful Yankee girl," became the slogan. It brought train loads of Know Nothings from Boston, Salem and Taunton.

The mayor, a Know Nothing named Knowles, came to the convent to ask Mother Warde to order Miss Newell to leave, warning her that a crowd that could involve as many as ten thousand angry protesters was forming. Mother Warde said she would do that only if Newell wished to leave.

When the mayor insisted that he was helpless to control such a mob, Mother Warde told him, icily, "If I was the chief magistrate of the city, I should know how to prevent a riot and keep order." Meanwhile Bishop O'Reilly came up with his own solution. He quietly assembled two hundred men, mostly Irish laborers. In ones and twos, they stealthily filed into the convent carrying an assortment of concealed weapons including old rifles, pistols and sword canes.

All the elements were falling into place for what could have been the bloodiest anti-Catholic massacre in America. On the frosty night of March 22, 1855, powder kegs were added to the mob's growing arsenal. There seems to have been a fair amount of drinking underway on both sides. John O'Rourke, the convent's janitor, swaggered up to Mother Warde, revolvers dangling out of each of his pockets. He was ready, he announced. She warned him, sternly, that there was going to be no shooting.

Bishop O'Reilly made out his will and then instructed a few of his priests to put on rough clothes and infiltrate the crowd in a last-ditch effort to try and control the situation. At eleven P.M., after mob leaders made their third threat to blow up the convent and its occupants if Newell was not released, the bishop, a bulky man wearing a straw hat and a linen duster, appeared in front of the convent.

"The sisters shall not leave the house for an hour. I will protect them with my blood if need be," the bishop shouted, over the taunts of the mob. A thin cheer came from the crowd, mainly from O'Reilly's strategically placed priests. But the overall mood remained ugly. Then Mr. Stead, the owner of the house, appeared beside the bishop. He asked Mayor Knowles, who was also there, to read the Riot Act, which he proceeded to do.

That meant he was threatening to arrest the mob. But where were Knowles's forces? He had none. The crowd jeered. A few rocks were thrown. Then Mr. Stead informed the crowd that it was not an empty threat. "Let me tell you there are four hundred strong Irishmen here, armed with deadly weapons within the enclosure of the garden walls. At the least attempt at violence, they will defend it."

To underscore where he stood, this most heroic of all landlords added, "The first shot fired at this house will go through my body."

The crowd, which has been variously estimated at several hundred, appeared uncertain about what to do next. This was shaping up to be a real fight. Then an Irish woman pushed her way to the front and cheerily asked the bishop if she could "help scatter a few prayers among the heathens."

That should have been the detonation point, but it wasn't. One of O'Reilly's disguised priests angrily confronted her, telling the woman— who was probably drunk—to go home and pray the rosary. Then they were both mocked by the crowd, but the psychological moment for action had somehow passed. The men outside slowly melted away. The men inside eventually put down their weapons and enjoyed a late supper, served by the nuns.

In retrospect, one of the most telling threats in this face-off may not have involved the fear of the law or a bloody fight. It involved something else that Yankees respect: their property. In his speech, Mr. Stead cleverly reminded them of their peculiar vulnerability. Most homes in Providence had Irish servants. Burn down the Mercy convent, he noted, "and your homes will be fired."

Miss Newell decided to leave the Mercies several months later, but remained part of the Catholic community in Providence, which grew along with the Mercies. Mother Warde's life again evolved into routine. Schools were started and staffed. Sister Austin Carroll was put in charge of instructing the widening stream of young novices how to teach school.

In the spring of 1858, two bishops came to the convent with a problem: Manchester, New Hampshire, a factory town, was developing a substantial population of Catholics. But the Know Nothings retained a robust and sometimes imaginative presence. Once they had surreptitiously cut through the supports of a temporary chapel there, so that when the building filled for Sunday Mass, the priest, the altar and the parishioners all slowly descended into the basement.

In 1854, they noted, the Know Nothings had staged a riot, driving Catholics from their homes, dragging the sick into the street and stoning the windows of St. Anne's, a newly built Catholic Church. Thanks to the intervention of some non-Catholic leaders, the church was saved, and the local priest, a heroic man named Father William McDonald, was building a convent alongside it.

But the head Know Nothing, a fanatic who styled himself the Angel Gabriel, had vowed that "no woman wearing religious garb shall ever enter the territory." The two men, Bishop Francis McFarland of Providence and Bishop David Bacon of Portland, Maine, went on to explain how Father McDonald had to stand watch nightly as the convent was being constructed to keep it from being burned to the ground.

In retrospect, it seems clear that the two men were trolling for Mother Warde, who had already volunteered for the Manchester mission before they launched into their scary tales about the Know Nothings. Bishop Bacon, who sometimes referred to the assembled nuns as "my children," became even more patronizing. "You see, Sisters, it is a big task we are presenting to you. Don't feel obliged to make good your offer of some minutes ago."

This was like waving a red flag in front of a bull. Mother Warde volunteered again. "Perhaps we need to remind him [the bishop] that his 'children' have already had some experience with the Know Nothings right here in Providence," she told her sisters. She picked four from those who volunteered. Then she resigned as the superior in Providence and made preparations for the trip. Hitting the road again, after a career of founding new convents, gained her a new nickname among the younger nuns: "Mother Exodus."

On July 16, as the volunteers climbed into their waiting carriages, Bishop Bacon was there to steel them for the journey, talking about the risk of "persecution, burning, stoning to death." All this seems unnecessary for Mother Warde, who was already pumped up for Manchester. This time, she had told her sisters, there would be no sneaking into town. They would come in wearing their habits.

For some reason the Angel Gabriel and his minions were not waiting for them when their train pulled into Manchester station. Instead the Catholics of Manchester, dressed in their Sunday best, were there to greet them. Many knew of the Mercy nuns' work in Ireland.

Father McDonald brought the sisters to a neat, brick building next to his church, where a dinner was prepared. Assuming this was to be their convent, Mother Warde was squinting out the window at their new surroundings. What was this large brick building on the other side of the church? she wondered. "It seems to be a college."

They were in the rectory, said Father McDonald. What she was looking at was her new convent. Protestants had been looking at it too, as it went up. There was a large number of small rooms upstairs. Downstairs, in the basement, there was one small dark room with a high window overlooking a brickyard. They had decided this was the dungeon, but a careful examination did not reveal any trapdoors or secret passages.

Father McDonald had one more parting gift, a wad of bills that he pressed into her hand. It contained over one hundred dollars. "Keep the wolf away from the door," he whispered.

Rather than wait for the wolf, the new walking nuns of Manchester took to the streets the next day. It was uneventful, except for one minor incident where a woman tossed back the veil of one sister and spat in her face. That evening, as the sisters had dinner, Mother Warde noticed a small crowd forming outside the convent. It was time for a stroll in the garden, she announced.

They turned out to be neighbors who were curious. They had never seen nuns before. One woman wondered about their "unusual garb," and Mother Warde's sisters staged an impromptu fashion show, explaining the symbolism of each item of their habit. "The black represents the life of poverty which we profess to follow," one explained. "Our veils signify the life of chastity which we have chosen."

This show-and-tell went on until well after dark. Dozens of people had questions. Mother Warde finally had one of her sisters sidle back into the convent to ring the bells. The sisters had to excuse themselves, Mother Warde explained, because they were being summoned to chapel.

This seemed odd to one skeptic, talking to his colleagues after they left. "Anomalies," he said, "but at any rate, they are friendly, and who could detect in the face of even one of them a look of unhappiness?"

Mother Warde realized she had hit on the right formula for resolving the fears of the curious in Manchester. She staged regular Saturday tours of the convent to let citizens have a more systematic probe of its hidden mysteries. No hidden passageways were discovered. The small, bricked-in room in the basement turned out to be a bakery.

She offered to give private lessons in French and to teach music to adults. Several accepted, including the wife of Manchester's mayor. Later, after the city grew more comfortable with its new nuns, it turned several of its more troubled public schools over to the care of the Mercies.

At night the convent offered instruction in the Catholic faith to adults. This was still touchy business. One night an angry Scotsman burst into the convent, interrupting a ceremony where his Presbyterian wife and his nine-year-old child, who had been converted by Mother Warde, were being baptized as Catholics.

As he sputtered, Mother Warde turned the full force of her charm on him, persuading him to stay and see the ceremony. Later she converted him and his brother.

Then she organized a Sunday school, an elementary school for girls and finally an academy for young women that attracted well-to-do Protestants because it offered a full liberal arts curriculum, including music, Latin, French, Italian, and German, painting and typewriting. "Differences in religion will not be regarded in the admission of pupils who are willing to conform to the general regulations," said the brochure of Mount Saint Mary's Academy.

There were misgivings from some Catholics, including some of her sisters. But Mother Warde shared Catherine McAuley's view about the worth of entrepreneurial activities. The select academies for young women helped the Church build bridges to the larger community and were "a tremendous help in breaking down bigotry."

The bishops had misgivings, too, but they seemed to have one surefire solution to expanding the Church in troublesome cities: Bring in Mother Warde. In the spring of 1861, Bishop James Frederick Wood of Philadelphia sent an emissary to Manchester. He asked whether Mother Warde could send a delegation of her sisters to take over a Catholic school there.

The vision of the earlier church burnings and book roastings in the City of Brotherly Love was all that it took to put "Mother Exodus" on the road again. In August she arrived in force, bringing ten sisters. She liked Philadelphia so much that the following month, when Bishop Wood and a guest, a bishop from Kentucky, visited their new convent, she told him she had appointed herself to be the superior of the Philadelphia convent. It would be run as a branch of Manchester. It was part of her plan to unify all the houses of Mercy in America under one leadership.

"Conversation was light" until Mother Warde explained her plan. Then Bishop Wood "evidenced great displeasure," but didn't argue about the matter apparently out of deference to the other bishop. Two weeks later, however, he returned with his top aide and laid down the law to the nuns. This was a matter of turf. "She [Mother Warde] had no right to exercise any authority from the moment she arrived in his diocese."

With that, Mother Warde went back to Manchester. There were other bishops, other opportunities. She sent delegations to Vermont, Omaha, California, New Jersey and Maine, where, in her seventies, she was taking canoe trips to start schools among the Passamaquoddy Indians. They dubbed Mother Warde the "Great White Mother." Meanwhile her previous convents in Providence, Chicago and Pittsburgh were rapidly spreading the order through the South, the Midwest and the West.

By 1881, there were more than two hundred convents with ten thousand Catholic sisters in the United States. Among these women, Mother Warde founded 120 convents, schools, hospitals and other institutions of social welfare, "more than any other religious leader of the Western World."

At about the same time Mother Warde's favorite enemy, the Know Nothings, had all but disappeared from the nation's political landscape. With all of their bilious fulmination and vicious nonsense, they were dead right about one thing: Mother Frances Warde was definitely one of these women who saw visions and dreamed dreams. "No one," writes Kathleen Healy, "was more personally involved in the realization of Catherine McAuley's dream in America than Frances Warde."

5

"THE NORTH LADIES"

On a balmy May evening in 1862, a heavy rain beat a tattoo on the roof of the Hammond General Hospital in Beaufort, North Carolina, as nine women, all dressed in black, arrived in a small boat. Stark figures sillhouetted against the muddy sky, they walked single file down a long wharf to the hospital, a rambling, three-story structure built on pilings over the Atlantic.

Just three months earlier it had been the Atlantic Hotel, a swank, new summer resort catering to the families of rich Southern planters. Now, as the women neared the beach, they saw signs of its current distress. Debris from what had been a grand piano, bits of shattered chandeliers, pieces of broken furniture and shards of what had been the hotel's elegant dinnerware lay underneath the dock, rolling lazily back and forth in the surf.

It had been one helluva party. A few weeks previously, the hotel was sacked in a midnight raid by the Union Army. A few days after the wine cellar had been drunk and the furniture had been thrown from the rooms and the tiers of porches that hung over the sea, the boats began to arrive with their sad cargoes. Two hundred men in blood-caked uniforms— Union casualties from multiple battles raging on the nearby Virginia peninsula—were carried in to mark the final stage of the transformation from a pleasure palace to a ruin filled with pain.

Until the women arrived, it had been one of the Civil War's many horrible medical innovations—a do-it-yourself hospital with no nurses, no soap, no candles, no lamps and a few sticks of furniture. Placed in charge of all this was a "steward," a suspicious, illiterate, barefoot man, a woodcutter from Maine named "Kit" Condon. He tended to rule the place from his perch on a wheelbarrow near the kitchen door.

Who were these women? some of the soldiers wondered. Widows, others concluded, more wives from the north seeking the remains of their husbands. The medical consequences of the war were now reaching a level of butchery that had not been seen in land warfare outside the Orient. By the time the shooting stopped, there would be 1,094,453 casualties, including 634,026 dead. At the outset of the war the carnage from mechanized weapons and more accurate artillery completely overwhelmed the slender medical capabilities of both the Union and the Confederacy.

The army had renamed the Atlantic Hotel after Dr. George A. Hammond, a hardworking, innovative Baltimore doctor who was Lincoln's new surgeon general. He was struggling to reorganize the Army's medical bureau. This was the day that Kit and his scruffy crew—who were busy making bread on the dirty marble top of a broken billiard table they had dragged into the kitchen—discovered that their daily drill was about to change. One of Dr. Hammond's prescriptions was the introduction of Catholic nuns as nurses.

These were no widows. They were Sisters of Mercy from New York City, Irish women led by Mother Augustine MacKenna, who was educated in a hedge school and had run an infirmary and a home for homeless girls. An unusually tall, handsome woman, she would explain to people, "I am the daughter of an Irish giant." After surveying the filth in the hospital, she told Kit she was taking over and presented the Army with her list of demands, which included brooms, tubs, kitchen utensils, castile soap, cologne, dressing gowns, towels, sponges, starch, lamps, kerosene and better food.

Neither Mr. Kit nor the Army liked the idea of being ordered around by these strange women, but an order from Washington soon followed, putting the sisters in charge of everything but the medical department. Then a steamer arrived from New York laden with the goods they demanded. Clearly, the Atlantic Hotel had now been taken in a surprise raid by the Sisters of Mercy.

This was a novelty to the soldiers, who had been nursing each other, sort of. Some were Harvard men, members of the 45th Massachusetts Volunteers. They had made a dashing entrance with their crisp new blue uniforms, landing accompanied by one of the best bands in the Army. Then the Confederate artillery had dashed them into the mud. One of the hospital's patients, a sixteen-year-old private named Hiram Hubbard, was found screaming because his wool shirt had become encrusted into a festering back wound. His mates were trying to scrub it free using a rough towel soaked in cold water. Suddenly he felt a gentle hand take over, applying warm water and soap with a soft sponge. The shirt came off the wound. Private Hubbard stopped screaming, but his face was still pressed hard into the pillow of his bed.

"Who is doing that?" came his muffled voice.

"A Sister of Mercy," she said as she dressed his back in soft, old linen.

"What are you!" exclaimed the boy, turning, astonished to see a woman dressed in black with her face framed by a stiff white collar. She was Sister Mary Gertrude Ledwith. She had seen her fill of frightened, shattered young men while serving as a nurse in the Crimean war, but she patiently explained to him that a Mercy's job was to help those who suffer. The opposite poles of the emerging America stared at each other: the Harvard man, the immigrant Irish nun. Private Hubbard finally settled back on his bed, his pain eased. "I don't care what you are," he sighed, "you are a mother to me."

More supplies appeared. Accumulating layers of filth were scrubbed from the walls and floors. A new doctor arrived. The food improved and meals were served on time. The Hammond had a number of black women, freed slaves, who had come to work at the hospital. To them this was an amazing phenomenon: women in strange uniforms ordering around the conquering Union soldiers! At night, when everyone else was asleep, the blacks held impromptu skits in the kitchen, mimicking the authority and the Irish accents of the Hammond's new masters as they issued cryptic commands to imaginary officers. They called them the North Ladies.

Dr. Hammond sustained some political wounds from his bold effort to recruit more nuns for the hospitals. Army surgeons, who had often worked with them in hospitals before the war, seemed to prefer sisters.

They were disciplined, organized and would calmly volunteer for the dirtiest, most difficult tasks.

However, Protestants, especially some of the Protestant women who were also struggling to control the chaos and the pain in the hospitals, were suspicious. They argued that sisters showed partiality to Catholic soldiers and withheld "the consolation of the Bible from men of other faiths." But Dr. Hammond, too, was a Protestant. What he liked about the sisters was that they worked. He lined up on their side, digging in and fighting the multiple efforts to banish the nuns.

"What Protestant nurses could compare with the Sisters of Charity in efficiency and faithfulness?" asks one contemporary account of Dr. Hammond's bureaucratic battles.

Nursing was still a long way from a recognized profession; "the prevailing opinion [was] that fulltime service in hospitals was not respectable work for women," notes an expert on the medical efforts of the Confederacy. What the prevailing opinion overlooked, however, was that sisters brought something to the battlefields that was rare: more nursing experience than the armies had. In early 1861, the Union Army operated one hospital in Fort Leavenworth, Kansas. Catholic sisters ran more than twenty, many of them started in converted barns, hotels, warehouses—exactly the conditions the Union Army was confronting in 1862, when it was saddled with more than two hundred hospitals and few trained staff.

The Confederate Army's situation was worse. It was building a medical bureau from scratch, with much less in the way of money and supplies to support it. For many of the wounded men in gray, the sight of Catholic sisters was even stranger. "Who are they?" gasped a group of bystanders as five Daughters of Charity arrived in Marietta, Georgia, in 1863 to care for the wounded. Their black habits and the coronettes, their distinctive, white-winged headgear, had given the order the nickname "God's geese" in the slums of Paris. In the dust and chaos of wartime Marietta, they seemed like women from Mars.

"Are they men or women?" asked another.

"Surely the enemy will run from them," contributed a third.

Of the 3,200 female nurses who served in military hospitals in the Civil War, at least 580 were sisters, coming from 12 religious orders. The most, more than 300 nuns, came from the Daughters of Charity, then the largest order in the nation. The second largest group, about 100

*A Daughter of Charity nurses soldiers at the General Hospital in Richmond,
Virginia, during the Civil War. (From a sketch made by a Union officer who was
convalescing there as a prisoner of war.)* (COURTESY OF THE ARCHIVES OF THE DAUGHTERS
OF CHARITY, EMMITSBURG, MARYLAND)

women, were volunteers from 7 different congregations of Mercies,
including Pittsburgh and Chicago. "God's geese" and Frances Warde's
"swans" were mobilized.

Working conditions were brutal. Roughly three out of five casualties
were caused by various infectious diseases, including dysentery, typhus,
malaria, smallpox, measles and tuberculosis that ran rampant in the camps
on both sides. The medical profession was still in the dark about the
causes of most infections, but their practice did include one effective and
easily administered cure: amputations, which limited gangrene, and were
the preferred remedy for even minor wounds.

In May 1863, the poet Walt Whitman gave us a portrait of a field hospital near Fredericksburg, Virginia, describing a moonlit spring night where the grass was carpeted with blood and bodies contorted in various conditions of agony. He called it a "butcher's shambles."

"O well it is their mothers, their sisters cannot see them—cannot conceive, and never conceiv'd, these things. One man is shot by a shell, both in the arm and leg—both are amputated—there lie the rejected members. Some have their legs blown off—some bullets through the breast—some indescribably horrid wounds in the face or head, all mutilated, sickening, torn, gouged out—some in the abdomen—some mere boys . . . the surgeons use them just the same."

Whitman's sense that women couldn't "conceive" of such conditions was the orthodoxy of his day. The truth of the battlefield was that some women dealt with this situation nightly. It was a "hard, wearing life; those who had lasted for any length of time seemed scarcely young and delicate," notes one account, adding that even the most righteous of the women nurses almost always carried an additional burden: the slander that they were ladies of easy virtue. The Union Army paid them forty cents a day. The Confederate Army paid nothing.

Needless to say, there was a high burnout rate, but many of the nuns stuck with it for the duration. The other orders shared the sense of the Mercies, that the hardest sacrifices were the most pleasing to God. Their habits and their organization protected them from the slander of easy virtue and, as the war ground on, it became abundantly clear to others on the battlefields that they certainly weren't out there for the money.

What bolstered Dr. Hammond in his requests for more and more nuns were inspection reports from the field. A hospital in Sedalia, Missouri, had been established in an old store and an adjoining house. A general had taken fifty of its hospital beds for his staff, leaving the wounded lying on the floor amid overfilled spittoons and reeking chamber pots. "Floors, bedding and men needed 'scraping,'" said one report. "Doctors felt helpless for want of nurses; the sick were left to the care of the sick."

A later inspection report from Sedalia found proper food, better cooks and new beds arriving. The difference, the report noted, was that Sisters of Mercy had arrived.

At a hospital in southern Illinois, a doctor's wife stepped nervously around a soldier whose face had been reduced to a stretch of mangled flesh and an orifice of gurgling blood. She had opted to treat a less gruesome patient. Then a sister from the Congregation of the Sisters of the Holy Cross, a teaching order, took her aside, gently reminding her of Christ's admonition that "whatsoever you do for the least of mine, you do to me." From then on, says the Holy Cross account, "the woman could never do enough for wounded soldiers."

There are few records of what properly-brought-up young women of this era felt when, say, they were asked to wash the bloody, dirt-encrusted bodies of soldiers. In the few diaries they made during the war, the sisters don't talk about this routine, which they must have performed tens of thousands of times as they prepared young men for the surgeons' knives. It was the part of their service that they offered up to God.

But Louisa May Alcott, who later went on to write *Little Women,* left us this account of her experience with a young sergeant at Union Hospital in Washington, D.C. She was thirty, approaching burnout as a nurse. He had hardly begun to shave.

> The next scrubee was a nice looking lad, with a curly brown mane, honest blue eyes, and a merry mouth. He lay on a bed, with one leg gone, and the right arm so shattered that it must evidently follow: yet the little sergeant was as merry as if his afflictions were not worth lamenting over; and when a drop or two of salt water mingled with my suds at the sight of this strong body, so marred and maimed, the boy looked up, with a brave smile, though there was a little quiver of the lips, as he said: "Now don't you fret yourself about me, miss; I'm first rate."

By late 1862, both sides had begun to catch up with the massive heaps of wounded. Washington, D.C., had hospitals in churches, schools and warehouses, some 25 in all, with 25,000 beds. One, Stanton Hospital, was installed in a long row of one-story frame buildings. It had 130 soldiers. Confederate and Union soldiers brought in from the battles in northern Virginia lay side by side.

President Lincoln visited there and later wrote: "Of all the forms of charity and benevolence seen in the crowded wards of the hospitals, those of the Catholic Sisters were among the most efficient. I never knew whence they came or what was the name of the Order." The order was the Sisters of Mercy. They came from Pittsburgh.

In Richmond, the capitol of the Confederacy, there were twenty hospitals. The best and the biggest was the sprawling, eight-thousand-bed complex of tents and buildings called Chimborazo where the Daughters of Charity served throughout the war. The account of one young sister who served there gives the sense that it was prayer and faith that kept her going: "after heavy battles we would not retire until 10 or 11 o'clock. We were called during the night, as short as it was; but we always rose at 4 o'clock. When the condition of our sick would permit it, our blessed exercises [Mass and prayer] were resumed with renewed fervor."

There is no record of any nuns being shot—but several died from infectious diseases. Sisters served on the battlefields and also on river steamers fitted out as troop ships and hospital boats. A troop ship carrying an Irish brigade from Chicago, the *Sioux City,* was ambushed by Confederate troops near Glasgow, Missouri, in the summer of 1861 and riddled with bullets. "I continued to say my office [a required daily prayer] through all the firing so that I might have it finished before being shot," recalled a Chicago Mercy.

Although they were fortified by the power of prayer and their vows of obedience, there were times during this terrible war when even the sisters refused to work. Father Francis Burlando, a priest who worked with the Daughters of Charity, wrote in 1862 of "very frightful" conditions on ships where "more than four or five hundred sick and wounded lay heaped on one another." The sisters would have continued, but "they were deprived of all spiritual assistance; no mass or communion; even when they entered the port, it was hard for them to go to church," said the priest. They were later transferred to a hospital.

In the case of the Mercies, it's hard to tell whether they were burned out or just burned. An account from the records of the Sanitary Commission—the huge and sometimes unwieldy volunteer office that served the medical needs of the Union troops—notes that Mercies on one hospital ship went on strike because they had no chapel and no keys to their rooms. In true Mercy fashion, the demonstration was very tidy and well organized: "They sat on their trunks 'clean and peaceful with their forty umbrellas and their forty baskets,' but unable to help with the incoming tide of battle casualties."

In the bloodiest battles of the war, however, sisters were in the thick of the action, sometimes working alone. In April 1862 after the battle of Shiloh, the first large battle of the war, the Cincinnati Mercies arrived on a commandeered steamer, the *Superior,* at the nearest port, Pittsburgh Landing in Tennessee. Waiting for them was a scene that might have been taken from Dante's vision of hell: the writhing bodies of five thousand wounded piled around a "hospital" that consisted of a few tents and a log hut.

A steady rain fell as officers pulled soldiers from a mob trying to escape on the boats and ordered them to take care of the wounded, who were left lying in the mud. The men soon walked away, notes a Mercy account. Some ladies from the area stayed on, but when smallpox cases appeared among the wounded, even they fled, "leaving the Sisters to continue alone their labor of love and danger."

The Daughters of Charity had the peculiar problem of having to cross the battle lines as they surged back and forth while their sisters were serving both sides. Having made a major commitment to serve the Confederates in Richmond, the Daughters also responded to a call from Washington to supply nurses to a Union hospital in Frederick, Maryland.

They pulled sisters from Catholic schools in Baltimore to serve in a grimy stone barracks crammed with wounded. There was little furniture and the rations were served on broken crockery with rusty knives and forks. The soldiers often joked "that they got their daily dose of iron in that manner."

The joking stopped one bright day in September 1862 when dust clouds boiling on the southern horizon revealed that the men could be soon getting their iron in a more dangerous form. Gen. Robert E. Lee's artillery columns were approaching. Washington sent every available wagon to Frederick to haul away the wounded and their supplies, leaving the Daughters and four doctors to care for the worst cases. Confederate scouts appeared on September 6 to demand the surrender of the men in the hospital.

Just after they surrendered, "a flood of nearly 400 sick Confederates" poured into the hospital. Since the supplies were taken by the North and the South brought none, the Daughters appealed to the citizens of Frederick, who gave them some food. Some women volunteered to help the sisters with their new burden.

Daughters of Charity in front of Saterlee Hospital, West Philadelphia. (COURTESY OF
THE ARCHIVES OF THE DAUGHTERS OF CHARITY, EMMITSBURG, MARYLAND)

The fact that Daughters had to frequently cross enemy lines led to
rumors that some were Confederate spies. Replying to a letter of accusa-
tion from a Union Army major general, Mother Simeon of the order sent
back a tart note that her sisters might be serving Confederates, but they
were also nursing Union troops in Albany, St. Louis, Milwaukee, Baltimore "and other places."

She went on: "We take the liberty to remark that the duty of the Sisters of Charity is to strive to save their souls by the exercise of charity
towards their fellow-creatures, the poor and suffering of every nation, independent of creed or politics."

The sisters' belief that they were doing the Lord's work made them
stand out in a crisis. When a hospital ship carrying seven hundred
wounded from the battle of Shiloh ran aground on a shoal within range of
Confederate guns, the captain ordered the nuns on board to abandon ship.

"None would think of doing so," the captain was told by Sister
Anthony O'Connell, leading a group of Daughters from Cincinnati.
When the ship's doctor, just about to go over the side himself, heard this,
he had second thoughts. To cover his embarrassment he delivered himself
of one of the more comfortable opinions of the day: "Since you weak
women display such courage, I, too, will remain."

If there were any remaining doubters of their courage, the bloodiest battle in the war showed what the Daughters could do. The Battle of Gettysburg happened virtually on their doorstep. Sister Matilda Coskery recalled riding through the battlefield in a wagon after the shooting stopped, maneuvering this way and that to avoid dead bodies, then seeing a red flag with a board under it "marked '1,700 wounded down this way.'"

Fifty thousand casualties were strewn about, largely untended, on the rolling farmland. After the warm summer night, the bodies of the wounded were covered with lice and maggots. "We could hardly bear this part of the filth," she remembered.

Yet they persevered. While General George Meade, commander of the Union Army, was encamped in their chaplain's house, the Daughters continued their indiscriminate triage. The men who needed their help the most got it. The sisters were among the very few treating the wounded, frightened, helpless men in gray. When their bandages ran out, they used their undergarments to bind wounds.

When the federal assault columns began to ravage the South, the North found more cases of "disloyalty" among the Mercies. Several convents had been established there with the most prominent one being in Vicksburg. There another seemingly improbable Catholic nun, Frances Sumner, was teaching school when the dark tentacles of the war wrapped around her and five other sisters.

"Fannie" Sumner was born into a wealthy, well-connected Unitarian family in Baltimore. Her mother was the daughter of a prominent merchant; her uncle was Charles Sumner, the distinguished senator from Massachusetts. Fannie was a Baltimore socialite until the late 1850s when a group of Mercies from Pittsburgh established a convent in Baltimore. They were looking for bright, well-educated young women.

For Sumner, the Mercies had the same magnetic attraction that had drawn in another socialite, Frances Warde, a generation earlier in Dublin. The Mercies sent Sumner to Washington to train as a nurse in one of their hospitals. From there she went with a group of five others to Vicksburg to teach at a local school. Ironically, one of her fellow sisters was another strong-willed young woman, Stephana Warde, Frances Warde's cousin.

Their teaching mission ended in December 1862, when they decided to convert their school into a hospital to care for the rising number of Confederate casualties. When General Grant's gunboats laid siege to the city in May 1863, they retreated into caves with their wounded as famine ravaged the blockaded city.

The battle lasted for six weeks. The Confederates repulsed eight attempts to take the heavily fortified city on a high bluff above the Mississippi. Meanwhile the sisters and their patients sometimes watched the incoming shells glisten in the sun as they formed their deadly arcs. Then they were "descending with ever-increasing swiftness, and falling with deafening shrieks and explosions."

When Union generals offered to evacuate the Mercies under a flag of truce, they refused in order to stay with their patients. Later they escaped with Confederates, traveling in cattle cars with the wounded. The Army was starving, but a clever steward kept the healthy soldiers out of the nuns' small store of food and supplies by periodically poking his head out to ask the men clinging to the car whether they had had smallpox, indicating there was a case inside.

Their journey on the very edge of the battlefields took them to Jackson, Oxford, Canton and back to Jackson, which Grant's and later Sherman's troops had devastated, turning it into what the soldiers called Chimneyville. A forest of chimneys was all that was left of the fire-gutted houses. They nursed soldiers in camps, barns and abandoned railway stations.

They worked without medicine, supplies, food and even shoes, when they wore out. But an enterprising priest, Francis X. Leray, who accompanied them, had some new shoes made for the women from rabbit skin.

By Easter 1865, the war was staggering to its end. Drunken Union soldiers prowled the streets of many Southern towns. General Sherman's officers posted a guard at a Mercy convent in Columbus, Georgia, as his soldiers laid waste to the town. But a group of soldiers overpowered him. One of them barged into the doorway of the convent, looking for "hospitality," until a nun planted both fists in his chest, "knocking him flat on the sidewalk."

Later, another Army delegation arrived at the doorway with a stack of documents. They were clerks carrying oaths of allegiance to the federal government. They watched as each sister read one and signed it. "And thus," one of the nuns later wrote to a friend, "we who had never been rebels were reconstructed."

The group of nurses from Vicksburg were eventually captured with their Confederate patients. Some of them managed to negotiate their way out, but Union Army officers saw something suspicious and threatening in Sister Stephana Warde, who was described by her peers as "colorful and enigmatic." The nun was taken into custody as a prisoner of war.

In the winter they released her. One evening a gaunt figure, a woman dressed in a tattered Union Army officer's coat wrapped on the door of the Mercy convent in Pittsburgh. As they would for any stranger, the nuns welcomed the woman and invited her in for supper. As the woman recounted her strange adventures, culminating in a stay in a military prison camp, there were some doubters.

Could this really be Stephana Warde, who had left the Pittsburgh convent years earlier to go to Baltimore? But then the POW reached inside her ragged shirt and produced a soiled little bag that she always wore around her neck. She opened it and spread a tattered document on a table. It contained the vows she took when she entered the Sisters of Mercy.

After a few days of R&R—rare for nuns in this war—Sister Stephana Warde, thirty-four, left Pittsburgh with a new habit. She also had a new mission. She was on her way to Stanton Hospital in Washington to nurse the Union wounded.

6

TALE OF
TWO CITIES

In a bright afternoon in April 1869, Sister Austin Carroll was sailing down the Mississippi on the steamship *Mollie Abel* with a small group of young sisters. Since the boat had no chapel and the weather was warm, the nuns said their morning prayers on deck. The passengers on the ship had become accustomed to the daily ritual. Some of them even began to join in when the sisters sang Latin hymns.

Mollie Abel's paddle wheel slowed. Her deckhands began unspooling the ship's big hausers, preparing for a landing at Cape Giradeau, Missouri. Suddenly the passengers noticed a group of rough-looking men standing near the dock. They were waving and shouting and pointing at the sisters who, dressed in their black and white habits, were easy to spot on deck. Some of the passengers grew nervous. While they had enjoyed the singing and shared the spirit of the young women, they knew Catholics in general and specifically Catholic nuns had long been targets of bigotry in the United States.

As the ship drew nearer the dock, the passengers could see the group more clearly. They were hulking stevedores and scruffy rivermen, but now they were quiet. To a man, they had removed their hats as a sign of respect. Some stood at attention. Others threw military salutes. Some were still shouting, but these were not catcalls. They were thanking the sisters for their nursing during the Civil War.

It was a new era for Catholics in the U.S. While bigotry certainly lingered on in the nation's many social nooks and crannies, the searing experiences of the Civil War had demystified Catholics for the average American. Soldiers on both sides had fought alongside Catholics and found they carried their share of the battle. As for the sisters, they were heroes to hundreds of thousands of young men who had never met a Catholic. But they had seen nuns working under fire and in the blood, gore, pain and chaos of military hospitals.

The rivermen shouted and waved and the Mercies waved back. The group of nuns was one of a number heading for new assignments as the order expanded to new cities. Their mission was New Orleans, and the woman charged with establishing a Mercy presence there was Sister Carroll, now called Mother Carroll.

This sort of greeting was definitely a new experience for the thirty-four-year-old sister from Tipperarary, who had come to Providence, Rhode Island, just in time for the long nights of jeering and rock throwing. She was one of the order's great adventurers, a small, cheerful, confident woman with a sharp eye for detail and a wry, understated sense of humor. Mother Carroll was equipped to deal with whatever came.

She was a teacher, a skilled organist and a prodigious writer who chronicled many of the Mercies' early American activities in a series of books and articles that sold well. She used the money to support her religious work. The spring day and the warmth of the reception at Cape Giradeau no doubt provided a comforting thought. She was escaping the harsh winters of the north and perhaps, harsh people. New Orleans was the one city in America where the dominant culture was Catholic.

What she found was a level of poverty, violence, despair and corruption that eclipsed her previous experience, even in Ireland. For the poor in those days, urban America was a raw, smelly, brawling, often heartless place. This and the following chapter are about the establishment of Mercy missions in three of the roughest cities: New Orleans, Chicago and San Francisco.

Know Nothings, Mother Austin discovered, were not the problem in New Orleans, which had honored sisters since 1815, when a French order, the Ursuline Nuns, created the nation's first military hospital. During the Battle of New Orleans they turned their convent over to wounded American and British soldiers, earning the thanks of General Andrew Jackson—soon to become President. The grateful city offered Catholic sisters free passes on its fleet of horse-drawn streetcars.

New Orleans was one part of America that wore its faith on its sleeve, celebrating the birthdays of saints, even the more obscure ones. One local historian notes that citizens sometimes got into heated arguments, even fights over which saint was the most democratic:

" 'Saint Rita—that's a stuck up saint!" one woman cried to another. 'What does she know about poor people?'

'Hunh!' her neighbor retorted. 'Saint Rita forgot more about the poor than your saint ever knew. She's as plain as I am. I talk to her woman to woman!' "

Austin Carroll quickly discovered why women in New Orleans needed their saints. Many of the town fathers were not exactly role models. They were cheats, thieves, pimps, gamblers and killers. They shared a deep French cynicism about the prospects for fairness and order. Still, they managed to run things with what another historian defined as "a careless air of grace, a sort of 'I know I'm stealing your wallet, but we might as well be friends in other things' attitude."

It was a town where gentlemen carried weapons and where the sewer system was the street. It had its own peculiar brand of nimbleness. When a town ordinance was passed attempting to confine rampant prostitution to the upper floors of two-story downtown buildings, the town's enterprising merchants soon built a spate of brand new three-story buildings. The "toughest two blocks in America" was Gallatin Street in the French Quarter where no business was legitimate. Law and order finally materialized in the form of regular armed patrols of the Union Army. They were there to keep other soldiers from being victimized.

The soldiers in blue also served another purpose. They were the protective cover for another form of artful dealing, Mother Carroll discovered, as she walked with her nuns on their weekly visits to the city jail and the adjoining insane asylum. Over the local government, which was largely corrupt, the U.S. government had imposed a new layer of politicians. They were carpetbaggers from the North and it took them very little time to become proficient at the local art of helping themselves.

While the Northerners sometimes tried to do the right things, like starting schools for black children and desegregating the city's streetcars, everything they did was deeply resented, and in 1877, when they left, most of it was quickly undone.

The poorest Catholics were the newcomers, Irish and German Catholics who, in the 1850s, had begun pouring into the cities at a rate of thirty thousand per year. Mother Carroll located her convent in a neighborhood called "Irish Channel," where people did not always appreciate some of her earliest works, which were to start parochial schools for black children.

She opened one in a German parish and a week later it burned down. There were more threats of arson, both from the Irish and German Catholic communities. Mother Carroll took the threats very seriously because, as most citizens of New Orleans knew, the city's volunteer firefighters, the "Firemen's Charitable Association," was corrupt. The shiny pumpers and the hook-and-ladder wagons looked splendid in parades, but the men who ran them tended to reserve most of their heroics for customers who paid them the most money.

So Mother Carroll developed her own brand of nimbleness. For example, she invented a kind of fire insurance by putting a school for blacks in a building attached to her convent. Burn the school and the convent burned down with it. That school escaped both the arsonist's torch and the sweaty palms of the Firemen's Charitable Association.

She found visits to the jail depressing—most of the artful criminals were on the street. The one "gentlemanly inmate" who roused himself to show the sisters around had killed his wife "with extraordinary barbarity." But Mother Carroll saw in him and his companions a kind of truth, a photographic negative of the mores of the city. It showed broken people who had become, in their minds, the people in society who had given them hope.

"Among these victims of frenzy or hallucination, here was a famous boxer, there was a man who had headed a riot; the daughter of General Lee and his mother stood apart; the only lineal descendant of George Washington, a burly negro, sat in silent majesty in a doorway."

As Mother Carroll and her sisters made their rounds, various singers, including one styled as the fabled Jenny Lind "warbled about the corridors with vigor minus melody." The nuns bowed gravely to an assortment of "military officers, lawyers, bishops, governors." A sick black woman told them not to worry much about her condition. Her husband, General Ulysses S. Grant, was coming for her in a week.

Young women were attracted to Mother Carroll and the order's works because the objectives of the Mercies were highly visible, even when they failed, like the burned-out school for blacks. By 1877 she had opened six Mercy convents in outlying communities, places as far away as Pensacola, Florida. She had started an orphanage and then started a row within the Church when she complained that teaching salaries at parish schools were being cut back.

This provoked a response from another of the city's self-centered institutions. The archbishop of New Orleans had recruited a number of priests from Germany to work in New Orleans. Instinctively, some of them did not relate well to the teeming, mostly illiterate Irish. And here was an Irish *woman* telling them what to do! One rector, Rev. Nicholas Jaeckel, took it upon himself to inform Mother Carroll where her place was in the Church's pecking order: "It is simply the duty of the sisters to obey, as this is the natural order of things, the fathers, not the sisters, being pastors." He added, "as long as the sisters remain fervent religious, docile and obedient children, so long will the fathers stand by them."

Yellow fever paid periodic visits to New Orleans, and when it did, there was panic in the streets and a great deal of applied quackery. Although doctors had only a vague notion of what the fast-moving disease's real cause was, New Orleans was a city of appearances. It paid people who appeared to have a cure.

In 1853, when the population of New Orleans was 150,000, yellow fever, or Bronze John, as it was sometimes called, carried away 9,000. Among the remedies tried were burning fires of tar and firing cannons on street corners to cleanse the air of "effluvia." One account of this notes that "Doctors were ordering cold treatment, hot treatment, open windows, closed windows. One decided that there was some mystic efficacy in the juice of fresh oysters. Coatings of lime were spread along the banquettes [sidewalks]; 'its exhalations were supposed to be antiseptic.'"

In 1878, when the disease returned, Mother Carroll and her sisters were in the thick of it, nursing the sick and preparing the bodies of the dead when their families and public authorities didn't. The fever did its damage quickly, leaving victims who vomited putrid, coagulated blood that, she recalled, resembled coffee grounds.

"Wherever this awful pestilence spreads a panic follows. Orphans are left desolate. Households are extinguished as by a breath, and family names completely obliterated," explained Mother Carroll, writing with a kind of numbness about the sad flow of daily events. "A week later, the health officers have fumigated the premises and the notice *à louer* [for rent] is up. How many such cases have we not known?"

Throughout these weeks of misery, the doctors provided nuggets of black humor that kept Mother Carroll reaching for her notebook. "An English doctor, attacked by yellow fever, died on the application of his 'unfailing specific' to himself. A New York doctor stricken in like manner, ceased to breathe while being treated with his 'newly discovered remedy.' "

She remembers a Dr. Kibbee, the inventor of a water-dripping treatment, applying it to a young, feverish Irishman until he had no temperature at all. "This was in the interest of science," Mother Carroll wrote, "but we felt that James Lingan was murdered."

The great literary accounts of plague start with Daniel Defoe's gripping *Journal of the Plague Years*, which traces the course of the black plague in London in 1665. Mr. Defoe's first-person accounts of the quackery and devastation are stunning, but they're not his. He was only six years old at the time. Mr. Defoe, who became a novelist and hired writer of political tracts, later explained that he'd derived his *Journal* from a diary kept by an uncle, Henry Foe.

Mother Carroll's accounts of a deserted New Orleans, where the rich had fled, leaving the poor in the death-grip of Bronze John, were taken from her own eerie experiences as she and her sisters went from house to house amid the stench of death. "Not a bell rang, not a note of music—the very songbirds have deserted us," she wrote. Among the outsiders moved by her newspaper accounts was John Pierpont Morgan, the New York financier. He sent her a check for one thousand dollars.

Watching the native families deal with the disease, Mother Carroll bet her thin resources on her hunch that women who had previously had a mild form of the disease were more able to fight it off. She sent her young, local recruits into the worst areas of the pestilence and held back Irish-born sisters.

Mother Mary Austin Carroll.
(COURTESY OF THE SISTERS OF
MERCY OF THE AMERICAS)

Her hunch worked. Of the four thousand people who died from this round of yellow fever, there were thirty priests and fifty-nine sisters. Of the Mercies, only three died and thirty-one eventually recovered. As far as Mother Carroll was concerned, the assumption of such risks was simply part of the job of being a religious. Priests, she wrote, must administer the sacraments to the dying. "That Sisters of Mercy should serve the stricken till they themselves fall, is doing nothing more than is appointed them." God will give them the grace, she concluded, to carry on.

There was a fun-loving side to Mother Carroll. She like to hang around with news boys, crap-shooting free spirits who lived on the streets. While she admired their independence, she cajoled them and taunted them to finish school. When local businessmen gave her free tickets, she would take the newsies or a group of orphans to see vaudeville. When this happened on Sundays, it provoked another outburst from the Germans in the archbishop's office. There was Mother Carroll setting another bad example. The archbishop frowned on entertainment on the Lord's day.

By 1885, the Mercies had a strong presence in New Orleans. Mother Carroll had formed eight convents with seventy-eight sisters. But she had also persisted in fighting against cutbacks for teachers' pay, which continued, and she pressed to build more black schools, which the archbishop opposed. When Archbishop Francis Leray—the priest who had made rabbit-skin slippers for Mercy sisters nursing Confederate soldiers during the Civil War—refused to allow her to start a mission in Belize, she went around him and got permission from Rome.

The next archbishop, Francis Janssens, deemed that a sign of disobedience. To punish her, he obtained a letter from Rome that removed her as the mother superior in New Orleans. He came to her convent with it and scolded her in front of her nuns. "It would take a volume to describe the scene—all the sisters were crying and sobbing. His Grace abused them roundly, not a kind word or even a courteous word," she recalled.

He ordered her to open a new convent in Selma, Alabama, deep in Baptist country, where her innovations, her sharp tongue and even sharper pen would not be in such obvious collision with his authority. So in 1891 Mother Carroll, then fifty-six, left the city she had come to love and was packed off to a convent in rural Selma, where the furniture consisted largely of vegetable crates. There, once again, she flourished. By 1900 she had opened thirty-three schools, many for black students, and nine convents.

While the priests considered her a "little haughty," the news boys decided she was just right. In New Orleans, where they saw excuses for parties every night, in 1881 these young men threw a big one. They held a banquet to commemorate Mother Austin Carroll's twenty-fifth year as a Sister of Mercy.

"We hope you will have twenty five more regular editions of this day, besides a whole lot of EXTRAS," went one testimonial. "And that there will be some of us boys around to cry them out for you." Though her life was never easy in this city "with an air of careless grace," the Lord did deliver a few of those EXTRAS. She died in 1909.

AT THE END of the Civil War, Chicago had a different character from New Orleans and an entirely different character from the dismal frontier town it had been. It was on its way to becoming a factory center, a railroad hub and a complex of stockyards and slaughterhouses: Carl Sandburg's celebrated "City of Big Shoulders." It was also on its way to becoming predominantly Catholic.

New Orleans might have its saints. People from the Windy City had a tradition of bragging about their miracles. The city fathers would eventually make the Chicago River run backward and build a stretch of gleaming skyscrapers along a stretch of Michigan Avenue that they renamed the Miracle Mile.

But after the Civil War, as it was filling up with Catholic immigrants, Chicago was starting out with smaller miracles. Usually nuns were involved in them, one way or another.

One night in 1859, in the deserted chapel of Mercy Hospital in Chicago, Sister M. Victoire, who ran the hospital, was sure that one of life's greatest mysteries was being revealed to her. A curious woman, a French-speaking Canadian who came to Chicago to join the Mercies, Sister Victoire found herself becoming absorbed in the lives and the daily experiences of her patients. What she yearned to know most about them, however, was "how those who died fared after death."

Two priests who had died at Mercy—Chicago's first hospital—had promised the nun that they would try to find a way to come back and tell her. And now at two A.M., in the dim, flickering light of the candle in the sanctuary lamp hanging above the altar, she could make out the outline of a figure she had never seen before. It was a man, dressed all in white. He was lying prostrate before the altar. I am going to see a ghost at last! she thought.

But, as she later put it, feeling a "leetle timid," she went first to get a candle. Upon closer examination, the "ghost" turned out to be Dr. Patrick McGirr, one of the hospital's first doctors, who had retired. As the nun discovered, his custom was to lie before the altar every night in his white cashmere dressing gown and pray.

Just why Dr. McGirr did this was not explained, but there was certainly plenty to pray about in Chicago. On just one day in 1857, 3,400 immigrants had arrived by train. The Irish, who had first begun arriving in the 1830s to dig the canal that connected the Chicago River with Lake Michigan, were creating huge slums out of abandoned lumber and packing crates.

Needless to say, they were not happy campers and the hospital saw evidence of that almost every night. Gangs of Irish Catholic youths and local Protestant toughs, "both sides armed with butchers knives and carpenters awls," notes one historian, held "weekly street brawls." Gambling, prostitution and other forms of corruption were protected by the city's corrupt police department. Ten years earlier a survey showed that 74 percent of the heads of families in the city were "destitute." Meanwhile, the nation teetered on the brink of civil war.

But the war turned out to be an economic and social boon for many in Chicago. Sisters of Mercy from Chicago became famous for rescuing boatloads of wounded from the battlefields of Shiloh. Many Midwest businessmen made fortunes from the war and set off a wave of boosterism in Chicago that continues to this day. Some of the emerging new rich, mostly Protestants, opted to send their daughters to St. Agatha's Academy, an elite boarding school for women started by the Chicago Mercies.

If Dr. McGirr had survived the war, however, he would still have found much worth praying about. The announced policy of the hospital was not to take free patients, but sick people would come with a meager deposit and then linger there for months, even years. "Now this frequently happens," says one history of the Chicago Mercies, but the order "does not advertise such works of charity."

The Mercies, among the earliest settlers of the city, owned some lakefront property that became quite valuable as Chicago's population literally exploded. But a succession of bishops challenged the women's right to own property. Finally one of them, Bishop Anthony. O'Regan, had demanded the deeds to the property; the sisters capitulated and gave them to him.

When Mother Warde brought the Mercies in, in the 1840s, the city had 30,000 residents. By October, 8, 1871, a Sunday, there were 334,000 sprawled over eighteen square miles. Chicago had become the fastest-growing city in the world. Demands for medical care were soaring. The Mercies had just taken out a big mortgage to build a new hospital, which was now rising, north of the city.

At nine that evening, the sisters were at prayers in the chapel when they heard the sound of commotion. Mother Mary Vincent looked out the window and saw flames burning in the distance. "It's the secessionists!" she announced, certain that the South had somehow risen again and that the Confederate Army was about to inflict vengeance upon the Windy City.

While Chicago's fire department was not corrupt the way New Orleans's was, it was small, only 185 men. The city had rejected the department's recommendations for a tougher building code, more pumps, fireboats and larger water mains because it felt the higher taxes would be bad for business.

Business was the credo upon which the city was built. It was the "grand junction" of more railroads than any other city in the world. It styled itself as the "Empire City of the West." To appease the city's fathers, the department had adapted a new strategy to cover its shortcomings. It was to get to the fire "before it gets the start of you," explained the city's fire marshal.

But that night they didn't. Dispatchers sent the first pumpers to the wrong location. Before they could react, the blaze had shaped into a giant wall of flame throwing fiery debris as high as five hundred feet into the air. The city of superlatives, which had been parched by a long summer draught, was about to fuel one of the most powerful firestorms ever seen, prior to World War II. Trees exploded. Steel melted. Marble turned to lime. What was downtown Chicago disappeared in about five minutes.

That night faith nearly killed the Mercies. From her lookout at the window, Mother Vincent made a variety of pronouncements including "The Blessed Mother of Mercy will not let this house in which she is so honored, burn!" By midnight, though, fires were approaching from three sides.

In the streets there was bedlam. "A fiery pall was extending over the doomed city. Bells were ringing, walls were falling with many a heavy thud, flames were leaping from doors and windows of public buildings, the very fire-proof edifices were melting in the burning air, the light was dazzling in intensity," was the way Mother Austin Carroll later put it, piecing together accounts from various sisters who were there.

Nonetheless, the business of Chicago went on. Drivers of hacks, wagons and carts, anything that rolled, were charging "outrageous prices" to haul people and their possessions away from the advancing flames. Once stacked with goods, some of the wagons mysteriously departed, never to be seen again.

Yet at about the same time, a procession of wagons and buggies began to appear in front of the convent. The men of Chicago, some of them covering their heads and backs with wet blankets, had not forgotten the Mercies. They took forty young women from the Mercies' home for women, fifty students from its boarding school and sixty sisters. Mother Vincent, who had finally become convinced that the convent would indeed burn, was among the last to leave. She was clutching her most valued possession, a tin box of cloth scraps and sewing items given to her by her sister, when one of the men pulled her into his buggy.

"He drove furiously through the scalding air," says Mother Carroll's account of this—presumably taken from Mother Vincent—and then dropped her off a few streets away from the new Mercy Hospital, which was quickly filling up with victims from the blaze. Mother Vincent was furious. It was against the rules, scandalous for a sister to be walking the streets alone, at two A.M.! How could she explain that to her sisters? She demanded to be taken all the way to the hospital. But the man whipped up his horse and dashed back into the fiery streets for another load. She never found out who he was.

The fire left a path of charred debris over four miles long and almost a mile wide. Three hundred people died. A hundred thousand people were left homeless that night and 17,450 buildings were destroyed. The Mercies invited the homeless into their new but only partially completed hospital. "Every available spot from cellar to attic was brought into requisition," says one account. Among the victims the Mercies were most proud of saving was a certain Dr. Hess, who had seen all of his property go up in smoke. Certain that life without wealth in the ash-strewn city was pointless, he aimed a pistol at his heart and pulled the trigger.

"Providentially, though a physician, he mistook the true region of that vital organ, and shot into the lower left lung," wrote Mother Carroll, in her short, but medically precise account of the event. The dazed man, seriously wounded but quite conscious, managed to hang on for three months in Mercy Hospital, casting his professional eye on the bedside manner of the women who nursed him. They didn't care whether he had any wealth at all.

He had never seen nuns before, and first treated them with "aversion." But by degrees they won over the doctor. "He died a Catholic," noted Mother Carroll.

7

MOTHER AND THE
MAGDALENS

Father Hugh Gallagher was a resourceful man. Following the path
of many of his American peers, in the summer of 1854 he went to
Kinsale, Ireland, to recruit some Mercy nuns for his hometown,
which was San Francisco.

It is hard to know at this distance what he must have told them. Easily, San Francisco was then the toughest town in North America. It had a
population of about fifty thousand, many of them absentees who had left
to prospect in the gold fields. Some of the would-be gold miners had left
destitute wives and children who were free to run in the muddy, garbage-
strewn streets.

The city, perched precariously on a series of green hills overlooking
the Pacific, was half makeshift buildings and half tents. "It was famous for
three things," recalled one early settler, J. D. Borthwick, "rats, fleas and
empty bottles." The law there was like the weather; it often experienced
heavy fogs. Between 1849 and 1856, more than a thousand homicides
were committed and the courts saw seven convictions.

Unlike Chicago and New Orleans, built at least in part from the sweat of blue-collar laborers, San Francisco had a service economy. It was based primarily on two industries: prostitution and gambling.

Whatever Father Gallagher told the Irish nuns, it must have been exciting. Twenty-nine women, nearly the entire population of the convent, volunteered to go with him to San Francisco. After considerable wrangling, they chose eight sisters, to be led by Kate Russell, a strong-willed, bookish woman from Killough, a small fishing village in the north.

Kate had just finished her novitiate, or the two-year preparation period to become a Mercy, but she was the obvious leader in the group. So she was given a ponderous name, Mother Mary Baptist Russell, and sent off with her charges and the impressive-sounding Father Gallagher to this San Francisco, wherever that was. She was only twenty-six years old.

The first part of the voyage was harrowing enough. They missed their assigned ship, called the *Arctic*, which was good because it collided with another ship and took all hands to the bottom of the Atlantic. The next ship took them to New York, where the real journey began. They transferred to a steamer bound for the trackless, fever-infected jungles of Nicaragua. There, after a three-week journey by boat and wagon across the isthmus, Father Gallagher was faced with his most difficult decision.

Bobbing in wait for them just beyond the Pacific surf was a skiff that would take them to the *Cortes*, a steamer bound for San Francisco. But the priest had learned that the standard means of getting passengers of the "weaker sex" through the surf was to have them carried by members of the local Indian tribe, men who customarily worked naked. Always protective of the sensitivity of his young traveling companions, Father Gallagher arranged to have the Indians dressed in shirts and pantaloons.

Just who was more surprised when the passengers emerged from the jungle wearing their long woolen habits is not recorded, but the Indians completed their task. The sisters arrived in San Francisco on January 2, 1855, and took up residence in a small house near the county hospital.

San Franciscans, at that time, seemed to have considerable difficulty over what to make of them. Because only eight thousand of its fifty thousand citizens were women, any new additions were of considerable interest. But the women in the city fell largely into two categories: prostitutes and wives. And these women, stalking the sloppy streets in clothes that made them look like some great, lost breed of penguins, concentrating on the sick and the prisoners in the jail, did not fit in either category.

A local Methodist newspaper broke through this impasse by attacking Mother Russell and her sisters for being agents that were foreign to "our Protestant and Republican country." A few days later a reader of the paper took this a step further, responding with a letter arguing that the sisters really did mesh with the spirits of the city: As "proof," he noted that they "did not keep the Sabbath and drank hard" during their incoming voyage on the *Cortes*.

This roused Captain Thomas B. Cropper, the skipper of the *Cortes*. He wrote the *San Francisco Herald* that the nuns had dined at his table every day on the voyage from Nicaragua and displayed "extreme propriety." He called the letter "the most detestable calumny I have ever heard or known."

The argument over just what these women were all about raged back and forth until September 5, 1855, when Asiatic cholera broke out in the city, bringing death to many of its victims within twenty-four hours. The city's solution was to pile patients inside the State Marine and County Hospital, a converted hotel which, according to a Methodist minister who visited it, stank with filth and was managed by incompetents. "The nurses were generally low men devoid of sympathy, careless, rude in the care of the sick, and exceedingly vulgar and profane."

When Mother Russell volunteered to staff the hospital, the city jumped at the offer. The nuns, who had had experience treating the disease in Ireland in 1849, cleaned out the hospital and its staff, inspiring the *San Francisco Daily News* to write the following account of their efforts: "The Sisters of Mercy, rightly named, whose convent is opposite the hospital, as soon as they learned did not stop to inquire whether the poor sufferers were Protestants or Catholics, Americans or foreigners, but with the noblest devotion applied themselves to their relief . . . the idea of danger never seems to have occurred to these noble women."

At the peak of the outbreak as many as a dozen people died daily and more than five hundred were in their graves by the time the force of the plague was spent. By that time the sisters, as one history of that period puts it, "had earned the community's allegiance." The San Francisco Board of Supervisors, however, remained steadfast in their ways, one of which was to contract out the treatment of the poorest hospital patients to the cheapest bidder and then to default on their payments.

In 1857, after nine months of trying to get payment for services rendered from the city, Mother Russell canceled the contract and ordered the patients put there by the city to leave. Then she bought the hospital, renaming it St. Mary's Hospital. It treated the poor for free, but those who could pay were billed. She even installed hot and cold running water and "made St. Mary's the city's finest medical facility."

The Mercies went on to open an orphanage and a number of schools as well, but the institution that made the most intimate fit with the peculiar needs of San Francisco was called the Magdalen Asylum. It opened its doors in 1861. Its mission: to care for ex-prostitutes.

Drawn by the presence of thousands of miners with gold dust in their pockets, prostitutes led a busy but ugly life in the city by the Golden Gate. They came in all colors, from as far away as France, Chile and New Orleans to help the pimps and madams "mine" the miners. It was a very competitive business. Some houses specialized in girls as young as fourteen. Others featured women in acts of bestiality. In 1855, the government counted more than one hundred bordellos in the area of Portsmouth Square.

"They showed up Sunday mornings outside Grace Episcopal Church . . . and at St. Mary's Cathedral just down the hill . . . to try to pick up men as they were leaving services," says one history of the early city. Some worked in parlors with thick carpets, polished brass and oil paintings. These were places where the guests were served high tea by a colored maid and entertained with music played on a grand piano while various women were displayed and prices were negotiated.

But most women worked in the "cribs." These were often shacks with a front window, a tiny "reception room" and a rear "workshop" where, lying on a small iron bed, a woman sometimes saw as many as eighty customers before dawn. Cribs were money machines; one brothel owner managed to jam 450 of them into a three-story tenement called the Nymphia. The women worked in two shifts.

There were a few glamorous madams, who tended to feed the gossip mills and to set the city's fashions with their imported gowns, but "the life" was a one-way street for most women. It led to poverty, drug addiction, alcoholism, disease and sometimes suicide. "Most died young and few ever escaped the life, before the 1890's," concludes one account. Among the first who did escape was one Amanda Taylor, described as a

Protestant girl from New Orleans "who had become completely disgusted with the life of sin she was leading."

In August 1856, she came to the hospital and begged Mother Russell to let her stay, even if the only room available was a coal bin. Mother Russell assigned her a room, where she lived a life of "indulgence," letting the sisters make her bed and sweep the floor. But after some weeks when a second prostitute, a very young girl, sought shelter at the hospital, Ms. Taylor found herself moved to help her.

Taking the responsibility to help a fellow being made Ms. Taylor a "changed person, industrious and devout." The word spread that Mother Russell would give shelter and protection to ex-prostitutes. By 1859 there were 24 at the hospital, enough to occupy an entire wing. By 1874, there were 150, so many that Mother Baptist had to find a separate building to house them. She then convinced the city to pay for some of their upkeep.

A newspaper reporter who visited the Magdalen found it to be almost conventlike, with freshly scrubbed dormitory rooms where the curtains and bedspreads looked like "inland snow." Passers by the big brick building sometimes heard them singing. They would call each other "sister," reserving the term "sister of honor" for the Mercies who ran the asylum. Women who had known only one way of earning a living, lying on their backs in the most degrading conditions, earned money from making lace and other fancy needlework that the sisters taught them.

"Are you an inmate here?" the reporter asked a woman with beautiful eyes and a "far away expression" who was washing windows in the parlor.

"Yes, ma'am. I'm a Magdalene."

"Been here long?"

"One year. But I shall never leave it."

"Are you happy?"

"Oh yes, perfectly. Nothing would take me back to the world again."

Mother Russell enjoyed a good relationship with the bishop of San Francisco, Joseph Sadoc Alemany—a Dominican who was her superior, but, more importantly, who became her friend. As the city's often-crooked politicians and businessmen finally gave way to a generation of more honest burghers, she and Bishop Alemany often teamed up to push them for tens of thousands of dollars of donations for the poor. But

Mother Russell also pushed herself to an extent that shocked her peers, including the bishop.

She once gave her tiny cot in the hospital to a mentally troubled woman who fancied it. On another occasion she dragged her mattress downstairs to give to a sick man she found lying on a straw pallet in the street. The nuns in the hospital gave her another mattress, with "Reverend Mother" written on it to make it more conspicuous should she give it away again.

"Legend has it," says one account of her efforts, "that Mother Baptist would pull up her petticoat and wrap the hospital bed linens around her waist and stuff them in her sleeves. When she reached the home of a needy family, she would pull the linens out and make the beds. She did this so often that the sisters put locks on the linen closets."

The bishop once chided Mother Russell in a letter, saying "your heart is bigger than your purse." She might have lacked the money to properly support some of her causes, but when it came to courage, that was a different matter. After she persuaded the city to let the Mercies take over San Francisco's "Pest House," during the smallpox plague of 1868, she assigned herself to start the mission.

The Pest House, a rough wood building slapped up outside the city, was a ghastly place, according to San Francisco's *Daily Evening Bulletin*. It resolved its staffing problems by simply locking up the smallpox victims without help after ten P.M. Mother Russell came there to live until Bishop Alemany ordered her back to the convent, saying that a "general's place was at headquarters directing operations, not exposing herself as a common soldier."

She complied until the day when one of the nuns she had assigned there broke under the strain of coping with endless misery. Then "the general," as she was known, returned until the plague ended nine months later. She never wrote about her work with the patients of the Pest House, but one of her companions, Sister Mary Francis, gave this account in a letter to Ireland: "The eyes of the greater number are closed, pus running down from them to their cheeks. Their throats are so sore that to take a drink almost chokes them, the tongue in most instances so swollen that one drop cannot pass down, their hands so sore they are helpless and the stench so terrible that they themselves cry out they cannot endure it."

The Mercies taught in some of San Francisco's first schools. Mother

Russell accepted payments from the city for her teachers until the city council created a requirement for an annual teachers examination, to be administered by politicians. Two other orders of teaching nuns complied, along with Bishop Alemany, but Mother Russell had a grim flashback to Ireland and what state control over the schools had done to Catholics there. So she refused, opting to finance her own schools. The other orders soon followed. It was the beginning of the parochial school system in San Francisco.

She visited the jails constantly, petitioning the governor in 1871 to let the Mercies be the first women to be admitted to San Quentin. Mother Russell's was a familiar face to the convicts there on death row until 1893. When other sisters did the visitations, she would tuck up her habit, put on her apron, and do the cooking, cleaning and scrubbing in the convent.

As Sister Mary Howley, one of the sisters who came with her from Ireland, put it, Mother Russell's example tended to end grousing about the smell, noise, inhumanity and poverty that the sisters wrestled with on a daily basis in San Francisco. "I would look at her working and scrubbing and feel ashamed of myself and say 'She is a fine lady, and see what she does; so how can I complain?'"

In April 1898, the city by the Golden Gate embarked on the next of its many adventures. War was declared against Spain, and San Francisco became a logistics center for the war. Amid the war fervor, whipped up by San Francisco's newspapers, and the thump of the marching bands that accompanied the regiments of young soldiers to the docks, Mother Russell was sometimes seen weeping. She knew from long experience what was coming next.

The military hospital at the Presidio was soon overwhelmed when typhoid and pneumonia broke out among the troops. Four Mercies volunteered as nurses and served for the duration. Major W. S. Matthews, the hospital's chief surgeon, later wrote that the nuns refused to accept payment from the Army, "exhibiting a most self-sacrificing and patriotic spirit. Their work is as good as could possibly be desired."

Mother Russell died on August 5, after suffering a stroke. More than fifty priests participated at her funeral; thousands of mourners packed the chapel of St. Mary's Hospital and jammed the streets outside. Pushing aside war news for the day, San Francisco's papers gave her full-page spreads. The *Bulletin* called her "the best-known charitable worker on the

Mother Mary Baptist Russell:
"The Best-Known Charitable
Worker on the Pacific Coast."
(COURTESY OF THE ARCHIVES OF
THE SISTERS OF MERCY,
BURLINGAME, CALIFORNIA)

Pacific Coast." The *Call* said, "No death in recent years has been heard of with more regret in this community." The *Chronicle* proclaimed that Mother Russell's "life of self-denial and good works has crowned her in a city's memory."

After all that, San Francisco's memory of Mother Baptist and the adventures of the early Mercies amid the wilds of the young city was to be very short. Many books have been written about that period, including several biographies of the city's most famous madams. But hardly any, not even church histories, mention the contribution of Mother Russell, according to Sister Katherine Doyle, a Mercy who is writing a book about Mother Russell.

"It has been very perplexing to me not to be able to find in any of the contemporary writing any references back to the Mercies or their charities. There is just a silence." One of her theories is that people tend to see nuns as a kind of faceless branch of the Catholic Church and not as individuals. "History tends to be written about individuals and not groups."

In a way, Mother Russell's fruitful life didn't need a history, for it was written on the ground in the form of the institutions that she and the San

Francisco Mercies built. Shortly after her death, they included six major hospitals in California and Arizona, eighteen schools and colleges and twenty-five convents with more than four hundred sisters.

After her funeral in St. Mary's Hospital, Mother Russell's body was taken to another of her monuments. The place where she had asked to be buried was St. Michael's Cemetery, the burial ground attached to the Magdalen Asylum.

8

WILD IN THE WEST

In February 1878, Mary Agnes Warde, a young slip of a girl, climbed the long flight of steps leading up to St. Mary's Academy in Manchester, New Hampshire. While she was only ten years old, she had superb credentials to become a future Sister of Mercy. She sang and played the harp. More to the point, she was the grandniece of Mother Frances Warde, who ran the academy. The students there had carefully prepared for Mary's arrival and expressed great interest in her musicianship.

They would be delighted to hear her play the harp, they explained. They said the best acoustics were in the front parlor of the convent, so she set up there, with the older students of the academy seated all around her. Nervously, she began to play. There was a knock at the parlor door, then Mother Warde appeared, swept the room with a steely glance and then softened as she saw the youngster. "Is that you, my dear? I was just looking for you. I wanted to see you."

In her office, Mother Warde explained to her young relative that the front parlor was off-limits to students. Whoever had put her up to playing the harp there had violated the rules. When they returned to the parlor, they found it was empty.

It is not advertised, but a certain amount of fooling around has always gone on in convents. Most of the students in St. Mary's Academy were teenagers or younger. They could not have fully appreciated the significance of this tired, kindly, elderly principal, who seemed to be spending most of her days tending her garden. To some of them she was simply an authority figure. To others, she might have seemed colorful, a woman shrouded in legends. She sometimes told funny stories during recreation, but rarely talked of her adventures.

By 1881, after only thirty-eight years in America, the ranks of the Mercies had grown to ten thousand sisters living in two hundred convents, more than in Ireland and everywhere else put together. Mother Warde had personally founded more than 120 convents, hospitals, schools, orphanages and other social institutions. According to one account, more "than any other religious leader of the western world."

At Mother Warde's funeral, just three years later, she was praised as a "free spirit," a woman ahead of her time who, in 1843, had seen endless opportunities in the raw, new nation across the Atlantic. For ambitious young sisters, eager to pick up her torch, the 1870s offered one place in America where they could face hardship, risks and challenges equal to any that their mentor had faced. That was the Wild West.

Some of them went on to become heroic figures, women who braved desperados, bigots, chronic poverty and grueling distances to establish a social network of schools and hospitals that gave many frontier towns the first glimmer of civilization. Others were headstrong people who were sent west, in some cases, because various church leaders had deemed they couldn't be properly controlled in more civilized places.

For the Mercies, the West was won out of Omaha, where Mother Warde had sent seven sisters in 1864. As always, there was a certain amount of overselling involved to lure them out there. The local bishop had promised them a fully furnished convent. What they found when they arrived was an empty brick building featuring barren walls, barren floors, a stove and, perhaps as a gesture to compensate for that, a piano.

But the local paper, the *Nebraskan,* gave them a welcoming boost in an editorial. It said that, finally, Omaha would have something besides a railroad and a large assortment of saloons to attest to its place as a seat of culture. The sisters "are accomplished in every branch of science and will attract scores of young ladies from every portion of the West," the paper said, adding that "no one thing adds more to the importance of a place" than schools.

On their visits to the jails they found Otway G. Baker, a store clerk who had been charged with killing the store's bookkeeper with an axe, taking his money and then setting fire to the store. To further support his story that the store had been held up by a robber, who succeeded only after a vicious fight, Mr. Baker had shot himself in the arm. It was a well-thought-out story. His problem was that few in Omaha believed it. So Mr. Baker was arrested and convicted of first-degree murder.

When the Mercies found him, he was on death row, full of "cold ridicule and sarcasm." After they continued to call on him, however, he gradually softened. He was baptized in his cell. The money was returned. Then Baker was hanged, leaving very little to remember him by, save for a handwritten note saying his final wish was to die as a member in good standing with the Catholic Church "as it was their instruction alone that brought peace and hope to my soul."

At their school, the Mercies found some gentlemen callers from the American Protective Association, a group concerned that "moral wrong-doing" was being spread by Catholic nuns. The sisters encouraged them to stay for an entire day, eating breakfast with the children and lunch with the principal, who informed them, sweetly, that she would welcome any suggestions for improvements.

The Omaha Mercies were led by Mother Mary Ignatius, thirty, a bright, ambitious woman who was an alumnus of Mother Warde's convent in Manchester. Her birth name was Julia Lynch. Raised in Ireland by wealthy parents and given an extensive education in the arts, she proved to be a handful for most of the authority figures she came in contact with. "She enjoyed leadership," says one account, "and was quite uncomfortable when she was not in charge."

She rattled the bishop in Omaha by taking out a $40,000 debt to build an orphanage, so in 1878 he decided to send her and six sisters on a mission to Yankton, South Dakota to teach the Indians. There she took out a $35,000 loan to start a school. When local parents refused to contribute, the nuns began begging for money on the street.

That bothered Bishop Martin Marty, the bishop of the Dakota territory, but while he was simmering over the debt, an even more prickly problem arose: one of Mother Ignatius's sisters, Sister Mary Paul Kierns, had run off with a Russian doctor, Dr. V. Sebiaken-Ross. They took solemn vows of matrimony before a Protestant minister. Still later, Sister Mary Paul came strolling back to her convent, pretending nothing had happened.

The tryst was exposed in a San Francisco newspaper, detonating an explosive scandal that set tongues wagging all over Yankton. According to one account, Sister Mary Paul's escapade turned the bishop's hair gray "within a week after he heard of it." An enterprising Yankton tobacco store began selling "Mary Paul Cigars."

The blame for all of this came down on the head of Mother Ignatius, who stubbornly refused to give up her school when the bishop demanded it. That forced Father George Willard, the vicar general of the Dakotas, to denounce her one Sunday from the pulpit for "resisting the authority of the bishop." He forbade Catholic parents to send their children to the school taught by the Mercies. "They are no longer Sisters, they are renegades who deceive the people by wearing the habit of religion," he said.

Mother Ignatius changed her name back to Julia Lynch, but continued to teach in Yankton, giving music lessons to the children of wealthy parents. She appeared regularly at Sunday Mass and took up residence with Dr. Sebiaken-Ross and the newly famous Mary Paul. This being a Catholic tale, sins were eventually forgiven.

The bishop later appointed Dr. Sebiaken-Ross to be the doctor for a group of Benedictine sisters who had taken over the Mercy school. And Julia Lynch, the so-called renegade, was welcomed back into the ranks of the Mercies in Omaha in 1898. She "came back like Queen Victoria, elegantly dressed in black," says one account. Her new name was to be Sister Mary Anselm.

Some of Mother Warde's progeny did better. Mother Mary Baptist Meyers moved north and west from Omaha, opening up convents, hospitals and schools in the Denver area. Her specialty was mining towns, and in 1894 she brought her Mercies by stagecoach to the one that may have been the wildest: Cripple Creek, Colorado.

The railroad hadn't quite arrived, but gold fever had the town digging furiously for the stuff that would soon bring it. There were five hundred gold mines in the area and eight thousand miners hacking away in makeshift tunnels and jury-built shafts that often collapsed on them. This posed a problem because, while the town had erected some seventy-three

Nuns 'n' Guns: Sisters of Mercy patrol the main street of Cripple Creek, Colorado, a wild mining town that featured seventy-three saloons and, until they came, zero hospitals. (COURTESY OF THE COLORADO HISTORICAL SOCIETY)

saloons and a selection of gambling dens and whore houses, it hadn't gotten around to building a hospital.

Mother Meyers, who had some of Mother Warde's gift for diplomacy, convinced local businessmen to help her turn one of the town's biggest buildings, a ramshackle, two-story structure, into St. Nicholas Hospital. The building was soon filled to capacity with twenty-five patients.

In 1886 a fire broke out in Cripple Creek, and lacking water, volunteer firefighters began to use what they had—dynamite—to keep it from consuming the town. As the sisters began to evacuate St. Nicholas, a number of other dynamite-bearing volunteers began to appear. In theory, they were there to blast structures to the ground, so they wouldn't feed the fire. In fact, they were going around town to settle old scores.

One of them, who happened to be a member of the American Protective Association, brought his dynamite into the hospital. Amid the confusion of the evacuation, he managed to stuff his charge into what he assumed was St. Nicholas's most vulnerable point, the stove that heated the building.

When he lit the fuse, instead of collapsing the hospital, the exploding dynamite shot a fierce blast out of the stove door, severing the dynamiter's leg. So the nuns trundled him off along with their other patient to a private hospital outside the range of the fire. It was run by a doctor, but the sisters lingered to nurse the dynamiter.

"He was badly injured and the experience of being cared for with compassion by those he had sought to injure motivated him to express sorrow for his deed," says one account of this. The sisters retrieved one of his heavy black shoes, which had landed in their teapot, and kept it among their memorabilia. St. Nicholas, which escaped the fire and treated 307 patients during the brief but exciting gold rush in Cripple Creek, hardly suffered at all.

Not all of Mother Meyers's undertakings were as rewarding. One deal with a mysterious and rich French priest, Jean Baptist Francolon, eventually left the order in charge of a hulking eighteen-room Victorian palace, called Miramont Castle, in Manitou Springs, a fashionable Colorado resort. Among other amenities, Miramont featured a cuckoo clock that marked the hours by producing one of the twelve apostles. To mark the quiet solemnity of midnight, Christ's entire following appeared.

Burdened with expenses, but intrigued with its possibilities, the sisters tried to run Miramont as a sanitarium and later as a kind of boarding-house for rich tourists. After receiving pressure that came from as far away as Rome to close it, they decided to turn it into a vacation house for sisters in the Mercies' Omaha province who, Lord knows, sometimes needed a rest.

But Mother Meyers, like Mother Warde, was indefatigable. On August 29, 1901, returning from a long road trip to raise money for a hospital in Denver, she arrived at the convent to learn that a novice, a beginner in the order, was dying in Durango, another mining town.

Taking a younger sister as a companion, she jumped on a train that crossed the mountains on a narrow-gauge railway. Their car became detached and then flipped over on her, dragging her to her death. Among the Omaha Mercies, she became legend. She was known as "the founder par excellence. She was willing to take the risk when she found a need to be met."

Another of the order's great western risk-takers was Mother Mary Francis Sullivan, who led the Mercies into another wild mining town, Joplin, Missouri. With few supporters in the largely non-Catholic town teeming with lead and zinc miners, she walked into the House of Lords, the town's richest gambling casino. She told the owner, Gilbert Barbee, that what he needed to do was to give her a building for the town's first hospital. He agreed.

The sisters later opened a school. "One could be a teacher during the day, a social worker in the evenings and on weekends, and with little or no notice, be whisked into hospital work with no preparation," says one history of their efforts in Joplin.

The nuns also dabbled in engineering. When they dug a ditch that ran from their convent to a nearby stream, Joplin found itself with its first sewer. Drunks returning from the downtown saloons on Saturday night didn't always appreciate the sisters innovations, however. For when they would sometimes stop by at the convent seeking further entertainment, yelling and banging on the doors, Mother Sullivan had devised another piece of engineering. It was a bell that roused Patrick McGaurin, a burly Irishman who lived across the street. One ring and he was over there, promising to throttle unwanted visitors.

Despite their success in Joplin, the Mercies were sometimes mystified by it. In 1907 one nun, Sister Mary Isabel O'Brien, dashed off a postcard to a sister in Chicago that confided: "Atheists meet you on all sides. The doctors at this hospital are fine men, but not one Catholic among them."

Among these women who helped win the West, the one who came closest to a John Wayne–sized stature was a five-foot-three Italian immigrant named Blandina Segale. Catholics, many of them immigrants from large European cities, had warned this twenty-two-year-old Sister of Charity about the nefarious ways of cowboys. As the young nun started her journey from her home in Cincinnati to Trinidad, Colorado, another desolate mining town, that image of the evil cowboy began to prey on her mind.

The daughter of an Italian fruit vender, Sister Blandina had been sent to a school run by the Sisters of Charity and became enthralled by stories of their adventures, especially their heroic service on the battlefields in the Civil War. She had prayed to become a sister and, after that, prayed to be sent to a mission outpost somewhere out West.

In the fall of 1872, she got what she wished for and all the problems that came with it. The first one was her father, who clamped his hand on her arm in a painful grip and asked her, point blank, if he had ever denied her anything. Her answer was no. Had she ever disobeyed him? She said she hadn't.

Then the fruit vendor assumed a tone of command. "You must not go on this far away mission. Are you going?"

"Yes, Father," said the daughter, feeling her heart ache as his tears began falling.

After she reached the end of the regular train routes, Sister Blandina shifted to a rough construction train, hauling Irish laborers to the uncompleted portion of the railroad. Surprised to see a nun traveling alone, they quickly took off their hats as a sign of respect. When she boarded a stagecoach at the end of that line, Sister Blandina realized that that world where men would treat her with respect was ending. She was entering a new one, populated by treacherous, heathen cowboys.

Her biography explains that she became so frightened about this that she couldn't eat as the stage rumbled into the early darkness of a December evening. Around midnight the coach stopped, the door opened, and a tall man wearing a buffalo robe climbed in. He plopped down on the seat next to her and asked her if she would like to share part of his "kiver." Before she could answer, he'd thrown it over her lap. The stage door closed, and as the coach lurched forward into the dark emptiness of the night, there she was, snuggled up alone with a cowboy.

She had been warned over and over in Cincinnati that "no virtuous woman is safe near a cowboy." Various other thoughts raced through her mind. "I made an Act of Contrition," she said, referring to a prayer begging God to forgive her for all her sins. She thought of the archbishop who had blessed her for this journey in Cincinnati, saying, "Angels guard your steps." But could even an angel save her now?

She had doubts. She changed her position "as would put my heart in range with his revolver. I expected he would speak—I answer—he fires, the agony endured cannot be written. The silence and suspense unimaginable."

As the young sister prepared herself for almost certain doom, the cowboy roused himself and spoke.

"Madam?"

"Sir," said the nun, icily, steeling herself for the worst.

"What kind of lady be you?"

"A Sister of Charity."

"Whose sister?"

"Everyone's sister, a person who gives her life to do good to others."

"Quaker-like, I reckon?"

"No, not quite."

As she gave a more elaborate explanation, it slowly began to dawn on Sister Blandina that she had nothing to fear from the man. Soon she had turned the conversation around. Why did he become a cowboy? The man said he'd read about it in books and run away from home to ride the range. Sister Blandina felt control of the situation shifting toward her. She admonished the cowboy to write his mother. He promised he would, saying he was "powerful glad" to have spoken with her.

After he got out, the stage rattled onto the washboard streets of Trinidad, a haven for escaped criminals from New Mexico, just twelve miles away. Some of its leading citizens were rustlers, land sharks and miners who lived in dugouts. When she alighted from the stage, Sister Blandina kept the new feeling: This might be a place of desperados, but she was the one who was going to be in control.

Her first outpost was Public School No. 1, where she had no difficulty explaining that bad things happen to people who break moral laws. A drunk, robbed of his land by a land shark, shot him. They hung the killer on a makeshift gallows just outside Sister Blandina's classroom window.

When the town's hulking sheriff had to face down a lynch mob, Sister Blandina stood with him. Later she found a way to repair the school, a crude adobe hut where the roof dripped cockroaches on her students' heads. After the locals told her that there was no money to fix it, Sister Blandina took a crowbar and climbed up on the roof to do the job herself. At the sight of that, six men arrived with tools and adobe molds. They took over, telling her that women were only fit to do white washing. This was man's work. Still, she showed them how to make plaster.

When the local whore, Crazy Anne, came to the convent to die, Sister Blandina provided a room and nursed her. Sometime after that, the nun started a baseball team, and one day, while she was crouched behind the plate calling balls and strikes, some of her students came to her with a warning. Two gunslingers were riding into town. They were gang members of the notorious Billy the Kid. We have seen this scene in a thousand westerns: The townspeople scattered and shopkeepers began to board up their windows.

But Sister Blandina went downtown to have a look. She found a man called "Schneider," loping into town on a fancy horse. Schneider was a tall, arrogant man dressed in red velvet knee breaches and a green velvet short coat. He was seated on a gold and green saddle and accompanied by another fierce-looking outlaw, who bore the odd-seeming moniker of Happy Jack.

Something as small as a raised eyebrow could trigger a gunfight with this pair, so the few townsmen who lingered left them pretty much to themselves. The two gunmen started drinking, then quarreling. At the height of the argument, both drew and, as Sister Blandina recalled it, "each got the drop on the other. They kept eyeing and following each other for three days, eating at the same table, weapon in the right hand, conveying food to their mouth with the left hand."

On the third day, at dinner, "each thought the other off guard, both fired simultaneously." Happy Jack caught a slug in the chest and died. Schneider was wounded in the thigh. Then men of the town took their revenge, heaving him into an abandoned hut and leaving him there to die.

After weighing what to do, Sister Blandina entered the hut lugging a load of food and clean bed linens. It was a contest between two toughies. "I see that nothing but a bullet through your brain will finish you," the diminutive nun told the gunman, who responded with a faint grin.

Schneider, who had worried that he was about to get a lecture on repentance, was amused by the nun, as she bustled around the hut. She had the appearance that nothing would shock her, so Schneider began telling her some stories. He told her how he had preyed on travelers on the Santa Fe Trail, helping those who appeared to be lost by leading them to a remote campsite, where he robbed and killed them.

Once, when he was caught at this and about to be hanged, the would-be hangman took pity and relented. So then, explained Schneider, he whipped out his hunting knife and scalped the man on the spot. Sister Blandina suggested that, horrendous as these things were, God would forgive him. Schneider found that hilarious. He said he was proud to be going to hell.

While he roared on about that, the nun left the hut. Soon she returned carrying a live coal in a shovel. If he had the courage to deal with hell, she suggested to Schneider, why shouldn't he give her a little preview and touch it? The discussions between the nun and the gunfighter went on in the hut for four months. "I do not speak on religious subjects to him unless questioned," recalled Sister Blandina.

One day she arrived at the hut to find three strange men hovering over Schneider. She recalls Schneider's introduction of two of them: "Billy, our captain, and Chism." The activities and the identity of Billy the Kid in the West have become shrouded in legend and some confusion. Sister Blandina provided this portrait of him. "Billy has steel-blue eyes, peach complexion, is young, one would take him to be seventeen—innocent-looking, save for the corners of his eyes, which tell a set purpose, good or bad."

Chism and the other men deferred to Billy as he ranted about how he was going to scalp the four doctors who worked in Trinidad because they refused to remove the bullet from Schneider's thigh. At one point, though, he revealed a more gallant side. He offered Sister Blandina his hand and said he would grant her any favor. All she had to do was name one.

Fine, said the nun, completing the handshake. She asked him to forget about scalping the doctors.

Sister Blandina had several other encounters with the Kid during her days in the West, which included assignments to missions in Santa Fe and Albuquerque. Once, meeting her on a highway, the Kid performed horse tricks for her. Another time, when she visited him in the Santa Fe jail, he was still gallant, although in an awkward position. He was chained to the floor and bound hand and foot. "I wish I could place a chair for you, sister," he said, greeting her.

Sister Blandina found the West to be a place where stereotypes about women could be bent to serve a good cause. She once pried a teacher's salary out of Santa Fe's school board and used it to buy school supplies. She raided the bishop's garden to get vegetables for hospital patients and shinnied up a drainpipe to put out a fire at the hospital by pouring salt on it from the roof of the second floor. At a railroad camp where twenty-four men were surrounded by an angry band of Apaches, she negotiated a truce, holding the cross in front of her as she approached the astonished Indians.

"I doubt not the men think I'm either a saint or a witch," she recalled.

To be sure, not all sisters were as bold as she was and there was a certain amount of prayerful flimflam involved in getting some women to come to the more remote parts of the West. In 1885, for example, two elderly sisters of Mercy from Michigan were on their way to retirement in California, but they got off the train at the bleak outpost of Fort Scott, Kansas.

Their objective was simply to go to Sunday Mass, but they ran into Father Francis J. Wattron. The silver-tongued pastor at Mary, Queen of Angels church, knew a gift when he saw one. He brought them into the rectory. Why did they want to go all the way to California? he asked them. Kansas's climate was better. "It was drier and had even more days of sunshine than Los Angeles."

Sister Mary Bonaventure, who had developed a touch of arthritis in Michigan, went on, but Sister Teresa Dolan, recovering from pneumonia, became intrigued with the possibilities in a balmy, sun-drenched Kansas. She returned with some younger sisters and started a foundation that eventually extended to four hospitals and ten schools.

No story about how the West was won by nuns would be complete without a discussion of what were called the wanderers. These were truly renegade nuns, rejects who tended to drift from convent to convent. While sharing the women's zest for adventure, they also had a tendency to wear out their welcome. The most infamous was probably Sister Mary Joseph Davis, another alumna of Mother Warde's convent in Manchester, New Hampshire.

Born in Ireland, she went to Yreka, California, with a delegation of other Mercies and later turned up in Montana and in San Francisco, where, somehow, she appears to have become addicted to opium. A large woman, who played piano, violin and harp, she had ambitions of becoming a founder, like Mother Warde. She was on her way to leadership in a Mercy convent in Salt Lake City, but then she was caught shoplifting while on a trip with a younger nun to San Francisco. The bishop of Salt Lake City discreetly arranged for her to be transferred to Pocatello, Idaho, someone else's diocese. There she found a great deal of work to do, usually around the hospital supply room.

Once the bishop there, Daniel Gorman, discovered her problem, he

Heading West. Sisters of Mercy break for lunch during a journey through the Oklahoma Territory in the late 1800s. (COURTESY OF THE SISTERS OF MERCY OF THE AMERICAS, ST. LOUIS, MISSOURI)

swore the other nuns to silence and had the Mercies finance a one-way ticket back to Ireland for Sister Mary Joseph. Back on the Olde Sod, she quietly left the order.

Wanderers enjoyed a certain popularity in the West because they could be used quickly to fill vacancies in convents, but having too many of them made convent life hell. Mother Angela Hostetter discovered this in Stanton, Texas, in the early 1920s when her community broke down after one of these much-traveled sisters complained about convent abuses to the local Ku Klux Klan. There was an effort to transfer the nun, a Sister Cincilli, to yet another convent, but the local bishop refused to allow it, asserting the woman was "out of her tracks."

For the many sisters who stayed on their tracks, their lives of service in the West brought some of them to the day when they realized that their mission was accomplished. But with it came the feeling that the magic, the state of being on the very edge of life was waning. This was sometimes difficult for them to absorb. There was a kind of swagger in what they did. Sister Blandina, the friend of Billy the Kid, once defined her mission as "to teach and meet emergencies as I saw them."

For her, the fateful day came in 1892 when she returned to Colorado and found that Public School No. 1—the school that she'd rebuilt, financed, taught in and served as a janitor for most of two decades—was under the control of a school board that included some of her former students. They insisted on teacher examinations and, further, that any sisters who taught could no longer wear their religious habits.

The teachers examination didn't phase Sister Blandina, but the business about not wearing her habit provoked a verbal shootout with the head of the board. "I looked steadily at the chairman and replied: The Constitution of the United States gives me the same privilege to wear this mode of dress as it gives you to wear your trousers, Goodbye."

With that, she turned and rode off into the sunset. Hollywood would have ended it right there, but Sister Blandina went on to take over a parochial school in Pueblo.

9

CUI BONO?

On a steamy day in July 1871, the Catholic Church in Baltimore held a parade. The archbishop gave a speech. Thousands of Catholics, members from nearly every parish in the city, lined the streets as young women, dressed in the dark, neat uniforms of St. Frances Academy, began to march north. They were going to what were then the outskirts of the city, to a new building that would become their new home.

These were black children, students from the nation's oldest Catholic school for African Americans. They were led by two black nuns. A group of older people, alumni of the school, marched with them. They were the beginnings of Baltimore's black elite because they had learned how to read and write and much more at St. Frances. It was a gift that made them stand out from the crowd. Emerging from the chaos and wrenching changes wrought by the Civil War, 90 percent of America's black population was illiterate.

But the object of most of the attention was the person riding behind them in a horse-drawn hack. She was a frail-looking, eighty-eight-year-old woman who had achieved an impossible dream. She had made St. Frances happen in an age when educating black children was considered unnecessary and even held to be a criminal act in some states. In some churches—the Catholic Church looming large among them—the reigning consensus was that it was pointless.

The battles to civilize the American West were minor events, mere horseplay compared to the struggle that this woman had been through. Winning the West had taken a mere twenty years. This tiny woman with the high cheekbones and the proud, penetrating eyes had been fighting the effects of racism in America and in the Catholic Church since 1818, when she opened her first school for black children in Baltimore.

Her struggle would go on for almost another hundred years. When she was a young woman she fought alone, losing more often than she won, working against the weight of law and custom and the inertia of well-bred people. They chose not to question side effects of a custom—slavery—that had made many of them rich and comfortable. Many upper-class Baltimoreans had always had colored servants and saw no need to improve them. They were fine, just the way they were.

In the middle years of her struggle, this nun saw gains she had made over decades disappear in a heartbeat. With the whim of a new church administrator or the death of one of her courageous benefactors, she often found herself back on square one.

She carried all this with her as her carriage rumbled over the streets. Now in her old age, she knew her battle wasn't over. In Baltimore, the segregated ways of the South were still enshrined in little black and white compartments. They were in stores, auditoriums, hotels, even in Catholic churches and hospitals, sections where black people were not welcome.

This parade was a kind of intermission, a truce where neighbors could acknowledge that the faith and determination of this fragile-looking woman, Elizabeth Lange, a French-speaking Creole from Haiti, had begun to reach their hearts, if not their minds or their wallets.

Still, there were people who seemed to sense the solemnity of the day and vied with each other for a role in it. A Jewish man volunteered to help the nuns move, but he would move only religious items used in the chapel. St. Frances being what it was—and still is—this meant a lot of baggage. He hauled over nine cartloads. There were heavy pews, woodwork, religious statuary, altars, bundles of crosses and stacks of hymnals. When he was finished, according to one account, he "refused to take a cent of money for doing it."

There are more than a million African American Catholics in the United States. At this time, Baltimore was one of the centers of their world. Like all Americans, they came from many places and embodied many cultural and racial variations. The man who volunteered to haul her hymnals probably didn't know it, but the evidence suggests that Elizabeth Lange was partly Jewish.

Her grandfather was Marcdoche Lange, a plantation owner in what was later to become Haiti. There he was known by his nickname, the Israelite, and he had accumulated a considerable amount of wealth, some of which he sent with his granddaughter when she fled the island's bloody revolution led by Toussaint Louverture. Baltimore was one of the ports of entry for these French-speaking Catholics, seeking peace.

The world where Elizabeth Lange grew up had many combinations of color and classes. In the America she found there were two: black and white. In the conventional wisdom of Baltimore the woman had arrived with three strikes against her. She had colored skin, spoke only French and had the desire to enter a religious order. In 1818, when she and a few similarly minded women opened a school to teach refugee children for free, the rules were that the only place for a "black" person in a religious order was in the kitchen, in the fields or among the weeds in the garden.

The Jesuits planted the faith in Maryland and started this precedent by owning slaves. Being Jesuits, they developed an intellectual rationale that some of the lesser minds of the Church later found useful. Bishops in Georgia and Louisiana would anaesthetize the consciences of wealthy members of their flocks by preaching that slavery was far from evil. It was simply another marvelous aspect of the Lord's work, they explained. Slavery was an "eminently Christian" way "by which millions pass from intellectual darkness to the brilliance of the Gospel."

Elizabeth Lange knew this was wrong. She had prayed that she could some day form her own order of Catholic sisters, women of color who would consecrate their lives to educating impoverished people of color. This was unthinkable in the Baltimore that she found. There were no public schools for African Americans in the city until after the Civil War.

But she persevered until she met a white man who listened to her. He was a Sulpician priest, Father James Hector Nicholas Joubert. He was a strapping man, a former soldier, and French, all good reasons why he didn't mind flaunting the city's English-speaking establishment.

Father Joubert had also fled the rebellion in Haiti. He felt that the long-term solution to the poverty of the refugees was to form a school that would educate colored girls. Ms. Lange's dream to form a religious order and run such schools made sense to Father Joubert, as he later confided to his diary, because the objective of a permanent school "would be more assured and promise far more good" if a self-perpetuating order ran it, rather than just one person.

He sold the idea to Archbishop James Whitfield, who was even more of a radical visionary than he was. The archbishop saw inevitability, even divine symmetry in the black order and its school. "The finger of God is in this thing," the archbishop predicted. Father Joubert drew up the papers and sent them to Rome.

In 1831, Elizabeth Lange's order, the Oblate Sisters of Providence, was sanctioned by Pope Gregory. She and Father Joubert selected a habit that consisted of a black dress and cape and tight-fitting white bonnet inspired by the simple garb of Mennonite women they had seen in western Maryland. St. Frances Academy started in a rented building with Sister Mary, as Elizabeth Lange was now called, two other sisters and twenty students.

This was regarded as revolutionary, in the worst sense of that word. The mere sight of black women wearing a religious habit was shocking to the point of being sacrilegious in Baltimore. Father Joubert came to realize that shocking people was dangerous. Baltimore was a city where outraged mobs sometimes formed so quickly and over such trivial matters that it was known as Mob Town.

It wasn't just Father Joubert who had this chilling feeling. The landlord of the rented school building suddenly announced that the sisters must leave because he had decided to rebuild it. Other houses for rent in the neighborhood became unavailable, once the color of the proposed tenants became known.

Father Joubert and Sister Mary managed to keep St. Frances running, but they had more than a few moments when it seemed to teeter on the edge of existence. On October 8, 1834, after Know Nothings burned a convent in Charlestown, Massachusetts, the priest realized he had created

Mother Elizabeth Lange
(taken from a painting).
(COURTESY OF THE OBLATE SISTERS
OF PROVIDENCE)

the ultimate magnet for America's crazed xenophobes: colored nuns who taught the Catholic religion in French! That night he and two other priests slept fitfully in the parlor of the Oblates' convent, waiting for the torches, the drunken shouting and scuffling of feet that seemed inevitable. But Mob Town failed to live up to its reputation. "The night passed very tranquilly," he informed his diary.

In the 1840s, as Father Joubert's health began to fail, so did the stream of money that he managed to find for the school. The sisters did kitchen work and took in washing, mending and sewing to keep going, but it wasn't enough. When he died in late 1843, it looked as though St. Frances, which had begun to produce trained teachers for other private colored schools, would be abandoned.

Seeking help, the Oblates sometimes stood out in the street in front of a neighboring Catholic parish, cold, hungry and discouraged. But parishoners walked past them without giving them a second look and Father Joubert's French-speaking order had no more priests available to help them.

This was treatment that some of Mother Lange's sisters could not abide. One of them was Almaide Duchemin, a tall beauty, the daughter of a French-Haitian nurse and a Baltimore patrician, Major Arthur Howard, a member of one of the city's leading families. Almaide, who became Sister Therese, had her father's fair blue-eyed complexion and the fiery, Latin temper of her mother. In Baltimore, where race mattered a great deal, she was categorized as an octoroon, a woman with one-eighth black heritage.

As the Oblates went begging on the street, Sister Therese struck out on her own, accepting an invitation to teach at a parochial school in Michigan. She had all the right credentials, an education in the classics, fluency in English, French and Latin, and something that most members of the Oblates didn't have: She could pass as white. So she did. In Michigan, where she assumed people would not categorize her, she founded an order of white sisters. Now she was Mother Theresa, the superior of the sisters, Servants of the Immaculate Heart of Mary.

Meanwhile, the sisters of her old order, the Oblate sisters in Baltimore, were rescued. When Father Thaddeous Anwander, a twenty-three-year-old immigrant priest from Bavaria, discovered their plight, he went to members of his order, Redemptorist priests, newly arrived from Vienna. The Oblates had started a tradition of education among colored families in Baltimore, he argued. They were saving souls, saving lives from destitution, saving a culture that would otherwise be crushed. How could this work be allowed to end?

His order sent him to the archbishop, a man named Samuel Eccleston. Where Archbishop Whitfield, who was English, saw the finger of God, Archbishop Eccleston, who came from Maryland's eastern shore, prided himself on his more intimate political sense of what was happening in America. He also had a tendency to show off his Latin by summing up things in pithy phrases.

Educate black people? *"Cui Bono?"* was his response to the fledgling priest. In other words, what good did it do to educate youngsters who were destined for lives of servitude? Father Anwander, who had been ordained just nine months, did not let his youthful pride or his sense of outrage get in his way. He got down on his knees and begged. The bishop was moved by that. Father Anwander could be the Oblates' new protector.

It *was* as if the finger of God had pointed. Father Anwander, who was still learning English, went door to door, begging for the school. He brought in his superior, Father John Neumann—a man destined to become a saint—who gave the nuns financial and moral support. With their help the Oblates recruited 10 new sisters and their school exploded, going from 20 students to 160.

The experience of other orders of nuns in America was that, after a period of trials, they reached a kind of tipping point where young women began to join them and where bishops from other cities invited them in. That eventually did happen to the Oblates. But in 1871, as Sister Mary rolled through the streets of Mob Town in her little parade, she had ample evidence that the tipping point hadn't yet arrived. For the Oblates, the trials were going to be longer and harder.

They had recently started schools in Philadelphia and New Orleans, which were soon forced to close for lack of funds. In the City of Brotherly Love, the citizens made the failure even more painful by forcing nuns off the sidewalks and into the muddy streets because they were colored. Sometimes they were pelted with garbage.

In the 1880s the Oblates took over an orphanage for homeless black boys in Leavenworth, Kansas. They found them sleeping on boards covered with straw and using old pieces of carpet to keep warm. To get more space they moved the orphanage onto an eighty-acre farm in the country. One morning after they moved in, they found there was no milk for the hungry boys, so one of the nuns put on her Oblate habit and a big black bonnet, grabbed a bucket and went to a neighboring farm to borrow some.

The farmer's wife saw this strange, dark apparition coming up the driveway and went inside and slammed the door. Through the closed door, the woman directed her to another farm where another woman did give milk. While rural America wasn't quite ready for the Oblates, the Sisters of Charity in Kansas were. They gave the new orphanage a present, a cow.

The nation had gone through a bloody war over slavery that had changed its laws, but the policies of the Catholic Church were slow to adjust. Catholic leaders remained leery of the anti-Catholic leanings of the Abolitionists, who were mainly New England Protestants. The Church's most outspoken leader, Archbishop John Hughes, announced in New York in 1861 that Catholic soldiers would fight to the death to support the Constitution. But they would "turn away in disgust," he said, if the cause was simply the abolition of slavery.

There were some bright spots, though, and they were evident in Sister Mary's parade. By 1871 the Jesuits in Baltimore had turned around on the issue of race. They were led in this by none other than the former bishop of Pittsburgh, Rev. Michael O'Connor, the man who had frequently come to the rescue of the Sisters of Mercy. In Baltimore he had achieved his dream of becoming a Jesuit; now he began to indulge in his other obsession: making the world a safer place for nuns.

To help Sister Mary's order, he raised $6,000 to buy an old Universalist church, which he turned into St. Francis Xavier's Church for the Colored, the city's first. The parade was en route to his next project: a new convent and school for the Oblates, which he had helped construct on vacant land on nearby Chase Street.

The Oblates continued to spread, opening parochial schools for African Americans elsewhere in Baltimore and in nearby Washington, but some of these proved to be fragile undertakings. A new pastor, arriving at one of their schools in Baltimore in 1880, summarily dismissed the Oblates. *"Cui bono?"* was an attitude that continued to haunt and taunt Sister Mary.

She died in 1882, seven years after Baltimore's African American Catholics celebrated her golden jubilee by hanging a giant bell woven with flowers over her place of honor in the chapel. "The sisters wanted her to have a gold crown, but Sister Mary would not allow it," says one account. She took pride in one thing, though, an indulgence that would have inflamed the Know Nothings in their heyday. "I am French to my soul," she confided to the young women who attended her final hours.

In retrospect, her crowning achievement was to build a foundation for action in perhaps the most difficult frontier the nation faced. Her life's work and the depth of faith that kept her at it sent a message to Catholics. It was that *cui bono* was hardly a Christian response for a church that claimed the allegiance of more American Christians than any other.

Sister Mary inspired no great rush to take on her mission, but people who saw the wisdom of it, like Father Joubert, kept turning up. The next was a young woman, Katharine Drexel, who knew all about the comforts and the inertia of the well-bred. She was about to become one of the richest women in America. For her, Sister Mary's dream proved to be a pathway to sainthood.

She was one of three daughters of Joseph Drexel, a clever man who started as a currency trader on the Ohio River in the 1830s. He built the business into Drexel & Co. in Philadelphia, one of the nation's largest investment banking firms.

He died in 1885, leaving his daughters $14 million in a will that was tightly drawn by lawyers because he knew his estate would make his daughters magnets for ersatz European noblemen and others who made careers out of preying on rich American women.

One or two had already tried, but there were to be no dukedoms or other airy titles for Katherine, a pensive, twenty-seven-year-old beauty with a round face and waist-length brown hair. When her inheritance payments started flowing, she was on her way to becoming a nun.

Just which order she would join raised a difficult question for the heiress, who was more familiar with couturiers in Paris than she was with the tangle of religious orders that was growing across America. Her spiritual advisor and family friend was a Philadelphia parish priest, Father James O'Connor, who happened to be the brother of Rev. Michael O'Connor. Father James gently introduced Katherine Drexel to the face of poverty in America. In 1887, just after she and her sisters returned from one of their grand tours of luxury hotels in Europe, he took her on a trip to visit Indian reservations. The shock of what she saw was so profound that Katherine later informed Father James that she was determined to form her own order, "a missionary order for Indians and colored people."

The priest's response was to send her to the Sisters of Mercy, the Pittsburgh branch of Ireland's fabled Walkin' Nuns. The discipline established there by Frances Warde, he felt, would give her the best training in the ways of helping poor communities. She applied in April 1889. A year later the heiress had her debut, as a substitute teacher for a class of colored children in a school taught by the Mercies. The students gave the new nun the standard treatment they reserved for beginners.

One young man whipped out a whistle and blew it. A comrade across the room replied with another whistle. Fearing that she was losing control, Sister Katherine pulled out her ultimate weapon, a rattan switch. "Hold out your hand!" she commanded the first young man. He simply ignored her, folding his arms. He whistled again. At that, two other boys started a fight. A third strolled over, unbidden, to build a fire in the fireplace.

Sister Katherine had carefully watched her Mercy instructors control a class like this with a few mild comments. She struggled in vain to keep her cool. "Children! No more lessons until there is perfect silence in this room!" she found herself shrieking. The entire class broke out in a song. Another nun, realizing it was a prank, came in to subdue the giggling students. Sister Katherine, who had a gift for understatement, later wrote Father James—by then a bishop in Omaha—about her new experience: "The children are very interesting."

In 1890, early in the planning for her order—which would be called the Sisters of the Blessed Sacrament—she reached a seminal question: Should her new order accept African American woman? It would have been a pioneering step. After much debate among her advisors, she decided against it. Part of the reason was, out of deference to orders like the Oblates, she didn't want to compete with them for recruits. But a major part of it was her feeling that neither her church, nor the nation was ready for that step. Most Catholic religious orders did not begin accepting black candidates until the 1960s.

One of her biographers, Lou Baldwin, gives us this rationale: "We must look at this decision as an 1890 decision, just a quarter century after the Civil War. Remember, Lincoln only freed the slaves, he didn't invite them to tea."

Katherine Drexel went on to develop and finance parochial schools all over America, with most of her money flowing into black communities, both in the urban North and the rural South. She saw firsthand how the segregation in her sprawling church continued to divide parishoners into orderly, sometimes invisible black and white boxes that determined where they sat and, no doubt, how they felt about themselves.

During a visit to St. Peter Church in Charlotte, North Carolina, she found that African Americans could receive communion only after all the whites were served. In Glencoe, Louisiana, she discovered how deep-seated this practice was. One of the white benefactors of a school she had

Saint Katherine Drexel, age sixteen. (COURTESY OF THE ARCHIVES OF THE SISTERS OF THE BLESSED SACRAMENT)

built for colored children became outraged when a black child stepped out of place to receive the Host. "Would you allow a nigger to go to Communion at the same time as your daughter and not resent it?" he asked her.

Many rural churches, she found, required African Americans to sit in the balcony, or behind the seats reserved for whites. That separation was not enough for white parishoners in Rayne, Louisiana, she discovered. The rule there was that blacks could only observe Sunday Mass on Thursdays.

In 1932 Mother Katherine Drexel wrote the pope, asking him to help her promote an auxiliary group of lay Catholics she hoped would help support her work among the Indians and blacks. In the letter, she made note of the evangelizing opportunity: Half of the nation's twelve million African Americans had no church. The pope was enthusiastic, but the auxiliary found few volunteers.

She could not beat the Church's system of segregation, but she did do something that eventually helped break it down. The Oblates and other emerging orders of African American sisters were facing a kind of catch-22 in the early 1900s. To expand, they needed to have high schools. State laws said they needed college degrees to teach high school, but no Catholic university would accept African American women.

When Southern University, a state-run school near New Orleans, came up for sale in 1915, Mother Katherine bought it, reopening it as Xavier University. She watched the dedication ceremony from a seat in the balcony, making sure that her name would not be mentioned as its benefactor.

As one of the historians of the Oblates put it, the new university brought "incalculable benefits" because many of the order's later leaders, supporters and recruits later graduated from Xavier. In the 1920s some Catholic colleges followed suit. Finally, in 1933, Catholic University opened its doors to Negroes.

These two women, Elizabeth Lange and Katherine Drexel, their schools and the lessons they taught had a profoundly uplifting effect on the lives of the many people they touched. Sister Majella Neale, seventy-two, an Oblate sister, vividly remembers her parochial school in North Baltimore. It was St. Peter Claver. All of the students were black; the sisters were white, members of a Franciscan order. Her fondest memories are of her first-grade teacher, a sweet-natured woman named Sister Majella, who obviously loved her students and frequently treated them to lemonade. When Ms. Neale left elementary school, in the 1940s, it was like walking off a plank. No Catholic high school in Baltimore would accept black children, so she went to the Oblates' St. Frances Academy, which by then had turned into a prep school for African American women. When she decided to become an Oblate, she was required to pick a new name, a saint's name that impressed her. She took the name of her memorable first-grade teacher.

In 1952, the year Sister Katherine Drexel died, Sister Majella was assigned to teach at another St. Peter Claver's, a rural elementary school in Ridge, Maryland. It was a town of farmers and watermen that had one of the schools Mother Katherine supported. On a holy day, Sister Majella took her eighty students to a predominantly white church nearby. They took up a whole side of the little church, including the front-row pews. No matter, she thought. "I figured they have a whole side for their kids and we'd have a whole side for ours."

It mattered. The rule at that church was that African Americans could not sit in the front rows of either side. Sister Majella found herself in hot water and the priest, a Jesuit, who ran her school was threatened with the loss of his job.

The world then was certainly a different place from the one in 1818, when Elizabeth Lange started her quest, or from 1890, when Katherine Drexel founded her order. This was the Atomic Age. Nations had changed. Customs had changed. People had changed. But in one crucial respect, despite heroic wake-up calls from two saintly women, the Catholic Church in America was still sleeping.* This is one reason why the average white Catholic was so profoundly shocked when the Civil Rights Movement erupted in the late 1950s. Hadn't we played by the rules?

---

* On October 1, 2000, Katherine Drexel was canonized in Rome, becoming Saint Katherine Drexel. The case for the sainthood of Elizabeth Lange is under preparation.

10

SERFS AND TURF

On July 14, 1874, Bishop Michael Domenec, the newly appointed head of the Diocese of Pittsburgh, summoned the leaders of the Sisters of Mercy in his region to a meeting. By this time the order, established in Pittsburgh thirty-one years earlier by Frances Warde and her "swans" from Ireland, was flourishing. There were 173 sisters running a network of schools and hospitals. The original mother house had sprouted eight branches.

Their growth in murky, sooty Pittsburgh was not unusual. Orders of religious women were busy building the infrastructure of the Catholic Church from the piney woods of Maine to the deserts of California. For them, bishops were like the weather. They came with the territory. They came in endless variety. And they had to be coped with.

Some bishops were creative figures, visionaries like the O'Connor brothers who understood the womens' abilities to nurture, manage and build. Being in a position of authority over nuns posed a variety of daunting questions. Sometimes orders went too deeply into debt and needed assistance.

Sometimes they ran afoul of the authorities or riled the local bigots and had to be rescued. The more progressive bishops realized that they were in one of the first large American organizations to harness the management capabilities of women. Thus, there were no handbooks or formulas on how to manage these managers. They were dealing with an unknown force of nature. Sometimes the most productive solution was simply to get out of its way.

But this was a solution that Bishop Domenec could not abide. He was one of a less imaginative breed that tended to proliferate in America as the Church's bureaucracy grew. For them, dealing with the women of the Church was not especially difficult or challenging because all of their knotty questions could be resolved by one simple approach: asserting the bishops' God-given authority.

Bishop Domenec showed the Mercies a paper. It was an order bearing his seal that would reorganize them into three independent branches, each under his control. His order concluded with this message: "I hope that you will make no opposition to these measures that I have laid down. If you do, then the community will suffer . . . on account of your resistance to lawful authority."

When the sisters began to protest, he gave them an imperious wave. He was from Spain, where bishops sometimes mirrored the arrogance of their class and their government: "No," he told them, crisply. "I have said it."

An account of the episode says the sisters were left in a state of shock. "Some in tears; all sat silent and motionless, stunned and amazed." To them, this was an outrage. This was America, not Spain. The reason some orders had come to the United States in the first place was to get away from European tyranny. Here there was, supposedly, no room for the kind of authority that had inspired the Inquisition. Americans had rights.

But this episode was playing out against the background of Canon Law, the legal structure that governs the Catholic Church throughout the world. Here their rights were less clear. Under Canon Law the local unit of government is the diocese and it is run by the bishop.

To be sure, the Mercies and many other orders of sisters do have rights under Canon Law. They are governed by constitutions or "rules" that have been approved by the Vatican. Any major interference with the rule has to be approved by the pope. The Pittsburgh Mercies pointed that out repeatedly. Bishop Domenec told the nuns that if they wanted to appeal his decision to Rome, fine. He had cultivated many friends in the Vatican hierarchy and they would be eager to support him. Make my day, was the bishop's attitude.

The Mercies' superior, Mother Mechtildes O'Connell, was known for her patience and strong faith. First she tried an all-American approach. After polling her sisters, she found that all but two agreed to petition the bishop to reconsider. So she drafted a petition and handpicked a delegation that included nuns who were Irish, French, German and American-born to deliver it to His Grace's office. He didn't even bother to give them a reply.

So then Mother Mechtildes drafted a longer version of the petition and sent it to Rome. The bishop was threatening to depose her as the leader and assume control over the order's property, which had been developed by the Mercies' money and their hard work. As she put it, these were "things we never dreamed any bishop had the power to do."

The bishop had another power, a travel budget. He gave himself permission to go to Rome and lobby for his side of the case. After several months of this, he sent a letter back to Pittsburgh in 1875 explaining how he had met with cardinals and even the pope. All, he reported, had listened attentively to his case. "The Mercy are beaten. I have gained a complete victory over all and my wishes have been granted."

So he returned to Pittsburgh in triumph, and began to reorganize what he regarded as his nuns. But there are many wheels in the machinery of Rome and some were beginning to turn in ways he did not understand. Until 1906 the Vatican considered the United States to be a missionary outpost and progress was measured by the growth in numbers of Catholics and Catholic institutions.

Somewhere in the Vatican there were maps stuck with pins showing the proliferation of schools and hospitals. Rome knew how many of those pins had gotten there: Nuns built them. Finally, in 1877, Pope Pius IX issued his ruling: Bishop Domenec was in error.

An autocrat to the last, the bishop tried to put the best face on it. He resigned after spreading rumors that his friend, the pope, was planning a much more important post for a man of his gifts than running a smoky, isolated place like Pittsburgh. The bishop returned to Spain to prepare himself for the rigors of this new assignment. It never came.

The fact that hundreds of different orders of sisters could carry out independent missions, working with, working around or working despite the orders of their bishops gave the church a flexible, innovative structure that coped well with the extreme challenges and opportunities in the new nation.

It gave the Catholic Church a resilience that allowed it to flow over obstacles and an innovative drive that had it constantly reaching out to new members and collecting arriving immigrants. These are characteristics that many Catholic historians fail to appreciate. They simply baffle most non-Catholics, who continue to view the Church as a monolith.

Dr. Roger Finke, who teaches the sociology of religion at Purdue University, is a Lutheran who has spent years tracking the growth of religions in U.S. Protestant orders. He found they had a distinctive growth cycle: Mainline religions would be established, then go into decline. New sects would spring up to attract members and mainline churches would reform, adopting some of their innovations.

But the Catholic Church just grew and grew. "I started thinking, how did Catholics avoid this cycle?" Then he began to focus on religious orders. The sisters were providing many of the innovations, spreading into every corner of the country. "What I found was they provided a tremendous amount of pluralism, a lot of diversity in terms of what's going on."

From our vantage point in the twenty-first century, having now seen gender wars rage in the U.S. military, in universities, in the professions and in major corporations, battles between nuns and bishops may not seem so shocking. But in the archives of orders of sisters these are seminal events, landmark battles that shaped their histories and their attitudes.

As the nation's first large, organized groups of educated women, the nuns were also the first to confront a long series of patronizing rules. They were like hurdles, put there by men like ex–Bishop Domenec, who were accustomed to feeling that, when it came to women, the bishops' whim had the support of the higher authority. Basically these women were charging into the unknown.

In Monroe, Michigan, it had been Mother Theresa, the woman who had been a member of the Oblates, the African American order of sisters in Baltimore. Passing as white, she had started her own order, the Servants of the Immaculate Heart of Mary, which had branched into Pennsylvania and was flourishing, until Bishop Peter Paul Lefevere of Detroit decided in 1855 he would take control, appointing a diocesan priest as her superior. When she protested and threatened to quit, he banished her from Michigan. He had to be wary of this bright, headstrong woman, he later confided in a letter to a fellow bishop, because she had "all the softness, slyness and low cunning of the mulatto." A second bishop later banished her from Pennsylvania, so Mother Theresa spent seventeen years in double exile, working with a third order, the Grey Nuns, in Canada.

In Wisconsin it was Marie Catherine Moes, a twenty-three-year-old who emigrated from Remich, Luxembourg, in 1851. In Europe she had been taught the dainty household arts of tapestry, wax work and embroidery.

In America no household was going to contain her. She craved action and movement. First she joined the School Sisters of Notre Dame, a German order, in Milwaukee. Then, having learned English, she quickly left that to join the Sisters of the Holy Cross in Indiana, where she taught in parochial schools for eight years.

As a parochial school principal in LaPorte, Indiana, she had gotten into a dispute with the pastor, who reported her to Bishop John Henry Luers. Sister Alfred Moes—that was her religious name—wrote a long, impassioned defense of her actions to the bishop, who was unmoved. Along with a demotion and a transfer to another school for "disobedience," he provided her superior with the following guidance: "As long as sisters & brothers keep their place, they are most useful & beneficial to religion, but when they begin to oppose the pastor [whose assistants they are] & seek to boss and rule him, it is turning things upside down, they loose [*sic*] God's grace & blessing & become a nuisance. . . . You will therefore do me the favor to recall her as soon as possible & without noise."

With that, Sister Alfred left with several other sisters from the Holy Cross order to found a new order, the Third Order of St. Francis of Mary Immaculate, in Joliet, Illinois. It was 1865 and now she was Mother Alfred Moes.

This was fine with Bishop James Duggan of the governing diocese, which was Chicago. But in 1870 he was succeeded by Bishop Thomas Foley, a man who liked to exercise his control at every level. When Mother Alfred again tangled with a local pastor, pulling her sisters out of his parochial school to protest something he'd done, the bishop came down hard, commanding that her order elect a new superior. It did, but Mother Alfred continued to run things. So then Bishop Duggan expelled her from the Joliet congregation.

In retaliation, Mother Alfred drained the parochial school system of most of its talent, taking twenty-three sisters with her to Rochester, Minnesota, where she had already opened a new school. The bishop of Rochester, apparently happy to get this windfall, appointed her the head of a new order, The Sisters of St. Francis of Our Lady of Lourdes.

She was forty-nine and still focused on teaching when, on August 21, 1883, a funnel-shaped cloud touched down and devastated Rochester. The wind overturned houses, flung carriages and lofted the Zumbro River Bridge, then mashed it into the ground, as if it were a child's plaything.

Dr. W. W. Mayo took charge of the thirty-four injured victims, arranging them in makeshift cubicles on the polished floor of Rommel's Dance Hall. He rounded up some volunteers to help nurse them, but they tended to come and go. That was a problem until Dr. Mayo hit on the idea of a more stable source of free help: nuns.

So he went to the convent of the Sisters of St. Francis and said in his characteristically shy, Minnesota way: "There ought to be a sister down there to look after those fellows." Mother Alfred took over the nursing functions. When the crisis had passed, she took the good doctor aside and confided something to him. She had been having this dream about how the two of them might build a world-recognized hospital in Rochester.

As Dr. Mayo recalled the discussion, he was flabbergasted. How in the world could he, an elderly country doctor, do that? Mother Alfred pointed out that he had two sons. They could become famous surgeons. Dr. Mayo fell back to another prepared defensive position. How could they hope to build a great hospital in Rochester? questioned the doctor. Even if her dream was accomplished, he argued. "How would the world know if we did?"

"With our faith and hope and energy it will succeed," said the nun.

The elderly doctor brought it down to brass tacks. It takes money to build hospitals. How much money could the sisters raise?

For Mother Alfred, who had no money, this was an easy question. She shrugged. "How much do you want?"

"Would you be willing to risk forty thousand dollars?"

"Yes, and more if you want," said the nun nonchalantly. "Draw up your plans. It would be built at once."

The resulting St. Mary's Hospital, opening in 1895, drew so many patients it spawned the Mayo Clinic and the rest, as they say, is history.

Mother Alfred Moes, foundress of two Franciscan congregations and St. Mary's Hospital, Rochester, Minnesota. (COURTESY OF THE SISTERS OF ST. FRANCIS, ROCHESTER, MINNESOTA)

The result was hundreds of basic medical innovations, but the foundation for all of them was the hard work, faith, obstinacy and frugality of nuns.

"Carefully Mother Alfred counted the nickels and dimes," says one history of the hospital. "The sisters wore rough, two-dollar shoes and habits of coarse cloth, and sat down always to plain, sometimes meager fare." Of course, there was still a price to be paid. Some sisters, tired of Mother Alfred's extreme austerity and the burdens of raising money for the new hospital, later complained to Archbishop John Ireland of St. Paul, Minnesota.

The archbishop, who was peculiarly fond of using ultimatums to settle disputes with religious orders, was quick to issue one. He demanded that her order elect a new superior, an election in which she would be ineligible. The sisters ignored Ireland, unanimously voting for Mother Alfred. Then the archbishop dropped all pretense of following the rules and flatly ordered another sister to take over her order.

In 1890 Mother Alfred retired, having founded two orders and a world-famous hospital while fencing with three powerful bishops. In a narrow sense, she was the loser in a series of turf fights. But sisters like Mother Alfred were not all that concerned about turf or in winners and losers. They were more interested in results. Bishops were not their motivating source or their scoreboard. God was.

There was Mother Dolores, a Dominican nun from Kentucky, who gave new meaning to the phrase *grace under fire*. Her self-reliance came from caring for the wounded during the Civil War. Sometimes she was caught in the middle of firefights and she knew the distinctive whine of a minnie ball. One had passed through her hair.

In 1876 she arrived in San Francisco with four teaching sisters and two novices and asked the archbishop for permission to start her own order. The archbishop refused, so, in the wee hours of July 14, 1877, Mother Dolores slipped out of the convent, leaving a note for the other nuns that she was taking an early train, the *Lightning Express*, back to Kentucky.

The other sisters found the note, raced to the station and boarded the train with Mother Dolores. They made it as far as Reno, Nevada, where they all left the train because one sister had become ill. Mother Dolores sought out the local bishop. Would he support a new order of sisters? He was interested, but first he wrote the archbishop of San Francisco, for Canon Law required his permission. "I shall give her to you as a present," was the most gracious response from the archbishop.

Mother Dolores was nobody's present. According to a manuscript in the Dominican archives, she was "continually in trouble with the priests and the bishop." The winner was Reno, which gained a new school, Mount Saint Mary's Academy, and a hospital, St. Mary's Regional Medical Center, which is still operating today.

Intimidation was a favorite tool of some bishops, though it sometimes didn't work very well. There was Bishop Richard Scannell of Omaha, who became so frustrated with the Mercies in his diocese in the early 1890s that he summarily handpicked a younger nun, Sister Mary Leo Gallagher, and decreed that she was to be their new superior. When she didn't defer to him, he simply picked another.

He threatened the Mercies with an order of interdict, which meant cutting off their access to priests and the sacraments, such as Confession and Holy Communion. Once during a church reception ceremony when he was supposed to present a clean white apron to a new sister, he flew into a rage, throwing it across the chapel. "Damn nonsense," he muttered.

Bishop William George McCloskey, who spent forty-one years reigning over the diocese of Louisville, Kentucky, liked to crack the whip. He deposed the head of the Ursuline Sisters for crossing the Ohio River without his permission. In 1904 he slapped the Sisters of Loretto with an order of interdict because they allowed a caretaker to live in a house on their property. "Women religious abandoned the diocese whenever possible," says one account of his tenure.

In Cincinnati, Archbishop John Baptist Purcell greeted the Mercies by telling them what to eat. His prescribed regimen was meat twice a day, always accompanied by beer. In the 1870s, he rearranged their finances, ordering them to pay a salary for a priest, whom they disliked. Then he offered to take over some of their property, promising to pay the mortgage on it. The sisters grudgingly complied, swallowing their resistance to the archbishop with a note saying they felt sure "your kind heart will watch over the interests of the community."

After that, the archdiocese went into bankruptcy and creditors hauled the sisters into court over the mortgage, which the archbishop had assumed, but neglected to take out of their name. His successor, Archbishop William Henry Elder, ordered the sisters teaching in parochial schools to submit to an annual evaluation by three of his priests. When the Mercies objected, he threatened to abolish them as a religious order. Poof, he explained, their status as nuns would vanish. "You become simply a family of pious women."

Some of these fights seemed endless. Mother Mary Xavier Malloy, clearly a headstrong women, dueled with two bishops for control over a Mercy-run hospital in Des Moines, Iowa, hanging on for thirty-one years until she died in September 1924. One of her antagonists, Bishop Thomas W. Drumm, of Omaha, referred to this epic battle, but only obliquely, at her funeral. "I would just say this, and everyone understands it, that I had no other thought—why should I?—than the welfare of the hospital."

Power corrupts, and in the case of bishops who preferred to lord it over sisters, it corrupted their priests, who sometimes aped the bishops' attitudes toward the women of the church. A classic case occurred in Yuma, Arizona, in the 1890s when a Father Gheldof asked the Mercies to take over his school. "Get what you can," he told them, "but do not send a bill and I will not speak of it in church. The sisters can live on very little and with what some of the families give, it ought to keep you." After a few years of living with this Catholic version of "Let them eat cake," the sisters withdrew.

There were a few women whose faith was so palpably strong that even the most power-prone bishops chose not to tangle with them. One was a short, frail-looking Italian woman with big, radiant eyes and a sweet smile. People always wanted to call her by her religious name, but she liked to be called Francesca.

She and seven other sisters arrived in New York in the spring of 1889 bearing a letter from Archbishop Michael Corrigan, who had invited them to come from Italy to start an orphanage in Manhattan. When they arrived, though, they found the archbishop had changed his mind. Since he had concluded that they weren't really needed, he coldly informed her, she and her nuns should return to Rome.

"No, Your Grace, that is impossible. I have come here with permission of the Holy See [the Pope]," said Francesca, sweetly.

Studying this serene, thirty-nine-year-old woman, the archbishop, one of the Church's more nimble politicians, had the good sense to back off. He issued another order: She could stay, but she couldn't start the orphanage. He had received letters complaining about it because it was to be located in one of New York's tonier neighborhoods.

As they say in the paratroopers, Francesca hit the ground running. Her order, the Missionaries of the Sacred Heart of Jesus, went straight for the orphanage, starting it right where the archbishop didn't want it to be. They went on to found sixty-six other institutions, a string of hospitals, schools and orphanages that ran across the United States, Central America, South America and Europe. She was a powerfully charismatic leader and a genius at raising money, buying land and making institutions that worked in poorer neighborhoods of big American cities.

Most of the men who played these imperious games with sisters are now minor footnotes in the history of the American Catholic Church, which has produced four saints. Three of them are nuns. One is Francesca, more formally known as Mother Frances Cabrini.

History, despite the way it is often taught, is more than a succession of battles. The difficulty for historians is that the quiet times, the rhythm of daily work, the stories of ordinary places, often go unrecorded. While there were, and continue to be, a fair number of gender battles in the

Saint Frances Cabrini. "No, your Grace, that is impossible." (COURTESY OF THE MISSIONARY SISTERS OF THE SACRED HEART OF JESUS, STELLA MARIS PROVINCE)

American Church, the atmosphere in some dioceses was not combative, but supportive.

St. Louis, Missouri, has a long tradition of this and it starts with Archbishop Peter Richard Kenrick, who invited the Mercies to work with French, Spanish, Irish and German immigrants who had crowded into the narrow, unpaved streets that led down to the levees along the Mississippi River. The heads of families were often deckhands who worked the riverboats, and they lived in a warren of saloons, cheap eateries and junk shops.

The Mercies were led by Mother Magdalen dePazzi Bentley, who was described by one of her former sisters as a "woman with a domineering personality and a queenly bearing." Her father was a judge in Ireland and her brother was serving as a priest in Rome and had reportedly developed strong ties with the Vatican. She never let people forget that.

She had been given a classical education in French convent schools and she ruled her convent in the grand style of Louis XIV. "Don't do what you think, Sister, do what you are told," was her advice to one underling. Many bishops would have seen her as an appealing target: someone to be put promptly in her place. But Archbishop Kenrick tried to be her friend.

Starting a religious foundation in America requires a certain entrepreneurial spirit. Even in the poorest neighborhoods, sisters tried hard to become economically self-sufficient. The Mercies had been trained to think that way. Following the earlier example of their founder, Mother McAuley, with her school and laundry on Baggot Street in Dublin, the Mercies started a laundry in St. Louis in the 1850s. They worked around the clock to get an income stream to support their charitable work.

But they never seemed to raise enough. Sisters went hungry and Mother dePazzi sometimes found herself telling the archbishop it was just too tough. She was going to quit. At times like these, the archbishop would literally buck her up, sometimes slipping her as much as one hundred dollars from his own meager resources. "God is only trying you," he would day.

When Mother dePazzi again came to the end of her finances and, as she was too proud to ask for more, was kneeling alone in her chapel, praying for money, mysterious men would sometimes appear at her door bearing more hundred-dollar bills.

As she became more ambitious, the archbishop steered her away from assuming big debts to buy land for schools, advising her to start an academy for the daughters of the well-to-do and to use the income from that to further her work with the poor. He wanted this woman with her queenly airs to become truly independent. It paid off. By 1861 the Mercies had 448 pupils, had found jobs for 2,848 people and were distributing a steady stream of coal, flour, meat and clothing to poor families. By 1871 they had started St. Johns Hospital, which grew to become one of the dominant hospitals of the region.

As the hospital expanded, Mother dePazzi noticed a curious thing in the convent; some of her sisters were sleeping on the floor. She assumed their beds had been sent out for repair; then more beds disappeared. After discovering her nuns were donating their beds to the hospital, Mother dePazzi countered by donating her own bed, but her sisters unanimously objected. She compromised and donated her pillow. Later, in a bit of inspired entrepreneurship, the hospital worked with the United Railways

Company, of St. Louis, to develop the first prepaid health insurance plan in the United States.

The archbishop's example, showing respect and patient support for this difficult woman, paid off in many other ways. By the early 1920s, the parochial schools in Chaffee, a railroad town outside St. Louis, had become so good that forty-nine students had transferred to it from the public school. They were coming primarily for the music lessons, another way the sisters raised money on the side.

This roused the bed-sheeted knights of the Ku Klux Klan, who burned a cross near the school. A negro was shot. A rally was held at a ballpark where an array of speakers raged against the many evils of Roman Catholics. One of the speakers tended to focus his venom on the nuns. "THAT'S A CONFOUNDED LIE!" shouted a stranger in the crowd, a man wrapped in a well-worn army trench coat.

"Throw him out!" demanded people in the crowd. As the local sheriff went for the man, he took off the trench coat to reveal a Roman collar. It was Father John J. Lonergan, the local parish priest and former World War I Army chaplain. He shook himself free, saying "You may throw me out, but not before you hear what I have to say."

The priest delivered a passionate defense of the sisters. Had these men no awareness of the selfless work that brought beauty and help to their community? Had they no respect for women who could be their sisters or their daughters? The fire in the crowd seemed to go out. Heads down, the once-angry men seemed to be studying their shoes, encrusted with the dust of the infield. Finally, the shoes shuffled away.

II

LIFE IN GOD'S MANSION

A long file of nuns lugging a variety of heavy suitcases and trunks trudge up Sixteenth Street to a stately brick mansion. It is perched on one of the city's few steep hills.

They had taken a streetcar from the cramped, downtown building they had been using as a school and a convent. They might have taken cabs to avoid this uphill climb from the streetcar stop, a mile away, but they are Sisters of Mercy, trained from the first day to squeeze every penny.

Besides, the order had just decided to splurge. It was about to buy the mansion for eight thousand dollars and then refurbish it to turn into a new convent and an academy for girls. The women were tired from the long trek, but they grew excited as the building, shaded by mature trees, came into view. Tall windows looked into generous-sized rooms including a ballroom. The house had servants' quarters, a carriage house, even a sunken garden on its spacious grounds that bore signs of once having been well landscaped.

The younger nuns had traded rumors about this for weeks. "The word went round that we were to have a new home on the edge of the city, a farm of considerable size, and—wonder of wonders—a mansion. True, God had not promised us a mansion, but He had promised us a hundred-fold and we accepted it humbly," recalled Sister Mary Xavier Reilly, who was one of those trudging up the hill. Just that morning she had taken her final vows.

This parade of baggage-carrying nuns might seem like an odd event in Cedar Rapids, then a largely Protestant town, the commercial hub for farming communities in eastern Iowa. But by this time it had grown accustomed to the ways of the Mercies. They had arrived in 1875, at a time when hundreds of other religious orders were settling into the towns that were springing up on the prairies. The nuns seemed to come with the landscape.

These Mercies had come from the mother house in Chicago by way of DeWitt, Davenport and Independence, Iowa, little towns where aspiring young women had swelled the order. Many of them were farmer's daughters, like Anne McCullough from DeWitt, who later became Mother Gertrude, a clever, funny woman who served as the leader in Cedar Rapids for almost a half century.

Like many ordinary places where the nuns settled, there were no grand adventures waiting for them in Cedar Rapids, a town first settled in 1846 by horse thieves and counterfeiters as the frontier rapidly moved west. There were no wild cowboys to tame or prostitutes to be saved; no power-mad bishops or denizens of the Klan to trouble them here. What Cedar Rapids wanted by the time the nuns arrived was what the Mercies brought, the promise of a new school and a second hospital, for the city's first, St. Luke's, a Protestant hospital, was severely overcrowded.

Mother Gertrude opened the first Mercy Hospital in a converted house in 1900. The *Cedar Rapids Gazette* praised the operating room as a "marvel of cleanliness, light and apparatus known only to the best in the country." The fifteen-bed establishment had a few drawbacks, which the boosterish paper was kind enough to overlook. The downstairs hallway was so narrow that patients on stretchers had to be carried partway out the front door before they could be turned and aimed in the direction of the upstairs surgery. The trip provided an additional bit of shock therapy during the fierce Iowa winters.

The following year, as business grew, Mother Gertrude laid out plans for a much grander institution. This would be a hundred-bed hospital. In a fund-raising letter she promised to equip it with the best equipment then available and staff it with people trained in the most up-to-date methods. "We will be content only when we have made it the peer of the best."

This version of Mercy Hospital opened in 1903 and during the first two years it treated 635 patients, 78 of them for free. Getting free treatment from Mother Gertrude, though, was not a matter of art, but one of need. "Although gentle and sympathetic, she could detect a malingerer at twenty paces," recalls Sister Xavier.

There was one major drawback: The sisters had no steady outside income. While they taught school for the local parish, Immaculate Conception, they did it for the first forty-four years for free. Protestants assumed the sisters were supported by the Church, which was wrong. The local priests assumed that the sisters were content to be self-supporting, which was not correct, either, but closer to the truth. Self-supporting they became, but it took a lot of Mother Gertrude's time and ingenuity.

The sisters survived on a combination of tuition from their pupils' parents, fees for music lessons and donations from benefactors. When this wasn't enough—and quite often it wasn't—they recycled newspapers to get money for schoolbooks. "Begging was not uncommon," says one account of their early history.

There were the "bees" where women and men from the community gathered with the sisters to collect and preserve chickens, corn, cherries, tomatoes and strawberries for the convent pantry. Merchants and physicians often provided goods and services at a discount or for free. Older sisters contributed their inheritances.

Then, as Mother Gertrude discovered, there were always the banks. She repeatedly bought property, assuming large mortgages and managed, somehow, to pay her debts on time. By the time she signed the mortgage for the mansion, the Mercies and their ways had become part of Cedar Rapids. Despite constant financial problems, they tended to blend right in.

In the cool of early summer mornings and evenings, younger sisters were regularly dispatched from the mansion to pick wild strawberries in the surrounding fields. One day a neighbor and a non-Catholic visitor were driving down a nearby road as three sisters, dressed in the traditional black habits and white veils of novices, stooped over to fill their baskets.

The newcomer was impressed: "The man who owns that fine herd of Holsteins is certainly well off!"

It was Mother Gertrude who was in charge of the "Holsteins," and humor was one of the tools she used to manage them. Once when two of her postulants (beginners) made off with a hospital bakery truck to drive around the grounds for a lark, she confronted them upon return. Having started their adventure, she told them, they should have made the most of it. "You should have gone to Fairfax."

Sometimes when she found a postulant deep in prayer in the chapel, she would sneak in and whisper in an other-worldly voice: "Every night before you go to bed, ask God for the grace of perseverance in your holy vocation."

Most of them did persevere. One of Mother Gertrude's biggest jokes was the mansion itself. The three-story building was built in 1856 by Judge George Greene, an Englishman who modeled it after the country homes of noblemen he had seen from afar while growing up in his native Staffordshire. When it came to developing Cedar Rapids, Judge Green was a kind of one-man embodiment of the American spirit of self-reliance. He surveyed its streets and promoted its real estate while also functioning as a state judge, lawyer, newspaper editor and railroad president.

Put all of that together and it spelled money. The judge used his to assemble Mound Farm. In the 1870s it sprawled over almost nineteen hundred acres. He hired an English gardener to landscape it, planting trees, a vineyard and an orchard. His house had sixteen rooms with four white marble fireplaces and black walnut woodwork. It was furnished with oil paintings and furniture the judge imported from New York.

For Iowa, in those days, it was a palace, but the judge had forgotten one crucial thing. He died in 1880 without leaving a will. That tied up the mansion in a long legal battle. Although it was foreclosed upon and offered at auction, none of the locals had the money to buy it. Meanwhile the mansion deteriorated. A nearby farmer found the ballroom was a handy place to store his wheat.

Mother Gertrude had done nothing to disabuse the young sisters, who continued to ooh and ah during their tour of the mansion. But once darkness began to fall, they found the long-neglected mansion took on a strange, haunted look: "A great gloom was settling over everything. It

Judge Greene's mansion, circa 1935. (COURTESY OF THE SISTERS OF MERCY OF CEDAR RAPIDS, IOWA)

was all just right for one of Poe's most horrendous stories," recalled Sister Xavier.

Then, as they settled into their beds, the walls came alive with scratching, scampering and squeaking. Their palace was alive with rats! They spent the night hunting them down with broomsticks, and the next day, the first of many cleanup assignments were handed out. Sister Xavier, like a good Mercy, fell into the spirit of the thing. "It was wonderful . . . to see the beautiful wood and marble come out from their coats of dust and dirt. And there's nothing like house-cleaning to keep up a spirit of camaraderie."

That morning Mound Farm had a new beginning. The mansion became Sacred Heart Convent and the hilltop was renamed Mount Mercy. What drove most of the women who took up life in the mansion was a much different spirit than the one that had propelled Judge Greene. His belief was that thrift and hard work accumulated wealth. The nuns were mostly farm girls who had learned from their fathers about the wild, popping sound as the first plows tore through the thick prairie sod. Hard work and thrift, for them, were part of daily life, part of the continuing fight to eke out a living off the land.

A Cedar Rapids schoolteacher, Grant Wood, later gave us the enduring symbol of this part of America in a famous painting called *American Gothic*. A simple, almost dour painting of a work-worn farmer and his wife, standing in front of their plain white farmhouse, it won a medal from the Art Institute of Chicago in 1930.

Wood had posed it, using his sister and his dentist as models, but the painting evoked something that was hauntingly real for millions of Americans. Unlike Judge Greene, who had prospered, all this couple had to show for years of backbreaking labor was barely enough to live on. There was richness in their lives, but for the couple in *American Gothic* it was not measured in dollars and cents.

The real models for *American Gothic* could have been found in almost any surrounding farm community. In Ryan, Iowa, a small town of immigrants from Germany and northern Ireland, there was Arthur L. Lyness, a farmer. The son of Irish immigrants, he didn't have shoes when he was a boy.

He was bright and did well in school, but after three years his family pulled him out because they needed him to help work the farm. During the first winter in Iowa, their farmhouse burned down. Lyness soldiered on with his father and brothers, stuffing hay into the walls of a draughty corncrib to keep warm and eating potatoes and salt pork.

Farming has always had an element of gambling in it, but in those days the odds were daunting. Farm prices went up and down like roller coasters and banks had a tendency to fail. In the financial turmoil of the 1890s, the Lyness family lost the farm, but Arthur and his brother later bought it back, heavily mortgaged.

Arthur married Catherine Devine, a skilled seamstress who was known to everyone in the small farming community as "Kit." "She had an infectious sense of humor and could make the best of any situation," recalls Lucille, their youngest daughter. Kit and Arthur made a go of the farm, but it sometimes brought them to the very edge of their endurance.

Lucille remembers her mother talked often of the early years when Arthur rose before dawn to milk the cows and to deliver the milk in the buggy to the local creamery. His chores continued through the day and well into the night until he "often collapsed from sheer exhaustion."

But Arthur was a survivor. He carefully plotted the peaks and valleys of crop prices and gradually worked the debt off the farm. His policy was a strict, pay-as-you-go process. If you didn't have the money for it, you didn't buy it. He had seen too many neighbors fail.

That meant the family lived very frugally. One exception he made was for books, newspapers and magazines. He would scatter them around the house, hoping to tempt Lucille and her four brothers into learning about the world beyond the farm.

Another exception came when others needed help. Arthur pitched in to sponsor church picnics and fund-raising drives. He built part of the Catholic church in Ryan. When the parish priest, a tall, broad-shouldered young man, Rev. John Malloy, appeared at the farm one night to explain that he had to have five hundred dollars, Arthur quietly agreed to mortgage his pigs. "My father never wanted attention. He just went about his life helping people," recalled his daughter. "My brothers would say they knew more about the neighbor's chores than they did ours."

Both Arthur and Kit were religious. Every Sunday morning, after Arthur finished the chores, they would put on their Sunday clothes, load up the family and make the seven-mile drive to church. One Sunday in 1918, as they were driving to Mass, the family car was struck by a drunk driver. Their oldest daughter, Mary, Arthur's favorite, was thrown out of the car and killed. It was their misfortune to become the victims of the first auto accident in the vicinity of Ryan. Mary was eight years old. She had just made her first Holy Communion.

It was a senseless tragedy that would have sent some fathers into deep depression, but Arthur didn't seem to falter. "People who knew us felt his love for Mary transferred to me. I just could do no wrong in his eyes," explains Lucille. At the time of the accident, she was only eight months old.

Her first vivid insight into this strong, silent man came in eighth grade when she won the county spelling bee. An older teacher whom Lucille didn't know came up to give her a hug afterward. The woman introduced herself. She had been Arthur's teacher when his family pulled him out of third grade.

Arthur had been such a promising pupil that the teacher explained how she had gone to his family, offering to give him private lessons at home. The family refused, saying there was no time he could spare from farm chores for that. "This hug," the teacher said, "is for your father."

From that point on, according to Lucille, the great goal in her life was to become a teacher. Using the power of learning to transform lives, she felt, was something she wanted to become involved with. Teaching also provided a path out, a way of ending the poverty of opportunity that she could see settling like a leech on the countryside in the early 1930s as the nation began to feel the despair of the Great Depression.

Lucille went to a Catholic high school, taught by Presentation sisters. On the farm she indulged in one of her passions, which was racing horses. Arthur was a superb horseman and he raised some palominos that she and her brothers would ride. She learned to drive the family Chevrolet and sought out opportunities to chauffeur her father on errands. Like many fathers, he kept a firm grip on the door handle as she tested the car's limits on tricky gravel roads. Arthur might have had to bite his tongue, but he said very little.

On Saturday nights Lucille went to barn dances, often accompanied by her two older brothers. The local "band" often consisted of a drummer, a violinist and an accordion player. But this was the age of radio; "Let's Dance" played on fifty-three stations every Saturday night in a coast-to-coast hookup. Players in small-town America could do fair imitations of a spectrum of bands, from Benny Goodman's swing to the rhumbas of Xavier Cugat. Dancing was what everybody did on the weekends. On warm nights in the early summer, Lucille learned the Charleston and the fox-trot, dancing on the rough-hewn floors of cavernous haymows, which remained empty until the first crop of hay was cut, dried in the fields and then gathered.

Prohibition had ended, but by law, Iowa was still a "dry" state. The sale of liquor by the drink was forbidden. Even the alcohol content of beer was regulated, but there were nights when the rules that governed the teenage society of Ryan were lubricated by some of the boys in the neighborhood, who would drive to Illinois, returning with a trunk load of more potent brew. Some of them were Lucille's boyfriends.

They're all dead now, but sometimes she finds herself thinking about them. By her midteens, Lucille was already seriously weighing the idea of becoming a nun. The boyfriends she'd had, the possibilities of becoming

Lucille Lyness and her family, including her father, Arthur (with bow tie), and her mother, Kit (seated to the right). The picture was taken in July 1935, two days before Lucille entered the convent. (COURTESY OF SISTER MARY ROBERTA)

a farm wife, she thinks, helped her make a mature choice. "I don't know how you can make a decision like that if you haven't had that kind of experience," she explains.

Kit helped with her decision. As Lucille recalls, she was a kind of perfectionist. "Whether planting a garden, raising chickens, or sewing, or performing the regular household tasks, she . . . had a strong sense of purpose. Her motto was that whatever was worth doing, was worth doing well."

Kit had been taught at an academy for women in Manchester, Iowa, that was run by the Sisters of Mercy. The experience had given her a love for music and the arts. On many nights in the kitchen, working with Lucille, Kit often talked about her experiences, how the Mercies would sometimes walk the neighborhoods, visiting the sick and helping the poor. "I was fascinated by that," remembers Lucille.

The idea of becoming a teacher burned in her mind. For that, she needed to go to college, but there was little money for college in the early 1930s and her father was seriously distracted by the crash of the financial markets. Lucille remembers going quietly downstairs one night and seeing him pacing the floor while Kit quietly said her rosary.

The local bank, which kept the money they needed to operate the farm, was on the verge of collapse. A few days later President Roosevelt declared a bank holiday and freed up emergency payments for farmers. The move saved the Lyness farm and made an instant New Deal supporter out of Arthur.

Still, the young woman knew that with four brothers there was nowhere near enough money to send one, let alone four, to college. She told her father she would go to work and save money for tuition. To her father, that seemed a dubious proposition. Jobs were scarce and low paying. College tuition was expensive.

Then, she let it all spill out. She wanted to become a teacher, but not just an ordinary one. She was determined to become a Catholic sister. Arthur, she recalls, was torn. "I remember him saying to me 'I would never come between God and a vocation [a calling to religious life], but I wish you would go to college for a year first.' I think he thought I was too young, then, to make the decision."

The dilemma was resolved when Lucille received an offer of a scholarship from a new school, founded in Cedar Rapids in 1928. It was Mount Mercy Junior College and it was located next to Sacred Heart Convent, a renovated brick mansion on a hill.

A year later, in 1935, Lucille Lyness became a postulant and began her life in "God's Mansion." That meant a day driven by the ringing of bells. She rose at 5:15 A.M. when the bells rang for chapel, then they rang for morning prayer, and after that, breakfast. Then it was time for chores, tidying up the mansion. Then the bells rang for study period. Then lunch with more prayers.

In the afternoon she attended classes in the newly built academy building, named Warde Hall, one more edifice to the memory of Frances Warde, the fiery young woman who had led the Mercies to America. Class time was followed by dinner and prayers at the mansion.

Finally, there was recreation. Sometimes it was sewing, sometimes it was playing baseball. The team's tomboy pitcher, Lucille Lyness broke her finger trying to make a catch. On snowy winter nights recreation went on Mount Mercy's splendid toboggan run. Then the neighborhood echoed with the shrill *EEEEEEEEeeeeee!* of excited young women as they shot down the hill and threaded their way through the trees. At eight-thirty there was lights out and no more talking until dawn, a period known to Mercies as the Grand Silence.

There was Mother Aloysius, an elderly, heavyset woman, who was in charge of the novices. She enforced various restrictions, including rules that severely limited family visits and prohibited trips in the outside community without an approved escort. She insisted on teaching the young women how to sew, although some of them sewed better than she did.

The transition from a life of independence on the farm to one where the convent bells measured each beat of your day, like some dictatorial metronome, must have been wrenching for some. In a 1997 interview, looking back at this from the vantage point of age seventy-nine, Lucille seemed to have blotted out that part. "I don't remember the don'ts as much as I remember the do's. They're like handrails that you hang onto when you're going up the steps."

That may have been Kit's influence, struggling to make the very best of any situation. The change may also have been eased by her new "family," many of them young, bright farm girls like Lucille. She no longer felt so isolated in her love for books. There was Mildred Lense, an only child, who read constantly and always seemed full of witty stories and puns.

When Mildred returned to her family's farm, on one of her rare visits after joining the Mercies, her family and neighbors were amazed to see this daughter—who had been a kind of scruffy, jack-of-all-trades at the farm—encumbered in her black habit, starched coif and white veil. Inside, however, was the same girl. When the windmill jammed, she shinnied up the tall, wooden structure in her habit and greased the gears.

There was Sister Dolores Eagan, an older woman, but another great teller of stories, who would accompany Lucille on her visits back home to Ryan. Kit and Arthur enjoyed her and treated her like a second daughter.

In a simple ceremony on April 12, 1936, Lucille was formally received as a novice into the Sisters of Mercy. Her dark hair was cut short. She went from the simple black dress of the postulant to the black habit, starched coif and white veil of the novice. At that point the order requires sisters to take a new name, a saint's name to complete her shift from her family into the larger "family" of her order.

Lucille suggested three to her superior. Her first choice, of course, was

Arthur. A second choice was Robert, the name of her youngest brother. Conveniently, it was also the name of Saint Robert Bellarmine, a famous teacher and writer.

This is how Lucille Frances Lyness became Sister Mary Roberta, the name by which her fifty-one future classes of students remember her. She was about to meet the first batch of them because, at the end of their second year of college, young Mercies were sent out "on mission" for a year of student teaching.

She went to Alma, Iowa, pop. 500, where the parochial school needed someone to teach thirty-five students in combined seventh and eighth grades. They sat at their desks in a long, narrow room dubbed "the boxcar" and, as Sister Roberta recalls, she loved every minute of it. She was finally doing what she had long dreamed of doing, teaching.

She took the same approach to lessons in the boxcar as her father had taken to farming. It was a privilege and at the same time a mystery because the growing of corn or the improvement of young minds were both complex, definitely nonlinear processes, only part of which was man's control. There were risks, but there was also beauty in it. Her father would sometimes go out and stare in wonder as his growing crops carpeted the bleak soil of winter with green. As his daughter saw it, her "crop" was students.

Sister Roberta has fond memories of those students in the boxcar. She can rattle off the names that went with the faces that greeted her there every morning over sixty years ago: Clarke, Gardner, Koblassa, Ferry, Heineman, Fencil, Shannon.

One of the year's most exciting moments came in the late winter of 1936. There was a presidential campaign starting and Franklin Delano Roosevelt, her father's great new hero, planned a whistle-stop trip through Iowa. The President of the United States was coming to Alma!

"That gave us a good opportunity to teach them a little government," she recalls. It was George Washington's birthday. The air was sharp with cold and drifts of snow lined the railroad tracks as the sisters marched 120 students, primed with information about the Presidents, down to the station. They were to stand on both sides of the main line. Little boys vied with each other to see who could dance on the tracks the longest as the lines formed. The sisters pulled them farther back worrying that, somehow, they would wind up getting sucked under the train.

That proved to be a good precautionary measure. FDR's campaign special first materialized as a moving dot on the horizon, but Sister Roberta quickly got this eerie feeling. The train was not slowing down at all. After all the preparation, could it be that the President of the United States was not going to stop in Alma?

mmmmmmMMMMEEEEEEEEEOOOOOOOOOOOoooooo. The students stood frozen in attention and shock as the President's steam-driven special roared through this tiny dot on the map of America. It was doing better than seventy miles per hour because FDR had fallen behind schedule and there were more important stops ahead.

Sister Roberta recalls a face peering out at them from a window at the rear of the train as they recovered from the mighty whoosh. She thinks it might have been the president. "We watched him as he went down the track."

The capstone of the day was not that. It was a little boy, one of Sister Dolores's kindergarten students. He was found leaping up and down on top of a snow bank shouting at the top of his lungs: "WE JUST SAW GEORGE WASHINGTON!" It was not quite what the sisters had taught him. Still, he had learned. And as Sister Roberta came to appreciate, learning was a gift, like her father's fields of corn, a marvelous thing to witness, a thing just slightly beyond anyone's control.

12

BREAKING
MENCKEN'S LAW

The bleakest moment in the history of the hospital that has served downtown Baltimore for almost 150 years came on the frosty evening of November 1, 1887. A group of doctors who used the hospital to perform surgery and to teach medicine came to the conclusion that it was doomed.

On the west side of the city the University of Maryland was developing a hospital with a medical school. On the east side a medical colossus bankrolled by a local merchant, Johns Hopkins, was beginning to rise. Parts of the center of the city, which included the waterfront, were becoming seedy slums populated by wharf rats and bums.

While the inner city had its romantic places, the doctors' diagnosis was that few people were interested in keeping their hospital going. The one exception was this strange order of Catholic nuns, the Sisters of Mercy. For some reason they had agreed to take over nursing chores at the hospital.

To the modern mind, City Hospital, as it was called then, was hardly a hospital at all. It was more like a charnel house or a kind of medical warehouse reserved for very sick people. It featured stark contrasts between life and death. Some students observed autopsies. Others could watch delicate surgery. And sometimes they could switch back and forth because the procedures were performed in the same room, often at the same time.

City Hospital was poorly heated, poorly lit, chronically short of potable water. Its patients, often street people, enjoyed what they might have considered luxury accommodations: dingy twelve-by-fifteen-foot boxes.

"Disorder in the highest degree and uncleanliness of the most repulsive type made the City Hospital a place to be avoided by respectable visitors," says one early account of its status. What mystified the doctors that night was that the nuns had come in at all. Since then they had cleaned it up and now they were pledging to help the doctors buy adjacent land owned by the city. They proposed to build a new hospital there.

These doctors were hard businessmen. Some were fine surgeons when they weren't drinking. It had seemed like good business to bring in the nuns. Since the Civil War the Mercies' nursing skills had become legendary. Plus, they worked for almost nothing.

But now they were offering to buy what amounted to an equity in the place! It was bad enough that the nuns' interest in the land had provoked the city's Protestant ministers to gather two thousand signatures on a petition to get the mayor to queer the deal. But now the doctors had to grapple with the frankness of the priest who had recommended the Mercies in the first place, Rev. William E. Star. A gentle soul who was chaplain at the state penitentiary, he had just let them in on a little secret: To back up their dreams, the nuns had no money, not a dime, zippo.

That night the doctors had a very noisy meeting, but Dr. Aaron Friedenwald, one of the elders among them, enjoyed a moment of quiet satisfaction. After all, it was he who had warned them that they should have never gotten into business dealings with the nuns in the first place. They had no contracts, nothing to assure that the sisters would do anything at all as their part of the bargain. Now the doctors appeared stuck. "I am sick of the whole affair," he confided to his diary.

Dr. A. B. Arnold, the dreamer of the group, presented this prognosis: The nuns wouldn't be involved with City Hospital if it didn't pay them. Sisters of Mercy, he reasoned, were no different from the doctors. They both had faith in the almighty five-dollar bill. There had to be money there someplace, he concluded.

But there wasn't. The priest, a respected man in Baltimore, had said as much. Some of the doctors were religious, some—like many of Baltimore's city fathers—put what little faith they had in the goals of the old Confederacy, and some were outright atheists.

What galled them all was that they had believed the leader of the Mercies, Mother Mary Benedicta, when she blithely told them if they committed to get the land, she would build the new hospital and make it "one of the finest in the Union." By the end of the evening they resigned themselves to the fact that they had all invested in a dubious undertaking that would probably take them all down with it.

Within a month, Mother Benedicta turned this completely around. She convinced the city council to issue a long-term lease for the vacant lot near the hospital for a thousand dollars. As for the petition from the Protestant ministers, it never made it to the mayor.

One account of the Mercies' explains this. The petition "fell into the hands" of Mr. John M. Travelers, a city council clerk, "and he being a gentleman of the highest integrity, and of uncommonly good sense, quietly dropped all the papers filled with signatures into his very capacious desk, turned the key and left them to mature."

After that, Sister Benedicta ventured off to New York and Philadelphia to inspect models for her hospital. She commissioned three architects to flesh out what her vision of it should look like. In short, the new hospital was happening. The following September, at the laying of the cornerstone, the political muscle that she'd used quietly to make it happen came on public display.

There was Baltimore's cardinal, James Gibbons, resplendent in white silk vestments. The new hospital, he told the crowd, would rival Johns Hopkins. Marching in solemn procession before him came the Knights of St. Vincent, Knights of St. Ignatius, Knights of St. Patrick, Knights of Holy Cross, Knights of St. Augustine and all of the other fraternal orders that bound together in a common cause the Irish, German, Polish and Bohemian Catholic parishes of Baltimore.

They marched with "green, red and white plumes and shining helmets," processing down Calvert Street "with floating banners and stirring music." One historian noted that the "little sisters in their saintly garb and innocent faces stood at the windows of the hospital" and cheered them on.

As for the skeptical Dr. Friedenwald, he had an epiphany, a realization that these "little" sisters were hardly innocent of what had happened. "Political influence is the magic wand to succeed in this," he confided to his diary, "and the Sisters manage to hold it, and also know how to use it."

The problem that remained was money. The clientele of inner-city hospitals is not an attractive or prosperous lot. A young reporter for the *Baltimore Herald*, H. L. Mencken, often visited the emergency room of City Hospital to gather what reporters call color. He usually found it. The doctors at the hospital were always helpful, he wrote, "for they did a heavy trade in street and factory accidents, and a very fair one in attempted suicides."

Police reporters, especially young ones—Mencken was then still in his teens—often develop a knowing, ironic stance to shield themselves from their daily ration of poverty, misery, gore and death. Mencken, a shrewd wit and gifted writer, was the prototype for many of the rest of us who followed in his profession.

Here is some of the color he gleaned from hanging around the emergency room at Mercy: "In those days carbolic acid was the favorite drug among persons who yearned for the grave, just as bichloride of mercury was to be the favorite of a decade later, and I saw many of its customers brought in—their lips swollen horribly, and their eyes full of astonishment that they were still alive."

Mr. Mencken's funny, smirky police reporting vaulted him into the literary stratosphere of his day, probably too high and too quickly. His prominence as the "Bard of Baltimore" helped perpetuate a lifelong set of prejudices. He ridiculed women who aspired to professions. People he called blackamoors were frequently shuffling around in the background of his accounts of Baltimore life.

But his most potent venom was reserved for religious reformers and moral spokesmen who preached that "service" to others was a useful, redemptive path. He was so convinced they were wrong that he later formulated what he called Mencken's Law: "Whenever A annoys or injures B on the pretense of serving or improving X, A is a scoundrel."

Had he gotten beyond the emergency room, what was going on in

City Hospital might have astounded the young reporter because it violated all of his emerging tenets. Working long hours to heal the sick in the dirty, crowded, segregated wards for blacks was Sister Mary Veronica, a woman who was later given this description by one of the hospital's doctors: "She was not an educated woman, but she was a sensible and very good woman, and no work was too hard or too long for her." Whenever an emergency arose, day or night, she was there "showing gentle kindness to every patient."

In the hospital's office sat Sister Benedicta, a professional hospital administrator. She spent many days there tracing the social wiring of Baltimore, thinking up schemes to connect the city's rich to the hospital in ways that would boost health care for the poor. She developed numerous contacts in Baltimore's business community, convincing them that they benefited from a hospital located downtown.

She nurtured people like Madame Jerome Bonaparte, wife of a grandnephew of Napoleon and one of the social arbiters of Baltimore. After the Mercies took control of the hospital, Madame Bonaparte was among the first laywomen to walk the wards. Noticing that the patients had no bed linen, Madame Bonaparte "supplied the need at once."

By 1899 Sister Benedicta's sources had given her enough money to build the hospital, but she needed to raise still more. What she had was an empty new building. She had to raise more cash to furnish it. Where was that going to come from?

Running downtown hospitals in American cities has always been a dicey, difficult business. Some of the most successful and stubborn practitioners of the art have been Catholic sisters. Sister Benedicta's problem, to use Mencken's word, was that she hadn't "annoyed" enough people in her quest to complete a first-class hospital.

First on her new list of new people to annoy was the President of the United States, William McKinley. She sent two sisters to Washington to tell the President that what she really needed was the services of the Marine Band, then directed by John Philip Sousa. This was close to mission impossible. Sousa and his patriotic march music were to the America of the late 1890s what the Beatles were in the 1960s. Everyone wanted them.

But Sister Benedicta figured the President owed her a favor. In July 1898 the McKinley administration sponsored a huge military exercise at Chickamauga Park, Georgia. More than forty thousand soldiers—the largest gathering since the Civil War—were encamped. They held grand parades on this old Civil War battleground and newspapers gushed forth many columns about the glories of the first large postwar exercise uniting soldiers from the North and the South. The men whose fathers had worn the blue and gray were now united in a grand new cause!

The public devoured such stories because it was the height of the frenzy of the Spanish American War. Unfortunately, there was also a less than glorious side to Chickamauga. Four thousand five hundred of its soldiers wound up on their backs in makeshift hospitals battling typhoid fever after drinking filthy water. President McKinley, who had read of the heroics of the nuns in the Civil War, invited some to come and nurse the soldiers.

His war department, which seemed to be afflicted with amnesia about the Civil War, resisted the proposal, saying the presence of ladies in the field hospitals would embarrass the men. As newspaper accounts of the horrible conditions at the encampment piled up, the war department relented. The nuns could come, but only if they enlisted under their family names and signed regular U.S. Army contracts for nurses.

Eleven Mercies came from Baltimore to join women from four other orders, led by the Sisters of Charity, who enlisted for the duration. When they arrived at Chickamauga, the Mercies were lined up, sworn in by a major, introduced to Army beef and bacon and assigned quarters in tents alongside a Kentucky regiment. The new enlistees were issued Army blankets for use as rain gear.

Sister Nolasco McColm, a forty-three-year-old Mercy nurse, was excited about her abrupt introduction to military life and recorded it all in her diary. The dismal part, she wrote, came when they were shown their ward in the Army's Third Division Hospital. There were more than four hundred patients, most of them fever cases, lying in tents, some without flooring.

"It was impossible to keep sheets and blankets out of the dust, which on a rainy day became mud," she wrote. Most of the tents were jammed with eight cots so it was "almost impossible to get between them."

The few male orderlies she saw did very little treatment and even seemed ignorant of the cause of the typhoid. She watched them carry bedpans out of the tents and dump their contents into a pit, dug near the camp's drinking water supply. The bedpans were then reused without washing.

"We did for those men what had never been done for male patients before; bathed them, washed, combed and cut hair, cleaning heads of vermin, rubbed them, dressed their sores, did everything with few necessaries and under very trying circumstances," Sister McColm noted.

Out of one hundred patients, the Mercies lost only six. While they had a few confrontations with bigots, the Mercies soon became comfortable with military life and came to call their new home Mushroom Town, after the beige canvas Army field tents that seemed to blossom everywhere. Their tent included a puppy they promptly named Theodore Roosevelt.

"We were loath to leave dear old Chickamauga," she wrote. "We had many privations, yet much consolation." Later, when the Mercies were recalled to Baltimore, they were miffed. "Everybody was distressed," she wrote, because the nuns wanted to go on to Cuba where the fighting was.

Still, they had had an adventure. "Uncle Sam sent us home in fine style," she remembered. After being mustered out, they were each issued tickets for sleeper cars from Atlanta and given three dollars each for subsistence on the way home. But there was a gap in their ranks. Sister Elizabeth Flannagan didn't make the trip.

After working around the clock in the fever wards of Mushroom Town, she was found to be infected with typhus. She had come home earlier in a metal coffin. Her fellow nurses wrote a poem about her. "And who, then, is Elizabeth?" it says. "The one who now doth rest in death! For God and country she hath died."

It seems clear that Mencken, with his low opinion of people who give service to others, wouldn't know what to make of this, but Sister Benedicta did. She planned a fund-raising "fair," featuring John Philip Sousa's band. All of Baltimore was invited. All the two nuns going to Washington had to do was carry her request to the White House. Once they did that, their mother superior had instructed them, President McKinley would take care of the rest.

They left Baltimore on the three P.M. express. "I was never in Washington before in my life. Never saw a President, except in pictures," recalled Sister Mary Borgia Leonard. When they arrived at the White

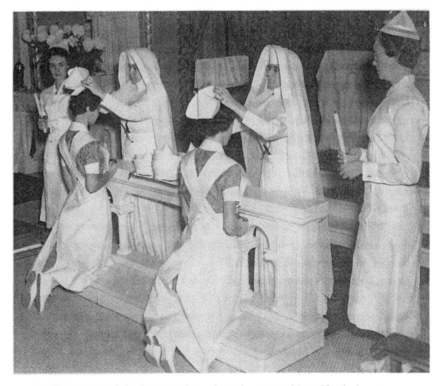

Instructors award the cap to newly graduated nurses at Mercy Hospital,
Baltimore, circa 1940. (COURTESY OF THE SISTERS OF MERCY OF THE AMERICAS)

House, they learned that President McKinley was out riding his horse and
was too busy afterward to see them.

They were then referred to the Secretary of State, who told them he
was the wrong man to deal with this. He sent them to see the Secretary of
the Navy. For many seekers of favors in Washington, this story might seem
terribly familiar, except that, for the nuns, it had a happy ending.

The following morning they met the Secretary of the Navy, who listened intently to the reason for their mission and then signed an order
commanding Mr. Sousa and the Marine Band to pack their instruments
and deploy to Baltimore. Sister Benedicta's fair was a huge success, raising
more than twenty thousand dollars. Now she had a new hospital *and* furniture.

The confusion over who really ran City Hospital was ended in 1909. Under the leadership of a formidable new administrator, Sister M. Carmelita Hartman, its name was changed to Mercy Hospital. She forged an even stronger alliance with the business community, and in 1911 her hospital sprouted a new wing.

Businessmen came to like her "take charge" attitude, which, for Sister Carmelita, came with whatever territory she happened to inhabit. Born Marie Estelle Hartman, she had had a reputation of being first, taking leadership positions and finishing whatever job she'd started. It started in grade school at Immaculate Conception parish in Baltimore, where she may have been the quintessential parochial school student—at least from the nuns' point of view.

A classmate later described her: "Being rather shy in her manners, she was not particularly attractive to the children, but she was most obedient and exact and was considered a most desirable pupil."

In 1893 she entered the Sisters of Mercy, where the classmate (who also became a Mercy, probably under her influence) assumed she was simply destined to run large organizations. "As a child she was born to command and this ran through her whole religious career."

In her second year in the convent she was made principal of a school. Later she was sent to Washington to open St. Aloysius, a school for boys. She focused it, laserlike, on street children. Her enrollment reached more than five hundred boys, many of them described as "overgrown, ungraded and undisciplined."

At Mercy Hospital, she transformed the business side, reinforcing the financial footings of the hospital and using part of the income to broaden its medical research and enlarge its medical team. She set about applying the Mercy formula with a vengeance: The poor came first, but the hospital had to generate the money to care for them.

She may have been the Mercies' ultimate grind. One analyst of her thoroughness traced it back to a relative who made a chance remark that she had overheard as a child. The remark was "Stella is a winsome little girl, but she never sees anything through to its end."

There was no facet of Mercy Hospital that Sister Carmelita Hartman didn't see through to the end. Under her hand "Mercy," as the locals call it, became a fixture of downtown Baltimore. Police and fire units made

Mercy's emergency room their hospital of choice. After Sister Carmelita left in 1917, to become the treasurer and later mother superior of the Baltimore Mercies, Mercy became the hospital-for-all-seasons for downtown Baltimore.

During the Depression hundreds of men lined up at the rear of the hospital at noon, when the nuns fed them soup and bread. After World War II, when many of the other hospitals in the city opted to move to the suburbs, Mercy Hospital raised $6 million and took on $30 million in debt to rebuild itself and remain rooted where it was, serving the inner-city poor.

The Mercies made sure their philosophy about running hospitals was contagious. They started a nursing school in 1898 that produced thousands of nurses in the region. "They were good nurses," recalls Sister Mary Thomas, who became one of the hospital's nursing instructors after World War II. "I don't know how many hospitals would simply take our nurses and never even ask for a recommendation."

In the late 1940s, Sister Thomas, among the youngest on the staff, recalls being summoned to the bedside of a very old woman. After pioneering as the first "Mother General" of the Sisters of Mercy in the United States, Sister Carmelita had come back to Mercy Hospital to die.

"She didn't know me, but she knew I was teaching the nurses. She wanted to see who I was," recalls the younger nun. It was a passing of the torch. Sister Thomas later became the hospital's administrator.

The story of Baltimore's Mercy Hospital is certainly not peculiar. It is a theme that has hundreds of variations in America. About 15 percent of the nation's hospital beds are in Catholic hospitals. They employ more than 774,000 people. Many of them, located in the inner cities, did not simply burst out of the ground. Sisters put them there.

Contrary to the doubting doctors, the prognostications of the young Mr. Mencken or the current proponents of "market forces" in medicine, it was not what they thought, but the force of the prayers, the sacrifices, the determination and the skill of these women in drawing help from the community that kept the whole enterprise going.

13

"THERE SHOULD BE UNIFORMITY"

One day in the early 1930s Mother M. Carmelita Hartman, a small, sharp-featured woman, arrived at a Mercy convent at Loretto, Pennsylvania. A small town nestled in the rugged Alleghenies, Loretto had already been a stage for some of the Catholic Church's more interesting historic figures.

The first was a Russian prince, Demetrius Gallitzen. Prince Gallitzen had abandoned a promising career as an officer in the Russian Army to become a simple parish priest. As the first American priest to receive all of his preparation in the United States, Father Gallitzen had thrown his heart and soul into developing Loretto, a colony of immigrants established in the early nineteenth century. He wanted to make it a model American Christian community.

He had laid out Loretto's streets, served as its main doctor and tried to set an example for its people by living simply in a log cabin, where he slept on the floor and wore homespun clothes. When he died, in 1840, there were six thousand Catholics in Loretto. One of the problems with Father Gallitzen's approach was that he was performing without a network. There was no backup, no continuing organization to assure that his example and his good works would survive after his death.

Later in the decade Mother Frances Warde, the strong-willed pioneer of the Sisters of Mercy in the United States, came in to fill the void. Part of her order's charm was its loose, free-wheeling organization and its continuing influx of young women. She established a convent in Loretto and gave it a mission, which was to to carry on Father Gallitzen's work.

And now, almost a hundred years later, here was Mother Carmelita. She was interesting, too, but in another way. In 1929 representatives of about 5,000 of the nation's 9,308 Sisters of Mercy had created a new post and then elected her to fill it. She was named the order's first Mother General, and given the task of unifying the Mercies. At the time the order operated out of sixty independent mother houses. They were scattered all over the United States.

Mother General Carmelita, then fifty-seven, may have lacked some of the humility of Father Gallitzen or the innovative flair of Mother Warde. What she brought to Loretto was her strong sense of order. As one account of her arrival describes it, the convent was filled with excited young women wearing white veils. They were nervously awaiting her arrival and milling around. Many of them were novices and they had composed a song of welcome for the Mother General.

Their problem was that Mother Carmelita had arrived early and their regular piano player, who had rehearsed the song, had wandered off somewhere. So a young woman from Kansas City, whose specialty happened to be jazz, was substituted. There were lots of giggles in the room as she banged out an up-tempo version of "You're Welcome to Loretto." It was a Mercy moment. The tradition of good-humored silliness in music and verse in the order went straight back to the order's founder, Catherine McAuley, in Ireland. It was regarded as one of the strengths of the Sisters of Mercy, a lightheartedness that kept them together in difficult times.

But for Mother Carmelita, strength was in order, not in fooling around. As the singing went on, she whipped out a ruler and began measuring the novices' habits. The rules were that they should be only so many inches off the floor and could have only so many pleats. She quickly identified some that were out of compliance "I doubt she heard a word," recalls one of the young nuns, Sister M. Regis Leahy. "She was so busy getting them to look alike."

Making the Mercies look alike and act alike was a daunting task in the 1930s. The goal of the unprecedented 1929 convention, held in Norwood, Ohio, was to establish the Mercies' first national organization, the Sisters of Mercy of the Union. Leaders representing over a third of the members of the order had indicated their preference by simply not responding to the invitation.

The absent leaders were from parts of New England, the Midwest and the West Coast. Among them was Cedar Rapids, where the leadership was absorbed in community work and leery of interference by outsiders. Others had been instructed by their bishops not to join. But the Norwood meeting went on without them, driven by a concern that there needed to be closer cooperation among the American Mercies.

One pressing reason was backseat driving by bishops, who were creating a crazy quilt of rules, newly invented variations and add-on customs that Mother Carmelita was elected to straighten out. In Massachusetts, for example, a bishop had decreed that it was in the best interest of the Church to ban the Mercies from visiting the sick, one of the things they were founded to do.

Bishop O'Connor, who had helped Frances Warde start the Mercies' first foundation, in Pittsburgh, had warned her that this might happen. Uneasy about the order's rapid growth, he wrote Mother Warde, reminding her that she had had phenomenal luck in attracting and trusting wise people. But splinter groups sometimes left the Mercies to form their own foundations, seemingly when they felt like it. If she couldn't provide some control over the order's structure, he warned her, Rome would. "Until all the world enrolls in the class of the prudent, checks and guides will be required for the common run," he told her.

By the turn of the century patches of imprudence began appearing in the Mercies' far-flung organization. In Oregon, several Mercy hospitals and schools had had to close because the nuns had made no provision for training young nurses and teachers. Just what the "checks and guides" should be for problems like this, however, was a tough question for the nuns.

Sisters in the South, accustomed to working in largely non-Catholic communities, had a relaxed attitude toward the rules that was not shared by their Yankee sisters in New England. And what the Mercies did in New England shocked the Mercies in Cincinnati, where the leaders were super-strict. Mercies in the West, many of whom had frontier adventures fresh in their minds, acquired a swagger that resisted rules. Who needed rules from afar? What they saw of the Church, they had built.

Many other orders of nuns were also struggling with this amalgamation process at about this time. A lot of them failed, remaining fragmented and unable to resist the multiple whims of bishops. But the Mercies had chosen a woman equipped to operate on a national stage.

Mother Carmelita had a shrewd business sense that had helped build a major hospital in Baltimore and she was later elected to head the overall Mercy establishment in Baltimore, which included schools, a novitiate and a college. In this job she became known for her "born to command" style.

But the emergence of Mother General Carmelita and her campaign to make her order a strong, independent voice in the Church left many U.S. bishops unimpressed. While they were the spiritual heirs of Father Gallitzen, the Russian prince who humbled himself before his flock, humility did not adequately describe their approach. Some of these men simply felt that they were born to command nuns.

According to the Mercies' history of the amalgamation, George Cardinal Mundelein of Chicago fiercely opposed the idea of a Mercy union and ordered the Mercies in Chicago not to vote on the matter at all. Bishop Karl J. Alter of Toledo, Ohio, convinced the majority of Mercies in his diocese to vote against it. Bishop August J. Schwertner of Wichita pressured the Mercies in Fort Scott, Kansas, to vote against it and then sat in on their vote to make sure they did.

When Mother General Carmelita asked to meet with him about this in 1935, Bishop Schwertner refused and raised the familiar issue of turf. He sent word that she was forbidden to meet with the sisters in their convent at Fort Scott, which was in his diocese. So she held a discreet meeting with Mother M. Madeline Feely, the head of the Fort Scott Mercies, on a train.

Eventually a compromise, of sorts, was worked out. The Mercies could vote to become a chapter in the new union as long as Bishop Schwertner could keep his position presiding as the head of this otherwise all-female assemblage. He might have felt uncomfortable in the position of self-appointed honorary nun, but he still had what many bishops prized most: the appearance of control.

The Mother General relentlessly pushed her point that, under church law, the sisters had a right to govern themselves. Shortly after her election, she brought in reinforcements. She petitioned the Vatican to name an Italian cardinal, Pietro Fumasoni-Biondi, as the union's "cardinal protector" in Rome; in 1933 her request was granted. When Rome weighed in on behalf of the Mercies, that made a difference.

For example, in 1936 Bishop Alter informed the Mercies in his district he was having second thoughts. They would get another chance, by secret ballot, to vote on joining the union. This time they decided to join.

The idea of belonging to a larger organization, one that was no longer strictly under the thumb of the local bishop, was exhilarating to some of the younger nuns. "I felt ten feet high. I was thrilled to belong to a huge organization. I felt secure," recalled one of the Ohio sisters involved, Sister M. Vincent Frazer. The new organization also gave Mother General Carmelita a freer hand to spread around her resources, to move sisters from one diocese to another and to standardize the training of young sisters.

She also gained some financial resources, asking each of the six provinces of Mercies for donations to help her buy a headquarters for the newly forming union. Just how they were able to respond so generously as the country entered the Great Depression is not clear, but in 1930 Mother General Carmelita plunked down $400,000 for a handsome Italianate villa in suburban Montgomery County, Maryland, just outside Washington, D.C.

Sited on a thousand acres, the villa included a large manor house, several other dwellings, a garage and some well-equipped barns. What the previous owners had used it for is also not clear, but the place had a mysterious, Gatsbyesque air about it. Neighbors had become accustomed to the roar and clatter of lavish parties and had witnessed a lot of fast cars and fancy people coming and going at all hours of the night during the heyday of Prohibition.

It took the sisters a few days to trace the source of a strong, sweet odor that tended to drift through the cavernous house. After they found it, according to the union's history, it took federal agents "three days to bottle the whiskey found in the cellar and cart it away in U.S. government trucks."

After that the Mother General and her staff constructed a chapel on the polished floor of the manor's ballroom and built a suite of offices where they put in long hours developing the order's first complete set of personnel files. Seeing this budding seat of power growing in his back-yard, another critic of the union, Archbishop Michael J. Curley of Balti-more, ridiculed it, referring to it as "Vatican City."

Mother General Carmelita set up a standard bookkeeping system and authored a set of uniform rules for the sisters. She banned night meetings, even for religious or educational purposes, with people in the community. Automobile rides for "health or pleasure" were strictly forbidden. Sisters could visit their families "only in case of trouble, illness or death."

The Mercies' new union was divided into six provinces and the Mother General spent a lot of her time traveling from one to the other, examining each to make sure her new rules were uniformly observed in the many mother houses in her domain. There was no court of appeals for her decrees. She was like the inspector general touring her new army.

In the chapel in Webster City, Missouri, for example, she found there were no kneelers for the sisters who prayed there. She ordered some to be installed. She also found the sisters there seemed to be undernourished. They had been fasting too much, she decided, to sustain them in their work. Their diet was improved.

When she wanted to, she could be very charming. When a priest refused to meet her in Paducah, Kentucky, saying he didn't want to meet any "big bugs," she went out of her way to persuade him, getting him to drop his opposition to the union. She could also be quite abrupt. When the bishop of Ogdensburg, New York, informed her that he was ordering the sisters in his diocese to take a special set of college courses, Mother Carmelita just said no.

She could be autocratic and petty. She banned fancy tombstones for departed sisters. "There should be uniformity in the cemetery," she wrote. Among the many letters she dashed off to leaders of the Mercy provinces is one to Mother M. Kilian Baptist of St. Louis complaining that her sisters made use of hand fans in the summer, a practice that did not conform with Mercy regulations.

When Mother Kilian responded that the weather got "oppressively warm" in St. Louis, the Mother General responded regally. Mother Kil-ian, she wrote, shouldn't feel obliged to explain the order. She should just carry it out: "In writing to the various houses you may say that it is my wish to have the use of fans by the sister discontinued."

A lot of the letters she received were requests to modify the sisters'

Mother M. Carmelita Hartman, the first Mother General of the Sisters of Mercy.

habits. Sisters had begun to drive by the 1930s and the Mercy veils, designed for an earlier century, blocked their side vision.

The veils also presented other dangers. During a 1938 ceremony welcoming new novices in Cincinnati, one of the nuns strayed too close to a candle and caught fire. "As she had the two white veils on her head with the two celluloid veil boards, it made quite a fire for a few minutes. However, we got the veil off her head and got her out of the chapel without causing too much commotion," reported Mother M. Carmelita Manning, then the head of the Cincinnati province.

But the Mother General denied most requests. Could hospital nuns wear white shoes and stockings? No, she wrote, adding a tart footnote: "I suppose the next request will be to wear low neck and short sleeve habits, no coif, etc."

By the late 1930s she began to see signs of the uniformity she had worked so hard to achieve. But it came with a price; the rigidity of her controls had put a strain on two of the Mercies' great strengths, their strong ties to the Catholic community and the spirit of spontaneity and humor that made the order continually attractive to a large number of young women.

As one of the younger sisters who joined the order then in Chicago, Sister M. Martina Schomas had memories that later proved prophetic: "Am I wrong in believing there was a growing tightening in discipline, an increased focus on unimportant minute details? Mother McAuley said, 'We must not make too many laws. If we draw the strings too tight they will break.' "

In 1941, Mother Carmelita was replaced by Mother M. Bernardine Purcell, a leader of the Cincinnati province, who brought some new tools to the job of running the fledgling union. One was resilience, another a sense of humor. As the strain and the pain of World War II afflicted the country, both would be much needed.

A former student recalled Mother Bernardine conducting a science experiment in 1913. It involved demonstrating the power latent in flowing water by using a wheel, run by a faucet. Nothing went the way the textbook said it would. The top of the faucet popped off and the powerful spray shot out at the nun, leaving her standing in front of her class, a sodden, dripping mass of black wool.

There were suppressed giggles as she crisply excused herself and sloshed out of the classroom. When she reappeared a few minutes later in a dry habit with a freshly starched coif, it was still funny. So she sat down and laughed about it along with her students.

Mother Bernardine also came to the mother generalship with a degree from Catholic University, a rarity for religious women at the time. She had seen, firsthand, how the jumble of daily required prayers and compulsory meditations in the chapel, added on over the years, gave young sisters very little time to do their main job, which was to prepare their lesson plans for students.

Throughout the war, finding ways to better prepare the teachers for the demands of their job—which was the Mercies' largest mission—was one of her top priorities. After the war, when the soldiers came home and the baby boom began, her concerns about this became even more pronounced.

Catholic school systems were exploding at the same time as what the newspapers referred to as the Atomic Age was beginning. Not many people understood what *atomic* meant in those days, but they did see that the society they knew was rapidly changing. During the war, women had become fixtures in the workplace. They performed men's jobs, earned high wages, drove cars, wore pants, jitterbugged with wild abandon and became accustomed to an unprecedented degree of personal freedom.

Could a religious order with hard rules that focused on long, often unpaid hours of teaching and nursing compete? Could women dressed in the penguinlike garb of Irish ladies from the 1840s attract the wild bobby soxers of the Atomic Age? This is what Mother General Bernardine was worrying and praying about. Like much of the Mercy experience in America, she knew she was in for another uncontrolled experiment. Somehow, the Lord would provide.

Sharon Burns usually wore bobby sox. On occasions that called for nylons, which were scarce during the war, she did what many young women did who preferred not to pay black market prices. She would paint her legs with pancake makeup and then have someone carefully draw long lines down the back, simulating the seams.

She was just sixteen when the war ended. One of the signs for her that society was changing was seeing thousands of young men, soldiers, returning from the war. They poured out of Union Station in droves and explored the streets of Washington, D.C., where she worked. To her, they were catnip.

A tall, striking strawberry blonde with blue eyes and a radiant smile, she'd done her patriotic duty during the war, working long hours, buying war bonds and attending USO dances where she would meet servicemen going to or coming back from the war. To her, they were so many young faces in a sea of uniforms. Then came one winter day in early 1946 when she found a young soldier staring at her in St. Aloysius Church. She had just gone to Confession and was walking up to the altar to pray. The soldier, a tall Army private with auburn hair, came to kneel nearby. She assumed then that when she rose to leave, he would.

This called for some serious meditation. Almost out of the blue, Sharon Burns, who had gone to public school and knew almost nothing about nuns, had decided she would become one. This young man presented a problem. "I said to myself, Burns you're going to enter the convent. But then I thought, wait a minute, even nuns ought to be able to admire a good-looking man."

The adagio in St. Aloysuis continued. When she rose to leave, he got up. When she reached the outer door, he was holding it, smiling at her. She smiled back. He said he was lost. Could she help him find the center of downtown?

Sharon had been hearing this from soldiers for weeks. "With all the others I would just tell them where the center of town was, but with him it was different. He was just so clean cut and sort of boyish," she recalls.

She decided to walk with him down South Capitol Street. St. Aloysius was just a few blocks north of the Capitol. It was early evening. The bustle of Washington was slowing. The trees around the gray, soot-encrusted Capitol building glistened with fresh snow. The streetlights came on, lending their sparkle to the moment. His name was Henry Hopkins. He was on his way home to Rhode Island and, when she got to her bus stop, he wanted to ride home with her.

"Oh, no you don't!" she blurted out.

The soldier was determined to get on the bus with her.

"Why would you want to do that?"

"I want to ask your mother for her permission to take you out."

"Oh, well, you don't really want to."

"Why not?"

"I'm going to become a nun."

She had supposed this was the time for the dance to end, but that didn't seem to phase him. "I have a cousin who's a nun," the young man said, nonchalantly, "and she's a hot sketch." (In the teen lingo of the twenty-first century, "hot sketch" translates roughly into "cool.")

"What kind of nun?"

"Oh, I dunno. She wears black and white."

"That's a big help."

So they took the bus to Seat Pleasant, Maryland, where she lived. Throughout her life, Sharon Burns has always tended to overprepare for things. She recalled as the bus rumbled north how she once brought home a stray collie. When she and the dog arrived at the door, her mother promptly sent it away. What would her mother do with a stray soldier?

While they were Catholic, Sharon's parents did not share their oldest daughter's enthusiasm for the convent. Her father had worked sporadically in factories during the Depression, moving the family from Pennsylvania to California and back to Washington in search of decent, more dependable jobs. Now he was heading a security guard unit at the U.S. Treasury. He went armed to protect armored cars. Defense always seemed to be uppermost on his mind.

He had devised a bulletproof career for Sharon, the eldest of his three daughters. His idea was that she should try to get a dependable office job in a government agency. As Sharon recalls: "He said go for the Veterans Administration. You'll always have work if you work for the V.A."

So that's what she had done, straight out of high school, starting as a secretary for the V.A. A year and a half later, when she announced that she had made up her mind to become a nun, her parents were really upset. "You're established in your work! Why do you want to lose a steady job?" her father blurted out.

He was shocked. Sharon cried. So did her mother. After twenty minutes, though, the storm was over. Her father was on his way down to the corner grocery to buy the ingredients for a luxury the family always indulged in on important occasions: hot fudge sundaes.

The result of all this was that for Mrs. Burns, the sight of Private Hopkins coming home with her daughter was a burst of sunlight. It was like old times. There were always young people from Maryland Park High School hanging around the house, hoping to see her daughter. Mrs. Burns liked the fact that there was plenty of action.

Her rule was no steady dating, and it was easy for Sharon to comply with. She had three boyfriends. She was on all the sports teams. She was the "canary," the popular, sweet-voiced lead singer who would front the high school's swing band, the Swing-O-Paters, and croon wartime hits such as "Don't Sit Under the Apple Tree."

She later attracted a following at Catholic Youth Organization dances where she would jitterbug with the best dancer in the school, a boy she had a crush on. This handsome young soldier who followed her daughter home was simply obeying a force of nature, concluded her mother. Why didn't he stay for dinner?

"We're Catholic. We're not eating meat tonight," she warned, reaching for another plate.

"That's okay. I'm Catholic." After dinner they had Mrs. Burns's permission to go to the movies.

Just how Private Hopkins led Sharon Burns to the Mercies is a convoluted story. Sharon's idea of becoming a nun began, as it does with many young women, with her father. Almost every day, before work, he took the streetcar to St. Aloysius to early Mass. He was an unusually kind man, always preparing breakfast for her and gently waking her in the morning with a wet face cloth.

While he never asked her to join him at morning Mass, Sharon found herself becoming intrigued. Where did all that love and gentleness come from? She began accompanying her father to St. Aloysius on their way to work.

There were nuns at St. Aloysius, but the idea of becoming one didn't take, at least not right away. "I was so glad I hadn't gone to Catholic high school," she recalls. "Nuns were almost forbidding looking. You'd see them walking downtown in twos, shopping or something, very self-possessed and distant. They didn't wear any makeup. I didn't see them as really being human."

The early mornings spent in prayer in church began to change that. She discovered there was a deep spiritual side to her life. Somehow she felt she was being called to spend her life working for God. She consulted a priest. How does one become a nun? He had shrugged. There were hundreds of orders.

He wrote out a list of eight that he felt she should visit. She should not appear overeager, he warned her, because the orders were all trying hard to recruit young women. By the time she met Private Hopkins, Sharon had visited two orders. She was working her way down her list.

Later that winter, after visiting several more, she went to the pastor of her church and told him she was about to enter one of them, the Sisters of the Holy Cross. The pastor, after noting that the Sisters of Mercy were last on her list, told her to be patient. "Wait on God's good pleasure, you don't have to hurry this."

Sharon went home that night in tears. Was it really God's good pleasure? Or was it the fact that the pastor was Irish and he was trying to steer her toward the Mercies because his sister was a member in Ireland? How was she to know?

She arrived home to find a thick letter waiting for her. It was from Henry Hopkins's cousin, who was about to take her final vows as a Mercy in Rhode Island. The woman who was described affectionately as the "hot sketch" was now a novice named Sister Mary Consilii. Her letter was full of enthusiasm for the Mercies and their mission.

The fact that Sharon had the Mercies last on her list was just right, wrote Sister Consilii. She compared it to the wedding feast at Cana where Jesus had saved the host from the embarrassment of running out of refreshments by making some excellent wine out of water. Sharon had "saved the best until last."

In the spring of 1946 Sharon finally reached the end of her list, trudging up a gentle hill in Georgetown to the Mercies' convent at Holy Trinity Church. Some orders had given her ponderous pitches on their mission and their traditions. One, which ran a university, had taken her to their theater to see a Greek play.

At the Mercy convent a young nun simply welcomed her by offering her milk and cookies. She was moved. "They were the only ones who fed me!" All that remained was to bring her parents to the convent to introduce them. The family didn't have a car, but that was not a serious problem. Sharon had one of her boyfriends drive them over to the meeting at the convent.

To this day Sharon Burns can't say just what it was that reached her heart and brought her into the Sisters of Mercy. She admits she had no idea what she was getting into. "I guess you could say," she explains, flashing her pyrotechnic smile, "that I felt there probably wouldn't be any more hot-fudge sundaes."

14

THE LITTLE BUDS

Sister Sharon Burns's first taste of teaching was an unruly class of seven-year-old boys at the Mount Washington Country School for Boys, a military school run by the Sisters of Mercy on a campuslike patch of North Baltimore. They wore blue-gray cadet uniforms, modeled after those worn at West Point. They were supposed to march in straight lines and to speak when spoken to.

At least that was the theory. After three years spent taking college classes at nearby Mount St. Agnes, the novitiate for the Baltimore province of the Mercies, the ex-bobby-soxer, was in love with theories. The learning experience fascinated her. Getting a college degree had once seemed impossible because the Burns family didn't have the money for sending one, let alone all three of their girls to college.

But by 1949 Sister Sharon was on her way to getting a degree in education. She could hardly wait. The parochial school couldn't wait. When she was still a "junior" sister, having taken only temporary vows as a religious, the order pulled her out of college. There was a vacancy in second grade that had to be filled. It later took her ten years of summer school to finish college. At first the change was terrifying. There she was facing this class of miniature officers. She knew she wasn't really ready to handle them.

"I found it so hard," she recalls. Practically every weekend she was in the superior's office crying. "They didn't tell us that I'd have to end up wiping up vomit all the time, pulling up flies and putting their boots on. I thought I would go in and teach and they would listen."

Next year, though, they did listen. It was another second grade class of thirty young "cadets," but these boys seemed to hang on her every word. There was Melvin Polek, who often volunteered to stay after school and clean the blackboards for her. He seemed perfectly at home, singing "Zippidy Do Dah" in a cloud of chalk dust as he hammered the erasers clean. Whap! "My oh my, what a wonderful day." Whap! "Plenty of sunshine headin' my way." Whap!

That was his way of trying to attract her attention, recalls Mr. Polek, now a systems engineer at Baltimore's Loyola College. "There wasn't a kid in that class that wasn't in love with that nun." As first graders, they had had a stern seventy-year-old as a teacher who made them march after school as punishment. Now here was this twenty-two-year-old beauty. "Aside from being pretty—and we couldn't see everything because she wore this habit—she was as sweet and kind as anybody we'd seen." The high point of his day came when she would sing to them in music class. "She had absolutely no disciplinary problems," he recalls.

After her rocky first year, Sister Sharon seemed more at home, as well. Standing in front of a class, she'd learned, was much more daunting than fronting for the Swing-O-Paters, her old high-school band. Still, she had gained confidence as a teacher and was beginning to enjoy it a little.

There was a creative side to Sister Sharon that tended to blossom when she was happy. In the novitiate, it involved dressing up her imaginary guardian angel in imaginary high-fashion clothes. Once, when she was marching her 1950 class of second-grade "cadets" to the classroom, one of them got excited about a caterpillar. This led her to write *Ikey the Milkweed Caterpillar*, an illustrated book for their science lesson. But it always seemed that just when she would begin to feel comfortable teaching one class in one school, the system would send her to another.

The next semester she was sent to the girls' school run by the Mercies at Mount St. Agnes. She was assigned to teach both fifth- and sixth-grade students, which meant twice the preparation time. She found the girls to

Sister Sharon Burns. "There wasn't a kid in that class that wasn't in love with that nun." (COURTESY OF SISTER SHARON BURNS)

be cool customers. She had replaced a popular teacher, and try as she might, she could not achieve the same rapport in the classroom as she had had with the previous class. Later she found that the girls had awarded her a nickname for her strenuous efforts. She was Sister Oh Be Joyful.

In the early fifties she was sent to Our Lady of Sorrows School. It was run by the Mercies for a Catholic parish in Birmingham, Alabama. That's where she learned more about the peculiar inner workings of parochial schools.

The school system was so overwhelmed by new students, it was running on the ragged edge. Just as she became accustomed to teaching sixth and seventh graders, her principal informed her they were hiring a lay teacher—one of the system's first. Because the new teacher refused to teach any grades besides fifth and sixth grade, Sister Sharon was being sent back to second grade.

That year, as she marched her class across the school's football-sized playground, she looked back to examine it. The file of youngsters stretched all the way across it. There were sixty-five of them, including one hyperactive boy who would regularly destroy her lesson plans and the classroom quiet she'd created because he was simply unable to stay in his seat.

She remembers turning and staring at the long line of little people following her that day, awed by the sheer amount of work they would mean for her in the year to come. "I said, 'This is my class?'"

The theory behind parochial schools, as they evolved, was that you can't have too much of a good idea. Various orders of sisters including the Mercies had had success running their own school systems, partly as a way to raise money. But beginning in the 1880s church leaders decided American Catholics needed a bigger, more uniform school system. It started with a nudge from Rome, which resulted in a decree from a meeting of American bishops, called the Third Plenary Council of Baltimore, held in 1884.

The decree said: "Near every church, when it does not already exist, a parochial school is to be erected within two years from the promulgation of this council, and to be kept up in the future, unless in the judgment of the Bishop the erection and maintenance of the school is impossible."

It seemed to be nearly an impossible task, being laid on a church that then consisted mainly of poor immigrants, but the decree sounded more onerous than it actually was. It left the matter of what was possible to be defined by the individual bishops. Within ten years after the decree the percentage of parishes with schools rose only slightly, from 40 to 44%, but the growth spurt was just getting underway. Catholic schools were rising everywhere.

In 1880 there were 2,246 schools with 405,234 students. By 1930 there were almost 10,000 schools with 2.5 million students. In 1965 the system peaked with 13,000 schools educating 5.5 million students. Roughly 12% of America's students, one out of every eight, were being educated in parochial schools. It had become the largest private-school system in the world.

There were several reasons for the growth. Immigrant parents worried that the culture of the boisterous new nation would erode their children's faith. Others were alarmed about the resilience of anti-Catholic bigotry. Still others, mainly the Irish, carried the gnawing fear that government control over public schools would inevitably lead to controls over Catholics that would force them back into poverty.

There were misgivings among some bishops, who wanted to spend more resources building bridges to the nation's non-Catholic majority, but the prevailing view in 1884 was to protect the faith by building a kind of educational fortress. As Bishop Bernard McQuaid of Rochester, New York, once described it, parochial schools were necessary to protect children from the "wolves of the world."

Other bishops were still more blunt about it. Archbishop John Hennessy of Dubuque, Iowa, would climb up into his pulpit and fulminate against public schools for being "breeders of infidelity and hot beds of hell."

But it took more than fulmination to build a rival school system. It meant bishops like Hennessy had to shake a lot of bricks-and-mortar money out of the pockets of the families sitting in the pews. They already supported the public school system with their taxes, but now they must also support the costs of constructing and staffing another school system. The essential ingredient that made this bold experiment work was the Catholic sisters. They did 95 percent of the teaching and administrative work in the schools from the very beginning.

Archbishop Hennessy's diocese, in eastern Iowa, was fairly typical of what was happening across the nation as the mission to build a national parochial school system gathered momentum. By 1900 there were seventy-eight schools, a third of them offering some high school. They were run by a spectrum of religious orders including the Sisters of Mercy, who ran schools in Cedar Rapids, Decorah, Manchester, Marion and Charles City.

Once the schools were built, the archbishop once explained to the Mercies during a meeting at Manchester, the rest was mainly up to them. "Guard well your school; it is the garden of God! The little buds are in your care! God will give the sunlight and the rain; you must enrich the soil and prevent the weeds!"

At the time, the lines between public and private school systems were blurry. Public school systems in New Mexico, Michigan and Pennsylvania sometimes hired nuns to teach because in those days religious orders had some of the most skilled teachers.

Their skill came from experience and instruction in the liberal arts, not education courses. Teaching orders of sisters set their own standards and ran a kind of medieval apprenticeship program, with older sisters passing on what they had learned in the classroom to young novices.

Harold A. Buetow, in his definitive history of Catholic education, *Of Singular Benefit,* points out that before World War I the teaching standards and the pay of teachers in parochial and public school systems were about the same. The real changes came afterward, when the huge teaching bureaucracies and networks of teachers' colleges that served the public schools began to grow. The growth of the parochial schools was also dramatic, but they did not have the money or the inclination to finance big bureaucracies.

Coming out of the 1940s, it was a system that always seemed to be flying by the seat of its pants, finding its way on the faith, idealism, common sense and on-the-job training of young women like Sister Sharon. For them, the school year was a series of adventures. They made up the rules to cope with problems as they went along. For example:

PROBLEM: Buckie LaPietra, captain of the football team at St. Matthews High School in Monroe, Louisiana, was running down the stairs. It was 1951. This beefy student decided he'd had enough of school.

SOLUTION: Although it was the same day that a snake escaped from biology class and that two students rehearsing for the class play found a newborn baby left in a basket on the school's doorstep, running right behind LaPietra was a five-foot nun, Sister Dorothea, then fifty. She caught up with him and got in his face. "I feel sure I sent up a hurried prayer before speaking with him!" she recalled in her memoirs. "At first there was no use in trying to make him change his mind." But he did.

Sister Dorothea, a member of Daughters of the Cross, taught for sixty years, a career she recalls as "this joyful life." Her teacher training consisted of taking over part of a sixth-grade class as soon as she joined the order. "I somehow knew instinctively, intuitively, that to get good results I had to hold the interest of the pupils."

Many of these women were paid hardly at all, given no vacations and accorded no retirement benefits. Of course, there were exceptions. In Iowa during the 1920s some county governments agreed to help support some parochial schools in remote, rural locations. The agreement was that the county would pay a salary for one teacher. The going rate was two hundred dollars a month. For the pastor of St. Patrick's School in Garryowen, Iowa, this was a splendid proposition.

He split part of the one salary among four Sisters of Mercy teaching there and tucked away the rest, giving himself the luxury of not having to ask his parishoners for anything that year. "Naturally, the counties objected to this, and the arrangements were terminated," notes a Mercy account of the incident.

Too bad, for splitting the salary among the sisters in Garryowen would have given them each fifty dollars a month, a scale of pay that the average parochial school sister working in the archdiocese of Dubuque didn't reach until the 1950s, and then only after a number of wrangles with the bishop.

The going rate was thirty-five dollars in the 1940s, when Lucille Lyness, now known as Sister Mary Roberta, started her career as a teacher in eastern Iowa. Then as now, she insists, money matters very little to her. She had the job she loved. She spent her summers at Mount Mercy College earning higher degrees. She loved her students. In short, she was living her dream.

The decade of World War II went by in a blur as she taught in a succession of smaller towns: Decorah, Dewitt and Charles City. On one visit back to her family's farm in Ryan, Iowa, she remembers blurting out to her mother that teaching made her so happy, she was fearful about dying "because I didn't think I could be so happy here and still be happy in the next [world]."

In some farm communities, such as Decorah with a large Scandinavian population, families of the students she taught often had at least one parent who was Lutheran. Still, the community took some of the edge off the sisters' financial situation. As Sister Roberta recalls: "Sisters didn't get very much money and the people knew that. They would always try to do what they could to help us." They gave "food showers," bringing canned goods, potatoes and other farm produce to the convent.

Meanwhile her mother, Kit, was sending packages from the farm: jam, a new pair of stockings, material for her to sew a new veil. When Sister Roberta needed money for something, a new pair of glasses, a dental bill, she would ask her mother superior.

Such extremely low overhead made parochial schools competitive and very attractive propositions for bishops. As the nation's economy revived after World War II, they began opening more and more of them. In retrospect, the self-sacrifice of the sisters had made the concept of parochial schools *too* attractive. As the numbers of schools rose, the building boom outpaced the growing flow of young women entering religious orders.

This added a major new source of disagreement to the normal tensions between bishops and nuns.

Sister Roberta was given an odd introduction to this part of religious life in 1951. She had been promoted to principal at Immaculate Conception School in Charles City, Iowa. Her superior at the mother house in Cedar Rapids was Mother Mary Maura Marron, a no-nonsense woman who had been relentlessly lobbying Archbishop Henry P. Rohlman to raise teacher salaries.

At the time the pay scale for a teacher in the archdiocese had risen to the munificent sum of forty-five dollars a month, slightly less than an enterprising seventh grader could earn delivering papers after school. The pay level was determined by the archbishop, but the salaries were actually paid by the parish priests, who were the sisters' employers.

Non-Catholics and scholars who insist on seeing the Catholic Church as a monolith might find this baffling, but this was another aspect of flying by the seat of the pants. Some pastors paid at the prescribed level, some paid less, some paid nothing at all, forcing their employees, the Mercies, to pay for the privilege of teaching.

The matter came to a head in 1949 when the Sisters of Mercy wrote a letter to the pastors in eastern Iowa. "It is no longer possible for us to stretch a nine-month salary over twelve months, nor is it possible for us to live on $45 a month," it pointed out.

In January, after the archbishop and a council of priests had raised the salary to fifty dollars for ten months, Mother Maura wrote Monsignor Leo Binz, who oversaw school matters for the archbishop. The pay raise was fine, she said, but a number of pastors hadn't cooperated with the old pay scale and were telling her they wouldn't cough up more until they were ordered to by the archbishop.

"Do you think there is any possibility of our being paid the back salary that is due us?" she asked him. Monsignor Binz, a tall, self-absorbed man who tended to weave back and forth in the pulpit as he gave long-winded sermons on morality, said there was nothing he could do. Nor was there much he could do after 1954, when he was promoted to become the archbishop.

There *was* something Mother Maura could do. She went to Charles City for a frank meeting with one of the freeloaders, Monsignor John Smith, the pastor of Immaculate Conception parish. Either he came up with some money, or the Mercies were leaving, she said. For reasons that are not known, the pastor refused to budge.

Sister Roberta, who knew little of these behind-the-scenes maneuvers, was told in January by Sister Maura that the Mercies' mission at the school was finished. After the school year, she and the entire faculty would pack up and leave for good. Sister Roberta was told not to tell anybody, not even her fellow sisters.

So in June Sister Roberta and her Mercies performed what amounted to a stealth withdrawal. The students and the parish saw nothing unusual in the nuns' departure. The sisters always went back in the summer to Mount Mercy, the mother house in Cedar Rapids.

Sister Roberta recalls her dilemma: "If we said we weren't coming back there would have been parties and going away things and we didn't want that. Many of the sisters loved their students and the people in Charles City and they were very saddened about the whole thing."

15

THE WAY WE WERE

SCENE: CEDAR RAPIDS, IOWA (POP. 60,000), MAY 1953

There were blooming spring days in the sophomore home room of Immaculate Conception High School when the perfume of what was happening outside swept in through the open windows like a drug and we all lost it.

Someone would crack a joke and the entire room would erupt in silliness—even some of the more restrained girls. The sister who taught us, a shy, scholarly soul, would try her best to quiet us down. She would try reason. She would try threats. Finally she would grow angry. When shrieking at us proved futile, as it usually did, she would leave the room.

There were a few more moments of delicious uproar before we could hear the rattle of the wooden beads and quick steps sounding in the hallway. That meant The Enforcer was coming. A slim woman in her late thirties, she would enter the classroom as if she owned it. She was definitely not amused.

She would simply stand in the front of the room by the teacher's vacated desk and stare us down. Then we'd get quiet because we all knew what was coming. She would begin her scold in a soft, chilled voice, saying: "The devil is in this room!"

What set apart Sister Roberta was her intensity. Other nuns might say that and we would think that was funny, too. But the demeanor of this woman told us she *really* believed it. The room went stone silent. What had seemed downright hilarious a few moments ago began to look, well, stupid. Nobody really meant to bring this on. People stared at their feet as the nun let the silence work for her.

In other classrooms, in other schools, in other years, this might not have worked. At the public school down the street, McKinley High School, *hell* was only a literary allusion or a theoretical possibility. But we had been brought up on tales of devils and angels, saints and sinners. When she started this, powerful imaginations kicked in. People would be looking around the classroom. Maybe, some of us thought, the devil really *was* in here.

None of us knew this woman then as Lucille Frances Lyness. Nor did we understand that being the disciplinarian was the part of her job that she truly hated. To us, nuns were just part of our landscape. We didn't know where they came from or where they went. At "I.C.," a plain, square brick building crammed with more than eight hundred students, most of us started in the first grade and finished as seniors. While the world changed around us, we could be sure of one thing: There was always going to be a sister standing in front of our next home room.

Like millions of Catholics passing through their schools in the 1950s, we took the presence of the nuns for granted. They lived in a large, World War I–era frame house next to our school.

Immaculate Conception drew its name from a nineteenth-century church doctrine that concluded that Mary, because she was the mother of Jesus, must have been conceived without sin. On the evening of May Day we would celebrate her purity, filling the street in front of the convent with a religious procession. To parents and non-Catholics we must have made quite a show, marching in procession dressed in white cassocks, carrying candles and singing ancient Latin hymns in honor of the Virgin.

A close observer, however, would see little boys pouring hot candle wax on each other's arms. These were experiments that ended with nuns flitting in and out of our ranks to pull selected ears. They *were* close observers. The proximity of their convent to the school, and their isolation from the rest of the business of the community, made it into a kind of giant lens, focusing their attention on us. We were their business.

Some of them knew us better than our parents did. Add to that the fact that the younger nuns were advised by older sisters who had taught some of our parents and it wasn't hard to see how they might be a step or two ahead of our schemes. A good bit of the corporate memory of the triumphs and failures of the Catholic side of Cedar Rapids resided in that convent.

As for Sister Roberta, she was the principal and a force to be reckoned with because she was younger and smarter than most of the rest of the faculty. Aside from the three priests who ran the parish, she was the authority figure for all eight hundred of us.

Because nuns were often the first authority figure for young Catholics, some of them later wound up as cartoons: knuckle-smashing disciplinarians or sex-addled policewomen in Broadway plays and other reminiscences of Catholic writers. These stories sell tickets and amuse readers, just as the Keystone Kops once did, but the reality on the beat, as in the classroom, was much richer and more multifaceted than the stereotype. There was justice and a considerable amount of love and hope in what they did.

We were city kids, most with working-class parents. Some of us came from broken homes; some had fathers who were alcoholics. We were definitely not the close-knit, self-help–oriented farm communities that Sister Roberta was used to. We sometimes referred to farmers as "shit kickers." Indeed, some of us used to brag that we'd never been on a farm. We were closer to being cartoons.

In high school it was not cool to say you admired nuns, although many of us secretly had in grade school. Some of the girls might still have said that, but for most of us boys it was better to smoke cigarettes, drink beer, shoot pool and pretend that our teachers came from Mars.

On the surface of things, the saints whom the nuns honored and the ones we revered were very different. They liked gentle Saint Francis, who gave away everything he owned and talked to birds. We would race junk cars on gravel roads and pretend we were James Dean, who ended his career by splattering his Porsche all over a California highway. Now *that* was cool.

If anyone needed more confirmation that nuns were weird, we had it on winter nights when we were in the vicinity of their mother house at

Mount Mercy. Roll down the car window and you could hear this strange *EEEEEEEeeeeee* sound in the air. Some people said that the sisters had a toboggan run up there. Nah. Not the nuns we knew, we concluded. They would never do that. It was some secret ritual they had.

One of the secrets that make parochial schools effective is quiet. Nuns had various ways of achieving it. To be sure, we did have one nun, an oxlike music teacher, who once silenced a student clowning during choir sessions by pinning him against the wall with a piano. But that was rare at I.C. Sister Roberta's palpable faith was her method of control. On days like this, she wielded it like a piano.

The nuns' workday went from early Mass in the morning until early evening. The younger ones would also take care of the retirement needs of the elderly, who in turn would pass on teaching tips.

Sister Roberta's mentor was a frail but wise former principal named Sister Mary Assumpta. She had emphasized some simple truths: Trust the students, always give them a second chance and, above all, never, ever raise your voice.

In her spare time after school, Sister Roberta was cramming for a masters degree in history, but none of us knew that, either. We certainly didn't tell her what we did after school. The priests knew more about our extracurricular activities. They kept an eye on the dances at the church Youth Center and monitored the road trips of the high school's basketball team.

In hindsight, though, the priests probably thought they knew more about us than they actually did. There were only three of them. Monsignor John Molloy—the same burley Irishman who had once talked Sister Roberta's father into mortgaging his pigs—was the pastor and spent most of his time handling financial matters. His two assistants, who taught religion, spent a lot of time talking to us about sex.

Even thinking about some of the things we thought about was a sin, they would insist. And they knew we were thinking about it because we told them so in the confessional on Saturday afternoon. They were celibate men and being crammed in a stuffy box for long afternoons to listen to the real and imaginary faults of hot-blooded teenagers was not pleasant.

They paid us back with visions of hellfire and brimstone in religion class. There was a kind of magnetic pull to these lectures. The central theme, however it meandered, always seemed to be drawn to violations of the Sixth Commandment (Thou shalt not commit adultery). To be sure, there was some sexual groping going on among us, but nothing like what they seemed to imagine. They were victims of a closed loop.

What went on in the confessional was secret, so the nuns were not in that loop. The sexual side of what went on at Immaculate Conception, though, was not entirely a mystery to them. From the time we were small they taught us to respect one another. Young women were temples. Each had a soul, a spark of God within, and they were not to be sullied.

While the priests were poised to pounce on the devil, the nuns took a different approach. They knew us more intimately. We all had certain gifts from God, and the nuns saw them as seeds in their garden. My high-school English teacher, Sister Mary Winifred, decided I had a gift for writing, which was news to me.

Neither writing nor any other academic subject was on the top of my agenda at I.C., but she was forever going on about it, praising me for what I'd done, pushing me to do more. A sharp-tongued, clever woman who took delight in showing us all the puns in Shakespeare, Winnie—as we called her—was hard to ignore.

Still, I thought I'd done a pretty good job of ignoring her until almost a decade later, when I graduated from law school and came to decide that life might be more fun, and more fulfilling, as a journalist. For some who knew me, it seemed like a strange career move. But it was an easy, pleasant leap to make. Winnie had given me the parachute to do it.

She and Sister Roberta were chums from their early days on Mount Mercy as novices. Sister Winifred was the tomboy who once went home and climbed up the windmill on her farm in her habit to grease the gears. Now approaching their forties, the two nuns used to sit in the late-afternoon quiet of the principal's office and discuss how to handle various students.

Sometimes they would grade test papers together. (When she wasn't being principal, Sister Roberta reverted to her real love, which was teaching American history.) Between the two of them, they had a pretty good sense of the strengths and weaknesses of our class.

It was the weaknesses that created the work for Sister Roberta. In the spring of 1956, when we were seniors, Sister Louise, our homeroom teacher, interrupted Sister Roberta's musings about her master's thesis. Here was a problem, she said, showing her a freshly processed print of the senior class picture that was about to go into the yearbook. Indeed, there was something strange about it. In the front row, several of the boys were seen to be grinning mischievously, extending the middle finger of their right hands at the camera.

As it happened, the photographer who took the picture was one of the town's more obvious homosexuals. A thin, officiously polite man, he was a great favorite of the nuns. That was two strikes against him for us. The idea to give him the finger came up in one of those hilarious moments. It was just nuts, putting the evidence on film like that, but sometimes life at I.C. went nuts for reasons we couldn't readily explain.

Neither Sister Roberta nor Sister Louise knew what the finger meant, but one of the older nuns soon enlightened them. That presented Sister Roberta with a political problem. The priests were her ultimate disciplinary backup, but one that she wanted to use sparingly. This was the Mercies' school. She wanted to be seen by us and by them as being in control.

If she took this picture over to the rectory there would be the spiritual equivalent of a thermonuclear explosion. So she handled it her way. The father of the boy who sparked this odd demonstration was quietly summoned with his son. After presenting him with the photo, Sister Roberta asked him to buy the negative and pay for the costs of another photo, a solution which the father promptly accepted.

The man, a crusty World War II veteran, explained earnestly that the sister must have been given the wrong information. The finger was not meant as an obscene gesture, but just a mild pejorative. For we were all good Catholic boys, weren't we? She took the money. He was allowed to save face. The offending boys got off the hook.

The negatives were destroyed and a new, more sober-faced photo was taken with the photographer grinning at us triumphantly as he set off the flash. There was no explosion at the rectory and Sister Roberta went back to her thesis. The score for that day, as for many others: Sister Mary Roberta, 1; the Devil, 0.

From that class half of us went on to finish college. Most of us married for life, raised strong families, and moved to various jobs all over the United States. Now, almost fifty years out of I.C., we have awkward moments when we meet at class reunions. But we always have something in common to talk about—the nuns. No one paid them for what they gave to us. No one could.

Looking back, this was an historic moment. In the late fifties and early sixties, the parochial school system was at its peak. It was a large, decentralized and peculiarly American machine finishing the Herculean task of lifting an entire class of poor and undereducated immigrants and their children into the middle class. For the most part, Catholics always assumed these schools worked. Few non-Catholic academics ever bothered to take a serious look at them, even though they were the nation's largest alternative school system.

That has since changed. Three sociologists led by James S. Coleman of the University of Chicago rocked the educational establishment in 1982 by trotting out a series of national test scores showing that students from widely differing economic backgrounds and from parents with different levels of education performed better, as a group, in Catholic schools.

The sociologists called it a "paradoxical result that the Catholic schools come closer to the American ideal of the 'common school,' educating all alike than do the public schools."

They found that the achievement gap between white students and minorities in Catholic schools was narrower than in public schools and that the higher level of discipline was "intimately intertwined" with achievement. More homework got done in parochial schools. There were fewer absences and dropouts.

The nation's highest performing schools were private prep schools, drawing from the nation's elite. But when the sociologists weeded out the extreme differences in economic backgrounds they found: "Catholic school sophomores perform at the highest level, sophomores in other private schools next, and sophomores in the public schools lowest."

Three education specialists, led by Anthony S. Bryk, professor of education at the University of Chicago, added more context to this in 1993. After visiting a variety of schools, they concluded that the level of teaching skills at parochial schools was "generally quite ordinary." They also found "limited fiscal resources" were a chronic problem at many Catholic schools, especially in the inner city.

Coming out of this, though, they found a curious kind of alchemy. Catholic students were higher achievers, especially in poorer areas, but they weren't necessarily the brightest students. They did better, in part, because their schools had stuck to a limited academic core where math and science were required.

Sister Mary Roberta.
(COURTESY OF FRANKIE BROWN)

Another discovery of the Bryk group: "Teachers are not just subject-matter specialists whose job definition is limited by the classroom walls; they are mature people whom students encounter in the hallways, playing fields, the school neighborhood and sometimes even in their homes."

They found parochial school teachers spent more time with each other and shared a set of values with the community that allowed them to set a base of moral authority. There were no layers of higher bureaucracy looming above a Catholic school. "Virtually all important decisions are made at individual school sites," they concluded, and "considerable deference is accorded to the principal."

Diane Ravitch, a senior research scholar at New York University, recently added another attribute that makes underfunded, under-equipped parochial schools shine in grimy neighborhoods: "steadfast resistance to the fads that sweep through the education world with alarming regularity."

The tragedy of these findings is that they began to accumulate as the part of the parochial system where the experts found the most unusual high achievers—schools in the inner cities—was rapidly fading into history. But in the 1950s, that cloud had not yet appeared on our horizon.

The force that gave the system smooth sailing, the influx of idealistic, faith-filled young women into religious orders, was still with us.

In 1953, Doris Gottemoeller, a tall, confident sixteen-year-old, one of the brightest in the graduating class of St. Joseph's Academy in Cincinnati, met a young priest. His name was John McDonough and he was an assistant pastor of a parish that the Gottemoeller family had moved into.

A funny, charming man, he had invited some of the young women in the parish to join a newly formed prayer group. As the individuals in the group got to know one another, he floated this suggestion: What would the young women think about a lifetime devoted to prayer? At first the idea seemed foreign to Doris.

The Sisters of St. Joseph who taught her at the academy seemed to be a stiff, overly formal lot. The priest told Doris to take a look at the Sisters of Mercy. They taught at the parish school and they were different. "When I looked around," she recalls, "the sisters in the parish were young and very attractive. I wanted to be a nurse, but I knew Mercies did a lot of different things."

Doris's father, an accountant for the local gas company, took the news stoically. His family had had a rough time in the Depression and he wanted his daughters to be self-reliant. Doris could follow her dream, as long as she finished school first.

To Doris, and to the thousands of other women who made this choice in the 1950s, it was all a very natural, seamless progression. One of her three younger sisters, Marilyn, had been talking about becoming a sister since she was in the third grade.

So Doris put on the black cap and the midcalf-length black dress of the postulant, and began attending classes at what is now called Xavier College—named for Frances Warde. She quickly discovered that there were a lot of little, annoying rules. She had entered, as she later described it, as part of an "affair of the heart" with God. But she found she had to ask her superior for permission to shine her shoes or to get twenty-five cents for a bus ride downtown to see the dentist.

On all such ventures outside the convent, she had to have a sister as a companion. It was lights out and no talking after 8:30 P.M., the start of the Great Silence. In many convents, sisters were forbidden to attend

Starting Out: A class of postulants, or first-year sisters, Sister of Mercy Novitiate, Cincinnati, Ohio, 1951. (COURTESY OF THE SISTERS OF MERCY OF THE AMERICAS)

movies or watch television. Thus, when bishops sponsored special showings of the classic Otto Preminger movie, *Joan of Arc,* starring Jean Seberg, Mercies had to decline.

"I remember thinking about some of it as being regressive and promoting a childlike dependency. I can remember going to bed at eight-thirty and thinking, If I was home, I'd just be going out about now," she recalls. But she soon shrugged it off. "I decided it was all part of the package. I was very accepting in those days," she adds.

She was assigned to teach at a suburban elementary school, St. Theresa's in Price Hill, which sounds as if it might have inspired a Bing Crosby movie. Learning was done by memorizing, and Father Anthony, the kindly, elderly pastor, would collar students on the stairway. " 'Recite the Psalm of Life,' he would say. If he or she couldn't remember it, the nun would get it," she recalls.

Sister Gottemoeller made sure her students got it. She was twenty-three, her forty pupils were thirteen. "I always thought the sun rose and set on those kids." It was a very Catholic neighborhood. "Whatever sister said was law." She remembers the camaraderie among the young nuns after school in the convent. "It's impossible to imagine this now, but when I think of how enthusiastic we were, how we prepared and how much fun we had . . ."

After the fifties ended, Sister Roberta went on to realize her dream. She was invited to join the faculty at Mount Mercy College to teach history. Sister Gottemoeller eventually became the head of all of the Sisters of Mercy in the United States. Most of us who were their students went out into the world and never looked look back. There was nothing special about the way they educated us, we thought. It was simply the way things were.

16
THE WAY WE
WEREN'T

On October 7, 1961, Claudina Sanz, a nineteen-year-old girl from Belize, landed in Baltimore. She was there to join the Oblate Sisters of Providence, an order of African American sisters founded by Elizabeth Lange in 1829. The order was flourishing.

One reason was that African Americans were discovering the benefits of parochial schools and joining them in record numbers. The order's 315 sisters were running St. Frances Academy, an elite school for girls in Baltimore, and teaching in more than 40 other schools from Maryland to Minneapolis.

Claudina had heard about the remarkable works of the Oblate sisters in St. Ignacio, her hometown in Belize. She was eager to join them, but her father, an archaeologist, was skeptical about her dream of going to America. Why was she going so far from home? he would ask her. Did she really know what she was going to find when she arrived in this strange place where the natives insisted upon usurping the name America? "He said you're not going to stay," his daughter recalls.

He was so sure she was coming back that he had given her a round-trip ticket. As soon as Claudina's plane landed in Miami, she went to the ticket office and cashed in the return portion. She is Creole, a mixture of Spanish, Mayan and African. She didn't know what she would find in America either, but she certainly did not want the lingering temptation of being able to run back home to Daddy. She was eager to learn all she could about this America.

Her first lesson came a few hours later, while she was being driven on a tour of Baltimore. An Oblate sister pointed out the car window. What they were passing was the Catholic cemetery reserved for whites, she explained. The cemetery for blacks was down the road.

Segregated cemeteries? Claudina recalls turning this over in her mind. St. Ignacio, where she had just come from, was a crazy quilt of skin colors. Her friends were Mayans, Creoles, Syrians, Hispanics, Orientals and Africans. They were all taught by an order of German nuns, who regarded the color of one's skin as being distinctly unimportant. In America, evidently, Catholics held it to be very important. But why would it matter so terribly much to people after they were dead? Claudina was wondering. So she raised the question.

There was silence in the car as it rumbled over the brick streets of East Baltimore. The Oblates, all of whom had grown up with intolerance, studied their new arrival as if she had just come to them from another planet. "That's just the way it is in this country," one of them said, shrugging.

Despite over a century of efforts by Mother Elizabeth Lange, Saint Katherine Drexel and many other individual Catholics to defeat intolerance; despite the fact that the Civil Rights movement had been brewing in the South and in the media since 1955, the Catholic Church had still not roused from its self-induced torpor about racial matters. The traditions that held it back were both deep-seated and mystifying, especially to outsiders like Claudina Sanz.

Racism is wrong. The Church's teachings going back to Christ are clear about that. These teachings had been taught and even absorbed, but selectively. For example, in 1945, a survey of Catholic high-school students in Philadelphia showed that 92 percent of them agreed that baptized African Americans were full-fledged members of the Church and had a right to attend any parish. In the same survey, 94 percent of these students also agreed that African Americans were, nonetheless, different. They should be "restricted to certain areas of the city."

To the Catholic mind of the 1950s, racial intolerance was being carried out in the South, and that was wrong. But the theory tended to break down as more and more African Americans moved closer to home. There were small groups of Catholics speaking out about the need to prepare for racially changing neighborhoods.

Dennis Clark, a member of the Philadelphia Catholic Housing Council, later recorded in his diary the reaction of one community group he had preached this to: "Silence, stone cold silence. . . . As I left I knew that they despised me because they believe I am against them."

In the 1950s in Iowa, where I grew up, we had no reason to be prejudiced. Few of us had ever known an African American. Yet some of us would talk knowingly about "niggers" being lazy and stupid. The few glimpses we had of real African Americans certainly didn't show that. I can remember the Harlem Globetrotters effortlessly blowing away a team of University of Iowa basketball all-stars.

I can still remember a dapper, resolute-looking black man with deep bags under his eyes getting off a bus in Cedar Rapids in the middle of a blizzard and leading his band into a dance hall filled with whites. Once he shucked his big galoshes and took his place behind the piano, he simply awed us with his music. He was Duke Ellington. He was a genius. Still, the image of "niggers" held.

As Claudina Sanz came to learn from her fellow sisters, racism was a kind of embarrassing scar on the body of the Church. It was concealed in different ways. In some places it was simply compartmentalized. Different people were supposed to be in different boxes.

At St. Mary's of the Assumption Catholic Church in Upper Marlboro, Maryland, where Sister Eleanor Marie Wedge grew up, there were two parochial schools. One was next to the rectory and the church and it was for whites. One was four blocks down the street, next to a bar. It had few amenities, no playground. It was for blacks. "We just didn't see each other," she recalls.

The point of connection were the Sisters of the Immaculate Heart of Mary, who taught in both schools. "They accepted you no matter what color you were," Sister Eleanor recalls, which was how she became attracted to the idea of becoming a sister. But neither they nor most other orders of Catholic religious would accept black candidates in the 1950s. So she became an Oblate.

Sister Elaine Frederick was born in Washington, D.C. The nation's capital had parochial elementary schools for black students, but once they reached ninth grade, it was like jumping into a void. There were no Catholic schools for African American high-school students. Somehow her father, a janitor, found the money to send her to St. Frances Academy in Baltimore. She liked it so much that she became an Oblate. One of her first assignments was Sharon, Pennsylvania, where she had a front-row seat to watch the nation's racial drama playing out. In the 1950s, there were hardly any African Americans there. But there was an attitude.

There was also Rev. Paul Francis Obenrader, an idealistic young white priest who was determined to use every power he had to change it. When older priests resisted his attempt to create an integrated parish, Father Obenrader used his family's money to buy and renovate a Jewish synagogue. Then he donated it to the Church upon the condition that he could attempt to run it as an integrated parish. It became Christ the King Church; to help make his point, the priest invited the Oblates to come up from Baltimore and teach in its school.

The experiment lasted six years. Sister Elaine, who came to teach music and choir, recalls them as happy years. The school was expanding, drawing white children from a neighboring parish, run by a monsignor, who complained to their parents. "The monsignor said he didn't want these women sending their children to those nigger sisters," recalls Sister Elaine. Within the church, the monsignor had more clout than Father Obenrader. Christ the King was eventually closed and the younger priest who founded it was transferred. "The people themselves," Sister Elaine recalls, "were not discriminating."

When Mary E. Dilworth was five, her parents enrolled her in St. Mary's School in Plainfield, New Jersey. She was the only black student among 150 pupils. She did well, bringing home glowing report cards to her father, a shipping clerk, who always seemed overjoyed to see them. One reason, she discovered later, was that he had a standing five-dollar bet with a coworker, the father of a white student at the school, that Mary's grades would be better. This was the 1950s and her father was trying to make a point. He was also making money.

One day in the second or third grade, she recalls, her classmates made a point. There was a birthday party and she was the only one not invited. She later asked the birthday girl about it, and was told that the girl's father had said that everyone could be welcome, except Mary Dilworth. The little girl asked her mother and got this reply. Some people "just did not like black people. And in my young mind, that was enough of an answer."

In the neighborhoods of Chicago, Detroit, Cleveland, Buffalo, Boston, Milwaukee, New York and other cities with large ethnic Catholic populations, the Church was divided by parishes that amounted to small nations. They were Polish, Irish, Ukrainian, Bohemian, Italian and German. They were often served by their own ethnic priests and nuns, and when the blockbusting of the 1950s began to panic others to move to the suburbs, these parishes were determined to hold their ground. John T. McGreevy, a history professor at Notre Dame, has written a valuable book, *Parish Boundaries*, describing the Church's racial struggles. He recalls these parishes were designed to be "fortresses."

One of the biggest was Visitation Church in South Chicago, where Monsignor Daniel Byrnes helped organize a civic group, the Garfield Boulevard Improvement Association. He held some of its meetings in the parish hall and broadcast its themes from the pulpit. Its overriding goal was to keep out African Americans.

Father Martin Farrell, a younger priest who was attempting to integrate Chicago parishes, recalled the monsignor's approach. "He had a way of giving a sermon without mentioning race once and everybody in the congregation knew what he was talking about. He'd put it up there and say 'clean up and paint up.'"

Other Chicago pastors weren't so subtle. In one parish African Americans, newly arrived from the South, were made to feel as if they were still home. They were greeted by a priest who invited them to sit in six pews on the right side "and let the white people who built this church sit in the center."

Despite all this, black Catholics saw value in the parochial schools. The schools tried to give every student a well-rounded education. They emphasized discipline, ethics and character building and their tuition charges were remarkably low.

In some neighborhoods, schools that were designed for white immigrant Catholics were becoming prep schools for upwardly mobile African American Baptists. In 1959 researchers counted 600,000 black Catholics, double the number in the 1920s. In larger cities there were more than twelve thousand conversions a year.

Most African American students didn't succumb to the religion, but they did get seduced by the teaching. Michele Foster, who later became a professor at Claremont College Graduate School of Education, recalls her nuns being tough and insistent on quality performance from all students. She attended St. Anne's Academy in Marlboro, Massachusetts, an all-white school, except for her. There, she recalls, "religion permeated the school environment."

Ms. Foster's mother took comfort in that. She was convinced that nuns simply couldn't discriminate among students "because if any of them failed to learn they [the nuns] would go to hell." Hell was, as her mother would always put it, "the best motivator."

Students at the all-black St. Francis Xavier School in Baton Rouge, Louisiana, had a different motivator, recalls Lisa D. Delpit, who later taught education at Georgia State University. "I recall pinches for misnaming the parts of speech and ruler hits for not forming a cursive capital A correctly." Her nuns, the Sisters of the Holy Family, an African American Order, pounded home the point that black students had to perform at a higher level than whites "if we were going to be able to do anything."

While modern educators would quibble with the methodology, it worked. In some cases it worked too well for the larger community. In the early 1960s students from her school were folded into a newly integrated Catholic school, where they outperformed some of the whites. The school was soon closed.

Antoine M. Garibaldi, who later became a vice president at Xavier University in New Orleans, recalls attending St. Augustine High School there in the early 1960s. The Josephite priests and brothers there taught that "discipline was a means to a greater end" and that if students learned that lesson, their dreams would be "fulfilled despite the lingering vestiges of segregation." Students who didn't learn that at his all–African American school had their ends introduced to the "Board of Education," a stout wooden paddle. Because they got results, the Josephites were regarded as "troublemakers" by some in the white community and occasionally received death threats. The Josephites, an order founded in England, have frequently come to the assistance of orders of African American sisters, such as the Oblates.

While the Vatican was prodding the American Catholic hierarchy to prepare their flocks for integration, many older bishops and cardinals tended to react with a collective shrug. They seemed to view it as beyond their powers. Racism was something too deeply embedded in America's culture for the nation's largest church to tamper with.

This is how Chicago's Archbishop George Mundelein, later elevated to cardinal, explained it in the 1930s. "Nothing will be accomplished for the evangelization of the colored in Chicago by scattering them among the whites in our churches and schools." Better to concentrate them, he said, in churches and schools "restricted to them."

Thirty years later, in the early 1960s, James Francis Cardinal McIntyre, newly installed in Los Angeles, shared some of the wisdom he'd acquired from years of working with New York City's parishes: "Kind lives with kind, Irish with Irish, Poles with Poles, Mexicans with Mexicans, Negroes with Negroes."

By the early 1960s, Catholic bishops, growing concerned about mounting racial tensions, had begun to issue collective statements denouncing racism as evil. But their flocks didn't seem to get the message. Alan Paton, the novelist, interviewed a white man he found in the aftermath of a riot at a housing project for African Americans in Trumbull Park, South Chicago. The man explained that he was there to get the "jigs" out of the neighborhood. Mr. Paton asked him how that goal squared with Catholic teaching. "The Church hasn't got a right to tell me who I should live next door with," the man responded, adding "and the Church knows it too, because it hasn't said anything about Trumbull Park."

According to Mr. McGreevy, the history professor at Notre Dame, it was Catholic sisters who finally brought home to the average Catholic the message of racial tolerance. It happened in the summer of 1963 when a group of white sisters in Chicago decided to picket the Illinois Club for Catholic Women, which had repeatedly rejected black applicants. Since the club was located on the downtown campus of the Jesuit-run Loyola University, local television stations were there to film the protest.

It was a revolutionary moment for Catholics in the city. Whether they were Irish, Polish, German or Italian, they all identified emotionally with the image of women wearing the habit. These were the same women who had taught them the basic principles of morality! They were their teachers and nurses!

What were they doing carrying signs and chanting out on the street? That night, after the nuns appeared on the evening television news, enlightenment struck. Phones rang, minds changed. Suddenly the Illinois Club for Catholic Women had a new open-entrance policy.

It was also a revolutionary moment for nuns, especially younger ones. Sometimes it seemed to them that there was little social payback from their quiet regimens of teaching or nursing, but here was social change carried out in a few hours! Many orders developed their own marching orders.

By 1965 more than five hundred nuns, a rolling sea of black and white, joined a civil rights demonstration in New York. The momentum continued to build. At Selma, Alabama, when Sister Margaret Ellen Traxler, a School Sister of Notre Dame, led a line of ten sisters into the front ranks of the demonstrators, she was followed by Benedictines, Sisters of the Blessed Virgin Mary and Sisters of Loretto.

Facing them, she later recalled, "rows of state troopers stood with their billy clubs in front of them. We formed a line, the sisters in front all the way across the street. People began to sing freedom songs and lined up behind us. The troopers stared at us, their necks red in the sharp March winds. I think of our singing now for there was a touch of prophecy 'No Man's Gonna Turn Us 'Round.' "

It was a moment made for television. The cameras caught a young sister marching jubilantly down Selma's Highway 80. She was shouting: "We are the Church! We are the Church!" For Catholics these were teaching moments.

But the images were wrong. The nuns certainly weren't the Church, at least not then. One of the facts that didn't make the evening news shows was that, throughout the tumult, Selma's Catholic parishes remained strictly segregated. The euphoria didn't last long, either. The following year, as Martin Luther King brought his civil rights campaign to the Catholic neighborhoods of South Chicago, a nun marching with him was struck by a rock and the crowd cheered.

In suburban Cicero a young man wearing a letter jacket of a Jesuit high school threw a brick at a marching sister. "And that's for you, nun," he shouted. Thousands of Catholic schools in inner-city neighborhoods were closing down as the young white families who supported them packed up and fled to the suburbs.

Sisters followed them. In Milwaukee, Father James Groppi led several of his civil rights demonstrations into white suburbs in 1966, marches that were often led by a phalanx of twenty-five sisters. "Marching," explained the priest, "is not only a protest. It is a prayer."

In 1968 the Ford Foundation supported "Summer in Suburbia," a project involving seventy-three sisters who went door to door in Cleveland's suburbs asking questions about racial issues. The idea was that their habits would give them entrée, but they reported that "a significant percentage of residents were clearly home, but failed to open the door."

The events of the 1960s were a disheartening experience for some sisters who had believed their examples would trigger a prompt change in Catholic attitudes about race. After 1968, thousands began to leave their orders. The civil rights marches were a radicalizing experience for others, who decided that direct social action, as opposed to the ways of the classroom or the hospital ward, would be their future mission.

At a warm-up rally before one of Martin Luther King's Chicago marches, a nun, Sister Mary William, stepped up to the microphone to suggest that racial justice for African Americans—as messy and embarrassing as it was for the Church to deal with—was only part of the agenda that was moving younger sisters. They had another issue.

"Why are sisters like Negroes?" she asked. "Because they, too, are segregated, ghettoized and because leadership is not encouraged in their roles."

The struggle to bring the church to civil rights cast a long shadow over the next generation of sisters. Barbara Schilling was twenty-two in 1967. A tall, jovial, tomboyish woman, she grew up in the white suburbs of Rochester, New York, going to parochial schools. Her father, an industrial engineer, was a recent convert to Catholicism who was still skeptical about many of its doctrines.

He loved her, but when it came to faith they developed an oddly contentious relationship. She would be doing her homework, studying a book called a catechism. It was full of questions and answers about Catholicism. He would be peering over her shoulder. "What does that mean?" he would ask.

"I don't know, why don't you ask the sister?"

"Why don't *you* ask the sister?"

So Barbara would ask the sister, who would, she recalls, "sometimes respond by saying don't ask questions, just memorize."

Her father had come from an old-style, authoritarian German-

Hungarian family where children were not allowed to voice opinions. He was determined that pattern would not be repeated in America. He wanted a daughter who would speak her mind, which she invariably did. She had been a devoted follower of the Civil Rights Movement since 1954. He was skeptical. They had raging, red-faced arguments over the dinner table. She frequently attacked his prejudice against black people.

He ridiculed her notion that the use of affirmative action would promote integration. Their battles were a regular event in the Schilling household until one day, in 1967, when Barbara dropped a small bomb. She told him she was about to enter the convent. He was stunned, but cautiously supportive.

So one day they drove up to the campuslike setting of the convent of the Oblate Sisters of Providence in suburban Baltimore. He let her out, telling her that his only desire was that she be happy.

She was. She was about to become one of two white women in an order of 313 African American nuns. Of course that was the part she hadn't told her father. Later, though, when she brought some of the Oblates home for summer vacation, Mr. Schilling grew to like them. "We'd play bridge," his daughter recalls.

17

OVER THE TOP

The great bronze doors of the papal palace swung open and 2,500 men, the collective world leadership of the Catholic Church, emerged. There were cardinals resplendent in red, followed by their entourage of theologians and canon lawyers. There were bishops, a shining river of white vestments that flowed into the massive square. Marching in carefully spaced rows, six across, they turned and entered St. Peter's Basilica.

For the American Catholics in the large crowd of spectators, it was the second sign that the 1960s held great promise for their faith. Two years earlier they had helped elect John F. Kennedy, the first Catholic President of the United States. Now they were watching the start of Vatican II, the deliberations that were intended to bring the Church into the twentieth century. It was the first church council in over ninety years.

For American Catholic sisters, the promise of Vatican II was more specific. They had labored for more than a century to build the American Catholic Church into a most remarkable institution. Now the sisters were looking for signs of respect from within the Church and a fairer, more equal voice in its governance.

Their case was a good one. Their schools, universities and hospitals were thriving. The numbers of young women entering convents was nearing an all-time high. It was as if they had climbed almost to the top of something very steep. But what the sixties turned out to be, for them, was a roller coaster.

In 1965, the year the council ended, there were 179,974 sisters in the United States, more than ever before and more, probably, than we'll ever see again. The following year began a long, downward plunge that has depleted them by over 60 percent and will soon cut more deeply because half of the remaining sisters are seventy or older.

For the millions of parents and students of parochial schools, it was a most puzzling disappearing act. In 1965 there were more than a hundred thousand sisters in classrooms. A generation later, nine out of ten were gone.

"Where did they go?" is a complex question with many answers. But it seems clear that some of the many hands that gave American nuns a push down this long, slippery slope were in this colorfully garbed assemblage of men. Processions were something the fathers of the Church excelled at. Dealing with the women of the Church, on the other hand, was not a matter that they gave much consideration. The seating arrangement that awaited them inside the basilica said as much.

Only fifteen Catholic women were allowed to attend Vatican II. Among them were leaders of conferences of religious women from eight countries. Mary Luke Tobin, a Sister of Loretto for more than thirty years, represented U.S. sisters. In one sense, this was progress.

More than eight thousand theologians and other experts had spent three years mulling over the agenda for the church council. None of them were women, but they had reached one truly historic decision in that regard. In previous councils Catholic women had been banned altogether. Now they were given a special status. They were "auditors."

What that meant, the women discovered as they took their seats, was they could watch the deliberations from a balcony high above the altar of St. Peter's. There they were, having devoted their lives to the Church, staring across the cavernous basilica at a balcony on the other side that was

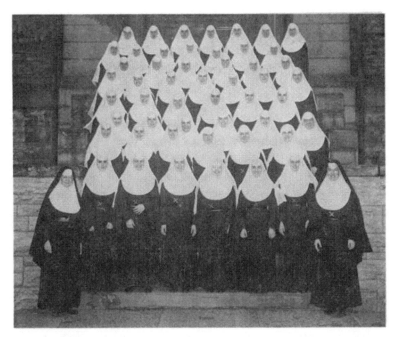

More sisters than ever. Young sisters in their third year of training at the Mercy Novitiate in Cincinnati, September 1965. (PHOTO COURTESY OF THE SISTERS OF MERCY OF THE AMERICAS)

filling with people who had been given equal status. These were the "official observers" from Protestant churches.

"They observed; we audited; none of us spoke," is the way Sister Tobin described this scene in her memoir.

The daughter of a gold miner, Sister Tobin had grown up in Denver and once wanted to be a ballerina. Instead, she became the leader of the Sisters of Loretto, an order based in Kentucky. She had fond memories of what she called a "high sense of morale" in the Church in the 1940s and 1950s. What she wanted out of Rome now was a seat at the table and some clear recognition of the sacrifices women had made to serve as sisters. When it came to making future decisions involving women's jobs and careers, she wanted the Council to explicitly say that in these matters women will have a voice.

From an American perspective, this doesn't sound like a very radical notion, but the men in Rome seemed nervous when she raised it. She recalls an American priest, then a Vatican official, taking her aside to give her a "scolding" after she held a press conference in which she called for women's rights. The priest's vehement attack and the shock of it brought her to tears. "I felt he was under pressure from somebody to get me in line. What was so difficult was being misunderstood and being unable to do anything about it. That certainly convinced me of my status as a second-class citizen in the Church," she later recalled.

In the summer of 1965, just before the last session of the Council, she made her move. She asked the administrative board of American bishops to use their muscle to support her. "I can still recall the great politeness of each of them when I paid my visit. But I could tell that for them to take our request any farther would have required enormous courage on their part and the hour was not ripe for that, so that was a painful disappointment. I expected more."

According to Xavier Rynne, the nom de plume for the American cleric who wrote one of the most-read accounts of Vatican II's deliberations, "surprisingly few American bishops spoke at the Council." Those who did tended to be hard-liners, such as James Francis Cardinal McIntyre of Los Angeles, who used up most of his rhetorical ammunition defending the Latin Mass and trying to limit the involvement of laypeople, positions that the Council rejected.

When it came to modernizing religious orders, the Council adopted a much-compromised, vaguely worded draft, boiled down from one hundred pages to four. A French bishop objected that Sister Tobin and the other "auditors" at the conference hadn't even seen it.

A Belgian, Cardinal Leon Joseph Suenens, argued: "We should give up the habit of treating nuns as minors, an attitude so typical of the nineteenth century." The author of an influential book on nuns, he wanted a more elaborate draft that introduced some form of democracy within religious orders and that called for the abandonment of outmoded garb and customs.

But the Church fathers, eager to get to what they felt were more important matters, approved the truncated version. It called for orders to engage in "adequate and prudent experimentation," revising their traditions and consulting with their memberships. The religious habit, it stated, was "an outward mark of consecration to God." It should be "simple and modest, poor and at the same time becoming."

Compared to other findings of the Council, these are fairly vacuous statements. Vacuums did not survive long in the peculiarly contentious atmosphere of the 1960s. Where the Church was silent, American sisters, including two in particular, used other resources to fill in the blanks and frame the issues.

One of them was Sister Mary Emil Penet, a short, thin-faced woman who led a major consciousness-raising effort in the 1950s about the status of Catholic schoolteachers. Larger orders, such as the Mercies, had begun to realize that the demands of the parochial school system were outstripping both the endurance and the supply of young nuns. But many orders remained in the dark about the larger picture until Sister Penet and her small team of nuns arrived. They toured the country in a battered old car they had christened *Raphael*.

Between September 1955 and October 1956 they put 44,268 miles on *Raphael*, visiting sisters in forty-two states. "What we found would make your hair stand on end," she later reported to her sponsor, a newly formed group called the Sister Formation Conference. She had a way of rattling off embarrassing statistics. Some nuns in Louisiana, she found, made forty-five dollars a month and were sending novices into the classrooms with no training.

Sister Emil, who had a Ph.D. in philosophy, also made speeches. "Are our sisters intellectual?" she would ask, noting that the teaching schedules imposed by bishops forced many of them to complete their degrees in short sessions in summer schools. A lot of them, Sister Emil found, were on the "twenty-year plan." It often took sisters that many years of summer school to get their college degrees.

She was certainly not alone in her suspicions that what the Church was doing in parochial schools was not sustainable. The Sister Formation Conference was begun in 1952 after a nudge from Pope Pius XII, who said Catholic sisters teaching school should have the same professional training as teachers in public schools.

Pressures for reform were building, but there was little in the way of response. In 1961 the Sisters of Mercy calculated that it cost them $1,587 per year to educate and sustain an average sister in teaching. The good news was that this teacher, once educated, would teach for forty-seven years. The bad news was that Chicago's parishes paid them only $1,000 a year for teaching. In addition, some bishops penalized orders that failed to recruit enough teachers to fill their assigned number of classrooms. They required the sisters to pay the cost of hiring lay teachers to fill their vacancies.

This was a treadmill that led to exhaustion and various orders found subtle ways to slow it down. They scraped together what money they had and began sending thousands of young sisters off to universities, many for advanced degrees. By the mid-sixties, when the final documents from Vatican II were still being printed, some of these women were already beginning to project their own versions of reform.

One of them was Sister Marie Augusta Neal, a member of the Sisters of Notre Dame de Namur, a teaching order. She is a sociologist. She and a group of forty reform-minded Catholic intellectuals wrote a book in 1965 called *The Changing Sister*. In it, Sister Neal said the old convent structure was no longer "relevant" and predicted that the future role of sisters would turn toward social action. Sisters who insisted on teaching school, she later determined, displayed a "pre-Vatican II" attitude.

In 1966 a group called the Conference of Major Superiors of Women, spun out of the Sisters Formation Conference in 1956, hired Sister Neal to construct a survey. It would be used, as she later put it, "to determine the readiness of sisters to implement the decisions of the Second Vatican Council."

The survey is a remarkable and monumental document—23 pages containing 649 multiple-choice questions. Parts of it have more than a passing resemblance to a "push poll," a tool being used by modern politicians to move voters toward a preordained set of opinions.

It was sent to 157,000 sisters, and 139,691 of them responded, many assuming that the poll was a church-sanctioned document, which it wasn't. Some of the questions it posed appear to have been drawn more from *The Changing Sister* than Vatican II. They raised issues that the gentlemen in Rome had never considered.

Sisters, many of them bone-weary after long hours of teaching or working in hospitals, poised their pencils over statements like these:

49. "I think that sisters who feel called to do so ought to be witnessing to Christ on the picket line and speaking out on con-

troversial issues, as well as performing with professional com-
petence among their lay peers in science labs, at conferences,
and on speaker's platforms."

99. "I feel that communities of the future should consist of small
groups of sisters living a shared life by doing different kinds
of work."

134. "When I think of social reform, I think of things I believe in
so deeply I could dedicate all my efforts to them."

495. "Do you think all sisters should be allowed to wear contemporary dress at all times?"

535. "Do you think some sisters in the United States should get
involved in civic protest movements?"

513. "Would you stand up for a sister's right in conscience to
speak, write, march, demonstrate, picket, etc. when this con-
flicts with a higher superior's or a bishop's wishes?"

644. "All authentic law is by its very nature flexible and can be
changed by the community in which it is operative."

This survey arrived at a critical moment, when many orders of nuns
were already absorbed in unprecedented disputes over whether and how
to change their habits and their rules in the wake of Vatican II. "I was a
novice when the questionnaire came out. I remember people staying up
nights to do it. It was the buzz," recalls Sister Mary Waskowiak, a Mercy
sister from Oakland, California.

In the sixties, there was a lot of buzz in the air. This is the memory of
Sister Doris Gottemoeller, who was then just beginning to teach chemistry in Mount Mercy High School, an all-girls school in a campuslike setting in Cincinnati. "I loved what I was doing. I was not unhappy. But as
new opportunities appeared, the rightness of them was self-evident and in
some ways exhilarating. When the Council started and you were in the
1960s, thoughts that you never had before were just part of the air you
were breathing."

Vatican II had called for religious orders to consult with their members and discuss what changes ought to be made. This, by itself, was a revolutionary opportunity. Discussions about rules just did not occur among
the Mercies. The Mother Provincial, the woman who presided over the
Mercies in the Cincinnati area, simply wrote in a book each year what the

sisters under her command would be doing the next year and that was it. She wrote it down. They did it.

At Mother of Mercy High School, where the book said Sister Doris should go, younger sisters, she recalls, were "aching" to discuss this assignment system and other matters. Up to that point, the rules of the congregation were whatever the school's mother superior, a respected woman, decided they should be.

Before the first meeting on the Vatican II changes, Sister Doris made an interesting discovery. Her mother superior had never held a discussion before and worried that the sisters might not welcome one. So Sister Doris and a friend volunteered to organize the meeting. The first omen of change that night, as the sisters assembled in the convent, was a young sister. She was sitting proudly in the front row minus her veil. "That was revolutionary in those days," Sister Doris recalls.

Meanwhile, many of the older sisters—the veteran teachers at the school—were collecting in the back rows. Many of them were hostile to the notion of discussing rules they had become comfortable with over the years. Some were heard muttering about it while the two younger sisters attempted to explain the agenda they had prepared. This made trying to explain something as complicated as Vatican II very difficult. "So we just moved our chairs to the back of the room," explained Sister Doris. Grudgingly, the convent's first discussion began anew.

Not all younger sisters shared Sister Doris's enthusiasm. Sister Joan D. Chittister, a Benedictine sister from Erie, Pennsylvania, remembers going home in 1968 to tell her parents she was quitting. She wasn't leaving religious life, she told them. "It's leaving me. Everything is falling apart. Nothing is the same anymore. There's no reason to stay. People don't want to teach; they don't want to wear the habit; they don't want to live together. I have to leave while I'm still young enough to be able to make a living."

Her father, a Protestant who had objected to her entering in the first place, suggested that she reconsider. "Who would take care of the older sisters if all the young ones left?" he wanted to know. It was a very good and timely question. His daughter returned to the convent.

The most disturbing part for Sister Mary Roberta, then in her early fifties, teaching college history in Cedar Rapids, was watching sisters who had worked with one another quietly for years beginning to split along

generational lines. The younger ones were pushing for more experimentation, fewer rules, fewer prayers. They were pressuring older ones to conform to what they saw as actions mandated by Vatican II.

"There were people whom you felt were good thinkers and you
watched them fall to the pressure. A friend who watched this with me said
she found it hard to believe educated people picking up everything that
comes along without asking why."

Fewer prayers? For Sister Roberta and many of the older sisters, the
quiet moments they spent together in the chapel were an essential part of
their day. They drew strength from it. They had seen the hopes of the
early sixties dashed by assassinations, riots and ominous rumblings from
the Cold War. Now this.

"I remembered sisters saying that we needed to have fewer prayers
and not spend so much time in chapel, strange statements like that. I can
remember a sister that I respected saying 'we're coming into serious
times. We should not be talking about taking away prayers but adding
some."

The wide-ranging discussions, she recalls, "were difficult for me
because my life had always been so happy. Everything was so positive and
then all of a sudden there was a disruption. The thing that was painful,
apart from changing the habit, was people going off to live in apartments.
That to me broke up our community spirit. . . . It was kind of do your
own thing where you were used to doing things together and sharing."

Sister Kathryn Rae Thornton, a younger Mercy who was one of Sister
Roberta's students, remembers a summer meeting among the Cedar
Rapids Mercies that took up a whole week in the summer of 1968. "There
was genuine conflict and disagreement. There was a lot of expression of
fear of losing what many people called our identifying factors, you know,
conformity. There was certainly a struggle over power and authority."

She recalls many of the younger sisters raising issues from Sister Neal's
survey. Informed debates, or "dialoguing," as she calls it, later became the
measure of her way of religious life, not rules laid down by some superior.
"If you believe that all of life is revelatory, then the will of the superior
isn't the only sacred voice." She was among the first of the younger sisters
to leave the convent at Mount Mercy to experiment with an alternative
lifestyle, living with a few friends in a nearby apartment.

Some of the most emotional "dialoguing" occurred over proposals to change the order's floor-length, 135-year-old black habit. While it was hot and unsanitary, blocked side vision and was, in its later polyester versions, a fire hazard, older sisters brought it into the debate as a symbol of stability and as a sign of their dedication. Younger sisters wanted an end to the habit altogether.

After considering more than thirty modifications and making sure that every sister had had her say, the order selected a midcalf-length model fashioned by a home economics teacher in Detroit. Gone was the helmet-like coif that framed the face and the starched white guimpe that concealed the bosom. It its place was a simple veil that exposed some of the sister's hair. Instead of the traditional black, it was dark navy blue.

The next hurdle, like all post–Vatican II changes, was to get it approved by Rome. American officials there were picky. It was too short, too form fitting, they said. But the Mercies, working through some Italian contacts, went over their heads and arranged a personal viewing for the Italian cardinal who decided such matters. He liked it and that was that.

Rome, in those days, was still supportive of Catholic sisters. While the Americans there kept pressing for more regulation, the Italians had a more relaxed, appreciative attitude. Mercy officials once watched two junior-level Vatican officials, an American and an Italian, tangle over how to deal with nuns.

The Italian's view was that the women's great success in America was a gift from the Holy Spirit, who guides the development of the Church. The Italian, a Father Gambari, finally silenced the American with: "Father, we can only attempt to assist, to further the Spirit's work. It is not ours to control or to dictate the Spirit's movements!"

After all of the debates over the habit, the new model lasted for only about five years. In the 1970s, at the urging of younger sisters, wearing of the habit became optional and many sisters opted for blue blazers, pantsuits and sometimes sweatpants and jeans. The velocity of the changes that were being implemented in many orders continued to accelerate.

American universities also had a hand in this relentless push for more changes. While the sister of the fifties may have started with the proverbial "school of hard knocks" and then labored through twenty years of summer-school classes to get her basic college degree, the young sisters of the late sixties and early seventies often had advanced degrees. Their immersion in higher education was occurring at the same time when the nation's campuses were becoming immersed in radical politics.

Maurice Isserman and Michael Kazin, two historians, have written a book about the 1960s, called *America Divided*. It talks about the forming of "an alternative America" that spun, in part, out of the campuses: "The dissenters advocated pacifism instead of Cold War, racial and class equality instead of a hierarchy of wealth and status, a politics that prized direct democracy over the clash of interest groups, a frankness toward sex instead of a rigid split between the public and the intimate, and a boredom with cultural institutions—from schools to supermarkets."

In their deliberations over how to modernize their rules, many orders drew on campus experts, ranging from psychotherapists to a group of reformers that became known as the "travelling theologians." One of the latter, Rev. Bryan Hehir, then teaching ethics at St. John's Seminary in Brighton, Massachusetts, addressed an assemblage of Mercies. According to the sisters' account, he told them that the hospitals and schools they ran were a "parallel presence" that had become "apostolically ineffective" because the government now provided similar services.

Then there were the sisters returning from the campuses, such as Sister Helen Rose, a Sister of Divine Providence, who emerged from graduate study in sociology at Columbia University to launch a behavioral study on why sisters had begun to leave her order in droves. "In the course of analyzing data, I became one of my own statistics," she explains in one of her books. She left the order and married a divorced man.

Later, in a further analysis of shrinking religious orders, she gives us a gentle reminder of her newly acquired faith. Orders of nuns might survive, she says, but she's not optimistic. "Miracles can happen; however such happenings are beyond the sociologist's abilities to predict."

Sister Joan D. Chittister, the Benedictine sister from Erie, Pennsylvania, who almost left her order in protest of Vatican II, was later sent to Pennsylvania State University to get a doctorate in communications. When she came back she was considerably more radical. After she became the head of the order, she persuaded her fellow nuns to begin preaching nuclear disarmament in its schools. Her sisters took a lot of "battering," she recalls, from priests and especially parents.

"They took kids out of our schools. The mail, day after day, said: 'You people are crazy. I don't want my family to have anything to do with a bunch of radicals.' "

In 1966 the Sisters of St. Joseph of Peace in Newark, New Jersey, sat down to review their order's history, following the dictates of Vatican II. They discovered the story of their order's foundress, an Englishwoman named Margaret Anna Cusack. She and her works had come under an order of suppression by the Vatican. She had written something Rome disagreed with.

"Before the sessions ended, the lid was off, and convent routine would never again be neatly laid out by superiors," recalled Sister Dorothy Vidulich, one of the nuns in the order. After reinstating Mother Cusack's memory, the order sold its New Jersey mother house and moved to Washington to take up its newly chosen mission: lobbying Congress about world hunger, the need for disarmament and human rights violations.

Sister Vidulich celebrated Holy Week by throwing vials of blood on White House pillars. She organized demonstrations against nuclear-tipped missiles and met with Sandinista leaders.

Under the old rules, the convent's walls and its routines tended to filter out the noise of the world and focus sisters on their mission. Under the new rules, the concerns of the day became paramount, and often, routine went out the window. Young sisters at Benedictine Sisters at St. Walburga Monastery in Elizabeth, New Jersey, bonded together on the roof of the monastery in 1968, after spending many forbidden hours there smoking and brooding about the assassination of Robert Kennedy and what they felt to be the horrors of the United States' role in the Vietnam War.

"When we got to the roof and began to talk about what was going on in our hearts, we really began to talk to God in a group," recalled Sister Kathleen McNany. During her order's deliberations over Vatican II changes, forty-three members of the roof group left the order and went to Baltimore to start their own order. Their new rules discarded the habit altogether and adopted a feminist liturgy.

The "sexual revolution" was also prowling the streets in the late sixties. Sisters sometimes brought that into their new deliberations. How should they deal with men? Sister Theresa Padovano was disturbed by rumors that Loyola University in Chicago had begun holding "mixers" for nuns and priests, so she refused to go there to get an advanced degree in theology.

Instead, Sister Padovano, a Sister of Charity from Leavenworth, Kansas, went to St. Mary's Seminary in Houston, Texas. There she fell in love with a priest, one of her theology professors, and eventually married him. "It was like being knocked off a horse, like [St.] Paul," she recalled.

At the time, Sister Sharon Burns, the former bobby-soxer turned schoolteacher, was opening a new chapter in her career. She was attending summer school at Notre Dame University, studying for an advanced degree in theology. There were a number of nuns in the class. There were also a number of younger priests.

While their teachers explored the nature of God as described in the Scriptures, some of the students found themselves exploring a less rarified form of nature: the forbidden magic of sexual attraction. "A younger sister who sat in front of me left her order. The one in back of me married a Jesuit. My roommate married a Jesuit. I began to think, 'Is something wrong with me?'"

Other sisters, she found, were going through the same turmoil. Some were upset at the change in the habit. Others said they were uncomfortable because this wasn't the order they had entered. "People were really suffering," Sister Burns recalls. She wasn't in love with wearing the habit, nor did she have any romantic notion of the nuns who taught her in high school, because she had gone to public school. "The reason I entered was to serve God in some way and God's people and that mission was still there. So I decided to stay."

In 1967, Mother Mary Regina Cunningham, the head of the Mercy Province in Chicago, found herself in the difficult position of referee in one round of this great intergenerational fight. Thirteen younger sisters, faculty members from Xavier College, sent her a letter saying there was "great suffering" among their ranks that might cause many to leave.

The suffering might ease, they suggested, if they could choose roommates, live in apartments and pick their own work assignments. That brought an emotional riposte from thirty older sisters who were teaching at Mercy High School on Prairie Avenue. "Those of us who took our vows thirty, forty or more years ago made a contract with the community. We have kept our part of it and expect the community we have loved and served to do the same."

Sister Mary Genevieve Crane, a nurse from another high school, accused Mother Regina of provoking the situation by failing to crack down on younger sisters. She complained of "the short skirts, the drinking and smoking in Regina hall till all hours of the morning. The sisters out in cars on the city streets late at night, even midnight, and the endless hours of watching television."

Sister Mary Monica Idzikowski, one of the Mercy High School teachers, said if the younger sisters "ultimatum" worked, she might hold her own demonstration. "If I have to take off and go to [downtown] Chicago, you will hear about it. I will take a portable amplifier, a good broom, a better shotgun and Squad Six and we will have ourselves a riot."

In sum, convents were not a peaceful place to be in the aftermath of Vatican II. Sister Judy Ward, a Sister of Mercy and a recovering alcoholic, now treats alcoholics in a hospital in New Jersey. She recalled that she . started drinking heavily in the late sixties. "These are the years of change. These are the years that most nuns left the convent. But I survived it all, and I might have Dewars to thank for it."

While the internal debates and the voting over how to comply with the true spirit of Vatican II went on and on, the numbers of young women wanting to enter convents suddenly dropped to record lows. Within the ranks of the Mercies, by 1971 nearly one out of six sisters had voted against religious life with her feet. It was much the same in other orders and this was just the beginning of the exodus.

The great, selfless machine that had spread hope, shaped young minds and nursed sufferers for generations in America had begun to falter. It had survived wars, plagues, frontier life, numbing poverty and mindless bigotry, but something about the tumultuous 1960s was beginning to destroy it.

This, of course, provoked a new round of questions from the intellectuals who helped spur the process of reform in the first place. Sister Marie Augusta Neal, the sociologist who prepared the influential sisters' "survey" in 1965, wrote a book in 1990. In it she raises a profound question: "Where have all the sisters gone?"

18

COLLISION

There is the call of a trumpet. It summons a thousand people who parade in hand-painted, brightly colored ponchos to hear Mass. As the ancient ceremony nears its end, they are engulfed in clouds of balloons. The balloons burst, showering the people kneeling in the pews with confetti. The worshippers file out, singing hymns, waving banners. A bagpiper leads them farther up a hill to a broad green lawn . . . and a party! There are tables laden with five hundred loaves of bread and five hundred baskets of fruit.

In the Catholic Church, May is the month of Mary, the mother of Jesus Christ. And Sister Mary Humiliata, who heads the order called the Sisters of the Most Holy and Immaculate Heart of the Blessed Virgin Mary, is not a woman who does things by halves. This is a full-blown festival, staged by her protégé, Sister Corita, an artist and one of the freer spirits of the 1960s. Scruffy men in coveralls—a CBS film crew—scramble to capture all these images as the order celebrates what many believe to be the beginning of a golden age of spiritual experimentation—the world after Vatican II.

The IHMs, as they are known, have traditionally drawn many young women from Los Angeles's Catholic elite. The order came from Spain in the 1870s and its teachers later became the mainstay of the city's parochial school system. From their lawn in Hollywood Hills, where the sisters and their many friends are dining, they can see their mission and the peculiar challenge it presents. The vastness of Los Angeles, then the fastest-growing city in the world, sprawls beneath them.

A young blond man who moves with the easy grace of a surfer takes off his many-hued poncho and drapes it over the shoulders of a white statue of the Virgin. "She looked like a woman, like a natural woman, who loved color and life," wrote Ned O'Gorman, who reported the scene for the *National Catholic Reporter*. He, like many others, was swept away by the joy of the day and the vibrant, palpable faith of the sisters.

But Mother Humiliata, sponsor of these revels, knew there was trouble just ahead. She had set her order on a path that guaranteed a collision with James Francis Cardinal McIntyre, the crusty ruler of the four-county Archdiocese of Los Angeles and one of the most outspokenly conservative leaders in the American Church. Within three years, many of the revelers on this Mary's Day field would be pitted against one another in a bitter civil war.

Historians have not yet settled their accounts of America in the 1960s, but one emerging theory is that it was the most culturally defining, divisive and "stormiest decade since the Civil War." Within a few short years an age of almost boundless optimism was suddenly transformed. Now, on a more darkly lit stage, a deep cynicism about government and a mistrust of all social institutions—especially churches—was spreading rapidly.

When it comes to confrontations, Mother Humiliata—who received this religious name from an obscure saint—is maybe humbled before God, but stubborn in her contrition. She does not intend to lose. Then forty-four, she had entered the order as Anita Caspary, the daughter of conservative German parents. She had earned a doctorate in English from Stanford and headed the department at the order's college, Immaculate Heart College.

In 1963 she was elected the head of her order, an office she says she did not seek or want. Up to then the IHMs were most famous for running an elite academy for girls and the college for women. As Monsignor Francis J. Weber later acknowledged in his biography of Cardinal McIntyre, the institutions of the IHMs were revered in the city. He said they were "among the most precious adornments of the Catholic Church in California."

In 1968 Mother Humiliata and almost four hundred of her sisters, two-thirds of the order, would reject their religious vows and leave religious life, an act without precedent in America. Priests, sisters, theologians, bishops and other Catholic thinkers have spent decades since then fencing with each other over the meaning of the deep fissure that suddenly formed within the order. Millions of Catholics would wonder how such an impasse could emerge so quickly and drain some thirty-nine area schools of the order's teaching talent.

Mother Humiliata still feels that she was only trying to add to the order's adornment. A parade of reform-minded theologians had convinced her that she was carrying out the will of the still-unfinished church council called Vatican II. The cardinal, a participant of Vatican II, felt otherwise. He thought some of these "reformers" were so radical that he refused permission for them to visit the IHMs, but Mother Humiliata received them anyway, in secret. It was just one of several clandestine experiments she had underway.

In the spring of 1965, when the cardinal was still shuttling back and forth from the Vatican II deliberations in Rome, he had already learned about some of the IHM experiments. He ran the Archdiocese of Los Angeles with an accountant's eye for detail and knew, according to Monsignor Weber, that there were an unusually large number of IHM sisters petitioning the archdiocese for permission to leave religious life.

Parents of schoolchildren and pastors of parishes that had parochial schools were reporting to him that IHM sisters were beginning to teach some strange new ideas in religion classes. There were even reports of IHM sisters seen riding bicycles and wearing pedal pushers.

A New Yorker, the son of an Irish mounted policeman who once patrolled Central Park, Cardinal McIntyre was an unusual combination of priest-comptroller. As a boy he had doted on Horatio Alger's rags-to-riches books. He worked his way through night school at City College and Columbia University by being a runner for stock traders on Wall Street. In 1915, when he felt the call to become a priest, he was twenty-eight years old and a property manager for a prospering attorney.

When he emerged from the seminary in 1921, he had an appealing combination of handsome charm, deep faith and the street smarts of a seasoned navigator of the financial district. Francis Cardinal Spellman soon put him to work overhauling the New York archdiocese's archaic bookkeeping system.

He later put Father McIntyre on the fast track to becoming a bishop. "He has been to me all things that one man can be to another," Cardinal Spellman was to explain later, after he had persuaded Rome to send Bishop McIntyre to take over the Los Angeles diocese in 1948.

By the 1960s Cardinal McIntyre, then approaching eighty and fighting various physical infirmities, had come to resemble, in the words of one of his priests, "an aging lion, who was no longer king of the forest." But he still knew a jungle when he saw one. When the fuss over the IHMs' experimentation first emerged, he quietly turned over the matter to the Vatican's Sacred Congregation of Religious. These were the Church's doctrinal police and they launched a "visitation," the Church's euphemism for an investigation.

In November 1965, Mother Humiliata was in Rome, just another happy face in the crowd watching the closing ceremonies of Vatican II. "I was in the middle of all the excitement when I got the call from home. There were visitations going on in all the convents. Teams of priests were being sent to ask questions of all the nuns."

"I came home fast," she recalls. When she arrived, she found sisters had been questioned about minute details of their daily lives. When and how long did they pray? What novels did they read? She was summoned to the cardinal's office, where McIntyre confronted her with summaries of the reports from the "visitators." He told her that her order wasn't leading a proper religious life. The cardinal concluded by giving her sixty days to straighten things out.

Mother Humiliata felt the investigations were unjust, but insists that at almost every turn she tried to placate the elderly cardinal. She sent him reassuring letters, but meanwhile consulted with her own theological experts. "It was no longer a regulated life that we were looking at," she says of the order's post–Vatican II plans. But before revealing these plans, she wanted to give herself more time to build support within the Catholic community.

Mary Kirchen, who entered the order in 1966, remembers the workshops and retreats. Vatican II, she was told, was going to shift the focus of the order to causes of social justice, like the Civil Rights Movement and the war against poverty. "We were all sitting there like little sponges saying yes, tell us about this."

Jeanne Cordova, then eighteen, rolled up in front of the mother house in Hollywood Hills in her father's gold Cadillac. It was September 6, 1966. Like many young women then, she had longed to be a nun since childhood, but she was trying to be cool about it. She was wearing her favorite James Dean–style sunglasses. Her father, a West Point graduate, liked what he had heard about the order over the years. The IHMs were, he told his daughter, "a disciplined outfit."

Nothing, she recalled later, turned out to be what she'd expected. Instead of a quiet time in the order's novitiate praying and learning about religious life, she was told that the novices would begin their religious life by living for a time in poor neighborhoods. Habits were sometimes regarded as being optional. And she would not get the religious name derived from the saints she had chosen—"Sister Paul Francis." Instead she would be, simply, Sister Jeanne Cordova.

There were constant struggles between younger and older sisters about many of these changes, but now everything was settled by votes. To her surprise, Sister Cordova found her vote was equal to that of the order's most senior member. "As the youngest members of the community, we were called into play mostly as guinea pigs. The changes were being wrought upon our lifestyle by liberals who thought our age put us on their side. I wasn't so sure whose side I was on—neither were the others . . . most of us were very attracted to the habit and the faith." Overall, she recalls, "we were ambivalent, confused and resentful."

She attended classes at Immaculate Heart College. She described it as "a radical intellectual oasis" where Sister Corita and her group of art students tended to set an atmosphere of spontaneity with few rules. The campus hosted frequent anti–Vietnam War demonstrations that would have shocked her father.

She was assigned to teach three times a week at a black school in Watts, where she learned a different kind of radicalism, which shocked her. "For weeks," she later recalled, "I endured 'honky do-goody' and 'stupid bitch,' to name two endearments I understand."

The fledgling nun gradually grew to care about people at the school, but life in the convent continued to unsettle her. There were few routines or schedules. She visited a downtown convent, near the cathedral, and remembers younger sisters sitting around in jeans, smoking and watching *Peyton Place* on television while a couple of older sisters, still wearing the order's blue habit, "walked around with a dazed look."

She began to think of the order as being "caught in a time warp, implementing a futuristic reality" that Cardinal McIntyre, she had learned, was dead set against. Although she was now teaching religion, she felt herself drifting away from it. Sister Cordova soon stopped going to Mass and devoted a lot of her time to reading news magazines and tracts by "new wave" theologians.

In the summer of 1967, while still answering questions from Rome about the first visitation, Mother Humiliata began yet another experiment. She had learned that the head of the Western Behavioral Sciences Institute, a psychologist named Carl Rogers, had received foundation grants for an ambitious experiment. He was looking for an entire school system that would agree to try his brand of group "encounter therapy."

The institute, based in La Jolla, California, had developed a technique of "nondirective psychotherapy" using sessions designed to get people to describe their inner feelings. Dr. Rogers, who had originally developed it to treat neurotics, thought it might be a way to improve communications in a large institution.

It was part Freud, part California, part sixties and part disaster, according to Dr. William Coulson, the leader of the institute's project with the IHMs. Another psychologist, Dr. Coulson helped train fifty-eight "facilitators" to conduct the sessions with the sisters and their students. About half of the freshly trained facilitators were priests or sisters from other orders. They, too, were eager to experiment with ways that might "liberate" people's thinking in the coming new age.

"I thought I was helping to make them [the sisters] more virtuous," explained Dr. Coulson, who used the fact that he was a Catholic and a University of Notre Dame graduate to sell the IHMs on the experiment. He found that the technique helped break down what structure remained in the IHMs. It attacked the notion of faith and quiet self-sacrifice that had made the order such a fixture in Los Angeles in the first place.

But evidence that this grand-scale experiment might be dangerous to the order came in only gradually. "Yeah, we attacked their faith," he admits in an interview, "but only in terms of a deeper faith, a Freudian faith if you will."

Two hundred and fifty of the sisters volunteered for the sessions, though Dr. Coulson says he found out later that some of the "volunteers" thought they had been ordered to attend. The "workshops" went off and on for three years. The psychologist recalls some fairly bizarre scenes.

There was a Sister Lucy, who taught a college course in educational methods. She invited a facilitator to hold an encounter session involving her and her class. After three hours in which the students freely aired their own feelings, for themselves, for each other, for old boyfriends—the sessions tended to be wide-ranging—the sister began to open up. As a sister and their teacher, she admitted, she found it very, very hard to talk about her own feelings toward them.

As the teacher began to cry, Dr. Coulson sat down beside her, taking her hand. Then one of her male students—the college had recently gone co-ed—held her in his arms, as she continued to cry.

One of Dr. Coulson's staff members reported a two-day encounter session in which an older, lay teacher, attacked one of the sisters for being too sure of herself. She was "much too good to be true. You're just like my sister!" the woman blurted out. The sister began to weep as the lay teacher continued on, flashing back to a traumatic experience of her childhood.

"This set off a period of sobbing which must have lasted twenty minutes," reported the staff member. The older woman left the room, followed by the principal of her school. After they had left, one of the younger lay teachers asked the facilitator, indignantly: "Do you think this sort of thing helps anyone?"

Dr. Coulson held a marathon session with IHM students at his home in La Jolla that lasted from eight P.M. Saturday to the following Sunday afternoon. It might have ended earlier, he writes, but the group got in such a "deep emotional situation" that he had to take extra time to work it out. "All in all, the group seemed to the participants as well as the facilitators as probably being deeper, more emotional, more 'violent' than was helpful."

The major participants in the sessions were a group of sisters who had been elected to represent the others in a formal chapter meeting where they would write the new, post–Vatican II rules for the order. As he listened to them talk, Dr. Coulson says he became aware that there were real, angry differences among these women, or as he later put it in his report, "evidence of organizational conflict." One bloc of sisters, a minority, resented the experimentation. "They felt compromised by the groups and were bitter that the school system had casually agreed to three years of much deep, personal experimentation."

The chapter meeting was held in the summer of 1967 and many more things were changed, but the main thrust of the document, at least as far as the cardinal was concerned, was a set of demands aimed at the part of the Church that he had spent much of his time developing. This was Los Angeles's parochial school system. While the growth of school systems in other parts of the country was putting strains on sisters, Los Angeles's system was literally exploding. Cardinal McIntyre was opening a new school every other week.

As the largest teaching order in the system, the IHMs thought they had enough leverage to change teaching conditions. They wanted class size reduced to between thirty-five and forty students per teacher. They wanted principals to operate full-time with full authority to run the schools. They wanted teaching contracts with parishes, adequate money for class materials, training and the right to withdraw from a parish that wouldn't accept their terms.

It amounted to a collective bargaining agreement, and had the cardinal accepted it, it would have cured a major defect in parochial schools and, perhaps, served as a model for the rest of the country. But that was not to be.

There are two versions of the cardinal's reaction in October, when he learned of the new rules. Mother Humiliata, who now uses her real name, Anita Caspary, says that one day after the sisters revealed their proposed rules, she was summoned to the cardinal's office. She saw his "Irish temper" explode, not over the demands about the school system, which she thinks he hadn't read, but over a rule that made the wearing of the habit optional. "He said, 'It looks to me that you're going into the schools

Anita Caspary (formerly known as Mother Mary Humiliata). (COURTESY OF ANITA CASPARY)

wearing secular clothes. If you do it, you're out of my schools.' We were fired. It sounds weird, but it really happened."

The head of the IHMs explained to the cardinal that she couldn't change the rule; the chapter's word was the order's law. Nonsense, she recalls the cardinal telling her. "That can't be true. I can change what my bishops do."

Monsignor Weber, the cardinal's biographer, insists that Cardinal McIntyre "paid scant if any attention to the habit issue." It was the threat of withdrawing from the schools that, he says, set off the cardinal during the October meeting. McIntyre, he says, considered it to be "an ultimatum that does not even admit to discussion." And, since the sisters had dared to make such a threat, the cardinal accepted it.

After the meeting, says Monsignor Weber, the cardinal wrote a report to Rome that said he had no intention of allowing "our convents to become hotels or boarding houses for women."

In October and again in December, a majority of the IHM chapter voted again to support Mother Humiliata's stand. Various attempts by the cardinal's bishops to work out a compromise failed. Most Catholic newspapers supported the cardinal. One paper called it "the first time in America that nuns ever tried to bully a cardinal."

The head of the IHMs then escalated the battle, taking her case to the press. She told the *Los Angeles Times* that her chapter's actions were a "major breakthrough" for Catholic nuns in America. *Newsweek* highlighted the dispute by featuring Sister Corita, the order's artistic sprite, in a cover article entitled "The Modern Nun." Mother Humiliata reemphasized the point with *The New York Times*. "We have many other sisters like her [Sister Corita] and we hope to have even more diversity and freedom."

Catholic intellectuals lined up behind the nuns. One of them, John Cogly, even went so far as to call the IHMs a "liberal light shining in the ultra-conservative darkness of the Los Angeles Archdiocese."

By this time the IHMs were the subject of a second "visitation" from Rome. The new investigator was Rev. Thomas R. Gallagher, a Dominican priest from Washington, D.C. After interviewing the sisters, he concluded that they no longer wanted to be a religious order under canon, or church law.

In February, based on Father Gallagher's finding, the Sacred Congregation of Religious in Rome issued its decrees. The papers of Vatican II, with their vaguely worded statements about the need for experiments by women's religious orders that had invited the reform movement in the first place, were barely three years old. There was nothing vague about this new directive. To continue to serve within the church, it said, the IHMs must:

1. Wear a uniform habit.
2. Have daily prayers and attend mass.
3. Recognize that the main point of education is to save souls.
4. Obey the Cardinal.

Mother Humiliata appealed the decision to the pope, reinforcing it with a drive to get the community and other orders of sisters to send supporting petitions to Rome. She sent a letter to all 7,500 parents of the students whom the IHMs were teaching, explaining that the cardinal had asked the sisters to withdraw from the schools. Cardinal McIntyre, who disliked dealing with the press, took it upon himself to explain his stand to the *Los Angeles Times*. He hadn't fired the nuns, they quit.

A panel of American bishops, asked by Rome to review the dispute, did what they could. But by this time the IHMs, once the "adornment" of Catholic Los Angeles, had been reduced to the ecclesiastical equivalent of Humpty Dumpty. The old organization was shattered. The bishops blessed an arrangement by which sixty dissenters within the IHMs were allowed to continue as a religious community and continue teaching—but under the old rules.

After the majority of IHMs left teaching, in June 1968, Mother Humiliata found herself in a box. "Our intention throughout this was to always remain, but to change whatever makes it difficult for us to operate in the modern world," she explains. But her faction in the order, about four hundred sisters, couldn't live with the decrees from Rome. In 1970, they requested to be dispensed from their vows. "This is unthinkable for most nuns," she notes.

The unthinkable was allowed to happen. There was a property settlement arranged between the two factions. A hundred and fifty sisters followed Anita Caspary into an order of women not considered to be a religious order by the Church. The majority of sisters caught in this collision between the unstoppable "reform" and the unmovable cardinal did what many young sisters were doing in the late 1960s. They faded away, joining the turbulent background of the age, leaving religious life altogether.

"Interestingly," Monsignor Weber points out in his brief for the cardinal, "there was never any great groundswell of support for the sisters in many other [religious] communities locally or nationally." That appears to be true. Most other orders of nuns simply sat on their hands during the three years of turmoil.

This may have more to do with America than Rome. The shocks the late 1960s delivered to the nation were profound. A parade of demonstrations, riots, assassinations and rebellious rhetoric had left the nation divided but in a distinctly conservative mood. The majority in 1968 voted for the more conservative candidate, Richard Nixon. Catholics in Los Angeles were no different. Most wound up supporting their cardinal.

To be sure, there were plenty of Church intellectuals still eager to put their fang marks on the flanks of the old lion. Rev. Andrew Greely, the sociologist, called Cardinal McIntyre a reactionary. The Church's decision to drive the majority of IHMs out of the Church, he insisted, "was one of the greatest tragedies in the history of American Catholicism."

Whatever it was, there were to be no more joyous celebrations of Mary's Day on Immaculate Heart's parklike campus in the Hollywood Hills. Without the Church's support, donors and incoming students shied away. Lacking the resources to support itself, the college was sold in 1980. Its buildings and its setting now belong to the American Film Institute.

Sister Corita, the producer of the holy festivities and, supposedly, the prototype for the "modern nun," later left the order to become simply Corita, a full-time artist. She died in 1986 leaving a legacy of bright prints, often with poetry, philosophy and song lyrics imbedded in the graphics. Her most famous work: the design for the twenty-two-cent "Love" postage stamp.

Jeanne Cordova, the novice who was troubled but also shaped by the chaos and noise of reform, left the order to become the president of the Los Angeles chapter of the Daughters of Bilitis, a support group for gay rights.

Dr. William Coulson, the Catholic psychologist who led the encounter therapy experiment with the IHMs, later spent a considerable time apologizing for his techniques, yet boasting of their power. "We corrupted a whole raft of religious orders on the West Coast in the sixties by getting the nuns and the priests to talk about their distress," he once told the editor of a conservative Catholic magazine. (Anita Caspary insists he "exaggerates" his role. "I would have never remembered William Coulson specifically if he had not promoted his own inaccurate and negative critique of our community decisions.")

Cardinal McIntyre resigned in 1970, once his ordeal with the IHMs had ended. He became a simple parish priest at St. Basil's Church on busy Wilshire Boulevard. He heard confessions, answered sick calls and could be seen out on the sidewalk kibitzing with parishoners after Sunday Mass, recalls one of his fans, Kevin Starr. Despite all the attacks on the cardinal for being a reactionary, Starr still sees him as the "embodiment of the type of priest and bishop who built Roman Catholicism in this nation."

Anita Caspary works with a remnant of her former order in a loose-knit community of 170 people, including a few men and non-Catholics. It is called the Immaculate Heart Community and it sponsors a high school, a medical center and a retreat center. It also has a college center that offers the nation's only master's program on "feminist spirituality," which dwells on many of the issues raised in the fight with Cardinal McIntyre.

Most of the community's members work at jobs in the city and live in apartments. The average age is sixty-eight. Asked whether, in retrospect, she would have done anything in the 1960s differently, Ms. Caspary brightens up and shakes her head. "I'm happy it was done. It would be much easier today. We would have the support of sisters in this country and others, too."

19

BREAKDOWN

In 1968, the seismic year of riots, radicals, demonstrations, assassinations, hedonism, drugs, moon landings and many smaller jolts that hit American culture, Mary Scullion, then sixteen, registered a little shock of her own. A slim, bright sophomore at Little Flower Catholic High School in Philadelphia, she had spent the summer working with inner-city children at a camp run by the Sisters of Mercy.

When she returned to her family's neat brick row house at the end of the summer, she told them: "This is what I want to do, be a Sister of Mercy." For her mother and father, Sheila and Joseph Scullion, this was a bit unsettling.

This was their little girl who excelled at math, had a habit of racing through the living room on her tiptoes and, when the mood struck her, did a little soft shoe to her favorite song, Simon and Garfunkel's "Feelin' Groovy."

She wants to enter a convent?

Like most Catholics in the late sixties, her parents had a sense that Mary would be swimming against the tide. Young women were leaving the convent in droves. Catholics weren't quite sure what was going on, but they knew it was extraordinary. Looking back, it is easy to see why they were concerned. After more than a century of steady growth, between 1965 and 1980, fifty thousand nuns—30 percent of the sisters in the United States—departed from religious life. It was a crippling blow to school systems, hospitals and other Catholic institutions that were geared to run on an ever-growing supply of young sisters. Meanwhile the numbers of Catholics and, for a while, the ranks of parish priests continued to grow.

The Scullion family worked out a compromise. Mary could go, if she still wanted to, after she finished her first year of college. And that she did, only to discover another ominous sign of the times. The Mercy's novitiate, in suburban Merion, Pennsylvania, had a dormitory built to accommodate as many as thirty incoming women a year. In Mary Scullion's year there were only four novices rattling around in there. Two of them later left.

Among the full-fledged sisters, there were still strong tensions over the changes the order had gone through in the 1960s. Memories of the head-on collision between the IHMs in Los Angeles and James Francis Cardinal McIntyre were fresh. The Mercies tended to side with the IHMs. Other orders of sisters were going through some of the same battles and experiments.

Meanwhile, the American hierarchy, the men who ran the Church, had seen Cardinal McIntyre's painful roasting in the press for interfering with "reform." They had also seen 10 percent of his parochial schoolteachers walk out on him.

While many bishops shared some of the cardinal's misgivings about reforms, in the 1970s bishops seemed to have decided that, for a while, it would be better for them to find something to worry about besides what was going on in the convents.

Meantime, there was this trickle of newcomers, the youngest nuns. "For those of us who were entering, the changes were welcomed by us because we didn't know anything else," explains Sister Anne Crampsie, who entered as a novice in the same class as Mary Scullion. "But the older sisters found it troublesome. We could see the unrest the changes had created."

In this charged atmosphere, the younger women quickly became leaders. Some found they could strike out and invent their own missions because the old rules of obedience and the rigid schedules of convent life were over. Nearly everything was determined by votes now, not commands. After she became a full-fledged Mercy in 1975, Sister Mary Scullion taught seventh grade in an inner-city school, St. Malachy's, where she had tutored in high school.

While she loved the children, Sister Mary, as the students called her, craved more action. She was kind of a throwback to an earlier era in America when sisters were drawn to the challenge of the frontier. A Jesuit priest, Rev. Ed Brady, got her involved in Saint Joseph's University's Justice and Peace Program, which was focused on urban homelessness.

About this time state mental institutions began releasing their patients. The reigning theory of the day was that most of the mentally ill should no longer be "warehoused." "Mainstreaming" them into society, it was felt, was a better solution. Sister Mary began working weekends to help the Mercies start a small hospice for the homeless who began accumulating in inner-city Philadelphia. She became fascinated with some of the people she found taking up residence on street corners.

There was "Duck Lady," an elderly woman who stationed herself near Wanamaker's Department Store. She made quacking noises at passersby and could not seem to open her clublike hands. There was Jealous Street, a Scripture-quoting former boxer who lived in a hole underneath the railroad tracks. Both of them needed food, housing and medical attention.

Still, neither of them wanted to come in off the street. They insisted that it was better to fend for themselves, outdoors. They were still needy people, but they were extremely distrustful of institutions. City and state agencies didn't know what to do with them. Sister Mary was excited. She had found her frontier.

All this fit right in with the new Mercy orthodoxy, which became less focused on running large institutions—a job that was becoming increasingly difficult—and more intent on small inner-city startups, like the hospice where Sister Mary was working. The net effect of this and the decision to make wearing of the habit optional, which also happened in the 1970s, was that fewer of the remaining sisters were seen in the parishes.

They were off working in non-Catholic areas of the inner cities, or they were working in the parish, but no longer as easily recognized as nuns. In either case the link with girls, who might see them and want to carry on their example—as Mary Scullion had—was being broken.

For many older sisters, life in the convents of the seventies was an adventure of a less pleasant sort. The meetings on how to reform the Sisters of Mercy in Cedar Rapids, Iowa, went on from the late sixties to the early eighties. Sister Mary Roberta, who was then teaching history at Mount Mercy College, remembers that "there were a lot of tears shed, some very emotional meetings," as the younger sisters gradually took control of the chapter and relaxed the old rules.

She always wore her veil in the meetings, as did most of the older sisters. She gritted her teeth as the rhetoric of some of the younger sisters took on a decidedly feminist tone. Some were saying women should become priests, even though the pope had ruled it out. Others, including some of the early rebels who had gone off to live in apartments, were now leaving the order. Sister Roberta couldn't understand how they could leave, just like that, after taking a vow to dedicate their lives to the Church.

"When I think about how long we studied our vows. For people to say they didn't know what they were doing or that the times have changed is incredible. The times have changed for everybody."

Other sisters who, like Sister Roberta, were then in their fifties, felt the significance of their vows had eroded. They were taking a look at their old faith through new lenses—as feminists.

As a young sister in the 1940s, Sister Mary Griffin, a former member of the Sisters of Charity of the Blessed Virgin Mary in Chicago, once felt her vows imparted a kind of zenlike beauty and detachment from the things of the world. She called the vow of poverty "a splendid kind of freedom. It makes one mobile, flexible, incorruptible. Like Thoreau, one wanders happily along the aisles of Bonwit Tellers [a fancy Chicago department store] viewing with delight all the things one has neither the means nor the desire to buy."

By August 10, 1973, however, she had gone the route of many reformers. The old rules were changed, the habit was abandoned, new causes beckoned (hers included the Alliance to End Repression, United Farm Workers and Alcoholics Anonymous). She'd gone off to live with others in an apartment. Then they left the order.

Finally Sister Griffin came to decide that she could no longer serve what she had come to regard as a "sexist" institution because men made the rules. She had worked for thirty-one years as a teacher. She had been dean and professor of English at Mundelein College, a prominent

Catholic school for women in suburban Chicago. Now it was time for her to leave.

Divorce from service in a religious order in the Church is an elaborate process. Her final step was to get a document that would officially release her from further obligations to the Church. It is called an "indult of secularization." It could only be issued by the vicar of the archdiocese of Chicago, a priest who functioned as its attorney general. She remembers going to his downtown office and meeting a rather smug young man. He gave her a document and asked her to sign it.

The document said she agreed that the Church owed her nothing for her past service, only a small sum in charity to prevent her from becoming an embarrassment to the Church. *Charity!?* The nun bristled, telling the priest that the Church owed her the money "in justice."

No, it was charity, corrected the priest. The precedent, he explained, was set in the seventeenth century in a case where an ex-nun had turned to prostitution to support herself, and thus proved embarrassing. She argued with him. The young man gently reminded her that he was a canon lawyer. He knew the law of the Church. This sort of discussion had obviously become a routine, perhaps even a trifle boring for him. Mary Griffin felt it was pointless to try to convince him that his law was wrong and stupid. "I sign my name. And it is over."

The most detailed study of the cumulative effect of the changes in orders of Catholic sisters was published in 1993 by two psychologists, Rev. David Nygren and Sister Miriam Ukeritis. Their work was financed by the Lilly Endowment and run out of DePaul University in Chicago and Boston University.

They surveyed almost ten thousand women and men in religious orders and also tracked the number of closings following the changes, which included a 23 percent decline in Catholic schools, a 15 percent drop in Catholic universities and a whopping 42 percent rate of closure of parochial elementary schools, most of them in poor, inner-city neighborhoods.

While religious orders had become "increasingly driven" by their new rules to tailor their missions to the poor, at the same time they had become "less able to respond to those needs through institutional means," the study concludes. When it comes to health care, for example, hospitals deliver much more treatment than hospices, but hospitals don't function well without hierarchical lines of authority and lots of willing young workers.

The net result of schools that no longer functioned and boarded-up hospitals, Father Nygren and Sister Ukeritis calculate, was a 25 percent drop in the delivery of education, health care and other services that primarily benefited poorer neighborhoods.

While the brothers and priests surveyed said the vow of chastity was the most difficult for them to live with, the most difficult vow for women was obedience. The study found that, despite all the post–Vatican II rhetoric, both women and men rated social work and the so-called "justice and peace" brand of social activism as the least attractive forms of service.

Meanwhile, the thrill of mission, the joy of serving others was rapidly fading away. That brought leaders of some religious orders to despair. "They [members] seem to have lost the original enthusiasm of their religious calling to life. Life has become drudgery for them and membership in our congregation a burden. Nothing we do, or try to do, seems to change the picture," responded one unnamed head of a religious order.

The survey found that nuns had more optimism and were more satisfied with their ministries in the Church than men were. They were the Church's anchor in many American communities. When sisters started moving away from positions they had held for more than a century, the whole composite face of the Catholic Church began to drift. The old ratio of three women joining the Church for every man had come to an abrupt end. Now it was one to one. Why? The authors cite "the experience of alienation of women in the church."

For women in their late twenties and early thirties, just getting into leadership positions in the 1970s, alienation was a factor that many of them wrestled with. Sister Doris Gottemoeller was finishing her doctorate in theology when she was invited to join a Mercy delegation to Rome. The goal was to get Vatican approval for changes the order was making.

For her, "feminism was largely a head thing and not a heart thing," she explains. She had read the literature, but she didn't begin to feel the force of it viscerally until she began dealing with, as she puts it, the "bureaucracy of males" that rules religious orders from Rome. "We were so subservient. 'This is what we want, will you please approve this.' We were hat in hand. It was all one way. It wasn't mutual at all."

According to Sister Pat Wolf, a leader of the Mercy province in New

York, alienation among women of various age groups made it more difficult to keep a community's spirit alive. In 1963, when she entered, there
were thirty-three women in her novice class. In the ensuing years of
reform, all but two left.

In the 1970s when she became the director of novices, their head
teacher, her classes consisted of one or two. "Training was practically one
to one. It made it very difficult for those who wanted to enter. They had
no peer group. The whole dynamic was really very difficult to support in
terms of nurturing people. People could leave, and they did. In some
cases the novices saw their leaders leave."

Feminism, she notes, has always been a part of the Mercies, dating
back to the founder, Mother Catherine McAuley, who made it a point to
serve the needs of the poor, especially poor women. Her system also
trained women to think for themselves and to support themselves. "We
founded institutions and ran the institutions and we ran them extremely
well. They were fertile ground for the training of women. It was an
enclosed system.

"If you were able to function in a department, you were going to
become the director. Right there you had to learn leadership skills. It
wasn't as if you were a dietician, you were THE dietician. The clergy forget that when they think about the image of religious women being sim-
plistic. People forget that there was nothing simple about founding
hospitals and running them."

All of this, the feeling of alienation from the Church and the rising
recognition of feminism, led to the election in 1977 of Sister M. Theresa
Kane, a real rebel, to be the leader of the Sisters of Mercy of the Union. As
the head of the order's New York province, she had been among the
boldest experimenters with reforms.

There was one item in her agenda that made her the favorite of the
more reform-minded nuns. Pope Paul VI had just issued a new pro-
nouncement that underlined the Church's long-standing position that
women could not become priests. Sister Kane was determined to try to
overturn it. Part of her rise, she admits, was politics. "Anyone being
elected at that time would have to be someone who was promoting ministry for women in the Church."

A vigorous, round-faced woman, she had grown up in the Bronx in
the 1940s, one of seven children. She still has more than a trace of the

clipped "Noo Yawk" accent she acquired playing stickball on the streets. When her brother wanted to be a priest, she got to thinking, Gee, if I was a boy, I'd want to be a priest.

But she wasn't, so she joined the Mercies in 1955. By the mid-sixties she was the administrator of St. Francis Hospital in Port Jervis, New York. At the tender age of twenty-seven, she was running an entire hospital. She remembers going to a state meeting of thirty hospital administrators. As she looked around the table she saw a long row of men in suits, mostly in their fifties. There were only two women, both of them nuns.

"Running a hospital wasn't unusual for a Sister of Mercy, but when I went out into the public sector, I found that wasn't going on in other places. That was the first question I had."

Some of her closest friends left the Mercies in the 1960s as reforms in business, medicine, law and other professions began to pry open new opportunities for women. But Sister Kane stuck to her vows and her guns; she was excited by change and determined to create new opportunities in the business of running the Church.

"I would go to a community meeting and people would ask what kind of changes do you want to make? Nobody ever asked me that kind of question before. . . . That was a whole new awakening for me."

Throughout the 1970s and '80s, the Mercies were the political leaders of feminist awareness among sisters. As the largest, most organized group, they had a considerable amount of influence. Given the mood of the times, Sister Kane's reformist stance made the Mercies' ideas even more attractive to emerging leaders in other orders. In 1979 she was elected to head the Leadership Conference of Women Religious. LCWR functions as a kind of trade association, a spokesman for most orders of sisters.

In Rome a vigorous new pope, Pope John Paul II, had taken over the reins of the Vatican. He had recently indicated that religious women should wear habits and remain cloistered, or relatively isolated from the community. He was preparing a visit to Washington, D.C. Sister Kane, who had been trying, unsuccessfully, to get a meeting with him, saw it as a splendid opportunity.

"We said to the men down in Washington who were planning the visit, 'We really think it's important for him [the pope] to hear from us that that [the habit and the renewal of the cloister] is not going to happen in this country,'" she explained.

As the chosen leader of most of the Church's professionals in the United States, i.e., the women who had literally built the American Catholic Church, it was hard to keep Sister Kane out of the proceedings of the historic visit. But the cardinals and bishops planning the pope's itinerary hit on a way to limit her role. Sister Kane was assigned to give a two- to three-minute greeting to the new pope at the Shrine of the Immaculate Conception in northeast Washington.

Even with that, the men of the Church were still worried about what Sister Kane and the women of the Church might do on Sunday, October 7, when the pope arrived at the shrine. Several hundred nuns were in the audience. Some sisters were outside demonstrating for women's rights.

Some of the demonstrators were inside, preparing to stand in silent protest or to walk out when the pope spoke. Sister Kane had asked the pope's American schedulers whether, after her welcoming remarks, she could go over and personally greet the pontiff. As she recalled, she was told: "Can't do that. Can't do that."

She carefully weighed what she wanted to say. The prayer service, she discovered, was being nationally televised. The pope had just spoken in Philadelphia, repeating his opposition to ordaining women as priests. "I'm thinking this is going to be problematic because he has just said it. I knew he was saying no for now, but he was not saying no forever."

As she sat in the church, waiting for her moment to speak and wondering what she might say, an older woman sitting in her pew started a conversation. She asked Sister Kane whether she was going to say anything to the pope about women. Sister Kane said she just might. "Good, I'm glad," said the woman, who then confided that when was the lone woman in her law school class, no one had given her any support.

Theresa Kane took that as an omen. She rose to tell the Holy Father that the women of the Church, contemplating its teaching about the need for dignity and reverence for all persons, felt the Church "must respond by providing the possibility of women as persons being included in all ministries of our Church."

Then she walked to where the pontiff was sitting, intending to shake his hand. When the pope, who seemed to be confused, did not respond, she simply knelt for his blessing and then returned to her pew.

There it was on national television: *An American nun dressed in street clothes lecturing the pope!* The press mobbed Sister Kane. "It was like an atom bomb going off," recalls Sister Doris Gottemoeller, who was one of Sister Kane's aides at the time. "Theresa handled it with a great deal of poise. She said what was in her heart and she said it respectfully. It wasn't in the slightest bit disrespectful or 'in your face.' Yet it got blown up to be the defining moment of her whole [LCWR] administration and of the papal visit."

Letters poured in from all over the United States, many of them reflecting a deep division among Catholics and Catholic women over whether women should become priests. Some of the most interesting letters were from nuns. According to the Mercies, two out of three sisters writing her supported Sister Kane. The intensity of the letters, both for and against, is stunning. In the church, which usually works out its internal differences in secret, there has rarely been such an emotional venting (to protect their privacy, the names of the letter writers have been deleted in the following extracts):

"I am very proud and grateful to be a member of the same great community as such a spiritual, God-fearing and courageous daughter of mother McAuley as you have proven yourself to be," said a Mercy, who defined herself as an "old timer" living in a retirement home in Sacramento, California.

"There are thousands who don't share your way of thinking. . . . If our Lord wanted women to be priests, He would have ordained His Blessed Mother. So the next time be specific in your statements, not general," noted a sister from the Immaculate Heart of Mary in Immaculata, Pennsylvania. She added: "I will keep you in my prayers."

"I wanted to let you know that a 43-year-old sister doing pastoral work in a little West Texas town has found new energy, a new impetus for facing the injustices within our church as a result of your courage," wrote a nun from Sweetwater, Texas.

"Obviously you are [the] Women's Liberation Army of the American religious. . . . Are we being 'liberated' from obedience? Are we being 'liberated' from charity? Why don't we throw out Jesus and the Father and just keep Mary and the sexless Holy Spirit?" asked a twenty-four-year-old Sister of Notre Dame.

"Your speaking out that Sunday gave me a renewed hope," wrote a young Benedictine sister from Kansas City, working in the field. "Day by day I become more and more pained by my experience in a male-dominated church. It is oppressive in so many ways. I'm discovering how much faith is needed to stay within it."

"You have given me the first unsavory opportunity in nearly fifty years of religious life to be completely ashamed of my general superior, and I have written to the Holy Father to tell him how ashamed I am," wrote a Mercy from Chicago.

"Undoubtedly you are receiving negative criticism from women who have been reared to glory in their service of man, but courage, redemption is in process and you are doing your part valiantly," said two sisters of the Blessed Virgin Mary from Rensselaer, Indiana.

"I am still in the classroom doing a full day's work where I have been doing so for the last fifty years. I feel quite satisfied and fulfilled. . . . Seeking another ministry has never been part of my thinking," wrote a sister of the Servants of the Immaculate Heart, from Immaculata, Pennsylvania.

"All I could say that Sunday morning as I watched on television in the kitchen of my apartment with three other sisters was: 'She is the only person all week who has really spoken to him [the Pope] in public,'" said a Sister of St. Joseph from Springfield, Illinois.

"If I did not write to you, I could not sleep. For the first time in my 50 years as a Sister of Mercy, I was sorry I was one. . . . My daily prayer for you until I die will be that you will NEVER be a priest," wrote a Sister of Mercy, whose angry scrawl made the location of her convent unreadable.

Two weeks after her brief but electrifying encounter with the pope, Sister Kane wrote a letter to the entire membership of the LCWR saying that, while she respected her critics' views, she regarded her speech as a "sacred moment in the history of our conference." She added that the outpouring of "hostile, unchristian and uncharitable" letters she received from Catholics caused her "to reflect again upon the violence which is so present within the human spirit."

Undaunted, Sister Kane wrote the Vatican in November 1979, seeking a three-hour audience with the pope to start what she called a Church-wide dialogue on the matter of women religious in the Church.

She is still waiting. Now in her mid-sixties, she teaches women's studies at Mercy College in Dobbs Ferry, New York, one of the many institutions that was forced to change during the long, rocky period of reforms.

Because of a shortage of both students and money, the Mercies were forced to sell it. Now it operates as a nonsectarian community college.

While her order has become a fragment of its former self, Sister Kane has lost none of her old political fire. She still thinks priesthood for women is just around the corner. "It's definitely coming. We are at the moment. We will all struggle with it and then we will rejoice."

Would she become a priest? "Absolutely, sure. If the service that I was doing needed that."

Will the next pope confront the issue? She grins mischievously. "Let's see who she is first."

20

CLOSING

In the summer of 1988, after fifty-two straight years of teaching, Sister Mary Roberta came to a fork in the road. The rule at Mount Mercy College required faculty members to retire when they reached seventy. She had managed to stretch the rule a little—she was now seventy-one. She was hoping to stretch it for a few more years. After all, she was still healthy and she still loved teaching.

But the college said this was it. She was, in effect, banned from her dream job. For the first time in her long, happy career, she was feeling a little angry and out of place. This was certainly not an unusual experience for Catholic sisters in the 1980s. Many of the communities they had built and that had had a vibrant life for more than a century, such as the one in Cedar Rapids, were going through a slow, bewildering agony that involved closing their facilities down.

The Sisters of Mercy in Cedar Rapids are a big family, proud of what they've accomplished. There have been 587 of them. Since 1855 the order estimates that they have schooled, nursed or otherwise touched the lives of more than a million people in eastern Iowa. But the 1980s were mostly downhill. The last young woman who joined the order to stay came in

1982. Since then somber funerals have replaced the joyous, weddinglike receptions of young novices as the regular events at Mount Mercy.

In the early 1960s, the Cedar Rapids Mercies had built a large new mother house with a gymnasium, an infirmary and a spacious dining area. The assumption was that the record numbers of women then entering the order each year would continue on into the future. The assumption was almost exactly wrong. Twenty years later parts of the building had yet to be occupied, so the sisters converted space that had been reserved for incoming novices into a new library for the college.

Since she couldn't teach, Sister Roberta was determined to get away from Mount Mercy, to try something new. She went to Evansdale, Iowa, where she heard they were looking for a sister to do parish work. She had no idea what that meant, but she went to see. It didn't seem very promising.

Evansdale is a blue-collar suburb of Waterloo, Iowa. It had begun as a squatters' town, a collection of shacks and other makeshift structures for immigrant workers seeking factory jobs. It had seen some good times; the shacks had since been converted to small homes. Some were still tidy with tiny, well-kept lawns, but many homes were sagging lumber and peeling paint. Battered pickup trucks peered from driveways.

The late 1980s had sent Evansdale back into an economic tailspin. The John Deere tractor plant was laying off workers and the Rath packing plant, long the major source of low-skilled jobs for the community, was closed, forever. "A lot of the people here were very defeated. Some of them were depressed. I recall one man who never left his house," remembers Monsignor Cletus Hawes, seventy-three, the pastor of St. Nicholas Catholic Church.

Many people in Evansdale didn't go to any church. The monsignor was looking for someone who could reach out to them and try to get them involved. He wanted to build a better sense of community. Then Sister Roberta came to inquire about the job. She recalls him telling her "Now just go down the street and start knocking on doors."

"I said, What? I went back to the convent and said I'm coming back [to Cedar Rapids], I can't do this. But they said he wouldn't ask you to do something he considered dangerous . . . give him thirty days."

So she began walking the streets, wearing the Mercies' modified habit with the midcalf-length skirt and the blue veil. "I would go out and knock on the door and say 'Hi. I just came to visit if you have some time.' First they thought I wanted to talk religion, but when they found out I was just a retired old schoolteacher who just wanted to chat, they'd put on the coffeepot."

She found a lot of people who were lonely or in need. She developed a list of community and church resources. She got people hearing aids and scholarships and medical appointments. She brought a fallen-away Catholic back to St. Nicholas. It was more exciting than teaching in the sense that when she knocked on a door, she had no idea what would happen next.

She remembers one scruffy man, a member of a local motorcycle club. He ushered her in and showed her pictures of motorcycles including his dream, a massive Honda Golden Wing. The nun thought it looked more like a jukebox on wheels. Someday, he said, when he had the money, he would buy a new one.

When she got up to leave, the man insisted on giving her a tour of the house, starting with the garage, the place he and his whole family had lived before they had the money to build the house. After that, as Sister Roberta headed to the door again, he stopped her again. "How would you like some jam?"

"I wasn't sure what was coming after that," she recalls. He showed her the apple and plum trees in his backyard and explained how he made the jam himself. About to leave again, carrying a jar of homemade jam, Sister Roberta found him barring the door. He had a confession to make: Since his wife died, he no longer went to church. "It's just too hard to go alone."

No problem. Sister Roberta went to his church, the local Congregational church, and arranged for him to join a support group. He went back to church the next Sunday. "Every day had its joys," she recalls, until one day three years later when she was diagnosed with walking pneumonia. The doctor said she had to quit her job.

She told Monsignor Hawes about it, and he said he would have to announce her departure at Sunday Mass. Sister Roberta made him promise that there would be "no big fanfare." Still, after saying Mass, he walked back to her pew and took her by the arm. The church was filling with applause. She could not refuse.

In an era when the Church's battle of the sexes still ran strong, the priest in his vestments and the nun in her veil walked out of church together. They were both creatures of more gentle times, and at St. Nicholas, they had made a good team. Outside, the parishioners filed past them to bid her farewell.

If you were a leader of an order of nuns in the 1980s, closings and leave-takings took up much of your time. They were delicate, often painful matters, recalls Sister Doris Gottemoeller, who was then the head of the Cincinnati province of the Mercies. A tall, confident woman, with streaks of gray beginning to show in her dark hair, she often found herself cast in the role of the heavy. She was the one who made the decision to close schools that the Mercies had built and operated for generations.

Without younger sisters, the economics of religious orders had fundamentally changed. Now it took money to pay lay teachers and still more money to care for the needs of the order's increasing ranks of elderly. Schools with declining enrollment could no longer be carried. She remembers closing McAuley High School in Toledo and St. Bernard Academy in Nashville, both big schools that had seventy-five years of alumni, many of whom were shocked and angry at her.

"It was hard, but when you can't maintain a quality program anymore and you're living hand to mouth, then it's time to close it." All the death signs were there, backlogs of deferred maintenance, declining enrollment, but when she arrived to make the announcement, faculty and students felt their world was being upended.

"I remember fifteen-year-olds saying this is the worst day of my whole life. You just have to say yes, I understand, honey, but there are worse things. People would come up and say things like they didn't know about financial conditions. At a certain point you can't tell people [about sagging income] because it creates a downward spiral."

Still more delicate was the matter of handling the departures of older sisters, some of the order's best leaders, who were leaving in the 1980s. These were often people she'd known for years, women she had hoped she could call upon in difficult times. Now they wanted out, for a variety of reasons. Sister Doris was the one who did the exit interviews.

While the temptation was there for her to urge them to stay, she decided her role was mainly that of a good listener. Some had joined the order for the wrong reasons. Some had achieved emotional stability in the Mercies and now wanted to go on to other things. Some felt they could no longer follow orders. She remembers one sister who left to play the stock market.

They were women, like her, who had joined the Mercies in their teens. She likens it to a reevaluation of an early marriage. "The reason you affirm marriage vows after thirty years is now you know her better. You've seen her in the light and in the shadows. You don't know that when you're sixteen." Some women were emotional about leaving; others weren't. "There is no formula for dealing with this."

One of the bright points of her leadership in the province was finding a way to save its eleven hospitals. Unlike schools, they often had some money. This was the age of Medicare and the law required sisters to take salaries. She helped consolidate their mortgages and installed professional business managers who centralized purchasing, hiring and management policies.

As more laypeople arrived to take over the work of the departing sisters, she developed uniform training programs that stressed service to the poor and other Mercy values. "You can't assume it will just rub off."

In other places, financial rescues didn't materialize. In Arkansas it was one shock after another. The Mercies closed dozens of parish schools, tore down their convent in Little Rock, a city landmark, and left Warner Brown Hospital in El Dorado, which they had run for almost a half century. Leave-takings were always hardest for the managers who had to organize them.

"That [turning over the hospital to new management] was the hardest thing I ever did," recalled Sister Mary Drilling, its last Mercy administrator. "We didn't close the hospital, we just moved out and left everything behind. There were no sisters then . . . and we had to close the door and leave the people there."

Familiar institutional faces of America were changing. The stately thirteen-wing mother house of the School Sisters of Notre Dame in Milwaukee became a Lutheran College. The campuslike home of the Gray Nuns of the Sacred Heart, which included three schools and a mother house outside Philadelphia, became an education center for the Federation of Jewish Agencies of Philadelphia. A Mercy mother house near Detroit became a training academy for the U.S. Postal Service. The empty novitiate building for the Sisters of the Most Precious Blood became the City Hall of O'Fallon, Missouri.

Sister Helen Amos, who headed the Mercy's Baltimore province in the 1980s, remembers jogging through the forested, seventy-acre grounds of the order's mother house and St. Agnes, their nearby college. Both were closed for lack of funds. The place, which had so many memories, was virtually empty.

"I'd be running on that hill and looking up at the beautiful trees, thinking how they needed to be tended. We didn't have the resources to get a tree surgeon. I just remember praying we would have the opportunity to get this in somebody else's hands who could take care of it." She later sold it to the USF&G Corp. The company turned it into a data-processing center.

Sister Pat Wolf, who headed the New York province in the 1990s, remembers the long ordeal of selling the order's mother house, a difficult negotiation that was completed in 1996. Then came the really hard part. "It meant that we had to move our sisters out of the infirmary. These were the women who had built the place. Some of them had lived in the same room for thirty years." They had assumed that they would always remain in communities of sisters, but she had no alternative but to send some of them to skilled nursing homes. "It was very difficult."

Parts of the parochial school system survived. But their new growth has been mainly focused in the suburbs, where more than two hundred new elementary schools have opened since 1985. More than a thousand Catholic schools have closed, most of them in inner-city areas where they were often attracting students from African American and Hispanic families looking for an alternative to the discipline-troubled public schools.

In Buffalo, for example, the diocese summarily closed the parochial schools of eleven parishes in 1971 and consolidated them all in two buildings on the site of a former downtown seminary for priests. It was defended as a way to save money.

"It was a huge mess," recalls Sister John Francis Schilling. As a newly professed member of the Oblate Sisters of Providence, she had changed her name from Barbara, the girl who had frequent debates with her father over the Civil Rights Movement. Now, as an Oblate, she was immersed in it. "People were very angry."

She and another sister from the Baltimore-based African American order were summoned to Buffalo to help resolve disputes among a stew of displaced religious orders represented on the faculty of the new megaschool and to help prevent further divisions among African American students from different neighborhoods who suddenly found themselves thrown together into the new student body.

When the nun appointed to head the school left, Sister John Francis, one of her assistants, was inserted in her place. She was only twenty-eight, in charge of a fractious new school with 350 students, about 10 percent of whom were Catholic. "We had open classrooms, but nobody had been trained to deal with them. I didn't even know how big a job it was," she recalls. She took on a teaching assignment along with the principal's job and coached the girls basketball and softball teams in what little spare time she had.

Backed by a core of African American leaders from the formerly white parishes where the students came from, the new "Diocesan Educational Campus" gradually managed to pull itself together. "It took us a couple of years, but our kids began getting high scores because of our emphasis on phonics and a highly structured program." Sister John Francis was right where she wanted to be. She stayed in Buffalo for eleven years. "I loved it," she recalls.

Many Americans, many Catholics, assume the Catholic Church might have kept the inner-city schools it had open because it is rich. But that, too, has changed since Vatican II announced its celebrated overhaul of Church teachings and practices in 1965. Before that, according to Charles E. Zech, a professor of economics at Villanova University, Catholics gave about the same percentage of their income—roughly 2.2 percent—to their church as members of main-line Protestant orders give to theirs.

Since Vatican II, many Catholics have grown richer, but their donations to the Church have declined by half. Modern Catholics, Dr. Zech notes, "contribute less money to their churches than do members of nearly every other major U.S. religion." If modern Catholics currently contributed at the level that their poorer fathers did, he calculates, the Church would have an extra $1.96 billion a year to spread around.

One of the most embarrassing financial ironies for the American Catholic Church in the 1980s was that this was the decade when the sisters—the women whose woefully underpaid help in the earlier years kept the public schools growing—became in need of some serious help themselves. Without the influx of younger nuns, the average sister was growing older. Few orders had retirement funds.

American bishops were the ones who might have gotten the money flowing, but when it came to the plight of religious orders, many of them had an out. They could plead ignorance. Since the dramatic blowup in Los Angeles over the actions of the sisters of the Immaculate Heart of Mary, many bishops had turned a blind eye toward what was going on in convents. Perhaps they felt it was better not to know.

After the strained welcome he had received from sisters during his 1979 visit here, Pope John Paul II appointed Archbishop John Quinn of San Francisco to head a commission to find out what was going on, especially the reasons for the sharp decline in religious orders. The archbishop's panel later reported that it found no major problems. But it added this revealing caveat: "most bishops have little understanding of religious life and still less understanding of what has taken place in religious life since the [Vatican II] Council."

Parish priests might also have generated more sentiment for giving. They often lived next door to convents and were frequent visitors to schools and hospitals run by the sisters and they saw how bad the financial situation was. But in many post–Vatican II churches, it was no longer considered politically correct for priests to bang on the pulpit and deliver the dreaded "Sermon on the Amount." So they found a variety of ways to avoid it, including deferred maintenance and, ultimately, closing schools.

Was there an ethical requirement, a moral obligation to help the sisters, who had often been the employees of the bishops running the school systems? Some Catholics, especially younger ones who no longer saw sisters in parochial schools, didn't see one. Four orders of sisters in Louisville, Kentucky, did some polling in preparation for a joint fund-raising drive and found younger Catholics were not likely to respond.

So the fund-raising campaign was dropped. "Laypeople say, 'What the sisters did, they did in charity,' and that's true. So it's kind of a hard case to make," explained Sister Helen Sanders of the Sisters of Loretto, one of the four orders.

In the mid-1980s, American bishops drafted a number of weighty moral pronouncements. One counseled American businessmen to be more sensitive to the financial needs of their workers. Another urged the government to take more heed of the plight of the poor in the Third World. By then there were multiple signs that some of the Third World conditions the bishops were complaining about afflicted the faculties in their own schools. The warnings started in 1973 when the bishops' department of education recommended that Catholic churches take a national collection to develop a retirement fund for sisters. The recommendation was ignored.

In the early 1980s a Washington-based association of Catholic donors and foundations, called FADICA, became concerned about the problem and commissioned a survey by Arthur Andersen and Co., the national accounting firm, to see how big the retirement shortfall was. By this time a task force appointed by the bishops was reporting that some orders were facing "a severe financial crisis," exhausting both their cash flow and income from sales of their property.

The Arthur Anderson survey in 1985 confirmed beyond anyone's doubt that the problem was staggering. The gap between the available retirement funds that the sisters had and the finances they would need to meet their financial and medical needs was $2 billion dollars and growing rapidly.

In the late spring of 1986—thirteen years after the initial warning—the National Council of Catholic Bishops (NCCB) came up with an emergency fund of $60,000 to help sisters in distress. Some of it was used to help a New York order that was in debt to its undertaker because it was unable to pay for the frequent funerals of its members. The bishops managed to find another $250,000 to establish an office in Washington where the Church could study the sisters' retirement problem.

All of this was being conducted behind closed doors. Bishop John R. McGann of Long Island, then the treasurer of the NCCB, remembers seeing the $2 billion estimate. "Across the board, our people were staggered. Maybe that's good," he later explained. But they weren't staggered quite enough until Frank Butler, the president of FADICA, put the study showing the Church's unfunded, $2 billion liability for retired sisters into the hands of a *Wall Street Journal* reporter. This revelation, appearing on the front page of the *Journal,* generated a frantic round of finger pointing.

Bishop McGann pointed to priests and parishes; it was really a "local" problem. Staff members of the NCCB pointed at me, the reporter who wrote the article. I was "distorting" the true picture. An archbishop mentioned in the story, too busy to comment before the story ran, later gave me this explanation over the phone: "Look, they brought this on themselves. They [the nuns] are the ones who abandoned the habit and went off to live in apartments."

There was discussion among the bishops over whether to mount a national church collection for retired religious, but once again that was shelved, perhaps on the assumption that the furor would die down. Many bishops felt there were already too many national collections.

In the wake of the *Wall Street Journal* article, a group of Catholics in Washington, D.C.—the first lay group to form without official Church sanction—started SOAR! (Support Our Aging Religious!). They began preparations for a nationwide fund-raising drive to help establish a pension fund.

Then the bishops announced they might reconsider. Sister Helen Amos, then the head of the Sisters of Mercy of the Union, remembers having a "skull session" with three friendly bishops who agreed to lead the charge at a meeting of bishops in Washington in 1987. She describes it as a kind of ecclesiastic football game. "You [the *Wall Street Journal*] sort of opened up a hole in the line there and we went through it."

Her argument to the bishops was simple. Over the years, younger sisters had functioned as a kind of pension fund. "In my convent of twenty-five sisters, probably five were retired and the other twenty took care of them." But by the eighties the ratio was turning around. What had been an exchange of love and care between generations was becoming an impossible burden. Older sisters had already given. Younger sisters were no longer there. Now it was somebody else's turn to give.

The three bishops managed to score a crucial touchdown for the nuns that day. The bishops reversed themselves, voting to establish an annual national collection for retired religious, to be taken on one Sunday every year. Instantly it became the Church's largest national fund-raising effort. Since 1988 the Church has collected over $351 million. By the turn of the century, the money had begun to make a change in the sisters' huge and daunting fiscal void. After decades of procrastination, confusion, benign neglect and worse, the Church fathers made sure that some checks are finally in the mail.

True to the checkerboard nature of the church, however, not all bishops opt to participate. In some dioceses the collection is barely mentioned from the pulpit. The most generous givers are found in the heart of the Rust Belt, in Buffalo, New York, where nuns man the pulpits on collection Sunday and where the campaign reaches out from billboards and resonates on local television news shows. Buffalo, which has sixty-three retired orders to worry about, donates more than $1 million a year. Bishop Edward D. Head, who initiated the campaign, explained that failure wasn't an option. "The issue cried out for resolution."

It still does. Sister Andree Fries, who belongs to the Sisters of the Most Precious Blood, runs the Church's National Religious Retirement Office in Washington. She estimates that the last big wave of sisters—the young women who filled convents amid the optimism surrounding Vatican II and the other events of the early sixties—are just beginning to retire. Gauged by the starkest, most conservative economic measures, the Church is still short some $6 billion to take care of them and the more elderly sisters. Sister Andree is convinced that as the economy improves and interest rates rise "that number will come down really fast."

At the moment, she uses some of her money to reach the orders that are the most needy. She's found a half dozen Hispanic orders in border towns in south Texas that have less than two hundred dollars in their checkbooks. "Their whole culture is God will take care of us and see us through the day." She estimates that there may be as many as two hundred other small communities of sisters that haven't yet identified their needs to the Church and continue to fend off poverty on a daily basis. "I call them my lost sheep."

Meanwhile the closings go on. In the 1980s Sister Pat McDermott, head of the Mercy's Omaha province, had to manage the departure of sisters from small towns all over the West. Their average age was seventy-five. Many of them had literally helped pioneer dozens of places, like Williston, North Dakota. As young women, they had been the order's real adventurers, the tamers of cowboys, the builders of hospitals and schools. Over the years, they had become deeply embedded in the life of their communities.

Now there was no one to replace them. Convent populations had dwindled in some places down to one nun. Even then, she says, they remained "vibrant in the community." When the sisters were no longer physically able to go it alone, she had to do the closing and arrange to put them in retirement homes. "As they came down to a small handful, there were some very painful and heart-wrenching decisions to make."

For the Mercies, she says, the unsettling of the West meant more than just retiring a few more nuns. "They had that rugged pioneer Western flavor. We're losing that. It's a loss for the Church and for what we're going to be about in the future."

21

FIGHTING FOR
LIFE

For Trinity College, a small Mercy-run liberal arts school in Burlington, Vermont, navigating the last thirty years has been like trying
to steer a ship rolling through an interminable storm. A fixture of
the community since 1925, it had undergone the usual experiments in the
sixties and seventies. Traditional courses were abandoned in favor of more
politically correct subjects like black history and creative writing. Many of
the sisters on its faculty left in the early eighties to take up parish work or
various social causes.

There were serious divisions within the order, causing younger
women to leave. "Religious life also felt the pain of many different view-
points and acted like wedges which separated congregation members, one
from another," explains Sister Marion Duquette in her history of the Vermont Mercies.

Trinity College had enough internal strength to outlast many similar
Catholic institutions, but by the fall of 1998, most of the familiar death
signs were there. Tuition payments were down, overhead was up. Despite
years of desperate attempts to raise funds, only a tiny endowment had

been assembled. A long-term president of the college resigned and soon so did her replacement. There were only two teaching sisters left on the faculty of the college, which continued to limp along on the basis of a big bank loan.

The quality of education remained high. In 1999 *U.S. News & World Report* ranked Trinity among the top regional liberal arts colleges, but this was not news you could take to the bank. Trinity's board of trustees declared a financial emergency in May 1999, exercising a legal maneuver that allowed it to lay off ten of forty-five faculty members. Two vice presidents quit.

That July, the board decided that things were desperate: The college would either have to merge with another school or close forever by June of 2000. It named Sister Jacqueline Marie Kieslich, then fifty-seven, to be the new president. She had not sought the job. She was the college's academic dean and had the feeling she was being forced onto the bridge of a sinking ship. "My question was why are we doing this and why do you want a permanent president now?"

She had grown up in Burlington, where her family ran a grocery store. She had gone to a Catholic high school, entered Trinity College and decided to become a Mercy. "We were the last class of postulants [beginners] to wear the traditional habit," she recalls. Then the reforms of Vatican II hit and Sister Kieslich remembers being plunged into the debates over the pending changes between younger and older sisters. "We were asking questions like mad," she says. Still, she had friends in each camp. Later she got a doctorate in education.

But guiding a college with 1,100 students toward closure, she discovered, was an experience that is not described in textbooks. The first question she faced was a moral one. Experts warned her that it would be crazy to disclose the board's decision to close or merge before the last academic year began in the fall. If they learned about the deadline, students would be leaving in droves, making it impossible for Trinity to find merger partners.

Nonetheless, Trinity promptly informed the students of the board's decision. "We were not being crazy," explains Kathleen O'Dell-Thompson, a Trinity vice president. "We're very close to our main mission, which is teaching people to tell the truth." Only two students left. The rest returned in the fall to a slimmed-down curriculum. Instead of twenty-eight majors, there were just eight, with a heavy emphasis on ethics and Catholic teachings.

The college received various offers. Real-estate developers wanted to buy the campus, with its twenty-three acres and seventeen buildings. Schools in Turkey and South Korea made bids to turn the school into an extension of their systems. An entrepreneur wanted to turn Trinity into a "center for technology."

The tradition of Mercies in Vermont goes all the way back to the order's American founder, Mother Frances Warde, who sent four young Irish nuns there in 1872. They braved cold and disease and overwork. Fourteen sisters died in the order's first ten years in Burlington. They and two other orders of nuns had helped nurse victims of the devastating flu epidemic of 1918 by turning their high schools into hospitals.

The older Mercy sisters, a group of sixty then living in retirement in the order's mother house, had acquired more than a little of the region's flinty character. When tuition payments weren't enough, they had run their schools by holding annual bazaars. In the sixties, when fee-hungry teams of outside psychological consultants offered their services to help guide the order through the reforms of Vatican II, the Vermont Mercies just told them no. They couldn't afford it.

After looking through all the outside offers, Sister Kieslich began to wonder. Turning the order's flagship, Trinity College, into yet another real-estate development or a technology center? "Sure, that would take care of things, but there was no room in any of these proposals for our mission."

An alumni group said there had to be another alternative, a way to keep the college open. But Sister Kieslich had been put in a box. On October 31 the college's $1.4 million line of credit was due at the bank, which had been extending it month by month. The new president fell back on the one resource she felt she could count on. She contacted nine other regional communities of Mercies and found they would replace the loan at better terms from their pension funds.

In the fall she went to the chapter meeting of the Burlington Mercies with this glimmer of hope. There was also interest from a local hospital in renting excess office space on the campus. She was not yet sure this was enough to rescue Trinity, but the older sisters rose and gave her a standing ovation. Then they voted to contribute $300,000 to the effort, assembling bits of money from various funds including some money that individual sisters had inherited. Sister Kieslich was shocked. "For some of them, to give twenty dollars was a lot."

Now she had an alternative plan to present during a board meeting that lasted a day and a half in November. The business types on the board were still skeptical. "They were expressing confidence in us, but at the same time they really wanted us to know that maybe we were dreaming."

It was Thanksgiving vacation, yet many students remained on campus to await the verdict. The press was banned from the campus while Sister Kieslich pleaded her case. "We thought this deliberation was just for family." She wanted the board to give her one more year. In the end the board agreed. "The place just went wild," she recalls. On Monday, as classes resumed, she reopened the college's admissions office, which had been permanently closed.

There was yet another near-death experience. In March 2000, the college held a two-day convocation with its students to plan the path ahead. Sister Kieslich had recently discovered that Gloria Steinem had been invited to give a campus lecture on the future of feminism in May, during final exam week.

Then she began getting calls from conservative Catholic groups. Some of them were outsiders, mobilizing in Vermont's capital, Montpelier, to protest pending legislation sanctioning gay marriages. To respond to the appearance of Steinem, a noted pro-choice advocate, they promised to organize national groups to demonstrate against her on Trinity's campus.

Then she had a call from someone in the bishop's office. If Steinem spoke, she said she was told, the archdiocese might remove Trinity College's official standing as a Catholic institution. That made it into a full-blown academic freedom issue. Sister Kieslich announced the dilemma to the convocation and arguments among students, faculty and sisters raged into the night.

Sister Kieslich and her team of administrators put this to them: Trinity's survival as a college was on the line, but so was its tradition. Whose tradition had they been struggling so hard to preserve? Was it Gloria Steinem's? Or was it the tradition of those sixty elderly women in the mother house who had just risked their last dollars to see Trinity sail on? The convocation voted to revoke Steinem's invitation.

Younger sisters were outraged. The spokeswoman for the college, a Vermont state senator, resigned in protest. But Sister Kieslich held firm. "As a Catholic institution, we are exploring our identity. We will sponsor events that support Catholic teaching," she explained at the time.

Hope and faith weren't enough to save Trinity. In July 2000, it announced it was closing for good. The uncertainty over its life or death had taken its toll. The school hoped for 120 new students, but only 30 signed up for fall classes. The gap between tuition and the school's operating expenses was too big for the sisters' charity to bridge. Sister Kieslich and her administrators finally had to admit they were beaten.

The school's seventy-thousand-book library went on the auction block. While the president of Trinity College and her advisors weighed how to dispose of the rest of the campus where they had spent much of their careers, they made some short-term rentals. One of the dormitories was leased to a local community group to provide temporary housing for fourteen homeless families. "It is a way to continue the mission of Trinity," Sister Kieslich explained during the wakelike hours after the final closing. "One of our hallmarks has been social justice and serving people in need."

MERCY HOSPITAL SYSTEM in Charlotte, North Carolina, went through a similar life-and-death struggle in the 1990s. When the end finally came, it wasn't about money because the hospital system in Charlotte and many Catholic hospitals in the nation have hundreds of millions of dollars in assets.

More valuable to the Mercies was the hospital's mission—to serve the poor—and the independence that allowed it to keep doing that. That was the sisters' bottom line. They knew they were in for a long, difficult struggle to protect it, but as Sister Pauline Clifford, president of the North Carolina Mercies, once put it, there was nothing really new about that. "Everything we have ever done has been a struggle."

Edward J. Schlicksup, the hospital system's last president, describes it this way: "There always was a certain tension between mission and margin. As time went on and all hospitals had to operate more and more along the lines of business principles, we found they came into increasing conflict with mission requirements. You may want to help the disadvantaged, but if you do too much of that, it puts you into jeopardy, particularly from the 1980s on."

Mercy Hospital in downtown Charlotte had shown the city its heart many times, starting in 1906 when a group of Mercies scrubbed up an old church hall and opened it as a hospital. A newer building helped carry the city through the 1918–19 epidemic of Spanish influenza, which took at least eight hundred lives. Mother Mary Raphael, who ran the hospital then, later wrote: "I don't know how we ever lived through that. . . . We put beds in the hall, beds everywhere. Everyone who came in to help got sick too, except Mother Bride and me. It was nothing but God's grace and strength that kept us going."

It was, by no means, the best-equipped hospital in town; Charlotte-Mecklenburg Hospital, owned by the city, and Presbyterian Hospital, a private hospital, had the edge there. But it was often first in things that mattered more to the nuns. In 1954 it was the first of the city's three hospitals to integrate.

In the 1970s Jack Claiborne, a columnist for the *Charlotte Observer*, gave this description of the city's hospital scene: "Some doctors called [Charlottee-Mecklenburg] Memorial a factory, Presbyterian a country club and Mercy the hand of compassion. Colorful exaggeration, of course, but there was some truth too. Mercy might be short of science at times, but the Sisters made sure it was long on tender loving care."

By the 1970s Medicare rules forced Mercy to develop a more businesslike balance sheet. The changing nature of the hospital business meant it had to engage in more serious competition with the other two hospitals, which were larger, for paying patients. As one local financial analyst put it, it was "expand or die."

That meant buying new equipment, constructing new additions. During the 1970s and the 1980s Sister Mary Jerome Spradley, the hospital system's chairperson, launched what seemed to be an endless round of major fund-raisers. Mercy Hospital was a class act. So were some of those who came to Charlotte to save it, including Frank Sinatra and Liza Minnelli.

In the early 1990s the hospital business changed again, bringing in "managed care," which tended to put large insurance companies in the driver's seat. They preferred to make contracts with full-service hospitals, which meant that Mercy either had to add new departments to its downtown hospital or, as many hospitals did, find a partner to merge with.

After two years of complex negotiations, on September 14, 1993, Mercy signed a "collaborative relationship" agreement with Charlotte-Mecklenberg. The idea was that Mercy could use the contracting strength of the larger hospital to bring in paying patients and still keep its independence and its own board of directors.

After a year of this, the Mercies decided it wasn't working. "It was uncomfortable for us," explained Sister Jerome. "We had been accustomed to being independent, very independent. To come to a point where we had to share decision-making and we were the junior partner . . . made a big difference."

In 1995, after a great deal of anguish, the Mercies agreed to sell their system, which by then included a suburban hospital and another in Asheville, North Carolina. It went to Charlotte-Mecklenburg Hospital for $197 million. The city-owned hospital, acknowledging the reputation of the Mercy system, agreed to keep the hospital's religious signs on display in the lobby and to continue to call it Mercy Hospital.

The sisters, whose convent is part of the hospital's nursing school, leased it back as part of the deal. In announcing the order's collective decision, Sister Pauline Clifford told the *Charlotte Observer:* "We've done our share of crying. It's like giving up the family home. Even though it's time to do it, it's still hard."

On May 18, 1995, the Mercies and the people who supported the hospital came together at St. Gabriel's Catholic Church to participate in a religious service. It seemed very much like a requiem for a hospital. The identities of the nuns, doctors, benefactors and others whose giving and struggles had made Mercy Hospital an essential part of Charlotte life for almost a century each seemed to hang, momentarily, in the lofty stillness of the church. One name followed another in slow procession as a choir recited them in the austere monotones of Gregorian chant: "Doctor Gerald Zimmerman . . . Colonel Frances Beatty . . . Beulah Squires . . . Mother Mary Raphael . . . Sister Stella Maris . . . Mother Mary Bride . . ."

Sister Jerome, a short, gray-haired lady, sat quietly near the altar. She insists it was not a requiem at all, but a rebirth. Following their theory that the hospital really belonged to the community, the Mercies had voted to use the money from the sale to endow a philanthropy: Sisters of Mercy of North Carolina Foundation, Inc.

She would run it along with Mr. Schlicksup. As she explained in an interview, "Mother McAuley never said you had to run acute care hospitals, she just said you had to care for the poor. So we decided we could provide more direct service with the sale."

There are 120 sisters left in her branch of the order, most of them near or beyond retirement age. On paper they look like millionaires who could have a very comfortable retirement. In fact, Sister Spradley insists, they are still Mercies. They are still bound by their vow of poverty, so they can't be millionaires.

They are still carrying out their mission of service, only now the money from the sale of the hospital will do the work for them. Since its start their foundation has given over $11 million to various causes in the area, many of them small start-ups working in the areas of health care and education for the poor.

For example, a program called Think College, which mentors inner-city children having difficulty in the public schools, got off the ground because the Mercy name still has respect in Charlotte. Kemal Atkins, the director of the program, says after the Mercies gave him $95,000, two other groups chipped in another $95,000. "It helped us considerably that we could say that the Sisters of Mercy Foundation is a supporter."

Since 1964, it has been Sister Jerome's practice to walk out of her convent, cross a courtyard and immerse herself in the daily bustle, the birth-and-death rhythms of Mercy Hospital. Now she leaves the same convent, crosses the same courtyard and passes the hospital complex that is filled with years of memories—even the grotto the nuns built behind the hospital to Our Lady of Lourdes, remains intact. Then she gets in her car and drives to a suburban office building.

It is a new building, filled with well-appointed offices of law firms and real estate dealers. The Mercy Foundation's office looks just like theirs except they're there to make money. She's there to give it away. They take risks; so does she. A recent $25,000 Mercy grant to a child-literacy program fizzled, and Sister Jerome says that is the nature of the Mercies' new business. It goes back to the order's very roots. "We will continue to take a chance on small organizations that are coming into being."

THE 1980S SAW a continuation of the struggle for sisters who had been fighting for reforms in the sixties and seventies. There was still a tension between the old ways of doing things and the new freedoms that were emerging. Sister Sharon Burns, for example, sometimes found herself accused of pushing the envelope, even when she hadn't intended to. As an elementary-school principal, she got into trouble once for appearing on television. She directed her students as they sang Christmas songs and then, asked to sing a solo, she did. She heard from the head of the Baltimore province of the Sisters of Mercy about that. Sisters didn't sing on television.

Later, as the battle raged over changing the Mercies' habit, she was criticized for wearing hers two inches too short and for having stockings that were too sheer. In the 1970s, when wearing the habit became optional, she began wearing makeup and jewelry. Some of the older nuns criticized her. The older nuns, having witnessed a steady stream of younger women leaving the convent, had begun to see the change in dress as an ill omen. "Start dressing up and soon you'll be leaving." Younger sisters tended to see every change as another opportunity. "We were sort of opening up to the world."

When the possibility for doctorates in theology—once an all-male field in Catholic colleges—opened up for women, she got into that. Later she was criticized for signing a statement critical of a new encyclical, Humanae Vitae, that had been written by Pope Paul VI. For a religious woman who had taken a vow of obedience, that presented a serious problem. Some U.S. bishops handed down career-ending punishments. In Baltimore, however, all it meant was that Sister Sharon had another audience with her superior to "explain" herself.

Her career was still headed upward, at least from the viewpoint of the reformers. By 1983 she had been selected to be the first woman chairman of the theology department at Jesuit-run Loyola College in Baltimore. For three years she had what she thought she wanted: a full college professorship, tenure and the power the run the department.

But something else had begun to gnaw on her conscience. An older sister had once told her about working with the dying. "Sharon," she had said, "it's so wonderful! You don't have to be afraid of being too tender." Sister Sharon found herself thinking about Catherine McAuley, the founder of the Mercies. Working with the sick and dying was something she regarded as a privilege, one that required "great tenderness above all."

That wasn't a message that was heard much in the 1980s. Then it was theology that was in vogue for both men and women. As the head of the theology department, Sister Sharon once discovered she had a hundred applicants for one teaching position. Meanwhile, she knew, hospitals and the nursing field in general were beginning to have severe shortages of skilled professionals. "I said to myself I'm not deserting theology, but I wanted so badly to do something hands on, to be close to suffering people." She mulled it over.

In the old days, her superior spared her from such agonies of choice by simply telling her what to do. Sister Sharon knew the order benefited from her large salary as chairman of the department. The new job with the elderly paid only a fraction of that. Her superior, Sister Helen Amos, told her to forget about the money. The choice was hers.

"That's when I found out how difficult the new way of being obedient was," recalls Sister Sharon. "You try so hard figuring out what God wants you to do." In the end, Sister Sharon opted for work with the dying, but she was destined to make one last curtain call at the college.

Literally. In 1985 she was cast in the lead for the college's production of *Hello Dolly!* Jim Dockery, a former Jesuit priest who taught English at the College, had insisted he would produce the play only if Sister Sharon took the lead. Dockery had once heard her singing a torch song for a college skit.

He decided this nun would make a perfect Dolly, and evidently, so did the audience. A former belle who leaves a lengthy widowhood to become a matchmaker, Dolly requires a woman with a great deal of presence on stage. She makes her most spectacular entrance down a staircase into a fashionable, turn-of-the-century restaurant, where the waiters, recognizing her from the "old days" when she was a femme fatale, burst out into "Hello Dolly!" the show's signature song.

"When Sharon Burns came down those stairs, it was fantastic," recalls Dockery, who says Sister Sharon has this peculiar chemistry. "You never got the feeling that Sharon was flirting with you, but she always came across as a woman who was charming. I guess that's what came out in the bright lights. The audience was in love with her, and she was with them."

For Melvin Polek that was certainly true. One of the boys who had fallen in love with Sister Sharon in military school, he was sitting in one of those audiences. When Dolly came down those stairs, he felt his jaw drop. "I didn't even realize it until she came out. I said 'That's her! She was my second-grade teacher!"

Another breakthrough: Sister Sharon Burns takes a bow as "Dolly." (COURTESY OF LOYOLA COLLEGE, BALTIMORE, MARYLAND)

In the 1930s Mother General M. Carmelita Hartman, a former head of the Mercies, would ridicule nuns who wanted to change their habit by telling them: "I suppose the next request will be to wear low-neck and short-sleeve habits, no coif, etc." Fifty years later, as Sister Sharon took her final bows to a sold-out house wearing Dolly's low-cut, short-sleeved, flamboyantly red dress, she had just rocketed through another barrier.

This time, though, she didn't get into any trouble. Among her admirers were a phalanx of elderly people who had been bussed over from Stella Maris, the retirement home where she now worked. They were waiting in wheelchairs in the lobby to give her a big bouquet of flowers when she emerged.

22
BECOMING HISTORY

The most festive occasion in the history of the Sisters of Mercy in Tennessee happened here in the spacious Cathedral of the Incarnation on the summery morning of June 11, 1966. A hundred years previously, six disoriented Mercies had entered this city, which was still in shock from the many wounds inflicted upon it by the Civil War. For their part, the Mercies were simply exhausted. It had been a long journey from their home in New England.

With their voluminous black cloaks and their clipped-sounding Yankee accents, they were certainly viewed as strangers and, more than likely, as enemies by the first townspeople they met. The folks of Nashville had been ravaged twice: first by the occupying Union Army, then by an efficient band of Yankee carpetbaggers known as the Alden Ring who were using their new positions in City Hall to loot what remained of the city's wealth.

So how did the people of Nashville receive these young Mercies? They loved them. While this city has aspects of a rough river town, it has a peculiar place in its heart for religious people. They tend to flourish here, from itinerant preachers and their tub-thumping companions who tout the Bible along the wharves jutting into the Cumberland River to fancy religious academies built in the suburbs where the elite of the city sent their daughters.

This chapter is about two such places, one run by Sisters of Mercy, the second operated by the Dominican Sisters of St. Cecilia. They both came from the North at about the same time and both started with academies and then established schools throughout the state.

In 1966, to commemorate their centennial here, hundreds of Mercies gathered beneath the red-tiled roof of the cathedral, filling the church's dark oak pews. Busloads of nuns had arrived from as far away as Kentucky, Ohio, Detroit and Chicago. They were commemorating community ties that were deep and broad.

At the altar the bishop celebrated high Mass with no fewer than eight priests. All of them had been educated in the state's twenty-one Mercy schools, a network that extended from Kingsport in the east to Memphis. There were 160 of the Tennessee Mercies there to help sing the "Gloria." Afterward they swapped stories with their visitors about some of the congregation's legends.

One legendary nun was Belle Baxter. She was a spoiled beauty who mesmerized many of the young men of Nashville in the 1880s. At the balls she attended they would line up, each aching to dance with her. After the swirl of her debutante season, she found another way to make them ache, this time all at once.

One morning they opened up the *Nashville Banner* to read "Miss Belle Baxter of West Nashville yesterday evening received the white veil at St. Bernard Academy in the presence of a number of friends. The young lady walked down the aisle attired as a bride and Bishop Rademacher performed the ceremony that wedded her forever to the work of the Church."

As a nineteen-year-old Mercy, Belle morphed into Sister Mary Columba, a parochial school teacher in Knoxville with zero tolerance for nonsense. "She used the ruler on altar boys who missed appointments," says one account.

Not far from the cathedral a large, old rectangular building sits on a hill in a campuslike setting, one that overlooks the buildings of downtown

Nashville. The building, an often bustling place of high ceilings and deeply polished floors, is the mother house and former academy of the Dominican Sisters of St. Cecilia.

Like the Mercies, they were also celebrating in the sixties, remembering the century of adventures, struggle and quiet faith. Over the years the two orders had competed for pupils in a community where only 4 percent were Catholics. Like the Mercies, the Nashville Dominicans also sent young women out to help build parochial schools across the state.

The Dominicans experienced a near-death experience in the summer of 1867, when their academy and all of its furnishings were sold at auctions to raise money to pay their heavy debts. Fortunately, the bishop of Nashville came to the auction and bought it back for them.

Women from the two orders helped nurse Nashville through a severe epidemic of cholera in 1873 that took about a thousand lives. Many people were fleeing the city as the nuns drove in, preparing to go door to door to provide what help they could to the elderly and poor who had been left behind.

"The silence appalled them as they passed through the streets of the city. Everywhere was the quiet of a graveyard. Not a sound save the rumbling of wagons filled with coffins or boxes to enclose them," says a history of the Dominicans. There was much for the nuns to do. The poor, especially black people, trusted the women in their distinctive white habits, but they no longer trusted doctors. People were dying so fast that the rumor quickly spread in ghetto neighborhoods that it was the doctors who were poisoning them.

The truth was that their well water was bad. In addition, some were suffering for putting their faith in dubious home remedies. A local newspaper, *The American*, advised: "use sulphur in your socks, one half teaspoonful in each sock every morning. This will charge your system with sulphurated hydrogen which is a bar to cholera."

After the sisters had been briefed by doctors on the proper ways to treat the disease, the mayor of Nashville lent them his carriage to help them make their rounds. Local women prepared food for the nuns, who worked around the clock. The epidemic finally began to ebb, but not before two of St. Cecilia's sisters were borne away in the line of coffin-carrying wagons.

The two orders of sisters had also shared the good times of Nashville. In the boom years of the later 1870s and 1880s, increasing railway and river freight turned the city's waterfront into a vast warehouse. The business brought the nuns more students.

Later, the bust of the Great Depression showed them the flip side of the economy. But these were women used to living in near-poverty conditions. For them the Depression was not all that different, except, like the cholera epidemic, it made the city's docks eerily still.

That changed, though, on Sundays when religion and, of course, country music became the solace of the city. If the South is the Bible Belt, Nashville must be near the buckle. *The WPA Guide to Tennessee,* written during the Depression, gives us this portrait of a Sunday on the riverfront of a city where people loved their religion and also loved to quarrel over the details: "Preachers mount boxcars and perch on the first story window ledges of the produce houses. Some lure listeners by mouthing French harps or strumming banjoes and guitars. Others whoop until a group collects. There is a constant crossfire of heckling between preachers and listeners. Furious men rush up to the preacher and shake fists, Bibles and canes under his nose. Some ignore the preaching and draw aside to roar Scriptural quotations into each other's faces. The preaching continues until about 9 o'clock at night, when the people, satiated and subdued, begin to leave."

The 1960s provided the two orders a splendid time to celebrate these and many other memories. Their novitiates were full of bright, shining faces, young women eager to bear the burdens of carrying on with the mission.

Then came the mixed messages of Vatican II and all the harsh social pressures of the sexual revolution and the antiwar, anti-authority days of the late sixties and early seventies. Young women stopped coming to the convents and both orders began to unravel. The Tennessee Mercies went down a familiar path, adopting reforms, abandoning time-honored customs including the habit, living in apartments.

Finally, those who remained became absorbed in the sad and difficult job of leaving or closing many of the institutions they had started.

But that is not what happened to the Dominicans. Their leader, an intense, wiry woman named Mother Marie William MacGregor, was no copycat. She studied the Vatican II papers carefully, especially the one that suggested that each order should go back and reexamine their basic traditions.

More than most, she appreciated the danger of the growing but ill-defined sense of rebellion. She had been a bit of a rebel herself. Fresh out of high school in the 1940s, Sister MacGregor had joined another order, the Sisters of Providence. When her mother superior caught her savoring a forbidden cigarette behind the convent's grotto, she kicked her out.

Then she joined the Dominicans. She found she could take the tough rules when they were accompanied by something rewarding. It was the deep spiritual life and the palpable, often joyful feeling of sisterhood among the Dominicans that attracted her. When she became mother superior in 1964, she was not one to snoop behind the grotto to see who might be smoking.

"She was a real leader in the sense that she had the vision, but she didn't let circumstances or ego distort that. She loved her sisters, no doubt about that, but she loved us enough to lead us well," explained Sister Christine Born, who was then a young novice. "She was fearless to say things that others didn't want to hear."

Other orders were hiring theological experts to explain the deeper meaning of Vatican II and retaining psychologists to help them discern just what it was that they really wanted, but Mother MacGregor wanted none of that. She took her sisters back to the twelfth century, getting them to pore over the books and documents that describe Dominic de Guzman, a young Spanish priest. He invented a new order designed to win back Catholics in southern France who had been lured away by street preachers of a rival faith the church called the Albigensian heresy.

The Dominicans, as his small band of priests came to be known, were monks in the sense that they lived by the rigid rules of the monastery, but they also carried their faith out to preach in the streets and the universities. They wore distinctive white habits and they were, in a sense, a grassroots movement.

Dominic, who later became a saint, stressed that they were all equal in the eyes of God. He installed a democratic form of government in the monasteries he founded. The monks elected their leaders and so did the sisters when Dominic began to form a companion order of nuns.

Trained to compete with the Albigensians where their recruiting was most effective, on street corners, the eloquent, white-garbed Dominicans drew crowds in Europe the way the street preachers did on the waterfront of Nashville eight hundred years later. The fame of the Order of Preachers, as the Dominicans are called, spread around the world.

It was the singularity of this tradition that Mother MacGregor resolved to fight to preserve in the late 1960s. Other orders might abandon the habit, but she argued that it was central to the Dominicans' identity; it was the sign by which the larger community, the people in the streets, recognized and trusted them.

Over the centuries, Dominicans had been martyred for wearing the white habit in the wrong places. Others had worn it in the right places at the right times and had risen to become pope. During the Middle Ages and the Renaissance, Dominicans were part of the background of great events.

She had seen that in the museums of Europe: paintings of men and women wearing her familiar habit. The faces in the paintings spanned many generations, some were players in history, others were simply there, part of the spirit of the age.

That habit, Mother MacGregor would argue during her order's meetings on reform, could not be abandoned just like that. It was an inherent part of the order's moral force. As she put it, "It is a leveler of men making indistinguishable the sons and daughters of the poor from those of the wealthy, the learned from the not so learned. May it ever be so!"

She was a good preacher, attentive to both the hearts and minds of her charges, recalls Sister Mary Angela Highfield, a novice who started under Mother MacGregor's instruction. "I remember her saying, 'Sisters look at the spirit of the law. We have to live it and love it. See those things that are essential and those things that aren't.' She always went to the source documents to show us what she meant." She got the annals out of the archives to show how the order held it together during the financial crisis of the 1860s and how it gave young women the courage to confront the cholera epidemic.

"Where does the strength for all this come from?" she once asked them. "It comes from a deep personal contact with Christ through prayer. How genuine is our love for people? It is only as genuine and real and deep as our love for Christ." The quiet moments, the regulated time for prayer and contemplation were another essential to religious life that must be preserved, she would argue.

Some of the younger sisters, women whose views were shaped by the social maelstrom of the late 1960s, simply didn't buy that. Sister Born, who was then twenty-four, was elected to represent the younger sisters during the deliberations. Some of them had just returned from universities filled with the skeptical, neo-scientific spirit of sociology or psychology.

Others came from meetings with other orders, where they learned the latest, politically correct interpretation of the reforms. There were some memorable debates at St. Cecilia's that left younger sisters dissatisfied and provoked disheartened older members to leave. "You felt your whole life was being voted on in front of you," Sister Born recalled.

Mother MacGregor kept prodding the sisters to understand the value of their heritage. She knew she was running against the conventional wisdom of the day, but she felt she was right. She wanted the young sisters to gain that feeling for themselves.

When preaching and gentle humor didn't gain their attention, Mother MacGregor would sometimes plead with skeptics. "I beg you . . . to protect the balanced life of prayer and work against the contemporary trend to reduce our day to one of mere convenience," she once wrote them. She issued a second letter to those who wanted out. They would have to wait for two months, because it took two months for Rome to process and approve their papers. As one history of the order puts it, those years "were not easy ones. It may seem simple now. There was nothing simple about it."

In the end, the Nashville Dominicans voted to remain in their schools and to retain their monastic tradition of regular prayer, obedience and periods of enforced silence. "The silence is so you can hear God," explained Sister Born. The vote to keep a slightly modernized habit carried 100 to 40.

She had kept her order intact, but Mother McGregor could not sell her tradition-minded approach to the pro-reform leaders of the Leadership Conference of Women Religious, the national group that represented the heads of most orders of sisters. After one tumultuous meeting in 1968 she wrote back to her order: "I am amazed and aghast at the senseless destruction of religious life in the United States."

Finally in 1971 she took the Nashville Dominicans out of LCWR and also left a smaller group, which represented the heads of Dominican orders of sisters. As the casualties began to mount from battles then underway in hundreds of other convents, there were some kindred spirits.

One of them was Sister Quentin Sheridan, then a young nurse at a Mercy hospital in Grand Rapids, Michigan. She and a group of seven other nurses were adamantly opposed to the Mercy leadership's aggressive role in reforming religious life. An eloquent, charismatic woman, Sister Sheridan sometimes verges on the theatrical when she describes the tumult of the sixties: "Oh, we all became so enamoured with ourselves and with all those little slogans. It was up with peace. Peace at all costs. Open the windows, let in the fresh air. Down with rigidity. Nothing was written in stone. Why, it was enjoyable! The habit doesn't mean anything! What is essential is what we do! We are the Church!" She pauses to catch her breath.

"You know, what we all needed then was a spiritual Pepto-Bismol, but we didn't have it at the time. We were in the middle of a nuclear bombardment, we were spinning. The elders . . . didn't understand what was going on. We saw it coming like a tidal wave. The youngsters were leaving in droves. What the slogans were suggesting became a morality. It was down with everything."

Her small group, which was being advised by a Jesuit priest, Father Francis Prokes, a professor at the University of Detroit, petitioned the Mercies to allow them to do some experiments. They wanted to form their own community within the Mercies that would emphasize the wearing of the habit, community prayers and meetings, collaboration with the bishops and formal obedience to a mother superior. They wanted to train their own recruits. The Mercy leadership was not enthusiastic.

In the early 1970s they flew to Washington to confer with the Mother General of the Mercies. They were greeted at the airport by a tall, cool Mercy, Sister Doris Gottemoeller, who was then a young assistant to the head of the order. As she recalls the negotiations that followed, there was not much room for compromise on either side. The semi-independent status they wanted within the Mercies, according Sister Doris, was "unprecedented."

The young sisters from Grand Rapids, who had set up a temporary headquarters in Alma, Michigan, refused to budge. "If you said black, they said white," recalls Sister Doris. Seeing no other option, the leaders of the Mercies began working on a financial settlement that would allow the Alma Mercies to leave the order altogether.

That left Sister Sheridan's group, which now calls itself the Religious Sisters of Mercy of Alma, with little more to start with than a borrowed farmhouse and their ideas. But their experiment and their conservatism soon attracted some highly placed friends. They included several of Michigan's bishops and the Papal Nuncio, Rome's ambassador to the U.S. Church. Working with the Vatican, they gained official standing in the Church as an independent order on September 1, 1973.

The Alma Mercies began meeting with leaders of other like-minded orders, which eventually included the Nashville Dominicans. Together they formed an alternative to the LCWR, which they named Consortium Perfectae Caritatis, after the Latin name of one of the Vatican II documents.

They began inviting priests and bishops to speak at their meetings. One of them, Father William Lori, then an assistant pastor of a church in Largo, Maryland, was asked to give a lecture on spirituality in St. Louis. He had never heard of the group before, he recalls, but they paid his way, so he went. This was 1979, the year Sister Kane shocked the Church hierarchy with her memorable greeting to the pope at the Shrine of the Immaculate Conception. The guns of the gender war in the Catholic Church were roaring.

In St. Louis, Father Lori found himself addressing a large audience of sisters. All of them were wearing habits. "I gave this talk and what I noticed was how many young sisters were in the room. To me it was an eye opener," recalls the priest, who soon became a regular visitor to meetings of Perfectae Caritatis.

Three years later, Father Lori was appointed secretary to Archbishop James Hickey, of Washington, D.C., and told him about the group. Intrigued, the archbishop came to see for himself. "He had worked with sisters his whole life. This was a natural for him," recalls Father Lori.

In 1989, after Archbishop Hickey became a cardinal, the women of Perfectae Caritatis found themselves with a champion in Rome. During a meeting of American bishops with Vatican officials the cardinal described the disarray of American sisters. "In some cases," he explained, "the very meaning of vowed religious life and its relationship to the church, both local and universal, remains as points of disagreement and even division among members of the same institute [order]."

Bishops, he suggested were partly responsible for this mess. He recommended that the Church open a formal channel of communication with members of Perfectae Caritatis and other orders of sisters who claimed their views weren't represented by the leadership of the LCWR. This raised a prickly legal issue. Under church law, Rome deals with one group of sisters representing each country. In the United States, the group that had been officially recognized since 1956 was LCWR.

But church laws can bend, especially when the pope thinks they should. On this matter, John Paul II appointed Cardinal Hickey as the official Church liaison with Perfectae Caritatis and asked him to see if he couldn't help work out its differences with the leaders of LCWR. Now Sister Sheridan and the other tradition-minded orders had two champions in Rome.

Cardinal Hickey, it would seem, had all the right tools for this mission. He had doctorates in both canon law and in theology. He had the full clout of the Vatican behind him. But, after presiding over two meetings as the intermediary, even he found it impossible to negotiate a way across the vast gulf of diverging opinions and hard feelings that lay between the two groups of nuns. "It was very hard," recalls Father Lori, who has since become a bishop. "There were years of divisions and a lot of water had gone under the dam."

Sister Quentin recalled one of the meetings, held in the Shrine of the Immaculate Conception in Washington. While the cardinal listened, three or four members from each side launched into a profound disagreement over the meaning of an abstruse section of the Vatican II documents. "They had their theologian. We had ours," she said, shrugging. Neither side budged. Afterward the LCWR representatives distilled ninety pages of argument into a six-page summary of differences. Perfectae Caritatis representatives refused to sign it. "It was not a pleasant meeting."

Sister Doris, who led the LCWR group, recalls it as "an altogether frustrating experience." LCWR, she says, "was trying to identify commonality and differences among us to see to what extent there were ways to bridge the gulf between us," but the other group, she says, kept raising the same obscure theological points.

She suspects the other group wanted the talks to fail, because they knew what was coming next. In 1995 Cardinal Hickey reported to the Vatican that he was at an impasse and got permission to form a second group, the Council of Major Superiors of Women Religious (CMSWR), to represent the members of Perfectae Caritatis and other, more traditional orders of U.S. sisters.

There was great joy among the more conservative group. "I was so excited I went out and took a ride up in a hot air balloon," recalled Mother Vincent Marie Finnegan, the leader of a Carmelite order in Los Angeles and then the chairman of Perfectae Caritatis's board. "It was a huge feeling of relief. If we didn't get that, I think we were going to see the death of religious life in the United States."

Since then they have been given at least equal representation with LCWR at meetings with Vatican officials in Rome. Sometimes they are allowed to bring two sisters to LCWR's one, which strikes Sister Doris and other LCWR leaders as unfair. "If they represent eight to ten percent of American religious, that's pushing it," says, Sister Doris, who once wrote Cardinal Hickey complaining about bias.

The stiffly formal relationship between the two groups continues, although they regularly send representatives to each other's meetings. One difference: At CMSWR meetings, Sister Doris notes, there is often a bishop or an official from Rome praising the more traditional sisters.

"It's so frustrating. It's as if they are regularly held up now as the model. You can ask what have they done that warrants that," she asserts.

Sister Nancy Silvester, fifty-three, a recent leader of LCWR, says the group continues to represent more than 350 orders of sisters in the United States and will continue to explore what she calls a "new synthesis" that integrates religious life with feminism, civil rights and respect for the environment. It does not necessarily mean teaching in schools.

"If you want sisters in your schools, you go get a CMSWR person." The goal of her group, she says, "is not to conserve orthodoxy in the Church. We just keep trying to figure out how we can continue to be prophetic and where we are willing to take risks. We haven't done it well, but we're still trying to figure it out."

A thin, intense woman who, like many LCWR leaders, often wears a sporty blue blazer with a tiny religious pin, Sister Silvester predicts that in the future, orders of religious women will look "very different." They will certainly be smaller, she thinks, and may include associate members, such as married couples, working together with celibate women.

The habit will not return, she says, because many religious women believe they can be more effective counselors wearing lay clothes. She resents the habit because it's "covering up your sexuality." She admits that one of LCWR's frustrations is in trying to explain its point of view to the media. "When television wants to portray a sister, they go out and find one in a habit."

The tension between the two groups appeared to ease at the end of the 1990s. As one leader of the CMSWR puts it: "We have cordial relationships with each other. It's just that we both have decided to be different." One telling difference is that CMSWR represents a relatively small percentage of American sisters, but it is attracting about 50 percent of the young women drawn to religious life. Over time, that could build CMSWR's presence and influence in the Church as the membership of LCWR diminishes with age.

Bishop Lori says he's been encouraged by instances of collaboration between the two groups, despite their doctrinal differences. "That's good. I think you've got to take the long-term view that eventually that's going to bear fruit. The Church thinks long term, and that's certainly the way I'm thinking."

In Tennessee the long term has already taken its toll; only a handful of Mercies remain. But over the last ten years the Nashville Dominicans have had an average of fifteen recruits every year.

While other orders are leaving or closing schools, the Nashville Dominicans are busy opening new ones, some as far away as Chicago. The audience for these freshly minted young "preachers" from the Nashville Dominicans is already formed: It has requests from five hundred other parochial schools to send sisters.

Part of this popularity comes from the order's supportive network of priests and bishops. And part seems to come from the powerful attraction of religious tradition to women in any age, including this one.

Sister Born, who recently stepped down as head of the Nashville Dominicans, is an embodiment of that. The fact that she is Catholic at all stems from the experience of her great-grandfather James Guthrie. He was serving as a doctor in the Confederate Army when he was captured by

Union forces during the Civil War. When he was pressed into service in the North, he discovered that Catholic sisters were on the battlefields serving as nurses for both sides.

Dr. Guthrie was so impressed, according to his great-grandaughter, that upon returning to tiny Tucker, Mississippi, after the war, "he and his whole family came into the Church." She joined the Dominicans in the early 1960s, right out of high school into the tough but abiding-love regime of Mother MacGregor.

"This is springtime for us," explained Sister Born, as she showed a visitor around the grounds of the mother house. "What is the attraction here?" I asked her as I watched a group of young novices, their long white veils flying behind them, as they played a game of Frisbee on the lawn. Sister Born, a shy, soft-spoken woman, smiled and looked down at her black, clunky shoes, standard nun gear for centuries. "Our shoes are very stylish right now," she said, grinning.

23

BLASTING OUT OF
THE ROUGH

As soon as spring temperatures reach forty degrees at St. Frances Academy, Darrell Hopkins gets the members of the school's golf team outside to hit some balls.

Never mind that it feels like it's freezing, he tells them. Never mind that the prisoners watching through the barred windows of Maryland State Penitentiary a block away are jeering obscenities at them. Never mind that the balls tend to get lost amid the weedy, garbage-strewn vacant lots and the graffiti-festooned buildings around their school. But no hitting police cars or the homeless women pushing grocery carts. They're out of bounds.

As coach of the golf team, Mr. Hopkins, a tall, genial man in his forties, prepares tough players for a tough league. They are all African American teenagers, some gathered from the meanest neighborhoods in the city. For many of them the battered, secondhand wedges they are learning to grip are the first contact they've ever had with golf. He tells them they'll be coming up against white kids from country club neighborhoods in the suburbs. The white kids have been playing the game all of their lives.

Many St. Frances boys start out as lousy golfers. Some start out seeing practice as a time to goof off. Some have learning problems. And some have a strong interest in starting fights. When that happens, Mr. Hopkins benches them.

He might make a nod in the direction where all the hollering is coming from, the penitentiary. You screw up here, his gesture says, and you end up over there.

There are a record six million adults in the nation's correction system, a number that might be just another statistic in the suburbs. In inner-city Baltimore, where half the African American men between eighteen and thirty-four are either locked up or before the courts one way or another, it is a fact of life that is often very painful.

The odds are pretty good that some of Mr. Hopkins's players have fathers or brothers in the slammer. He doesn't belabor the point. When his players are ready to learn, he reminds them, he's ready to teach them. Recently, one of his screw-ups became the team's best player.

"What you don't do is give up on them," explains Mr. Hopkins. "You never do that. I learned that from the nuns."

Until 1974, St. Frances Academy was an elite prep school for black girls. It had been that way since 1828, when Mother Elizabeth Lange and her evolving Oblate Sisters of Providence started it. In 1870 they had further flaunted the conventional, segregated wisdom of this city by moving their school to 501 East Chase Street, a quiet, well-to-do white neighborhood.

Pictures of those classes line the walls of St. Frances. They smile down at you, young black women wearing dinner dresses, gloves and big, fashionable hats. They came from all over the country and graduated into the city's black elite. There were thousands of them. Then, in the 1960s, this stable world turned completely upside down.

A freeway cut a gash through the inner city that soon became a fault line between black and white neighborhoods. One block west there are fashionable hotels and antique-filled row houses. One block east, the deteriorating row houses often have boards where their windows used to be. First, blockbusters chased out the whites and brought in the black middle class.

Then the theft-prone victims of the twin plagues of heroin and crack that have addicted sixty thousand people in Baltimore frightened away the middle class. They left behind them a kind of no-man's-land of the very poor and street hustlers with St. Frances planted squarely in the middle.

At the same time, the Oblates underwent their own series of crises. They couldn't stop the neighborhood from sliding downhill and they had no money to move their school out of it. The order's intake of novices—young, teacher material—suddenly dropped close to zero. On top of that, there was fierce new competition. In the 1970s other local schools that had previously shunned bright black women began vigorously competing for them. That made the job of filling each new class at St. Frances more problematic than the last.

Some white religious orders that faced this problem came up with the rationale that teaching in parochial school was no longer "relevant." So they sold their schools and sent their younger members off on what were well-intentioned but often short-lived new missions, to help the people who lived in what the newspapers called the ghetto.

That is not what they did here, explains Sister Claudina Sanz, who was elected the Oblates' superior general in 1993. St. Frances was their flagship school and they were not about to abandon it. They made a series of changes to adapt to the new conditions.

The first came in 1974, when they decided to admit boys to St. Frances. To make room for them, they moved their convent out of the building and put it in a series of renovated row houses nearby. "If we're only looking at saving money for our retirement, we're preparing to die," she explains. "We have to take half of our money and put it in recruitment and vocations and that's what we did."

By the early 1990s, Sister Claudina, who had come from her native Belize in 1961 to join the Oblates and learn about America, had learned quite a bit. As a teacher in a parochial school in northeast Washington, D.C., in 1968, she'd watched the mindless violence of the city's devastating riot following the assassination of Martin Luther King. "It was like a crazed moment. Blacks even burned each other out. There were Chinese stores, black, white all in the same block. They all just went down."

Back in Baltimore, living at the convent near St. Frances, she'd watched the structure of the neighborhood crumble under the allied pressures of poverty, crack and federal welfare programs that tended to remove the man from the house. They also, she says, removed the sense of family obligation from the man.

"Some men thought, Well, I don't have to run this family. I can have three, four different women with children. Neighbors would take care of the children, or they would be on the street. Then the drugs came along, which is really the curse of our earth. Children are born with addiction. That's what we are contending with now."

During the late 1980s, under the guidelines of Vatican II, the Oblates decided to review their history. What it told them was to dig in and fight. Other orders may have battled over whether or not to keep their distinctive habits, but the Oblates viewed that as a side issue.

They kept their black veils. "We have opted to wear our veil because there are few black nuns and we feel responsible to the Church and to our race as a role model. If a black person is walking around without a semblance of our religious order, nobody would know who we are."

Most importantly, they wanted the students of St. Frances to know who they were and what they stood for. They kept the faculty heavily laced with nuns and brothers. They are essential, Sister Claudina feels, because of the peculiar character of the neighborhood. "Laypersons are not equipped with the deep spirituality they need to look at the positive aspects of life here."

A stunning 98 percent of St. Frances graduates go on to college. Of those, about 80 percent go on to complete it. And they don't come from any black elite. When they arrive at the academy, 50 percent of the students live at or below the nation's poverty level. Only about 20 percent are Catholics. The white-glove days are mostly a memory now as St. Frances reaches out to children at risk.

"Most teachers want to work with children who are smart," says Sister Claudina, "but we have to have the patience to bring the children out of the mire and work with them and that's what we have done." To further that mission, in 1993 a popular teacher at the school, Sister John Francis Schilling, was named the new principal.

It made no difference to the Oblates that Sister John Francis was one of the two white women among the order's ninety-eight sisters. She had the right credentials for the job. As Sister Claudina puts it: "She is tough."

Tough love is the one commodity that St. Francis has in abundance. That's what the golf coach, Darrell Hopkins, found when arrived in 1976.

He came from a public housing project in the neighborhood. His was the first large class of boys to attend St. Frances. The first sister he would meet in the morning was Sister Paul, the vice principal.

A short, stocky, bowling ball of a woman, she would position herself outside the brick gate, the entryway into the academy. The students came to see her as part of that gate. "She would make sure you were neat and proper, or she wouldn't let you in the building. Not wearing the right color tie? You're not coming in. She'd check fingernails to make sure they were clean. She'd sniff you to make sure you were washed up. At the same time you knew that she cared about you."

Twenty-five boys entered that class of 1976 and thirteen of them graduated. Some left because their parents couldn't afford the tuition. It now runs to $3,600 a year, but the school finds ways to partially subsidize about 40 percent of the students. Others left because they started fights.

Mr. Hopkins can still see them in his head. "They sat outside drinking and using marijuana, you know, all that kind of stuff. The school had taken in a lot of kids from other schools where they had trouble. We had some people who got out of jail. They didn't stay very long. Caused too much trouble. The sisters were very strict. You got in one fight and you got put out of school."

The nuns, he recalls, had their own kind of fight. "I've seen them take on the worst kids and make them better. They'll be arguing with them, fighting with them and tutoring with them until they become better students." At some point, under this barrage of attention, the surviving students at the academy bonded together and identified with the goals of the school.

When he went on to college, Mr. Hopkins recalls that one of the things that shocked him was that there weren't any nuns. "I didn't realize how special they were until I went out in the world. You find that other people just don't care as much about you or how you do as much as these sisters did. Basically they were like your mother when you were here," recalls Mr. Hopkins. "No," he says, correcting himself, "they *were* your mother. When you go on to college, there's nobody doing that anymore."

There were no sports at St. Frances when Mr. Hopkins was there. That's why he came back recently and volunteered to start the golf team. His day job is as a fitness instructor in a local gym, so making St. Frances students stand outside and whack balls when it's forty degrees just seems natural to him.

"When I get into something, I really get into it." Suburban schools sometimes cancel golf matches when it's cold, but Mr. Hopkins's team plays its full schedule. Recently the team has begun to win a few games. They will win more, predicts the coach. "They're basically seasoned now, ready to play."

What might make the other teams in the league take him seriously is that basketball teams fielded by St. Frances have repeatedly won both the Catholic League championships in Baltimore—both the boys and girls teams—despite the fact that all of their games must be on the road.

They have no home gym to play in. They practice in a recreation center eight blocks away, when they can get floor time. Their success has helped put St. Frances on the map, especially for college basketball recruiters. When they arrive, they also discover that the principal, Sister John Francis, is tough.

She has read all the stories about the dismal academic records of most black athletes who go to college and she is determined that her students are not going to repeat them. She preps students before the recruiters arrive: "I tell them use basketball, don't let basketball use you." By her standard, winning isn't everything. It's nothing compared with winning a college degree. "I must be a coach's worst nightmare," she says, proudly.

Some educational experts claim Catholic schools are successful in inner cities because they skim the best students from their neighborhoods. That's not at all what St. Frances does, explains Sister John Francis. "We take kids that other schools don't want, kids that are disasters."

The typical student is usually two to four years behind on standardized tests. "I'm not giving a whole lot of credence to standardized tests, but that's a fact you can measure. It's not that the kids we get aren't capable, though, many of them are, but they're just not confident of themselves."

The students tend to come in two categories. Black families who move to the suburbs often find their children have trouble in public schools. "If they have attention problems, they usually find their way to us. That gives us a stable parent base," says Sister John Francis. The rest are boys and girls from inner-city Baltimore and there is often very little in their lives that is stable.

Patrick Lee grew up right around the corner from the school. His

Left to right: Sisters Mary Paul, Clare Terrance, Reginald Gerdes, and John Francis Shilling are teachers at St. Frances Academy in Baltimore. They are part of the team that has succeeded in turning youths from one of the city's toughest neighborhoods into college material. "We take kids that other schools don't want." Demetrius Charles, a St. Frances graduate and currently a junior at Duquesne University in Pittsburgh, stands behind Sister Clare Terrance. (COURTESY OF ST. FRANCES ACADEMY, BALTIMORE, MARYLAND)

father was in jail. His mother worked long hours at a downtown hotel. He has vivid memories of the boys he grew up with. By his count at least sixteen are dead or murdered; another thirty are in jail. Most of the deaths and the incarcerations are drug related.

Proving that you were tough and could compete in this world was what mattered to young Patrick, and in 1987, when he started public high school, his only interest was football. When he didn't make the team, he dropped out, which was not that unusual. The dropout rate for boys in inner-city schools was running at about 60 percent.

His good fortune is that he and his family had known the Oblates since he was a little boy. When the nuns heard that his father had gone to jail, they arranged for Patrick to get a scholarship to St. Frances. "Public school was fun," he recalls. "You just don't get the attention you'd like.

Here you get it whether you wanted it or not." He was two years below his class's reading level. They were doing research papers. "I'm one of the only ones in the class who didn't know what a research paper was."

He found the nuns would tutor him before school and after class. "All you had to do is ask for it." He never made it to the top of his class, he recalls. "But by the time I was a junior, you couldn't tell me I wasn't a top student here. I felt like one."

He was point guard and captain of the first two championship basketball teams from the academy. One of the downsides of not having a home gym is that the crowd is always against you. Sometimes the referees seemed that way, too, he recalls. But Sister John Francis was always there in the stands, rooting for the team, called the Panthers, and keeping tally on a score sheet.

Their coach, William Wells, was always reminding them that life could be a series of road games if they didn't do their best. Patrick can remember sitting on the bench, feeling besieged and hearing him pump up the Panthers: "We're not just the small school that sits by the side of the jail anymore; we're here to compete!"

After he graduated, Patrick went to Salisbury State University, on Maryland's Eastern Shore, a nearly all-white college. Patrick found just being there to be an amazing experience. "I didn't know anybody who went to college. I just learned about it on TV." He wanted to play basketball for Salisbury, but early in his freshman year he decided not to. "The message I got from Sister Schilling was: 'You've got people out there that's expecting you to fail right away, they don't know you, they just expect you to fail. Prove them wrong.'"

As he recalls, there were twenty black students at the school that year; eighteen were on athletic scholarships. He got to know them the following year. After figuring out how to cope with his course load, he walked into practice and made the team. "I saw guys with a lot of talent, but after the season was over, they just forgot about everything they were doing. I was determined that wasn't going to happen to me."

Most of his college teammates failed to graduate, but Patrick did. He could only get four tickets to the school's graduation, so he came back to the old neighborhood wearing his cap and gown, walking door to door to share his moment with friends and relatives.

He's still there, working as community outreach coordinator for St.

Frances, which has since doubled in size, growing to 270 students. Some of them are jammed in so tightly that there's only standing room left in the chapel. There is a long wait list of students hoping to get into ninth grade. Backed with grants from the state of Maryland and local foundations, the academy is building its first gym and a community center.

The new attention has brought along some criticism. One article that appeared in a local Catholic newspaper suggested that the tiny school performs so well on the basketball court because it bends the rules set by the Maryland Interscholastic Athletic Association (MIAA) to recruit athletes.

This provoked a tart letter from Sister John Francis. She responded that the school's admission standards have absolutely nothing to do with basketball. They were set long ago by Mother Mary Elizabeth Lange, a black immigrant to Baltimore from Haiti. She was a small but strong-willed woman. And when she founded the Oblate Sisters of Providence in 1829, she gave them a distinctive mission. They were to educate people, but "particularly the poor, the neglected and those with special needs to recognize, develop and live as respectful, responsible and just members of God's human family."

"Her standards, I assure you," wrote the principal of St. Frances Academy, "are higher than those set by the MIAA or the Catholic League."

24
GOD OF THE SMALL

I n the summer of 1998 a nurse wheeled the young man who came to be called John into the hospice section of Stella Maris, a suburban nursing home run by Mercy Medical Center in Timonium, a suburb of Baltimore. He was twenty-six but he looked more like eighteen.

John's problem was that he was born into an age in which there was much casual talk in the media about recreational drugs and recreational sex. These were things that were regarded as cool and John, a homosexual, had indulged himself. Life for him was a kind of pipeline of fleeting friends and momentary pleasures. Suddenly, here he was, all alone, coming out the other end. He had contracted AIDS from using dirty needles. The disease had already rendered him blind. Soon he would be dying.

John was entering a phase and a place that were very foreign to the world he knew. People still died, of course, but that wasn't regarded as cool in the 1990s. People didn't die on MTV; nor did they age much. The nurses that began to fuss over him at Stella Maris were no longer considered to be cool, either.

Admissions to nursing school had fallen off by 30 percent. Young American women and men were shunning the profession. Hospitals were trying to import nurses from as far away as the Philippines. While dot.com kings, software merchants and professional baseball players made an obscene amount of money in the 1990s, no one could accurse nurses of doing that.

The hospitals they worked for had become increasingly "market driven," in the lingo of the endless newspaper articles about medical "reform." Translated, that meant nurses were overhead and their salaries had to be clamped down. It also meant that it was no longer cool to accept many charity patients like John.

What John had going for him on the day he was wheeled in was that Stella Maris is owned by the Sisters of Mercy. They don't give a fig about what is regarded as cool. For almost 125 years they have emphasized nursing skills. Part of their mission is to care for the poor, and there is no market that drives that.

In the hospice, a place normally reserved for problems of incontinence, incoherence and the other incapacities of eighty-year-olds, John was a shocking presence with his straggly blond hair and his unlined, almost boyish face. Compared with the other patients, there were moments when he seemed almost angelic.

The comparison vanished, though, as soon as he opened his mouth. Then he would spit on the floor, chain-smoke and spew obscenities at whomever was around him. He told the nurses that he didn't want their help. He didn't trust anybody. They should all just leave him alone.

His favorite place for these harangues was on a porch that overlooked Loch Raven, a reservoir surrounded by wooded, rolling hills. One day as a thunderstorm approached, a nurse started to wheel him inside and he swore at her. He was screaming that he didn't need anybody so they should get the hell away from him.

So they did. He sat on the porch and got thoroughly soaked; only then did he ring the bell for someone to bring him in. This attracted the attention of Sister Sharon Burns, the chaplain of Stella Maris's hospice and the woman who trained the nurses and the nurses' aides in spirituality and medical ethics. She reached for his chart. It said John had no religion. John had never known who his father was. What little family John had, a mother and foster grandparents, lost track of him eleven years previously. He had no one.

Oddly, that made him cool at Stella Maris, where the drill that Sister

Sharon supervised was taken from the gospel of St. Matthew, chapter 25: "I was a stranger and you took me in. I was naked and you clothed me. I was sick and you visited me . . . as long as you did it for one of these, you did it to me." Sister Sharon would use this text to tell her students that it was a great privilege to work with the dying.

Although they might have to do some unpleasant things to help the elderly, she would tell the nurses that every act was holy. Sister Sharon could see that this drill wasn't working very well with John, so she decided to work with him.

She likes challenges. She has spent eighteen years caring for the dying, often shunned as the ultimate "burnout" specialty by nurses. As Sister Sharon tells people, she finds it fulfilling even though she goes home many nights exhausted. "I could die tomorrow," she explains, "and feel that my life has been worthwhile. . . . Not that I am eager to go, but I feel that good about what has happened in religious life for me."

One of her previous challenges was becoming the first woman to head the theology department at Loyola College in Baltimore, long a redoubt for Jesuit graybeards. Teaching the gospel of St. Matthew to young students there was interesting, but applying the gospel to the dying patients at Stella Maris reached her much more deeply. "It was the first time I understood it in my gut."

From the time she was a teenager, fending off the flirtations of returning soldiers in the wake of World War II in Washington, D.C., Sister Sharon had always been capable of charming men. At age sixty-nine the force was still with her—a hint of red in her hair, high cheekbones, bright blue eyes, a rich sense of humor and a dazzling smile. She brought this all into focus on John. He was blind, of course, but she knew there were ways she could still reach him.

She waited on him. When he wanted ice water, which was quite often, Sister Sharon brought it. When he was fumbling to light his cigarettes, she would run down to the sanctuary, come back with matches and light one for him. Every day she would wheel him out on the porch. He would sit and spit. She would shrug and wipe it up with a towel. When his Sony Walkman broke, she lent him hers.

After three weeks of trying to radiate love and kindness, it seemed to her that John had changed, but the way a glacier changes. There was only a little melting. He would still swear at the nurses, but not at her. When she arrived to light his cigarettes, he often acted as if she wasn't there, absorbed in a discussion with a newfound friend, a rasp-voiced, chain-smoking old woman dying of lung cancer.

Sister Sharon found herself growing frustrated. While the dying might appear vulnerable, she had trained her nurses to wait for the right moment. It would come. They should never talk about God to patients until they were sure they were ready. With John, she was frustrated enough to consider violating her own rule.

"I thought, I've been waiting on this person hand and foot for three weeks. He owes me. Tomorrow I'm going to talk to him about God!" When she entered the hospice the next day, everything had changed. The nurse told her that in the night John had had a vision. They heard him raving about how he'd seen Jesus. He had been shouting, "He's real! He's real!"

When Sister Burns came into his room, John was dozing. "I said he looks like an angel," she recalls. She was so moved she sang "Amazing Grace" to him, all five verses. After lunch she returned. He seemed a bit groggy. "I said, 'John, Jesus told a lot of wonderful stories and I'd like to tell you one.'"

"Tell me the story," he said. She picked the story of the Prodigal Son. A young man runs away from home, spends all his money, his friends desert him and he winds up at the very bottom rung of society, making slave wages feeding pigs. Yet, when he decided to return home, his father was there to welcome him lavishly.

"You've started back, John," Sister Sharon told him. "I want to assure you that you do have a Father who loves you." As John drifted back into slumber, she sat with him, holding his hand. Then she stepped out of his room for a few moments to finish some office work. Eight minutes later the nurse called her. John was dead. "I never got around to introducing God to him," Sister Sharon recalled. "God took care of it."

There have been many scenes like this at what is now called Mercy Health Services in Baltimore, since the Sisters of Mercy took charge of the city's run-down downtown hospital in the 1880s. During the last thirty years of its life, the hospital business has changed radically. As late as the 1970s, most hospitals were nonprofits and many, like Mercy, had religious affiliations.

The business is now dominated by for-profit hospitals, managed care and federal auditors and insurance companies who determine how money is spent. The combined effect has been a speeded-up in-out cycle so that the convalescing and the dying are usually done somewhere else.

What Sister Sharon did with John is called pastoral care, and it is an intangible item. It never appears in the system's $200 million annual budget. The nuns just absorb it, as they always have. Sister Helen Amos, a short, bright, pragmatic woman who is chairman of the hospital system's board of trustees, would like to find a way to support more of it. "Before I retire," she sighs, "I'd like to see Mercy for the first time in its existence have an endowment that is worthy of its name."

She sees U.S. hospital care headed in two directions. One is market driven and technology driven. It will pack hospitals with the latest equipment, drugs and doctors who can use them to prolong life, although it will be increasingly expensive. She says, "The average age is seventy-five; there are people who think we can make it a hundred and twenty. If you don't stop and ask yourself the question of whether longer life is an appropriate goal, then you'll just keep pursuing this retreating horizon."

Sister Helen prefers the other direction: "sustainable, affordable medicine." In part, this would apply more nursing skills and be more attentive to the desires of the patient and the patient's family. "Are there people who find it comfortable for you to hold hands and pray? Yes there are."

For Mercy Hospital, the late 1900s involved a long struggle to keep its traditions and its independence along with its financial footing. When other hospitals moved to the suburbs, the Sisters of Mercy raised the money to rebuild their hospital right where it was, in the heart of downtown.

Sister Mary Thomas, a former pediatric nurse, was the hospital's chief administrator for thirty-five years, ending in 1991. She recalls there were enormous pressures to move. The sisters had already purchased land in the suburbs. "I prayed and prayed and prayed to make the right decision." In 1968, as construction crews were finishing the new building, she climbed up to the top and remembers seeing the smoke of Baltimore's race riot, which was raging near the hospital.

She had risked the hospital's entire future on the proposition that the hospital should remain downtown. As she watched, she saw National Guard units and some of the hospital's clients from the adjoining African American neighborhoods. Together, they were protecting Mercy Hospital.

"We had sisters on almost every floor," she recalls, somewhat wistfully. They were mostly managers, or teachers at the hospital's nursing school next door. In 1973 the nursing school closed. Fewer and fewer young women were applying. The same was true for young women wanting to enter the convent. Suddenly, there were many other career choices.

In the 1980s, Sister Thomas launched a new effort for survival, a campaign to convince downtown businessmen that, despite all the changes, the hospital nearest them had some peculiar advantages. Sisters of Mercy might be older and most no longer wore their familiar white habits, but they were "still different from the rest of the world," she reminded one audience.

"We have different fundamental motives and goals. We are not working for personal salaries or personal gain. We are not paying off home mortgages or putting children through college. Our lives are centered in service to Christ and His people. We have sacrificed something. We serve as selflessly as we can."

If the businessmen didn't understand that, all they had to do was look at one sister. She was Flora Lancaster, a shy, smiling, thin-faced woman who was to the hospital's nursing staff what Derek Jeter later became to the New York Yankees. She was the heart of the team, the nurse that everyone else, especially the younger nurses, measured themselves against.

She came from rural Maryland and when she entered the convent, she took the name Sister Mary Thecla. Like the other nuns, she was sent away for a master's degree in nursing and groomed for a management role, but her first love was being with patients. Night and day, that's where she could usually be found.

Mr. Jeter and the New York Yankees are sometimes accused of playing "small ball," that is, concentrating on being near perfect in the fundamentals of their craft. That, in a nutshell, was Sister Mary Thecla's specialty. "She was about medium height, very thin, very humble," recalls Sister Thomas. "She was a supervisor, she didn't like it, but she did it." During off hours, she would roam all over the hospital, doing favors for people, making sure they were comfortable. "Her loveliness was in her

Sister Mary Thecla. Small things matter. (COURTESY OF THE SISTERS OF MERCY, REGIONAL COMMUNITY OF BALTIMORE, MARYLAND)

smile," recalls Sister Thomas. "If you were a patient and she came into your room, you'd never forget her."

Sister Helen Amos remembers her walking down the hall, carrying suitcases for stronger women and "running around the hospital at all hours of the night delivering things, doing laundry for patients." Sometimes she would just stand in the downstairs lobby, wearing the Mercy nurse's traditional white habit, and greet visitors and patients as they came in.

One of the doctors at the hospital swears Sister Mary Thecla was "bilocal" because she seemed to have the ability to be with patients on two different floors at the same time. "It was that attention to detail, that absolute focus on patient care, no matter what else was going on, that was very inspiring," recalls Sister Pat Smith, who watched her. For several years Sister Thecla had Sister Sharon's Stella Maris job, caring for the dying.

In the summer of 1998, it was time for someone to care for Sister Thecla, but that proved to be very difficult. She was dying of leukemia, though she insisted on being put in a double room at Mercy Hospital. She did that so she could get out of bed and help nurse the patient in the adjoining bed. At her funeral, the church overflowed with friends, flowers, prayers and former patients. A hospital employee, Josef Stefan, was moved to compose a song in her honor. It is called "God of the Small" and this is one of the verses:

> *A hospital can be a really big place*
> *She's still making her rounds*
> *While the sun's going down*
> *And she makes it a point to visit all of the floors,*
> *And some simultaneously.*

Mercy Hospital's plan for survival calls for a mix of suburban clients, business people from downtown and people from the poor neighborhoods that surround it. It will continue to modernize. In 1997 it won an award for having one of the best women's medical centers in the country. Mercy devotes $15 million of its income every year for service to the poor.

There have to be limits to that, notes Sister Helen. "We have to be a mainstream presence. You can't be one hundred percent serving the poor. In our society if you're only operating for the poor, society will let you become a poor institution, and I mean poor in every sense of the word."

Still, Mercy continues to buck trends in the hospital business. In 1996 it reshuffled its staff, cutting back on a proliferation of nurses' aides and technicians and using the money to increase the number of registered nurses on its staff by 40 percent. Later, it spurned a national wave of amalgamation, encouraged by managed care, and backed away from a proposal to merge with a nonsectarian hospital.

Such mergers have ended the identities of a large number of religious hospitals, but Thomas R. Mullen, Mercy's new chief executive officer—the first person to hold the job who is not a nun—wanted no part of that. "He said we had the best name, Mercy. We should keep it," recalls Sister Helen.

There were twenty-five sisters working in the hospital in Sister Thomas's day. There are about a dozen now, most of them in their late sixties or older. "If we're going to continue to fade as a presence, the only thing we can do is pass on the tradition to others," explains Sister Helen.

The person in charge of doing that is Sister Aine O'Connor. She is thirty-five. By quirk of fate, she's from Dublin. She's a Catholic and she used to pass Catherine's McAuley's house on Baggott Street nearly every day, but she didn't know what it was. Trained as a speech therapist, she came to the United States in 1993 for what she thought was an eleven-month stint doing research work at Emory University in Atlanta. Her plan after that was to go back to Dublin. "I'd always wanted to be married and have five children."

Much of her research took place at St. Joseph's Hospital, which was run by the Sisters of Mercy. In her spare time she volunteered for the hospital's outreach program, which sent vans carrying medical help into poorer neighborhoods. At the hospital she saw sayings of Mother McAuley inscribed in big letters on the wall of the lobby. "I thought, Who is this woman? What she says makes a lot of sense." As Aine (pronounced Anya) learned more about the history of the order's experience in America, she found herself being pulled into it.

Her job at the hospital is to teach the Mercy tradition to its two thousand employees, whom she meets with in small groups. For example, she gave the hospital staff little cards with pictures of nuns sweeping and cleaning the hospital, which generations of Mercies once did, very thoroughly, to set apart their hospital. "Our ordinary duties should be performed with all possible care and attention, none of which should be deemed trivial or unimportant," says the card.

What Sister Aine teaches could be described as small ball. Once it is acquired, it can be a very powerful tool. It was the credo of Sister Mary Thecla, and it is the example that Sister Sharon tries to set for the nurses who care for the dying at Stella Maris. Sister Sharon is now seventy-four. Her *Hello, Dolly!* days are over, but she has no plans to retire from her current post anytime soon. She does have a full agenda of things she plans to do on the side, including taking watercolor lessons and mastering Spanish. "So much to learn, so little time!" she says.

As time goes on, Sister Aine will become the keeper of the legacy of these skillful, vigorous women. She hopes to use it to perpetuate the soul of the hospital that watches over downtown Baltimore. As she puts it, it is a job that begs to be done. "Our tradition goes back to Ireland. We have sisters here in their nineties that keep passing on little bits of it to me. And I have to say, I can't let go of that."

In an age that abounds in connoisseurs of art, music, wine, food and travel, there are few people who are connoisseurs of hospital care, perhaps because most Americans would prefer not to think about it. Since 1972, Terrance Keenan has spent a lot of time walking hospital corridors and talking to nurses, doctors and patients. As a program manager for the Robert Wood Johnson Foundation, he has helped give away $3 billion to improve the nation's health care.

To him, the hospitals run by sisters are a kind of gift to America that is declining in value with age. "When you have a group of people who make a lifetime commitment to bringing caring and comfort and consolation to people in pain, you have a very precious asset that's been diminished."

The fading presence of hospitals run by sisters and other religious groups combined with the nation's nursing shortage, he thinks, has been a double blow to the state of medical care. His prognosis is bleak: Smaller hospitals, such as Mercy in Baltimore, that emphasize nursing skills, he predicts, "will find they have a mission that gets continuously more difficult to fulfill."

Other hospitals that have what he calls an "overriding concern with the bottom line," he thinks, will drive the nurses that remain out of the profession. By shortening the recovery period for patients with serious illnesses, he says, they put much more stress on their nursing staffs by leaving them with patients who are all very sick. "When you have all of our patients going through intensive care, the effect on nurses is very exhausting." That, plus pay scales that tend to be flat after the first few years, are why many experienced nurses are leaving in midcareer, he says.

"Nobody is looking at what's happening inside those hospital walls. A hospital is a nursing care institution. Who is there twenty-four hours a day caring for patients? It's the nursing staff. The doctors come and go."

In 1992 Mr. Keenan had an even more intimate view of this problem. He underwent heart bypass surgery at a hospital run by a large university. When he arrived home, his doctor advised him that he was still very sick and still needed attention. So the connoisseur of hospitals indulged himself. He checked into St. Mary's Hospital, a small hospital in his hometown, Newton, Pennsylvania. He was there for eleven days and the care he received there, he says, was critical. "You're very challenged when you're sick and you have to pull together all your will to survive."

The hospital is run by the Sisters of Mercy, and Mr. Keenan, a Catholic, found their presence comforting. But there was something beyond a mere physical presence, a feeling that seemed to permeate the hospital. Measured against the cost and sophistication of buildings, diagnostic machinery and exotic specialists, it was something small and immeasurable, but still, it was what brought him the most comfort.

What was it? "The feeling that all of the patients had there, was that there was the kind of compassion that it takes for someone who is ill to find himself and get well again. It's very had to put into words. It's an atmosphere of kindness and concern."

25
YEAST

It was a few nights after Christmas 2000 and all through the glittery downtown, grates were exhaling the warm breath of a busy, prospering city. A closer look at those grates, though, revealed a number of ragged, dirty people. They were standing, sitting, dozing, preaching, begging. Mark Bradley studied each one of them as he slowly cruised past them in his white, unmarked van.

It was a Code Blue night. In the parlance of people who worry about the homeless, that means a life-threatening environment. The windchill factor hovered at just ten degrees. The air was beginning to have a cruel bite. If some of these people spent this night unprotected, he knew, there could be bodies on the street by morning.

But bringing in the most stubborn of the homeless is an art form requiring great patience, compassion, attention to detail and, above all, gaining their trust through repeated visits. Mr. Bradley, forty-six, had been schooled carefully in this by a Mercy nun, Sister Mary Scullion. Starting in 1988 with an experiment to see if she could get a few homeless "bag ladies" off the street, by the turn of the century this short, wiry sister had managed to bring renewal to an entire section of north-central Philadelphia.

Stephen F. Gold, fifty-eight, a lawyer who had made arguments about the theory of the rights of the homeless, sometimes watched her, spellbound, as she methodically put it into practice. She made a map of where each person lived downtown and visited them frequently, bringing them food, always extending the possibility of rehabilitation.

"Mary does not have the kind of street smarts that I would like her to have," Mr. Gold notes. "She is not afraid to go out at any time at night and alone. An awful lot of those people know her. I've gone with her sometimes. I grew up in a tough neighborhood, but some of the streets she visits scare me.

"She'd say 'Hey, I think that so-and-so used to sleep down there by the railroad tunnel, let's go.'

"I'd say, 'Wait a minute, Mary, there are no lights.' She'd go. She's truly religious. She's not afraid for herself. Danger isn't on her radar screen."

With the backing of the Mercies, private foundations and more than a hundred volunteers like Mr. Gold, Sister Mary has formed a small empire dedicated to rebuilding shattered lives and the equally shattered neighborhoods of North Philadelphia. In a dozen years her Project H.O.M.E. had grown from an improbable, controversial idea into a valuable community institution with $34 million in working assets and eleven different operating centers.

The nun's efforts are especially appreciated on Code Blue nights. While the city's fathers are still not exactly enamored of the homeless, nobody wants the job of explaining why there are frozen bodies on the streets. Mr. Bradley, the outreach coordinator for H.O.M.E., was hopeful as he continued his cruise. Bitter cold, he said, might get some of his more hard-core cases into accepting a ride to shelter and, maybe, a start on rehabilitation. "Cold is a time of opportunity. It gets them ready to think of other alternatives."

At Eighteenth and Vine, he slowed down. There was Albert, standing on a grate, a familiar face. He took art courses sponsored by Project H.O.M.E. In one class he'd just made a bulldozer out of clay, showing considerable talent. But that seemed to be all the rehabilitation Albert could tolerate. Mr. Bradley got out of his van to talk to him. This was not the night to bring in Albert, he explained, getting back into the van. Albert had a home where he could sleep. Like many mentally ill, however, being inside made him feel trapped. This night he just preferred to be outdoors.

A radio call sends Mr. Bradley's van to a Wendy's on a fashionable street where a white, stretch limo with darkened windows pulled away from the curb, revealing a police car parked behind it. The police were inside the Wendy's talking to a customer the restaurant didn't want. He was a toothless, slobbering old man wearing a urine-soaked parka. He had difficulty keeping his pants up and seemed totally incoherent.

Mr. Bradley took him away in the van. The police seemed relieved. At Project H.O.M.E.'s headquarters the man tried on clean, warm clothes as Mr. Bradley and other volunteers checked a hospital bracelet found on his arm against city records on a computer. They make a lucky hit. His name was Alonzo and he had been missing from the boardinghouse where he lived for five days. Mr. Bradley took Alonzo home.

As they left, they passed a wall bearing the motto of Project H.O.M.E.: "None of us are home until all of us are home."

For Sister Mary, shelter is just the beginning of the meaning of home. When she realized that the homeless had multiple problems that required education, housing, jobs, counseling and myriad other services to resolve, she kept on expanding Project H.O.M.E., which is now, among many other things, in the process of rehabilitating a thirty-three-block stretch of North Philadelphia.

An African American neighborhood once marked by graffiti, abandoned houses and dismal statistics—56 percent of the families live below the poverty level—it now hears the bustle of construction crews as H.O.M.E. rehabilitates crumbling row houses and turns them into rental apartments for the poor.

Her goal is to build two hundred housing units for the working poor in the next ten years. She knows the neighbors and the neighborhood and has picked up the street talk. Giving a visitor a tour of the neighborhood, she complains about the time-consuming paperwork to get more abandoned housing from the city to rehabilitate. "Frankly it's a pain in the ass."

This neighborhood once had a rich community life, and while she's trying to revive it, she's done what she could to memorialize the past. It was once Irish Catholic, and the old church that was its spiritual and social heart—St. Elizabeth's—was torn down long ago for safety reasons after the Catholic Church abandoned it. The rectory remains and Sister Mary and a neighborhood group have tried to memorialize the church by building a neighborhood garden that marks its old outline.

Her main goal is to help community life become rich again and to see that, as it does, the message spreads. To that end, H.O.M.E. has formed thirty-three young people into a kind of human wakeup call. It is an award-winning drill team: the North Philly Foot Stompers. In the summer of 2000, Sister Mary celebrated her twenty-fifth anniversary as a Sister of Mercy. The Stompers stomped and the neighbors ate barbecue.

All this took work. When H.O.M.E. efforts first started, the people who live in the neighborhood objected to the idea of an outside group using an abandoned, former convent as a rehabilitation center for drug addicts. So Sister Mary took up residence there with the addicts. "I told them [the neighbors] you can have my number. If there are any problems, give me a call."

She had a variety of collisions with city officials and sometimes led street demonstrations. It was her complaint that brought in the U.S. Department of Justice to sue the city to force approval for H.O.M.E.'s headquarters, an abandoned casket factory, under the Fair Housing Act. Former Mayor Ed Rendell, often on the losing end of these efforts, once called her an "urban terrorist."

In one way what she has accomplished here fits squarely with the long tradition of the Sisters of Mercy. The order's founder, Catherine McAuley, and its American pioneers Frances Warde and Austin Carroll among them, would feel quite comfortable with the adventurous nature of H.O.M.E. But in another way they wouldn't. There are no younger sisters here ready to take up Sister Mary's cause.

Joan Dawson-McConnon, a tax accountant who cofounded the project with her, is a Catholic, but many of the group's dedicated army of volunteers aren't. Mr. Bradley is a Quaker; Mr. Gold, who has become her lawyer and chief political strategist, is Jewish, but not religious. Will O'Brien, her top assistant and a fallen-away Catholic, says he is religious, but has trouble defining just what religion it is. He thinks of himself as a kind of "Anabaptist." What does this mean for the future of the project?

Sister Mary Scullion (left) and Joan Dawson-McConnon, the co-founders of Project H.O.M.E. (COURTESY OF PROJECT H.O.M.E., PHILADELPHIA, PENNSYLVANIA)

"You have to have faith," shrugs the nun, dressed in her customary uniform of sweater, faded jeans and dirty white sneakers. "When Catherine McAuley started, it was just her and four or five other people. They had no idea how this was going to go."

Ms. Dawson-McConnon says the people in H.O.M.E. are tied together by a faith in what they do. "There is a strength in all of the people from an organizational standpoint. I think we exist and we grow and we nurture each other because of what's here. I think all of these people will carry this on and do well. New people will come in with new energy and new ideas."

As for the Sisters of Mercy, providers of the initial spark and the financing that ignited H.O.M.E. and countless other projects that help the poor, the next ten years will be Code Blue. It will be a life-threatening time for them and most of the other orders representing the remaining American sisters.

The Mercies are a mirror of the actuarial nightmare most of them face. In the Philadelphia area there are 430 Mercy sisters, but only about 25 are below the age of fifty. The schools where they served once numbered over

100; now there are fewer than 20. Their four hospitals have been folded into a huge, professionally managed regional health-care system called Catholic Health East.

Nationally there are 6,000 Mercies with only 240 of them under the age of forty-five. After years of inner turmoil over the meaning of Vatican II reforms and chronic failures to recruit young women, the prospect that their order might die or severely change its structure is something Sister Mary and many of the younger Mercies often think about.

"I don't know if the order will go on or not, but I believe there will be other forms of mercy, forms of standing in solidarity with the poor that will always exist if we, as a people, are faithful to God's call. It can't help but be that way," asserts Sister Mary. "We're all part of this. We all have to take a little responsibility."

Sister Marie Chin, the order's current president, thinks that something very much like Project H.O.M.E. is part of the Mercies' blueprint for the future. A trim, cheery woman who grew up in the mountains of Jamaica, she sees the small, neighorhood-centered project as a kind of return to the Mercy roots. Mother McAuley, she notes, started the whole order, working with the poor from one house on Baggott Street in Dublin in 1831.

Sister Marie and other leaders of the order are planning what they call the "1831 Project." The idea is to focus the remaining younger sisters on developing neighborhood centers to serve the poor that would attract volunteers the way Sister Mary Scullion has, from all walks of life. Sister Marie hopes to form fifty, maybe a hundred.

"What we need to do now is find who are these people who have a passion for this and who want to put their lives where their words are," she says. "If the life force is there, we can move with it. We want the immersion in the neighborhoods." Whether the model will exactly match Sister Mary Scullion's project or not, she's not sure. There could be other versions. Overall, though, she is very excited by the idea. "It's almost like a refounding moment, using Catherine McAuley's vision."

The idea of influencing the behavior of larger communities or organizations with a handful of sisters is part of the planning in other areas as well. "If you view religious life as a work force to carry on institutions, then I think we have a major problem because we don't have the folks to physically work in all those venues," explains Sister Katherine Doyle, fifty-five, a regional leader of the Mercies in Auburn, California.

"But if you look at religious life as a prophetic force that speaks to the truth that God is at the center of our universe, then what you need is highly passionate women who are committed to the lifestyle. It doesn't take a lot of yeast, you know, to make bread."

In recent years the Mercies have cast their bread upon the waters in a series of experiments to find new ways to address their mission. In 1981 their Denver branch bankrolled eight Mercy sisters with $500,000 to see if they could use it to provide better housing for the working poor, particularly those with families. Today the effort involves twenty sisters from various orders. They employ 513 people to oversee about $500 million worth of rental property in communities all over the West.

"Our mission is to create healthy communities. We're not just about doing housing," explains Sister Lillian Murphy, fifty-nine. "We want to have a voice in public policy. You have to have size for that."

The most critical part of the yeastlike activities of Catholic nuns will be in their hospital systems, where they definitely have size. Catholic health-care systems, most of them started by nuns, represent the largest source of free health care in the United States outside the federal government. Measured in economic terms, four of the nation's ten largest hospital systems are Catholic with combined net revenues of over $18.7 billion.

Meanwhile the number of sisters still actively managing these hospitals has shrunk to a relative handful. In this situation, they have found it can be a struggle to get the "bread" to rise. The nuns' strong sense of mission, the willingness to self-sacrifice, the long hours and their often penny-pinching ways are difficult to pass on to modern work forces, especially where there are labor unions involved.

California Mercies have folded in their hospitals with those of eleven other religious orders to create Catholic Health Care West, a $4.5 billion venture and the sixth largest hospital system in the United States. The system has fought a long and bitter battle with the Services Employees International Union, an affiliate of the AFL-CIO, which has been trying to organize the workers in the hospitals. The union has accused the system of hiring antilabor organizers and "failing to respect Catholic teaching, which supports workers rights to engage in collective bargaining."

The sisters managing the system responded that they were simply defending their workers' rights to choose whether or not to join a union. In April 2001, the two sides came to an agreement, but the tension between the two forces will likely linger.

Among the hospital managers, there is another huge gap that must be bridged. The Sisters of Mercy Health System in St. Louis, for example, started as a tiny downtown infirmary in 1871 where nuns did everything, including washing the bed sheets by hand in the basement. Now it is a $3.2 billion system, running twenty-four hospitals in eight states. Among its thirty thousand employees, fewer than sixty sisters remain.

"We will be down to thirty sisters in ten years," explains Sister Mary Roch Rocklage, chairman of the center's board. "We have to continue to make this accountable to what we are about. We've got to prepare the next group [of leaders] or we've lost the whole ministry to the Church."

"Otherwise we'll be doing wonderful social work, but it won't be the ministry of the Church." She sees about a "five-year window" to figure out how to pass on the Mercy torch. There will always be people from the community to continue the Mercy's work, she explains. "But do we minister? They don't see us. We don't touch them anymore."

About 16 percent of the nation's community hospital beds are in Catholic hospitals, which employ more than 617,000 people. According to *Modern Healthcare,* a weekly trade magazine that measures hospital size and income, Catholic hospitals are the fastest-growing systems in America. As a group, they also tend to run the largest operating losses.

Finally, there is a peculiar leadership gap within the ranks of the remaining sisters, organizations that are now top-heavy with elderly. The Sisters of Mercy are a prime example, with only a relative handful of their members under the age of forty-five. Recently the order sent all of them to a meeting in Miami. The goal of the meeting was to help them develop peer relationships, so they don't feel isolated in individual communities of older women. It was a way to give more strength to the yeast.

"We wanted to bring them together to give them opportunities to take on responsibility," explained Sister Doris Gottemoeller, who arranged it. "We want them to have the resources and the impetus for new outreach, not to be taking care of us."

"It was so brilliant!" said Sister Aine O'Connor, one of the members of the younger group. "It was like I'm not the only one attempting this."

While her predecessors drew strength from praying and bonding together in convents, Sister O'Connor's peers must often pray alone, but they try to keep in daily touch with one another via the Internet. "If you've had a hard time, someone will call."

Meanwhile, they prepare for the day when they will be the heirs of the vast Mercy system. "One of the things that people don't realize is that when you join Mercy, you have these wise women who've been around the block. There's a legacy that people have to offer us," added Sister Aine.

Few women have spent as much time or as much thought in preparing to transfer this legacy as Sister Doris, who spent the last thirty years in Mercy leadership, first in Cincinnati and later at the Mercy's national headquarters in Silver Spring, Maryland.

During her long career, as she watched many of her peers leave, she has had to manage much of the order's pain, first handling the departures and the closings of the seventies and eighties. As the head of the Leadership Conference of Women Religious, she fought for reforms and tried to keep the voice of most American sisters viable in Rome when Pope John Paul II seemed more swayed by more tradition-minded orders.

In the Mercies, an order that sometimes seems populated by smart, chatty Irish women, Sister Doris is something like an elder statesman: tall, reserved, sure of her ground, quietly dominant. "The first impression people get of her is, I think, because of her height," explains Sister Marie, who replaced her as the order's leader in 1999.

"You think that she's stern. Sisters used to come up to me and say, 'What is Doris really like?' She's a wonderful community person. She's bright, brilliant—oh, she'd be so embarrassed by all this. There is a wonderful simplicity about her. She's seen it all, yet she is so grounded in what really matters. She doesn't lose her equilibrium."

Between 1981 and 1991, Sister Doris headed a committee that eventually merged all of the communities of the Sisters of Mercy into one new unit: the Institute of Sisters of Mercy of the Americas. Most of what the committee did was driven by visions of a bleak demographic and financial future if the order remained Balkanized with seventeen independent communities.

In the days when the order was growing, the women who led it liked it that way. The smaller units gave them a sense of independence and community-based control. But as the order began to age and shrink, the

Sister Doris Gottemoeller: the Mercies' "elder statesman."
(COURTESY OF THE SISTERS OF MERCY OF THE AMERICAS)

enormous financial burden of retirement posed a question that seemed to have but one answer: To survive and to make sure sisters could retire in dignity, the Mercies needed an organization that enabled them to confront their financial problems together.

For much of their existence, the financial policy of the Mercies and other orders of sisters has been extremely simple: The Lord will provide. They were concerned about mission, not about money, and lived on the generosity of others. The result is a strange patchwork of plenty and poverty that is peculiar to the ways and values of America. The sisters who taught often earned barely enough to survive. Thanks to Medicare, which required that hospital officials be paid competitive salaries and given retirement benefits, orders and congregations that focused on hospitals are relatively well off.

The new organization, which is based on twenty-five Mercy regions, makes it easier for the rich ones to make loans to help the poorer ones and to take the lead in areas that are building joint retirement homes for multiple orders. To further that, and to shed more light on future financial options, the order is developing its first uniform national accounting system. That will give sisters a better grasp on what funds and what properties are available to bolster their retirement system.

Where their managerial ranks are thinning, the Mercies and other orders have begun to make use of an obscure part of Church or canon law, the "juridical person." It sets up a trustlike arrangement that will assure the management philosophy of the Mercies will to carry on, after they are no longer able to serve on the boards of the hospitals or the schools that they built.

Are the Sisters of Mercy preparing for their organizational death? "We're not paralyzed by the thought of it," says Sister Doris, with her characteristic coolness. "We've made plans to care for our elderly members. We're not consumed with anxiety about that. We have resources within the institute to care for ourselves, so we don't have to burden younger members to care for older people."

She does regret one thing: the long lapse in recruiting that left a huge gap in the ranks between older sisters and the few young ones entering. "We were really remiss in promoting ourselves and in inviting new members." In their early years of explosive growth, the Mercies found the United States to be their richest terrain for new recruits. Now the cycle is different. Mercy chapters in Third World countries continue to grow, but Sister Doris doubts whether there will ever again be six thousand Sisters of Mercy in America.

"But we want women in the future to have the opportunity to live this way of life. . . . The responsibility we have is to live the commitment we've made with as much authenticity and generosity as we can muster and then invite others to come and see."

She likes the idea of focusing more effort on Scullion-like community projects because it would make the Mercies visible again, in the way they were once accepted as part of the landscape in thousands of American communities. "Under the age of sixty we might have a thousand people. If we could take those thousand people and deploy them on forty spots across the country, it wouldn't matter what ministry they did. They'd be visible and we'd be visible. They would be seen as attractive. We have become so diffuse that people don't have a chance to see who we are. I think this is the kind of thinking we have to do."

Sister Doris's current job is senior vice president of Catholic Healthcare Partners, a $3 billion, thirty-hospital system that she helped put together during the 1980s. It is a composite of many of the different organizations that struggled to bring not-for-profit health care to the Midwest. At its core are eleven hospitals founded by the Mercies. There are also hospitals formerly run by the Sisters of Charity of Montreal, the Sisters of the Humility of Mary, the Franciscan Sisters of the Poor, the Diocese of Covington, Kentucky, several municipal hospitals and some built by Lutherans.

Her job is to work with Brian Connelly and Jane Crowley, two executive vice presidents of the new system, to help them make sure the dominant religious tradition of the hospitals permeates the training, promotion and incentives for all new managers and employees. They have prepared training films, such as one entitled *Value-Based Service in a Bottom Line World*, to convey the message to employees.

Such transitions are not new to either of them. Mr. Connelly remembers his first job as a hospital administrator in 1984 at Providence Hospital in Detroit. His first board meetings consisted of a dozen women, all members of the Daughters of Charity—who owned the hospital—and him. "I was sort of let inside this sacred arena and I was a little frightened," he recalls.

In the months to come, however, the number of sisters on the board dwindled down to two. One day at a ceremony to dedicate a new building, he found himself standing alone. The transition had occurred.

Ms. Crowley started as administrator at St. Mary Hospital in Richmond, Virginia, a small hospital run by the Sisters of Bon Secours. In the mid-1980s there were still eight elderly nuns working at the hospital, including one, Sister Mary Monica, who had been the hospital's chief executive officer before she retired. Some days she would plant herself behind Ms. Crowley's desk.

"I'd say, 'Sister, can I help you?' She'd say, 'I think we need to have tea.' There'd been some problem that she'd heard about from a patient."

One day Sister Monica ordered that a glass booth be built in the middle of the lobby for her. She wanted to greet patients as they came in the door. In theory, Ms. Crowley's job was to approve all construction work at the hospital and she thought it was an awkward location, but Sister Monica just went to the carpenter and told him to build it. "I was a little lost," recalls Ms. Crowley. But the booth turned out to be a great success. "People would line up to speak with her. She was such a visible presence."

Later Ms. Crowley began to rethink those meetings in her office. "She brought me very real feedback at a very formative stage in my career. At the time, I thought I was doing her a favor, but after ten years I realized that she was teaching me without me ever knowing it. When she died, I cried as if she was my grandmother."

Other orders, including the Daughters of Charity, which built the biggest Catholic hospital system in the United States, are having the same transition problems. "Our farm team dried up," explains Sister Carol Keehan, referring to younger sisters who once provided the system's workforce. She is president of Providence Hospital in Washington, D.C., which she rescued from near bankruptcy in 1989.

Most of the Daughters' hospitals are now in big systems, like Catholic Healthcare West and the even larger Ascension Health, which is the nation's fourth largest system. Sister Keehan is determined to keep Providence as an independent unit, serving poor neighborhoods in northeast Washington, D.C.

"You keep this going by building up the strength of the laypeople who work here. You have to spend the time and the money to make sure they have everything they need, not just degrees, but that they have the kind of spiritual development and theological exposure" that young sisters received in their education.

Every month, a busload of Providence employees visits the order's mother house in Emmitsburg, Pennsylvania, home of Mother Seton, the first American saint, and site of the order's heroic nursing efforts after the Battle of Gettysburg. "Many of them are getting to know some of the older sisters who are retired up there," says Sister Keehan.

In a sense, all Americans are heirs to the rich traditions of orders of religious women in the United States. But the most direct heirs are the few young women following their footsteps. In the Mercies they are a small but brave group. They are entering a mansion with many doors and hallways that lead to various forms of public service.

Sisters of Mercy have been role models for Sue Weetenkamp since she entered Mercy High School in Baltimore in 1962. The faculty was staffed with young sisters then. "Many of them were just out of college. They were very dynamic, very intelligent women, very much in touch with the world." Some of them became her friends for life. She remembers it "as an extremely happy time."

Later she went to Mount Saint Agnes College, which the order ran in north Baltimore. As she explains it, when eight women out of her close circle of about fifteen college friends decided to join the order, she was torn. They were the elite of the class. She wanted to go with them. "But I never really heard the call. I was kind of mad that I didn't, but I remember thinking that if I went, it would only be because they were there."

In the early 1970s this whole world began to turn upside down. Eventually, all of her friends and some of her former teachers left the convent. One of them told her that it was Sue, a class leader in college, who really had the right stuff to be a Sister of Mercy. But by the mid-1970s Sue was sure that was no longer in the cards. She had married a man she called Mister Right and they were having children.

Still, she remained close to her Mercy friends. She did volunteer work at hospices and signed up as a Mercy "associate," one of a group of people who help with the orders' missions. When her husband left her for another woman in 1985, she raised the children and put them through college herself.

That was hard. She had started a small used-furniture upholstery business, Sue's Redos, that seemed to take all her time. "I said damn if those kids were going to lose both parents. I made sure to get to every school meeting and every game. We struggled financially. There were a lot of bread sandwiches."

In the mid-1990s, as her business prospered and her children were finishing college, Sue started feeling that her life was suddenly changing. At first she suspected it was something physical, perhaps the onset of early midlife crisis. Then she began to sense she was being called to enter the Mercies. "In the back of my mind I said, 'Nah, I really don't want to hear this.'" But she continued to hear it. "So I sat down and decided if this was a business decision, how would I handle it? I sat down and did a list of pros and cons."

The pros won. She remembers having dinner with a friend, the head of the Mercy's Baltimore region, and nervously edging the conversation around to the point where she could pop the question: "What does one do these days to become a sister?" In the fall of 1999, Sue became one of a handful of novices entering the Sisters of Mercy.

At the novitiate, located in St. Louis, one of her first assignments was to load up with Bibles, rosaries, pens, crayons and crossword puzzle books and visit the jail, a Mercy tradition in the city that goes back to the 1850s when Sister Austin Carroll did it. In the order, she is among a group of new beginners that call themselves Sister Moms, because they have all had families.

Sue, now fifty-one, says she is happy again. Her problem is that there are so many vacancies open in the ranks of the Mercies that she's going to have a hard time choosing a new career. "It's like being in a candy store and loving candy, but you only have a nickle to spend. What do you pick?"

In the novitiate, she met Amy Ballard, twenty-six, who went to a Catholic high school in Little Rock, Arkansas, but stopped going to church at eighteen, when her parents divorced. After college, she volunteered at a center for teenage mothers run by a Sister of Mercy. After that "it just all kind of evolved," Amy explains.

She felt the same pull that Sue had. She wanted to join the Mercies. Her parents were skeptical. She remembers being "scared" to tell her friends, who might ridicule her. But times had changed. "They said we already knew you were going to do this and it's great." She was a year behind Sue in the novitiate. If she survived, she would be the youngest Sister of Mercy in the United States, an added bit of challenge for her.

A slim blonde who could be mistaken for a college cheerleader, Amy saw her future as a kind of puzzle with two big pieces that needed to be fitted together. She believes her generation feels that community service is important. "I think there is a craving for it. The question is how to bridge that gap between this [Mercy] tradition and theirs? Sometimes I find myself thinking, Why am I here? It's a struggle. Some days I just want to give up."

Other days, she felt determined to take the message of the Sisters of Mercy back out on the streets of America, where it began more than 150 years ago with the "walking nuns," where it still is with the North Philly Foot Stompers and where, Amy is convinced, it *has* to be to survive. "They never recruited before because people just came to them. Older sisters say vocations come from God and you don't need to go out there.

But I just think that we need to be more vocal about it, and more public about vocations," she told a visitor to the novitiate.

She got close enough to the Mercies to glimpse one of the solutions to the order's current difficulties, but she will not be a part of the dwindling supply of "yeast" that the Mercies and other religious orders will provide in the twenty-first century. Unable to bridge the gap between the feeling of obligation to do community service and the vows that would mean a lifetime dedicated to it, Amy left the order in 2001.

26

THE ROAD TO
ST. CECILIA'S

Every year around August 17 an assortment of cars enters the wrought-iron gate of the Dominican Sisters of St. Cecilia. As they climb the long driveway, they near a big brick building set on a hill in a leafy park, a fine place, perhaps, for a picnic. But what happens here in August is definitely not a picnic for most of the occupants of those cars.

These are families bringing their daughters to enter religious life, a bittersweet experience. Many parents are saddened or puzzled by the departure of a loved one who is attracted by a career that would seem to be an anachronism, like becoming a blacksmith or a telephone operator in a day of impersonal, automated bustle. Some parents come here strongly opposed, even frightened by the mysterious world of ritual and few tangible rewards. And many of the new recruits arrive here physically and emotionally drained from the teary rounds of saying good-byes to family and friends. It is as if they were leaving for another planet.

St. Cecilia's class of 2001 was culled from between 125 and 150 women who visit the convent every year. Of those willing to join the order, eighteen were accepted. Their average age is twenty-four and they come from all over the United States, explains Sister Catherine Marie, the order's director of vocations. Nearly all of them, she says, are looking for traditional religious life. "The top questions we get are 'Do you wear a habit?,' 'Do you have daily devotions?,' 'Do you pray the rosary?'"

Those selected in August are to become "postulants," the timeless name for women entering the four-year cycle of transition from their normal lives to the rhythm of religious life, which, they all know, will be very different. It was Shakespeare who said you must be careful what you wish for, and that, too, is on their minds as they pull their baggage out of the cars and brace for the final round of good-byes. Their dream—the vision that had impelled them to sell cars and stereos, to give away their clothes, to quit lucrative jobs, to pull away from friends, even boyfriends in order to come here and become a Dominican sister—was about to become a reality. A nun! In an earlier age, this would have been seen as a reasonable step, a normal progression for young Catholic women. They were customarily taught by nuns. Catholics would simply shrug and say that they had gotten the "call," as a sign from God to serve him in religious life.

But what happens here every August is no longer a reasonable step, but an adventurous—some would say reckless—leap of faith by women, some of whom started the journey with little or no religious background. The great majority of these young women have never seen a sister in a classroom. In school they learned almost nothing about the rich history of religious orders in America. Self-sacrifice? They come from an age of self-indulgence in which people seem wary of commitments, benumbed by television and bombarded with every conceivable form of electric communication promising instant gratification.

Yet here they are, standing in the driveway of a building dedicated to a second-century Roman woman who was rewarded for her faith and good works by being beheaded. They are preparing to walk through the doorway of a life where rules require silence, poverty and celibacy. From now on contemplation, prayer, song and giving will be the preferred ways to communicate. To be sure, a great deal has changed since the sixties, but there is one aspect that hasn't: One way or another, women continue to hear the "call."

It came to Ashley Sarradet, thirty, in her early twenties. "I kind of pushed it away because I felt it wasn't normal." She had seen many Catholic sisters in her community, in Mobile, Alabama, but they had all been elderly. "I couldn't figure out why God wanted me to be with older women." Her dilemma was how to scratch with this persistent spiritual itch, this unexplained yearning to become a nun. "I decided it wasn't for me, but the thought wouldn't really let me alone."

Ashley had plenty else to absorb her. She was a triage nurse at the emergency room of the hospital run by the University of South Alabama in Mobile. It was rated as a Level One trauma center by the state, which meant that the helicopters carrying burn victims from serious traffic accidents were vectored there. There were some Saturday nights when ambulance crews brought in a steady stream of people who were shot or knifed. Between them would come pregnant women in the last stages of a difficult labor, homeless drunks in the last stages of a difficult life. She, a sturdy, smiling, attentive redhead, stood ready at the door to receive whoever came in, to weigh their needs against others and steer them into the right channel in the bustling room. Around her eighty people worked, sometimes frantically, to diagnose, to save lives or ease pain. She loved the job and the people. "Emergency room people are adrenaline junkies. We have to make decisions quick," she explains. Over time, she discovered that many of her peers were religious. "They have to be because you see a lot of death and dying . . . and births."

In her late twenties, she felt the call again, this time growing stronger. She went to see a parish priest, who provided some advice. "He said that if I didn't see an order I liked, I probably didn't have a vocation." She regarded that as a kind of dispensation that would free her from further anxiety, for she never expected to see an order that she liked. "I thought I was home-free." But in 2000 she came to St. Cecilia's on a visit and discovered the Dominicans included many young women. "I knew as soon as I saw them, that was it."

Well, not quite it. First she told her parents. They were shocked. "It was hard for them to understand that I was going to have to leave. Vocations weren't talked about. Everyone assumes you're going to get married and have a family." She told her former boyfriend. "He felt it was okay." She sold her house. Now here she was, about to enter a life where she would live for the first few months in a stark dormitory cell, marked off by white sheets into eight-by-twelve-foot cells, each with a table, a chair, a bed. In the dormitory would be forty-five new companions—the women in St. Cecilia's novitiate.

Watching over the new arrivals was Sister Mary Angela Highfield, fifty-eight, the mistress of novices. She would set their rules and help them with the weaning from home and friends into a life that accepts St. Cecilia's as "home." "We do it pretty radically," she explains. From then on, her charges could not phone or send e-mails home; they must write letters. They were limited to four days of home visits the first year. In their new home, conversation time would be limited by periods of silence and channeled. "They're taught not to talk always about the past; they're not constantly talking about their former love life or whatever." (Television is forbidden, though the mistress of novices acknowledges she might make an exception if Nashville's professional football team, the Titans, made it to the Super Bowl.)

This is her third experience with novices. The first time came in the sixties when she was one. Mother Marie William MacGregor, something of a genius at molding young women, was her novice mistress then. Most of her peers came straight out of high school. Few had acquired cars, apartments or much of anything else to get rid of. Families were almost always supportive. In 1983, when she did her first turn as mistress of novices, the parting process was harder. Recruits were fewer, older, more experienced and more tentative about accepting the rigors of religious life. Now, almost twenty years later, she was looking at her second batch of novices. These women, whose age averaged in the early twenties, were different again. "These young women have seen the pendulum swing to the extreme of materialism, the drive to succeed and all that and yet they have come to a conversion." These were women from Generation X, a generation derided in the press as cultural dropouts and nihilists. Yet they came from all parts of the country, seeking a regime whose customs date back almost a millennium. Oddly, there seemed to be nothing tentative about them. They had already sacrificed much. They wanted in. About half of them, she knew, would make it.

Carolyn Hetzler, twenty-five, got the call in October 2000 while she was leafing through a copy of *Sports Illustrated*. It had an article about a professional basketball player, Shelly Pennefather, a six-foot wonder who had the gift of sinking three-point jump shots almost at will. At the peak of her career, in 1991, she discovered she had another gift. She shocked the world of basketball by joining the Colettine Poor Clares, one of the most strict religious orders in the United States. Here was a maneuver that had her fellow players completely faked out. They couldn't believe it. "She said she'd been called," said one of them. "I said, 'Well, did you have to answer the phone?'"

Ms. Hetzler knew immediately why Pennefather had done it. "She had wanted something more. I could really identify with that." After college Ms. Hetzler had achieved her own kind of quiet stardom. She became a high-school teacher in Washington state and fell in love with her job. "Teaching was my life. I could pour myself into it. Kids were just amazing." The magazine article went right to the heart of what was missing. She was living alone in a community where people who lived side by side often regarded each other as strangers. Like the basketball player, she knew there had to be something better. She found it here. "I saw the young sisters living the traditional life. They had the habit that really showed who they were in the minds of the world. I remember going out to the field here and sisters were playing ultimate Frisbee. I thought this is the most amazing thing in the world. These are normal sisters who like to have fun. They can run around and yet they have given their lives fully to Christ. You didn't have to be old to be a sister. You didn't have to not have fun."

Jacqueline DuPuis, twenty-two, went to a Catholic high school in Minneapolis. By the time she was a junior, she had pretty much decided she would do whatever was God's will. For years, she and her twin sister had had the same game plan. "We would be in each other's weddings." Then came the call. "Just out of the blue I felt that God wanted me to join the religious life. I didn't know what that meant at the time."

She spent some time visiting orders. "The religious life I saw was sisters who lived on their own in their apartments. I felt that, well, this was what God was calling me to. I felt I was going to have to live alone. What I really wanted to do was get married, but I was faced with this idea that I was going to live alone, just be a teacher and end my days living alone." When she arrived at St. Cecilia's, at the suggestion of a friend, she felt instantly at home. "It was always here, what I was looking for, but I never knew where to look for it."

In May of 2000, Lucy Sundry, twenty, had a friend who died in an auto accident. It got her thinking. "Her death struck me about how precious life was and how short it was." Her call had come to her initially in high school, where she had tried to ignore it. Her idea of religious life was that it was declining. "The question really stuck with me throughout the rest of high school. I never really stopped to ask God whether He wanted me to serve Him as a sister. I was afraid that if I asked, that I would receive an answer that I wasn't looking for."

After the death of her friend, though, she began looking. A priest gave her a brochure about St. Cecilia's. The women who appear here don't necessarily come from celebrated Catholic universities. Every year since 1997, around Easter a vanload of women usually arrives from Texas A&M. The Aggie women, several of whom are now sisters, call it their Nun Run, a way of checking out convents and a preferred alternative to a beery week on the beach during spring break. Ms. Sundry organized a similar venture among her friends at Winona State University in Minnesota. One of her friends opted to join a conservative order in Michigan, the Alma Mercies. Another joined an order in Illinois. Ms. Sundry came here, and then went home to tell her parents she was joining St. Cecilia's. "The life here was so familiar, without it being familiar."

The call has drawn a blackjack dealer, an ex–Army captain, several teachers and nurses, a lawyer, a ballerina, a linguistics expert and an assortment of women from other professions. Of the 190 sisters who call this home, half have come within the last ten years. Their median age is thirty-five. There are more eager young recruits here than in just about any other order in the United States. By comparison, the Sisters of Mercy, the nation's largest order of nuns, attracts about ten annually.

Sister Mary Angela's plan for the first two days is simple. She loads the women into vans and they go to a rural monastery often used as a retreat center. Just then, retreat is what they all need, she explains. "They spend the first two days more or less sleeping. They come in pretty exhausted with all the good-bye parties and so on." The bonding that begins among them is very important. They are given the black vest and the black pleated skirt that postulants wear and are taught to sing the "Office," the prayer that religious men and women say to begin their day. The preparation is done so that three days later, when they return to the convent, they can begin to fit into its rhythms.

They are introduced to the older sisters in the infirmary, women in their eighties and nineties, some in wheelchairs. They are also introduced to the Horarium, the Latin name for the schedule that religious orders established in the Middle Ages: up at five A.M., a half hour of silent meditation, then Lauds, a meeting in the chapel where the "Office" is sung or chanted together. At 6:15 A.M. there is daily Mass followed by breakfast in silence, accompanied by a spiritual reading. Then to work, which is usually attending or teaching school. After the school day there is soccer, Frisbee or volleyball for the younger sisters, followed at five P.M. by Vespers, prayers in the chapel followed by the rosary. Dinner is taken in silence, with more spiritual reading. Then, an hour of recreation. Next, at 7:45 P.M., there is Compline, or night prayers, in the chapel. After that, time to study and prepare for the next day. At ten P.M. begins the "profound silence," which lasts until dawn. "After a long day of teaching, when you're mostly hearing yourself speak, the silence is really restful," explains Sister Catherine. "There is too much noise in daily life."

The beauty of this is hard for outsiders to fathom. Some of the older sisters know full well what the postulants are going through. Sister Mary Justin, forty-four, a professor at the order's college, remembers the battle royale with her family when she announced she was joining St. Cecilia's in 1977 after finishing three years of college. Her mother and her three sisters all lined up against her. Her father, who was a Methodist, went into sullen rebellion. He had agreed to raise the children as Catholics because his wife was Catholic. "But this was not part of the deal!" he would rage to his wife. He refused to speak to Sister Mary, his youngest daughter, for six weeks. Then, one day, he did. He had been reading over the literature she had been sent from St. Cecilia's and discovered the one crowning reason why she would never make it as a nun. "Do you realize there is this silence?" he asked her triumphantly.

She persisted. Her mother recruited her three older sisters to make one final attempt to talk her out of it. They confronted her in her room as she was sorting through her clothes. She should reconsider what she was giving up, take more time to think it over. She should at least finish college first. "And I said to them, if you feel strongly that God is calling you, do you turn around and say to Him, 'No, you've got to wait?'" When the mother returned, the three daughters each had neat piles of clothes given to them by their baby sister.

Entering St. Cecilia's "was a very difficult period for me" recalls Sister

Mary Justin, "because my family didn't support me." That gradually changed "once my family saw my happiness and saw it wasn't a forced happiness. Then they were able to start to see the bigger picture of what's really here. . . . They've come to love the sisters very much. Father even came into the Church shortly before he died."

To the casual visitor who arrives here, the first impression is that you've made a wrong turn on the freeway and blundered into a time warp, a Brigadoon-like vision of life as it was in the fifties. This is the way convents used to work: There are young novices pushing the oldest sisters in wheelchairs, making sure that everyone gets to prayers in the rose-colored chapel on time. When they are singing here together, the mix of the new and old, the high young voices and the mellower tones of the order's veterans, has a peculiar kind of beauty, a unity that once filled Catholic churches. This is the way this community has always lived. "For us to throw away the monastic practices would have been like throwing away half our heritage," explains Sister Mary Angela.

What people do in the order is determined annually by the mother superior, who assigns people to various missions of the order, primarily teaching posts in the order's twenty-two schools, based on her judgment of their talents and the order's needs. While many religious orders now regard this as heresy, it is not all that far from what happens in a modern American corporation or on a baseball team. Their manager selects. They obey. The strength of the sisters in their order comes from their faith and their communal prayer life, not from their mission. The Dominicans believe the togetherness, the unity and the organization give them staying power at hard jobs in which individuals might eventually burn out. "You can go out and help the poor, that's fine. But you don't just go out and get yourself in a tailspin and wear yourself out," explained Sister Christine Born, a former leader of the order.

The women who watch the procession of new entrants have vivid memories of their own struggles that brought them here. For Sister Mary Celeste, thirty-three, a black woman who graduated from the University of Michigan and came to Washington, D.C., for a high-paying job as a data analyst with the U.S. Postal Service, it wasn't so much a tailspin as it was a void. She had all the perks, including an apartment in Cleveland Park, one of the city's fanciest neighborhoods. Still, she felt a strong need to belong to something. She joined a feminist group, but soon left. It wasn't a good fit. "I was against abortion and I liked men."

She joined a Catholic feminist group and started going to daily Mass. Then one day she was walking along the Potomac. "I was thinking, I'd kind of like to work for God." She came here on a religious retreat and saw younger women bonding with older sisters. That, she felt, was belonging. Now, as a Nashville Dominican, she teaches religion at an Oak Ridge, Tennessee, elementary school.

Sister Mary Sarah, thirty-four, was a college student in Missouri. When she came here, it was the prayer life that attracted her. "I was here two hours and I said sign me up, this is it." Now she is the principal of an elementary school in Chicago, but the assignment, she is quick to point out, is not why she became a nun. "The primary purpose of everything we do is to seek the face of God. Everything else will come from that."

Sister Grace Olde-Kemp is one of those who came here from Texas A&M when she and ten other women came in a van with a trailer in what was billed as the Nun Run of 1997. The following year, as a high school math teacher, she joined the second Nun Run with twenty-four women. She found that the visits to St. Cecilia's were having a kind of cumulative effect. The pull grew until she finally joined in 2001. Three more Aggies are preparing to follow her.

Sister Sandra Stang, twenty-eight, was a nurse at the Mayo Clinic in Rochester, Minnesota. Coming here, she says, was like falling in love. "Just meeting the sisters, you saw such beauty. We call that Dominican beauty; you knew that there was Jesus in them. . . . I feel that sisterhood is a treasure. You unravel it and God reveals the beauty more and more."

Sister Anna Grace Neenan, thirty-one, is a beauty. She spent ten years as a professional ballerina. As a lithe, dark-haired teenager, she danced the role of Clara in Tchaikovsky's *Nutcracker* three Christmases in a row. Later, as a professional, she performed for the Boston, Pittsburgh and Pennsylvania ballet companies. Life for her was all dance: a blur of *Swan Lake, Romeo and Juliet, Petrouchka*. Then, in 1995, rehearsing for Alvin Ailey's *The River,* she injured her hip.

"It was a blessing in disguise. I began to think about what sort of person I would be and what I needed to do to do that." She had an older sister who was a Nashville Dominican. After several visits here, Anna felt the call. Her two closest friends didn't understand. "I tried to discuss it with them, but there's only so much you can say. What do I make of this? I don't want to do anything except be holy." Sometimes, when the spirit moves her, she will portray the meaning of a prayer in dance for the other sisters. "Most ballet dancers are very spiritual. They're searching for beauty and they're searching for truth." She is studying to become an elementary-school teacher.

Sister Mary Dominic, forty-four, is the daughter of a Methodist minister in Birmingham, Alabama. She was in graduate school at Queens University in Belfast, Northern Ireland, working on a Ph.D. in linguistics in 1979 when she got the call. Her objective was to study urban dialects, but she also saw some urban terror. Prowling the streets were connoisseurs of the power of gasoline: Protestants and Catholics who had grown up using Molotov cocktails to torch each other's houses. Some graduated to attacks on passing British soldiers, a practice of pouring a stream of gasoline down from buildings and then igniting it with a torch just over a passing armored car. They called it "warming the troops."

But she had the good fortune to encounter a different kind of Irish warmth: A group of Catholics discovered that she was a musician and asked her to play in church. As she played, she began to feel the power of the liturgy; it was pulling her in. One of the essential elements of the Catholic faith is that Christ is present on the altar at Mass. As Sister Mary saw it, it had a kind of stark logic to it. "If you believe that," she explains, "there is no point in being anything but Catholic."

She is not a woman to do things by halves. She returned to the United States to teach linguistics at Auburn University. In her spare time, she began looking at convents. "When I came up here, it was like love at first sight. . . . I could see that these were the sisters who still had the charism [spiritual gifts]. There was something beautiful about the ways they loved the Church and taught the Catholic faith. I was attracted to the monastic life. After eight-hundred years, it's perfectly at home in the modern world." She teaches English and religion at a high school.

Sister Mary Thomas, thirty-five, was at Western Kentucky University getting a degree in engineering. "My goals were set. I knew exactly what I was doing." Then she met a Benedictine brother who intrigued her. He had a sense of "simplicity, peace and courage" that she'd never seen before. She was the pride of a rural farm family that had struggled to raise five daughters and five sons. She was one of the first to make it to college and she started thinking that the sacrifice her parents had made to get her there amounted to putting her on a "kind of platform upon which I began to think 'Am I ready to offer something more?'" She told a parish priest she was thinking about becoming a sister. He gave her a brochure of the Nashville Dominicans. "I walked in the door and I saw joy and a radical gift of happiness and service." Her friends told her she was throwing her life away. Her father, a dairy farmer, took it the hardest. He said she was turning her back on a successful career. "There are parts of this that you can't explain. There are elements of a call from God that you can't put into words. That's where the faith comes in." She teaches physics and calculus to high-school students.

Sister Mary Madeline, twenty-eight, thought she wanted to "be a doctor, get married and have a big family." She had a full college scholarship when she felt a call to become a sister. Her father, a Methodist from Baltimore, Maryland, was unhappy about it. So she invited him to come with her for a week to visit the Nashville Dominicans. On his way in, he met Sister Hildegarde, a member of the order for sixty years, stumping along with her aluminum walker. "She was funny. She told jokes. She made him think this place is really unique. We stayed for several days. I would say today he's my number one supporter. He says it's not as though you lose your daughter, you gain a hundred and fifty more." She teaches English and religion in a junior high school.

Sister Stacey, twenty-two, grew up in a Catholic family in a suburb of Cleveland. They were always forcing her to join Catholic youth groups and nagging her to go to church on Sunday. She didn't like it. Swimming was the thing for her. She had a scholarship at Ohio University, but what she saw of college life wasn't for her. "Sex, drugs, alcohol, partying every night. That really got to me." She went back to live at home and attend a community college. She came here on a four-day visit. "I knew in my heart I had to enter. I knew absolutely nothing, didn't know you had to be silent, eat in silence. I was just trusting. I'm just so happy to be here."

Sister Mary Diana, thirty-nine, had a masters degree in mathematics from the State University of New York. She was saying prayers one day when the notion hit her: She might become a nun. "Over time I started thinking that the Lord wanted me to give him my life. But I didn't know any sisters. I said, 'If that's what you want, you've got to show me some sisters.'" Then she attended a summer religious class taught, in part, by Nashville Dominicans. In 1988, she came for a visit. "When I met them I was absolutely stunned. Anything I had thought about in religious life seems to all be here." Still, she came here tentatively, taking a leave of absence from her job in 1989, without explaining where she was going. She left her car with her parents, who had mixed feelings about her leaving. Among the many things she's discovered since then is the inner peace brought on by the night-long silence. "It's wonderful." She's at Vanderbilt University, finishing a medical degree. Her peers wear white medical coats, she wears the white habit of Saint Dominic. "My patients don't seem to react much. I introduce myself as a medical student and we go along from there."

Sister Anna Laura, twenty-nine, was engaged. Her goal in life was to "get married and have a huge family." When a college professor suggested she might want to look at religious life, she drew a complete blank. She had never met any sisters. Intrigued, she visited several convents. Most of them, she discovered, were thoroughly reformed. "Most of the members of the communities were doing whatever they wanted instead of having a unity of vision, that vision of living religious life and giving your life to Christ." She came here in 1996 for a day and a half and was hooked. She teaches English to ninth-graders.

Sister Mary Edith, twenty-eight, felt the call while walking through a mall at the University of Dallas. She visited another order that, she says, gave her bad vibes. "They were not together. The older ones were still in habit, the younger one's weren't. They didn't love the Holy Father. . . . They were interested in women becoming priests." Then she came here for four days. "I was sold. They took me up to my room. I was just so keen on the place. It was just very, very beautiful. I was just taken in by the joy and how everyone did everything together." She went home, sold her car, had a garage sale to get rid of the rest of her belongings including her favorite rock-and-roll CD by the Indigo Girls. "I took one last trip to Mexico, and that was it." Every novice at Cecilia's has chores to do while they're learning to become a sister. One of Sister Mary's is to bake bread that the order gives to doctors, dentists, car repairmen and others who donate their services to the order.

Sister Mary Seton, thirty-two, liked the idea of service. Her first job after college was teaching kindergarten on the Navajo reservation. That was a struggle. The kids didn't speak English. She couldn't keep them in their seats. When she came home to Fairfax County, Virginia, her father told her she was going to become a nun. "I said, 'No Dad, there is more than one way to serve God.'" She thought about going to graduate school and took a job as a waitress until she sorted things out. On a vacation trip to Moscow she heard a Catholic priest say if you felt a call to religious life, come up to the altar. She went. She made out a list of things she wanted from an order. It would have to be one that wears habits. "The habit says you're a sister. I'd seen sisters in modified habits, or wearing no habits at all. It doesn't really say they're religious. Not that they aren't, but it doesn't speak the same way that the habit does. Habit speaks." Now she teaches school in Murfreesboro, where they hadn't seen a sister in more than thirty years. "I walk around the neighborhood. I don't say a word, but I have gotten a lot of comments. People see me in the grocery. People come up and ask me questions."

Sister John Mary, thirty-nine, entered a Catholic grade school in Chicago just as most of the sisters were leaving. There were still a few nuns, a mix from different orders. She was struck by the Dominicans. "They loved one another intensely." After high school she came here to see why and she found everything she was looking for. "They said the Office, wore the habit; the order had a community dimension. It lived together and everybody knew one another." Her mother was upset. If she wanted to help the poor, why didn't she become a social worker in Chicago? Her father was "very agitated about the whole thing. Father said 'If you came to me and told me you were going to be married, I could tell you about that. But you've come to me with an offer I know nothing about and that's frightening to me." Her parents bought her a brand-new ski outfit. It was a not-so-subtle reminder of one of her joys that she'd be giving up if she took this fateful step. "I looked at that and said 'I'll miss that, but Mom and Dad, I want this. I believe I will not be a complete individual unless I do this.'" Once they saw she was happy at St. Cecilia's, they supported her.

Like the other women who have come up the road to St. Cecilia's, Sister John was running against the spirit of her age. But the call she heeded is ageless. Like the other women at St. Cecilia's, she found a place where she gets plenty of support. She can use it. She has served as the principal of three grade schools during the last twelve years.

27

NO TIME FOR
DANCING

The legacy of more than 400,000 women who have been Catholic sisters in America is a peculiar kind of gift. They educated millions of us, healed millions more. They inculcated the spirit of giving and built the schools and hospitals that make healthy communities, and in that sense, they have given us living reference points that help define the quality of American life.

They have been a source of care and hope in nearly every American crisis, from the War of 1812 to the attack on the World Trade Center on September 11, 2001. They were there for us in the Chicago fire, the San Francisco earthquake. They stood fast amid the chaos and superstition of the yellow fever outbreaks in New Orleans and pitched in when others preferred to ignore the AIDS outbreak in the 1990s. Along the way they shaped our history. Without sisters it is fair to say our frontier cities and the Wild West would have been much wilder places. It is also fair to say that without them the American Catholic Church would be but a shadow of its current self.

Their gift is peculiar because it is largely unexamined. Older Catholics seem to have taken it for granted. Younger Catholics don't know much about it. This is partly because of the odd experience of growing up in a church that was built on the faith, courage, idealism, self-sacrifice and sweat equity of young women. Yet in parochial school when we read church history, we read about the pronouncements and the activities and opinions of elderly men.

Part of the reason for this is that, historically, sisters have been trained to be self-effacing. Their mission was to give attention, not to receive it; to cure poverty, not to complain of their own. Another part of the reason is that the American Catholic Church, which counts 22 percent of the nation as its members, is one of the country's most poorly understood institutions. Until recently, when educational experts began to take note of the peculiar merits of the parochial school system, few outside scholars have done serious research on the Church or its institutions.

Because of the sheer breadth of the experience of Catholic sisters in America, this book—with a few excursions—uses the journey of the Sisters of Mercy to tell the larger story. There is great diversity among the nation's four hundred orders of sisters, but members of most of them will see much in the adventures of the Mercies that is similar to their own experiences, including the more recent years. The current life signs of most orders of sisters are not good.

After studying a number of orders in the 1980s, Sister Patricia Wittberg, a member of the Sisters of Charity and an associate professor of sociology at Indiana University, found most of them "in a decline phase with many members experiencing alienation at the most profound levels." While she found the situation "extremely threatening to the orders," she also found that "both the membership and the leaders may prefer to deny that it exists."

Sister Wittberg's theory is that the growth and decline of religious orders occurs in 250-year cycles. The current decline, she notes, is "more precipitous than any since the French Revolution." Moreover, she sees an element of despair in it. During the 1970s and 1980s most orders failed to recruit, which she finds odd because the basic survival instinct of most organizations is to perpetuate themselves.

What was it that wrecked what had been a smooth-sailing ship, one that had survived, even flourished in the storms and battles of most of our history? Part of the sisters' crisis during the rise of what Tom Wolfe called the Me Generation may not be all that peculiar.

Who Cares for the Future? Sisters of St. Francis prepare a picnic for their orphans.
Dubuque, Iowa, 1898. (COURTESY OF ST. MARY'S ORPHANAGE, DUBUQUE, IOWA)

Robert D. Putnam, a political scientist and the author of the seminal study of the decline of American social organizations *Bowling Alone,* found that forty-five different groups ranging from the League of Women Voters to the Red Cross and the Boy Scouts all began steep membership declines starting in the 1960s. "It's not just that older people are pulling out," he explained in an interview. "It's that younger people aren't joining. Finally some of these organizations just age themselves out of existence."

Dr. Putnam began his research in the early 1980s in Italian hill towns and found an unusual correlation. Towns that had a high level of involvement by volunteer groups such as choral societies and football clubs also had better governments and more efficient economies. "People were healthier," he notes.

He sees the decline of groups, accompanied by a decline in church-going and a falloff in voting, as a kind of loss of "social capital," but *Bowling Alone* does not paint a bleak future because he, too, thinks these things occur in cycles. A hundred years ago, as many people from rural society flocked to the cities, he says there was a similar decline in social groups. Then, between 1900 and 1910, there was a vigorous period of renewal when many current fraternal organizations and labor unions were created to fill the void. He thinks it can happen again. Throughout American history, he notes, ours has been a nation of joiners.

But his research also shows that the decline of specific groups is not necessarily self-correcting. Renewal takes hard work. Young women were an essential part of the work of the Catholic Church when it was young in America. I think it is fair to say that if it is to become young again, it will have to figure out how to regain their attention and their strong nurturing skills.

That will take some creative thought and vigorous outreach. Old forms that work should not be discarded. New forms that reach out into the larger community should be encouraged. Yet, despite the obvious troubles many religious orders now face, this is not something that seems to have captured the attention or the imagination of the men who run the Church.

"You would think that when a lot of sisters begin leaving, that should be a matter of major concern for the Church," says Roger Finke, an associate professor of sociology at Purdue University. He believes that much of the steady growth of the Catholic Church in America stems directly from the innovative work, resilience and diversity of orders of sisters.

While he acknowledges that the period from the mid-1960s onward presented a more corrosive atmosphere for many organizations, he thinks the decline of Catholic sisters is peculiarly steep. The primary cause, he believes, is a self-inflicted wound brought about by Vatican II, the church council that ended in 1965.

Dr. Finke makes an interesting case. In Spain and Portugal, two nations where the church hierarchy largely ignored and didn't publicize Vatican II, orders of sisters continued to grow. The "cost" of entry into sisterhood—the vows of chastity, poverty and obedience—remained unchanged.

Yet, Dr. Finke argues, the findings of Vatican II cut heavily into the benefits of belonging. It blurred the status of sisters as an elite group—one that had obtained in church tradition for more than a thousand years. And Vatican II provided numerous opportunities for tinkering with the engine that gave sisters their peculiar focus and power: their life in a community of faith, common missions, intergenerational help and strong community recognition and support.

"Vatican II made far more revisions than were desirable for strengthening religious orders," thinks Dr. Finke. He says he understands why some Church leaders might have trouble comprehending why a 1960s council still praised for its "reforms" might be the central problem for sisters. "It's hard for some of them to get enough distance from that time."

Dr. Finke, a Lutheran, and Sister Wittberg have collaborated on a study that says one of the strengths of the Catholic Church in America has been a creative "tension" between religious orders and the church bureaucracy. It helped the Church attract and keep a diverse body of parishioners. The occasional collisions between the various groups, they argue, has been, for the most part, healthy because they provided a source of "internal revivalism" that Protestant churches lacked.

As this book attests, some bishops and cardinals overdid that. They tended to peel away the creative part of this tension by becoming petty overlords. If there were disputes, they had to win them. They were accustomed to treating sisters as their wards or their supplicants. For many sisters, that attitude came with their territory. To be successful, they learned to work around it. Sisters were often the real entrepreneurs of the Church, risking all to create institutions that still serve millions. Like Sister Mary Scullion in inner-city Philadelphia, Sister Mary Roberta in Evansdale, Iowa, and the thousands of sisters who have gone before them, they have been human catalysts who brought communities to life.

On top of that, nuns took the additional risk of working in an organization that lacks the retirement benefits that even the most amoral, tight-fisted corporations give to their loyal employees. To their great credit, America's bishops have recently begun to address this issue, but—at the rate that they raise money in the post–Vatican II atmosphere—they have billions to go before they can ease the poverty they helped create.

Sister Mary J. Oates, a member of the Sisters of Saint Joseph of Boston, has written a book about the odd holes in the Church's modern philanthropy. She notes that in her city, in 1991, 1.8 million Catholics gave about $11 million to support Church charities, about $6 a person. At the same time Boston's Jewish community—only 225,000 souls—donated $23 million to combined Jewish charities, about $102 per person.

While Catholic giving was more generous in earlier days when it was centered at the parish level, big area-wide Catholic charities, she notes, now derive a lot of their income from government funds. That seems to have contributed to the charitable numbness among the flock. She cites a 1993 Gallup poll that has 52 percent of a national sample of Catholics saying that they can be good Catholics without donating time or money to the poor.

So what is it that's missing? Among other things, she suggests it is a woman's voice. She says that in the 1970s, as sisters began closing their own institutions, despite their long experience, sisters were not welcomed into executive positions in Catholic charities, most of which are still held by men. "The long-term cost of excluding women from decision-making roles in the philanthropic sphere is incalculable," she argues.

This turf battle will not be a surprise to readers of this book, but it should also be noted that there have always been priests and bishops, many of them, who have gone to heroic lengths to promote the work and to give free expression to the talents of sisters. There was the doughty Bishop of Providence, Bernard O'Reilly, who coolly made out his will and then faced down an angry, drunken mob of Know Nothings bent on burning down a convent.

There was the Bishop of San Francisco, Joseph Sadoc Alemany, who collaborated with the headstrong, impulsively creative Mother Baptist Russell to tame the streets of San Francisco. When the going got rough for her, as it often did, he was there as a friend.

There was Father James Joubert, the French-American priest who risked his life and reputation to help start the Oblate Sisters of Providence, the first order of African American nuns, in a time of slavery. There was Bishop Michael O'Connor, who came to the rescue of both the Sisters of Mercy and the Oblates.

We certainly haven't run out of heroes. Today there are the bishops and parish priests in the archdiocese of New York who are helping to raise money for a novel experiment: a retirement home that serves five different orders of nuns who taught in parish schools. Such joint retirement homes will probably become an economic necessity in the future, notes Pat Wolf, the head of the Sisters of Mercy province in New York. But they have been slow in coming.

The one in New York started out as a dicey venture because no one knew how strong-willed women who had spent their lives serving in distinctly different religious communities might react to each other.

At first it was thought they might need separate rooms to pray in. Sister Wolf recalls the case of Sister Hilda, ninety, a Mercy nun, and Sister Kostka, ninety-nine, a Sister of the Blessed Sacrament. They eyed each other warily until one day they discovered that they were both rabid fans of the New York Yankees. "They have made a wonderful, wonderful friendship."

As far as I know, there are no plaques or statues commemorating the men of the Church for saintly acts of cooperation with sisters. There ought to be. It is probably expecting too much to think that the nation's longest-lived institutional gender war will throttle down, but some of the Church's role models need to be softened. A church where many religious women now style themselves as militant feminists and where some priests still admire imperious prelates like the late James Francis Cardinal McIntyre of Los Angeles does not seem to have the right stuff for internal communication, let alone for survival as a coherent moral force.

There is some tendency among the men in the Church to think that time alone will heal this wound. The theory seems to be that, by waiting, many of the more reform-minded orders of religious women will soon die off. To be sure, time and a failure to recruit have put sisters in a precarious position. But time does not appear to favor the men of the Church, either. In 1965 there were 994 priests ordained. In 2000 that number had shrunk to 442. Meanwhile the Church they serve grew by 14.3 million souls and 1,599 parishes.

Eighty-three percent of Catholic parishes report they are now short of priests and 2,334 have no resident priest at all. The age of the average parish priest is now fifty-seven; in the next decade, this average priest will near retirement age, considering there are more priests over ninety than there are under thirty. In 1900, when Catholics were poorer but gave more, the average parish size was 1,759. Today its size is 3,086 and these are mainly middle-class souls. But while this church has grown in size and wealth, its per capita charity is poorer.

It seems likely that the seismic jolt of the pedophilia scandal that struck the Church in 2002, along with strong evidence that the experiences of some of the more chronic offenders had been scrupulously ignored or covered up by the hierarchy, will make these statistics worsen in the months and years to come. Alarmists view the Church's future as the episcopal equivalent of a large ship deliberately running itself aground. Even staunch defenders of the hierarchy have had to admit that time does not seem to be favoring the policies or the path of the status quo.

The Church's primary solution to fill the growing vacancies in its rectories has been to import priests from as far away as Nigeria, Vietnam and the Philippines. It has pulled some thirteen thousand laymen out of the pews and made them deacons, which allows them to handle some tasks previously assigned to priests. If the question of priestly celibacy is reconsidered, as it probably should be, another large resource—thousands of married ex-priests—might become available. Finally, in the Midwest the men of the Church have been quietly tinkering with a still more radical remedy: They have been delegating some priestly tasks to American nuns!

Six years ago, after the last priest left Our Lady of Mount Carmel in a suburb of Toledo, Ohio, he was replaced by a "pastoral leader." She is Sister Marilyn Gottemoeller, a Sister of Mercy and the younger sister of Doris Gottemoeller, the former leader of the order. Sister Marilyn is one of nine sisters being used on an experimental basis to run parishes in Ohio. Elsewhere, there are another two hundred sisters doing the same thing. Sister Marilyn lives in the rectory, keeps the books and maintains daily contact with the parish's 210 families. A priest comes once a week to say Mass and hear confessions. He works for her. "Basically I'm the one who is accountable to the bishop," she explains.

Has there been tension with nearby priests? Of course, she shrugs. "Some priests just choose to ignore you. Part of it is they don't know what to do when talking informally with a woman. For those of us in pastoral leadership, in some ways we can be a threat to them."

"When we started," she says, "the big concern was our qualifications. Fortunately, every one of us has a master's degree in theology. I think that concern is gradually lessening." She has learned to ignore the tension. "I feel to get angry about it just doesn't accomplish anything. You just have to feel you can work around it. You can win over somebody better with kindness and gentleness than by pushing an angry agenda."

Her job, she admits, is an interim fix. "I know this is where God wants me to be right now. I also know this is very challenging. This is the first time I've ever lived alone. There have been some good things; you learn how to live with yourself. On the other hand, part of religious life is living in a religious community." She tries to maintain that part by meeting monthly with a network of sisters in the Toledo area. "I value that. I don't see myself living alone all my life."

While much ink has been spilled on the selfishness of the Me Generation and the supposed steeper decline in moral values among Generation X, there are some indicators that tend to point in the opposite direction. The scene in the driveway of St. Cecilia's convent in Nashville, for example, is either an annually occurring miracle or it shows that religious life and religious traditions do appeal to young women in America. The heroic response to the savage terrorist attack on September 11 showed us dramatically that the notion of joining and supporting organizations dedicated to helping others has certainly not been erased from the American spirit.

One question we are left with is which of these indicators do we heed? Another is whether the Church is ready to offer these opportunities to serve to a new generation, or if it will continue to watch its life force die?

There is not enough room in this book, nor am I equipped to deal with the knotty theological questions that are clustered around whether women should be allowed to become priests. Pope John Paul II seems to have gone out of his way to make this subject even more unapproachable. Ordination of women could drastically change the way that religious orders have traditionally operated, perhaps to their detriment. On the other hand, it would be a strong symbol in a church that badly needs to find one to show its women that their efforts are valued and that they have a voice that will be heard and respected in church councils.

There are thousands of women outside religious orders who might also be interested in that sort of message. Polls show increasing numbers of them now live alone in large cities. They are divorced, widowed or just plain leery of long-term relationships with men. Fewer women marry now than at any time in our history. They are frequently highly skilled, devote long hours to their jobs, but still feel lonely, unconnected and unfulfilled.

In short, they live with some of the hardships that nuns have traditionally assumed, but they don't get the traditional benefits, the spiritual strength, the bonding with a larger family. They may also miss the sense of service to others, adventure, influence and creativity that have made long and happy careers for thousands of Catholic sisters.

In a more perfect world, some of these women might become nuns. This may seem a radical thought, but a proper understanding of Church history shows that one of the strengths of the Catholic Church is that it has always had a few radicals around to prod it toward perfection. Some of them have been sisters, but one of the heroes that pushed it into the Civil Rights Movement was a priest, Monsignor John J. Egan, a Chicagoan of legendary courage.

He died recently at the age of eighty-four, but a few days before his death, he summoned up the strength to fire off one more rocket, a "last testament" that says the Church is now facing a similarly fundamental issue of justice. It must be committed to "the broadest possible inclusion of women in positions of leadership," he said, including further discussion of the ordination of women.

Polls show that only a minority of religious women aspire to priesthood, though a larger group probably thinks that the barrier against women is an anachronism that should be removed. Clearly it is not a matter to be decided by numbers or polls. The question it raises is more fundamental: survival. Orders of religious women have been the Church's largest reservoir of managerial talent and beneficial contacts with the outside world. If the Church intends to survive as a healthy community, the men who run it need to clarify the status of sisters and give them the opportunity for roles and responsibilities that use their full range of skills.

Universities, corporations, governments and other churches have applied this theory and prospered. The great paradox of the Catholic Church in America is that it was there before them, establishing itself through the use of the wisdom, the care, the patience and the sheer life force of groups of religious women. Now it is time for the Church to acknowledge that. That seems to be a most difficult step, one that the nimble theologians of Vatican II preferred not to take. They tended to dance around it.

Unless the Church can seize the current national mood in its fullness—

and that means reaching out to *both* young men and young women—its own statistics show that there's not much time left for dancing.

These are not just issues reserved for bishops or nuns, or even just for Catholics to ponder. Catholic sisters have had a long and fruitful relationship with America. If their voice further weakens or becomes silent, that will be a loss for us all.

NOTES

The notes for each chapter generally pertain to quotations taken from written sources, some published and some archival. (Quotations not referenced here are taken from interviews conducted by the author.)

1. SPIRITED WOMEN

1   "They were the Catholic serfs": Jay P. Dolan, *The American Catholic Experience: A History from Colonial Times to the Present* (Garden City, N.Y: Image Books, 1985), 289.

3   "Higher education . . . dangerous to a woman's health": Sister Mary Hermenia Muldrey, *Abounding in Mercy: Mother Austin Carroll* (New Orleans: Habersham, 1988), 336.

5   "No firemen, policemen . . . came to their aid": George C. Stewart Jr., *Marvels of Charity: History of American Sisters and Nuns* (Huntington, Ind.: Our Sunday Visitor, 1994), 80.

5   "Cholera-plagued Union facility in Indianapolis": Ibid., 202.

6   "My God, look at those women": Ibid.

8   Sister Lucy Dosh: Suzy Farren, *A Call to Care: The Women Who Built Catholic Healthcare in America* (Washington, D.C: The Catholic Health Association of the United States, 1996), 11–12.

8   Her sisters put an end to that: Matthew Russell, *The Life of Mother Mary Baptist Russell* (New York: The Apostleship of Prayer, 1901), 56.

8   "If you listen to the superior": Juliana Wadham, *The Case of Cornelia Connelly* (London: Collins, St. James Place, 1956), 234.

8   "I got a smiling, evasive answer": Ibid.

10 "I do know they are praying for me": Sister Austin Carroll, *Leaves: Annals of the Sisters of Mercy*, vol. 4 (New York: P. O'Shea, Publisher, 1895), 58.
10 "Never until you lie on your death bed": Ibid., 401.
10 "I am only afraid you are not wild enough": Ibid., 365.
10 "Have you ever been in Omaha": Kathleen Healy, *Frances Ward: American Founder of the Sisters of Mercy* (New York: Seabury Press, 1973), 307.
11 "I looked at the other two": Charles E. Nolan, *Mother Clare Coady: Her Life, Her Times and Her Sisters* (New Orleans: Academy Enterprises of New Orleans, 1983), 98.
11 "There was no stranger sight": Farren, op. cit., 63.
12 "My boy": Ibid., 66.
13 "We're just like the Army": Ibid., 133.
13 "A source of revival and reform": Roger Finke and Patricia Wittberg, "Organizational Revival from Within: Explaining Revivalism and Reform in the Roman Catholic Church," *Journal for the Scientific Study of Religion*, 2000, 154.

2. "THE WALKIN' NUNS"

21 "They all consisted of mud walls": Cobbett, as quoted in *A New History of Ireland*, vol. 5, *Ireland Under the Union, 1801–70*, edited by W. E. Vaughn (Oxford, England: Clarendon Press, 1989), 110.
22 29 percent of Catholics could read or write: Ibid., 91.
22 "Contrivance for the impoverishment": Burke, as quoted in Maire and Conor Cruise O'Brien, *A Concise History of Ireland* (New York: Beekman House, 1972), 78.
22 "Unbecoming to his character and position": Sister Austin Carroll, *Leaves: Annals of the Sisters of Mercy*, vol. 1 (New York: H. J. Hewitt, printer, 1881), 17.
23 "The celtic fire of her character": Ibid., 104.
23 "Often after an entire day spent without food": Recollection of Sister Clare Moore, a contemporary of McAuley's, as quoted in Mary C. Sullivan, *Catherine McAuley and the Tradition of Mercy* (Notre Dame, Ind.: University of Notre Dame Press, 1995), 100.
24 "With the perversity of madness": Ibid.
25 "Well I know what you would do": Ibid., 147.
25 She lived in what is usually called good style: Sister M. Bertrand Degnan, *Mercy Unto Thousands: Life of Mother Mary Catherine McAuley, Foundress of the Sisters of Mercy* (Westminster, Md.: The Newman Press, 1957), 46.
25 "If you would have a public institution be of service": Sullivan, op. cit., 150.
26 "Imbibed certain Protestant prejudices": Sister Clare Moore, as quoted by Sullivan, op. cit., 102.
26 "She . . . told us that she never intended": Ibid.
26 "Place no trust . . . in any man living": Ibid., 102.
26 "The scoundrels of society": W. E. Vaughan, op. cit., 198.
27 "She was his favorite": Carroll, op. cit., vol. 1, 202.
27 "Balls, musical concerts and theater": Kathleen Healy, *Frances Warde: American Founder of the Sisters of Mercy* (New York: Seabury Press, 1973), 19.
27 "Tall, well proportioned with a dignity": Ibid.
28 "Really, Miss McAuley": Carroll, op. cit., vol. 1, 31.
28 "She often said it was so hard": Degnan, op. cit., 114.
29 "Without the cross, the real progress": Carroll, op. cit., vol. 1, 186.
29 "Scarcely left the hospital": Sullivan, op. cit., 178.

29   "Johnny . . . get up and go near": Carroll, op. cit., vol. 1, 138.

29   "Oh Gran! Look at the tall wan": Ibid.

30   "Tim! Take yer curly head out of the light": Ibid.

30   "I seen 'em sittin' down on the settee": Ibid.

30   "Look at the fairest portion of creation": Ibid, 385.

30   "As a test of my humility, I have": Ibid.

30   "Sugar of the very blackest," "virulent scurvy": Clare Moore, as quoted by Sullivan, op. cit., 206–70.

32   "You've 15 hours from 6 to 9": Sullivan, op. cit., 249.

32   "Poorest and cheapest mode of travelling": Ibid., 114–15.

32   "We will soon have a valuable laundry": *The Correspondence of Catherine McAuley, 1827–1841,* edited by Sister M. Angelea Bolster (Dioceses of Cork and Ross, Ireland: Congregation of the Sister of Mercy, 1989), 56.

32   "Sister of Divine Providence": Sullivan, op. cit., 115.

33   "Ipso facto unsexed herself": The quote is taken from a display at the House of Mercy on Baggot Street. It is undated.

33   "Formed themselves into a body-guard": Carroll, op. cit., vol. 1, 107.

34   "As unweariedly to the service of God": Ibid., 268.

34   "We all loved her very dearly": Ibid., 292.

34   "What shall I do if": Ibid., 189.

34   "How many new beds": Ibid., 423.

3. FANNY AND HER "SWANS"

37   A bishop first, a Jesuit afterwards: Sister M. Benigna Doherty, *The First Hundred Years of the Manchester Sisters of Mercy, 1858–1958* (privately published, June 1968), 126.

37   "Now please write again": Kathleen Healy, *Frances Warde: American Founder of the Sisters of Mercy* (New York: Seabury Press, 1973), 204.

38   "The writer never knew": Sister Austin Carroll, *Leaves: Annals of the Sisters of Mercy,* vol. 4 (New York: P. O'Shea, Publisher, 1895), 238.

38   "She probably could not bound": Mother Juliana Purcell, as quoted in Carroll, *Leaves,* vol. 4, 282.

39   "Pittsburgh is like Birmingham in England": Dickens, as quoted in Stefan Lorant, *Pittsburgh: The Story of an American City* (Lenox, Mass.: Authors Edition, 1964), 89.

39   "All of Mother Frances' geese are swans": Healy, op. cit., 110.

39   "And with fear that they would add.": Sister M. Jerome McHale, *On the Wing: The Story of the Pittsburgh Sisters of Mercy, 1843–1968* (New York: Seabury Press, 1980), 31.

39   "Cleanliness was almost unknown": Carroll, op. cit., vol. 4, 85.

39   "Expressed a desire to become Catholics": Healy, op. cit., 165.

40   "Oh! You are the Bishop's Sisters": Sister M. Hieronyme McCaffrey, "Mother Frances Warde—The American Foundress—and the Early Days of the Pittsburgh Sisters of Mercy": *Mercy* magazine (May/June 1967)

40   "She always insisted that any teacher worthy": "A Few Leaves from the Book of My Remembrance," an unpublished manuscript by Sister Paul Xavier, a grandniece of Mother Frances Warde, discovered in 1939.

41   "By a rich lace veil that swept": Archives of the Institute of the Sisters of Mercy of the Americas, Silver Spring, Md.

42   "It looked quite smart in the evening": Carroll, op. cit., vol. 4, 232.

42   "Sieve in summer and a shell in winter": Ibid., 233.
43   "The poor mother, who at all times": Ibid., 235.
43   "Mysterious and terrifying": McHale, op. cit., 52.
43   "Oh! Sir . . . the next place we come to": Carroll, op. cit., vol. 4, 238.
44   "Superstition and priestcraft": Ibid.
44   "When the Sisters saw how ill": McHale, op. cit., 54.
45   "Overriding faith . . . in work": Lorant, op. cit., 102.
46   "It is estimated that a million Irish": Maire and Conor Cruise O'Brien, *A Concise History of Ireland* (New York: Beckman House, 1972), 103–104.
46   "Fever and dysentery cases came on board": Edward Laxton, *The Famine Ships: The Irish Exodus to America* (New York: Henry Holt and Co., 1997), 45.
47   "Killed all bigotry against the nursing Sisters": Healy, op. cit., 190.
47   "Joe Barker, a street preacher, was arrested": Lorant, op. cit., 120.
47   "Completely shattered": Carroll, op. cit., vol. 4, 123.

4. MOTHER EXODUS

48   The bishop of Cincinnati had his own: Mary Ellen Evans, *The Spirit Is Mercy: The Sisters of Mercy in the Archdiocese of Cincinnati, 1858–1958* (Westminster, Md.: Newman Press, 1959), 53.
49   By 1852 sisters had created 133 schools: George C. Stewart Jr., *Marvels of Charity: History of American Sisters and Nuns* (Huntington, Ind.: Our Sunday Visitor, 1994), 112.
49   "Hands up gentlemen!. . . . Oh! Well then, take two chairs, sir": Sister Austin Carroll, *Leaves: Annals of the Sisters of Mercy,* vol. 4 (New York: P. O'Shea, Publisher, 1895), 262–64.
49   Riots in Cincinnati, Louisville, Albany and Philadelphia: Stewart, op. cit., 94.
50   "Awful Disclosures of Maria Monk": as described in Stewart, op. cit., 91.
50   "Rome's Traffic in Nuns": Ernest Phillips, Protestant Truth Society, undated. London, England
50   "They belong to the type which dreams dreams and sees visions": Ibid., 5.
50   She had not been "docile" enough: Kathleen Healy, *Frances Warde: American Founder of the Sisters of Mercy* (New York: Seabury Press, 1973), 216.
51   "I did not know Mother Frances when I first saw her": Ibid., 229.
51   "One bright midnight when the glass of every window was completely shattered": Sister Mary Hermenia Muldrey, *Abounding in Mercy: Mother Austin Carroll* (New Orleans: Habersham, 1988), 32.
52   "However unpleasant it may be": Healy, op. cit., 242.
52   "Unlock your prison and free the beautiful Yankee girl": Ibid.
52   "If I was the chief magistrate of the city": Carroll, op. cit., vol. 4, 400.
53   "The sisters shall not leave the house": Ibid., 401.
53   "Let me tell you there are": Ibid.
53   "The first shot fired at this house will go through my body": Ibid.
53   "Help scatter a few prayers": Ibid.
53   "And your homes will be fired": Ibid.
54   Cut through the supports: Ibid., 177.
54   "No woman wearing religious garb": Doherty, op. cit., 2.
54   "You see Sisters, it is a big task": Ibid., 3.
54   "Perhaps we need to remind him": Ibid., 4.
54   "Persecution, burning, stoning to death": Ibid., 5.
55   "It seems to be a college": Ibid., 8.

55   "Keep the wolf away from the door": Ibid., 10.
55   "The black represents the life of poverty": Ibid., 16.
56   "Anomalies . . . But at any rate, they are friendly": Ibid., 16.
56   "Differences in religion will not be regarded": Ibid., 27.
56   "A tremendous help in breaking down bigotry": Ibid., 24.
57   "Conversation was light": Sister M. Henrietta Connelly, *Mother M. Patricia Joseph Waldron, Founder of the Philadelphia Sisters of Mercy* (Devon, Penn.: Cooke Publishing Co., 1985), 25–26.
57   "She . . . had no right to exercise any authority": Healy, op. cit., 288–89.
57   "More than any other religious leader": Ibid., 435 and 518.

5. "THE NORTH LADIES"

59   By the time the shooting stopped: The casualty figures are taken from Shelby Foote, *The Civil War: A Narrative*, vol. 3 (New York: Random House, 1974), 1040.
59   These were no widows: The account of arrival at Hammond General Hospital comes from George Barton, *Angels of the Battlefield: A History of the Labors of the Catholic Sisterhoods in the Late Civil War* (Philadelphia, Penn.: Catholic Art Publishing, 1898), 223–29.
59   "I am the daughter of an Irish giant": A more detailed account of the events of the hospital can be found in Helen M. Sweeney, *The Golden Milestone, 1846–1896: Fifty Years of Loving Labor Among the Poor and Suffering by the Sisters of Mercy of New York City* (New York: Benziger Brothers, 1896), 88.
60   "Who is doing that?": Barton, op. cit., 229.
61   "The consolation of the Bible": Quentin Maxwell, *Lincoln's Fifth Wheel: The Political History of the United States Sanitary Commission* (New York: Longmans, Green & Co., 1956), 68.
61   "What Protestant nurses could compare": Ibid.
61   "The prevailing opinion [was] that fulltime service": H. H. Cunningham, *Doctors in Gray: The Confederate Medical Service* (Baton Rouge, La.: Louisiana State University Press, 1958), 73.
61   "Who are they?": Sr. Mary Denis Maher, *To Bind Up the Wounds: Catholic Sister Nurses in the Civil War* (New York: Greenwood Press, 1989), 13.
61   Of the 3,200 female nurses: George C. Stewart Jr., *Marvels of Charity: History of American Sisters and Nuns* (Huntington, Ind.: Our Sunday Visitor, 1994), 190.
63   "O well it is their mothers": Whitman as quoted in Harold Elk Straubing, *In Hospital and Camp: The Civil War Through the Eyes of Its Doctors and Nurses* (Harrisburg, Penn.: Stackpole Books, 1993), 156.
63   "Hard, wearing life; those who had lasted": Maxwell, op. cit., 67.
63   "Floors, bedding and men needed 'scraping'": Ibid., 53.
63   A doctor's wife stepped: An account taken from the "Civil War Narrative" of the Congregation of the Sisters of the Holy Cross, found in Maher, op. cit., 88.
64   "The next scrubee was a nice looking lad": Straubing, 115.
64   "Of all the forms of charity": Kathleen Healy, *Sisters of Mercy* (New York: Seabury Press, 1973), 146.
65   "After the heavy battles we would not retire": "Annals of the Civil War," from the archives of the Daughters of Charity, quoted by Maher, op. cit., 88.
65   "I continued to say my office": Barton, op. cit., 225.
65   "They sat on their trunks": Maxwell, op. cit., 152.
66   "Leaving the Sisters to continue": Mary Ellen Evans, *The Spirit Is Mercy: The Sis-*

ters of Mercy in the Archdiocese of Cincinnati, 1858–1958 (Westminster, Md.: Newman Press, 1959), 91.

66   "That they got their daily dose of iron": Robert E. Denney, *Civil War Medicine: Care and Comfort of the Wounded* (New York: Sterling Publishing Co., 1994), 116.

66   "A flood of nearly 400 sick confederates": Ibid., 152.

67   "We take the liberty to remark": Stewart, op. cit., 205.

67   "Since you weak women display such courage": Maher, op. cit., 101.

68   A red flag with a board: The reminiscences of Sister Matilda are found in Virginia Walcott Beauchamp, "The Sisters and the Soldiers," *Maryland Historical Magazine,* Summer 1986, 130.

69   "Descending with ever-increasing swiftness": An unnamed eyewitness quoted by Foote, op. cit., vol. 2, 411.

69   "Knocking him flat on the sidewalk": Sister Austin Carroll, *Leaves: Annals of the Sisters of Mercy,* vol. 4 (New York: P. O'Shea, Publisher, 1895), 351.

69   "We who had never been rebels were reconstructed": Ibid.

70   One evening a gaunt figure: Sister Mary Paulinus, *Angels of Mercy: An Eyewitness Account of Civil War and Yellow Fever by a Sister of Mercy* (Baltimore: Cathedral Foundation Press, 1998), 21.

6. TALE OF TWO CITIES

73   " 'Saint Rita—that's a stuck up saint!": Harnett T. Kane, *Queen New Orleans: City by the River* (New York: William Morrow & Co., 1949), 310.

73   "A careless air of grace": Harold Sinclair, *The Port of New Orleans* (Garden City, N.Y.: Doubleday, Doran & Co., 1942), 289.

73   The "toughest two blocks in America": Ibid., 208.

74   The "Firemen's Charitable Association" was: Ibid., 281.

74   She found the visits to the jail depressing . . . "gentlemanly inmate" . . . "with extraordinary barbarity" . . . "among these victims of frenzy or hallucination": Sister Austin Carroll, *Leaves: Annals of the Sisters of Mercy,* vol. 4 (New York: P. O'Shea, Publisher, 1895), 386–87.

75   "It is simply the duty": Sister Mary Hermenia Muldrey, *Abounding in Mercy: Mother Austin Carroll* (New Orleans: Habersham, 1988), 146–47.

75   "Doctors were ordering cold treatment": Kane, op. cit., 206.

76   "Wherever this awful pestilence spreads a panic follows . . . a week later, the health officers have fumigated the premises": Carroll, op. cit., vol. 4, 469.

76   "This was in the interest of science": Ibid., 468.

76   "Not a bell rang,": Muldrey, op. cit., 178.

77   "That Sisters of Mercy should serve": Ibid., 179.

78   "It would take a volume to describe": Ibid., 238.

78   "We hope you will have twenty five more regular editions": Carroll, op. cit., vol. 4, 476.

79   "How those who died fared after death" . . . I am going to see a ghost: Ibid., 298.

79   On just one day in 1857: Donald L. Miller, *City of the Century: The Epic of Chicago and the Making of America* (New York: Simon & Schuster, 1996), 135.

80   "Both sides armed with butchers knives": Ibid., 442.

80   "Now this frequently happens": *Reminiscences of Seventy Years: Sisters of Mercy, St. Xavier's Chicago* (Chicago: Fred J. Ringley Co., 1916), 119.

80   Had demanded the deeds to the property: Kathleen Healy, *Frances Warde: American Founder of the Sisters of Mercy* (New York: Seabury Press, 1973), 204.

81 Get to the fire "before it gets": Miller, op. cit., 145.
81 Downtown Chicago disappeared in about five minutes: Ibid., 149.
81 "The Blessed Mother of Mercy will not let this": Carroll, op. cit., vol. 4, 305.
81 "A fiery pall was extending": Ibid., 303.
81 "Outrageous prices": Miller, op. cit., 150.
82 "Every available spot from cellar to attic": Carroll, op. cit., vol. 4, 307.
82 "Providentially, though a physician, he mistook": Ibid., 316.

7. MOTHER AND THE MAGDALENS

83 "It was famous for three things": Charles Lockwood, "Suddenly San Francisco: The Early Years of an Instant City," *San Francisco Examiner*, 1978, 24.
83 Between 1849 and 1856: Sister Matthew Russell, *The Life of Mother Mary Baptist Russell* (New York: Apostleship of Prayer, 1901), 47.
85 "Our Protestant and Republican country": Ibid., 154.
85 "Did not keep the Sabbath": Sister Mary Aurelia McArdle, *California's Pioneer Sister of Mercy: Mother Mary Baptist Russell* (Fresno, Calif.: Academy Library Guild, 1954), 34.
85 "The most detestable calumny": Ibid., 35.
85 "The nurses were generally low men devoid": Ibid., 39.
85 "The Sisters of Mercy, rightly named": Russell, op. cit., 155.
85 "Had earned the community's allegiance": Doris Muscatine, *Old San Francisco: The Biography of a City* (New York: G. P. Putnam's Sons, 1975), 242.
86 "Made St. Mary's the city's finest": Ibid.
86 "The government counted more": Ibid., 205.
86 "They showed up Sunday mornings outside grace": Lockwood, op. cit., 93.
86 As many as eighty customers before dawn: Ibid., 95–96.
86 A three-story tenement called the Nymphia: Muscatine, op. cit., 208.
86 "Most died young and few ever escaped": Curt Gentry, *The Madams of San Francisco: An Irreverent History of the City by the Golden Gate* (Garden City, N.Y.: Doubleday & Co., 1964), 58.
87 "Who had become completely disgusted": McArdle, op. cit., 90–91.
87 "Are you an inmate here?": Sister Austin Carroll, *Leaves: Annals of the Sisters of Mercy*, vol. 4 (New York: P. O'Shea, Publisher, 1895), 14.
88 "Legend has it": Suzy Farren, *A Call to Care: The Women Who Built Catholic Healthcare in America* (Washington, D.C.: The Catholic Health Association of the United States, 1996), 147.
88 "The eyes of the greater number": McArdle, op. cit., 110.
89 "I would look at her working": Ibid., 154.
89 "Exhibiting a most self-sacrificing and patriotic spirit": Ibid., 157.
89 "The best-known charitable worker": Ibid., 159.
90 "No death in recent years": Ibid.
90 "Life of self-denial and good works": Ibid., 161.

8. WILD IN THE WEST

92 "Is that you, my dear?": Sister M. Benigna Doherty, *The First Hundred Years of the Manchester Sisters of Mercy, 1856–1958* (Published privately, June 1968), 71, Archives of the Institute of the Sisters of Mercy of the Americas, Silver Spring, Md.

93 "Than any other religious leader of the western world": Kathleen Healy, *Frances Warde: American Founder of the Sisters of Mercy* (New York: Seabury Press, 1973), 518.

93 "Are accomplished in every branch of science": As quoted in Kathleen O'Brien, *Journeys: A Pre-Amalgamation History of the Sisters of Mercy Omaha Province* (Published privately, 1987), 75, Archives of the Institute of the Sisters of Mercy of the Americas, Silver Spring, Md.

94 "Cold ridicule and sarcasm": Ibid., 149.

94 "She enjoyed leadership": Ibid., 164.

95 Turned the bishop's hair gray: Ibid., 480.

95 "They are no longer Sisters, they are renegades": Ibid., 487.

95 "Came back like Queen Victoria": Ibid., 490.

97 "He was badly injured": Ibid., 482–83.

97 "The founder par excellence": Ibid., 270.

98 "One could be a teacher during the day": Ibid., 357.

99 "You must not go on this far away mission": Sister Blandina Segale, *At the End of the Santa Fe Trail* (Milwaukee, Wis.: Bruce Publishing Co., 1948), 13.

99 "I made an Act of Contrition": Ibid., 27.

99 "As would put my heart in range": Ibid.

100 "Quaker-like, I reckon?": Ibid., 28.

101 "Each got the drop on the other": Ibid., 68.

102 "I do not speak on religious subjects": Ibid., 69.

102 "Billy has steel-blue eyes": Ibid., 72.

102 "I wish I could place a chair for you": Ibid., 208.

103 "I doubt not the men think I'm either a saint or a witch": Ibid., 113.

103 She was caught shoplifting: O'Brien, op. cit., 590.

103 "It was drier and had even more days of sunshine than Los Angeles": Sister Mary Annrene Brau, *Mercy in the Heartland: Sisters of Mercy in Kansas, 1886–1986* (Kansas City: published privately, 1986), 29.

105 "To teach and meet emergencies as I saw them": Segale, op. cit., 261.

105 "I looked steadily at the chairman and replied": Ibid., 282.

9. CUI BONO?

108 "Refused to take a cent of money": Grace H. Sherwood, *The Oblates' Hundred and One Years* (New York: MacMillan Co, 1951), 140–41.

108 An "eminently Christian" way: Lucia Betz, "Schisms Within the Church: Catholic Attitudes Toward Blacks Before and After the Civil War," *Freeing the Spirit,* Fall 1979, 24.

109 "Would be more assured and promise": Father Joubert, *A Translation of the Original Diary of the Oblate Sisters of Providence, 1827–1842* (Baltimore: Published privately), 13.

109 "The finger of God is in this thing": Martha M. Lannon, *Response to Love: The Story of Mother Mary Elizabeth Lange, OSP* (Washington, D.C: Josephine Pastoral Center, 1992), 10.

110 "The night passed very tranquilly": Joubert, op. cit., 16.

111 *"Cui bono?"*: Sherwood, op. cit., 115.

112 The farmer's wife saw this strange apparition: Ibid., 195.

113 Catholic soldiers . . . would "turn away in disgust": Betz, op. cit., 25.

113   "The sisters wanted her to have a gold crown": Sherwood, op. cit., 173.

113   "I am French to my soul": Lannon, op. cit., 19.

114   "A missionary order for Indians and colored people": Lou Baldwin, *Saint Katharine Drexel: Apostle to the Oppressed* (Philadelphia, Penn.: Catholic Standard and Times, 2000), 65.

115   "The children are very interesting,": Ibid., 86.

115   "We must look at this decision": Ibid., 88.

116   "Would you allow a nigger": Ibid., 163.

10. SERFS AND TURF

120   "I hope that you will make no opposition": Sister M. Jerome McHale, *On the Wing: The Story of the Pittsburgh Sisters of Mercy, 1843–1968* (New York: Seabury Press, 1980), 136.

120   "Some in tears; all sat silent": Ibid.

121   "Things we never dreamed any bishop had the power to do": Ibid.

121   "The Mercy are beaten": Ibid., 144.

123   "All the softness, slyness and low cunning of the mulatto": *The Paths of Daring Deeds of Hope,* a collection of letters edited by Sister Margaret Gannon (Monroe, Mich: Sisters, Servants of the Immaculate Heart of Mary, 1992), 46.

123   "As long as Sisters & Brothers keep their place": Suzy Farren, *A Call to Care: The Women Who Built Catholic Healthcare in America* (Washington, D.C.: Catholic Health Association of the United States, 1996), 72–73.

124   "There ought to be a sister down there": Helen Clapesattle, *The Doctors Mayo* (Minneapolis, Minn: University of Minnesota Press, 1941), 62.

124   "How would the world know if we did?": Dr. Mayo's recollection of the conversation with Mother Alfred appears in Farren, op. cit., 74.

125   "Carefully Mother Alfred counted the nickles": Ibid., 249.

126   "I shall give her to you as a present": Ibid., 76.

126   "Continually in trouble with the priests and the bishop": Ibid.

126   "Damn nonsense": Kathleen O'Brien, *Journey: A Pre-Amalgamation History of the Sisters of Mercy Omaha Province* (Published privately, 1987), 171.

127   "Women religious abandoned the diocese whenever possible": George C. Stewart Jr., *Marvels of Charity: History of American Sisters and Nuns* (Huntington, Ind.: Our Sunday Visitor, 1994), 258.

127   "Your kind heart will watch over the interests of the community": Mary Ellen Evans, *The Spirit Is Mercy: The Sisters of Mercy in the Archdiocese of Cincinnati, 1858–1958* (Westminster, Md.: Newman Press, 1959), 117.

127   "You become simply a family of pious women": Ibid., 150.

127   "I would just say this, and everyone understands it": O'Brien, op. cit., 466.

127   "Get what you can": Sister Mary Athanasius Sheridan, *And Some Fell on Good Ground: A History of the Sisters of Mercy of California and Arizona* (New York: Carlton Press, 1982), 244.

128   "No, Your Grace, that is impossible": Stewart, op. cit., 278.

129   "Woman with a domineering personality": Ibid., 342.

130   "God is only trying you": Sister Mary Isidore Lennon, *Milestones of Mercy: Story of the Sisters of Mercy in St. Louis* (Milwaukee, Wis.: Catholic Life Publications, Bruce Press, 1956) 17.

131   "THAT'S A CONFOUNDED LIE!": Ibid., 62.

11. LIFE IN GOD'S MANSION

133   "The word went round": Sister Mary Augustine Roth, *Written in His Hands: The Sisters of Mercy of Cedar Rapids, Iowa, 1875–1975* (Cedar Rapids, Iowa: Laurance Press Co., 1976), 43.

133   "Marvel of cleanliness, light and apparatus": Ibid., 130.

134   "We will be content only when we": "Mercy at the Century Point," a brochure from the Mercy Hospital Web site, *www.mercycare.org.*

134   "Begging was not uncommon": Ibid., 160.

135   "The man who owns that fine herd": Ibid., 48.

135   "You should have gone to Fairfax": "Our Foundresses," an undated paper found in the archives of Sacred Heart Convent in Cedar Rapids, p. 6 (the author is not identified).

135   "Every night before you go to bed": Ibid.

135   "A great gloom was settling over everything": Roth, op. cit., 43.

136   "It was wonderful . . . to see the beautiful wood": Ibid.

12. BREAKING MENCKEN'S LAW

146   "I am sick of the whole affair": Alexandra Lee Levin, "When the Old Mercy Hospital Was New," *Maryland Historical Magazine,* December 1964, 332.

147   "One of the finest in the Union": Ibid., 334.

147   "Fell into the hands" of Mr. John M. Travers: "Mercy Hospital," an unpublished manuscript of the early history of Mercy Hospital in Baltimore, by Sister M. Borgia Leonard, 1902.

147   With "green, red and white plumes": Levin, op. cit., 337.

148   "Little sisters in their saintly garb": Ibid.

148   "Political influence is the magic wand": Ibid., 334.

148   "For they did a heavy trade": H. L. Mencken, *Newspaper Days, 1890–1906* (New York: Alfred A. Knopf, 1963), 24.

148   "In those days carbolic acid": Ibid.

148   "Whenever A annoys or injures B": Ibid., 38.

149   "Showing gentle kindness to every patient": Description of Dr. Harry J. Friedenwald, found in Sister Mary Loretto Costello, *Sisters of Mercy of Maryland, 1855–1930* (St. Louis, Mo.: B. Herder Book Co., 1931), 110.

149   "Supplied the need at once": *Mercy Hospital, Golden Jubilee* (Baltimore, Md.: Mercy Hospital, 1924), 13.

150   "It was impossible to keep sheets": The diary of Sister Nolasco McColm was kept from August to December 1898. It was bound with canvas from a field tent of the 3rd Kentucky regiment and found in the Archives of the Sisters of Mercies' national headquarters in Silver Springs, Maryland. The description of the field hospital upon their arrival is on page 47.

151   "We were loath to leave dear old Chickamauga": Ibid., 80.

151   "Everybody was distressed": Ibid., 110.

151   "Uncle Sam sent us home in fine style": Ibid., 125.

151   "And who, then, is Elizabeth?": Ibid., 47.

151   "I was never in Washington before in my life": "Mercy Hospital and Issues Related to Sponsorship," an undated speech given by Sister Mary Thomas, administrator of Baltimore's Mercy Hospital in the 1980s, 9.

153   "Being rather shy in her manners": Mary Regina Werntz, *Our Beloved Union: A History of the Sisters of Mercy of the Union* (Westminster, Md.: Christian Classics, 1989), 2.

153   "As a child she was born to command": Ibid.

153   "Overgrown, ungraded and undisciplined": Ibid., 3.

153   "Stella is a winsome little girl": Ibid.

154   "They employ more than 774,000 people": The source for this data comes from a "Fact Sheet" published by the Catholic Health Association of the United States in Washington.

13. "THERE SHOULD BE UNIFORMITY"

156   "I doubt she heard a word": Mary Regina Werntz, *Our Beloved Union: A History of the Sisters of Mercy of the Union* (Westminster, Md.: Christian Classics, 1989), 14.

157   "Until all the world enrolls in the class of the prudent": Sister Justine Sabourin, *The Amalgamation: A History of the Union of the Religious Sisters of Mercy of the United States of America* (St. Meinrad, Ind.: Abbey Press, 1976), 9.

159   "I felt ten feet high": Werntz, op. cit., 26.

159   "Three days to bottle the whiskey": Ibid., 13.

160   Automobile rides for "health or pleasure": Ibid., 11.

160   "There should be uniformity in the cemetery": Ibid., 20.

160   "In writing to the various houses": Ibid., 14.

162   "It made quite a fire for a few minutes": Ibid., 79.

162   "I suppose the next request": Ibid., 76.

162   "Am I wrong in believing": Ibid., 21.

14. THE LITTLE BUDS

172   "Near every church, when it does not already exist": Harold A. Buetow, *Of Singular Benefit: The Story of U.S. Catholic Education,* (London: Macmillan, 1970), 152.

172   In 1880 there were 2,246 schools: The statistics are taken from Anthony S. Byrk, Valerie E. Lee and Peter B. Holland, *Catholic Schools and the Common Good* (Cambridge, Mass.: Harvard University Press, 1993), 32.

173   Protect children from the "wolves of the world": Terence McLaughlin, Joseph O'Keefe, and Bernadette O'Keefe, *The Contemporary Catholic School: Context, Identity and Diversity* (Washington, D.C.: Palmer Press, 1996), 9.

173   "Breeders of infidelity and hot beds of hell": Mary Augustine Roth, *Written in His Hands: The Sisters of Mercy of Cedar Rapids, Iowa, 1875–1975* (Cedar Rapids, Iowa: Laurance Press Co., 1976), 65.

173   "Guard well your school": Ibid.

174   "I feel sure I sent up a hurried prayer": Sister Dorothea Olga McCants, *Chalk Dust and Pencil Shavings* (Shreveport, La.: Daughters of the Cross, 1982).

175   "Naturally, the counties objected to this": Roth, op. cit., 95.

176   "It is no longer possible for us to stretch a nine-month salary": Ibid., 169.

176   "Do you think there is any possibility": Ibid., 170.

15. THE WAY WE WERE

184   "Paradoxical result that the Catholic schools come": James S. Coleman, Thomas Hoffer and Sally Kilgore, *High School Achievement: Public, Catholic and Private Schools Compared* (New York: Basic Books, 1982), 144.

184   "Catholic school sophomores perform at the highest level": Ibid., 140.

184   The level of teaching skills at Parochial schools was: *Catholic Schools and the Common Good*, Anthony S. Byrk, Valerie E. Lee and Peter B. Holland (Cambridge, Mass.: Harvard University Press, 1993), 309.

185   "Teachers are not just subject-matter specialists": Ibid., 298.

185   "Steadfast resistance to the fads": Diane Ravitch, "Testing Catholic Schools," *Wall Street Journal,* October 1, 1996, A22.

16. THE WAY WE WEREN'T

191   "Silence, stone cold silence": John T. McGreevy, *Parish Boundaries: The Catholic Encounter with Race in the Twentieth-Century Urban North* (Chicago: University of Chicago Press, 1996), 91.

193   "Just did not like black people": *Growing Up African American in Catholic Schools,* edited by Jacqueline Jordan Irvine and Michele Foster (New York: Columbia University Press, 1996), 116.

193   "He had a way of giving a sermon": Ibid., 96.

193   "And let the white people who built": McGreevy, op. cit., 57.

194   "Religion permeated the school environment": Irvine and Foster, op. cit., 102.

194   "Because if any of them failed to learn": Ibid., 104.

194   "I recall pinches for misnaming the parts of speech": Ibid., 120.

194   "Discipline was a means to a greater end": Ibid., 135.

195   "Nothing will be accomplished": Ibid., 53.

195   "Kind lives with kind, Irish with Irish, Poles with Poles, Mexicans with Mexicans, Negroes with Negroes": McGreevy, op. cit., 220.

195   "The Church hasn't got a right": Ibid., 100.

196   "Rows of State Troopers stood": *Midwives of the Future: American Sisters Tell Their Story,* edited by Ann Patrick Ware (Kansas City, Mo.: Leaven Press, 1985), 132–33.

196   "We are the Church!": Ibid., 150.

196   "And that's for you, nun": Ibid., 212.

197   "Marching," explained the priest, "is not only": Ibid., 202.

197   "Why are sisters like Negroes?": McGreevy, op. cit., 219.

17. OVER THE TOP

201   "They observed; we audited; none of us spoke": Sister Mary Luke Tobin, *Hope Is an Open Door* (Nashville, Tenn.: Abingdon Press, 1981), 20.

202   "I felt he was under pressure": *Midwives of the Future: American Sisters Tell Their Story,* edited by Ann Patrick Ware (Kansas City, Mo.: Leaven Press, 1985), 191.

202   "I can still recall the great politeness": Ibid., 192.

202   "Surprisingly few American Bishops spoke": Xavier Rynne, *Vatican Council II* (New York: Farrar, Straus and Giroux, 1968), 70.

202   "We should give up the habit": Ibid., 388.

202   "Adequate and prudent experimentation": *The Teachings of the Second Vatican Council: Complete Texts of the Constitutions, Decrees and Declarations* (Westminster, Md.: Newman Press, 1966), 236.

203   "Simple and modest, poor and": Ibid., 245–46.

203   "What we found would make your hair": Marjorie Noterman Beane, Ph.D., *From Framework to Freedom: A History of the Sister Formation Conference* (New York: University Press of America, undated), 57.

203   "Are our sisters intellectual?": Ibid., 24.

204   *The Changing Sister,* edited by Sister M. Charles Borromeo Muckenhirn (Notre Dame, Ind.: Fides Publishers, 1965).

204   A "Pre–Vatican II" attitude: Ann Carey, *Sisters in Crisis: The Tragic Unraveling of Women's Religious Communities* (Huntington, Ind.: Our Sunday Visitor, 1997), 120.

204   "To determine the readiness of sisters": Marie Augusta Neal, *From Nuns to Sisters: An Expanding Vocation* (Mystic, Conn.: Twenty Third Publications, 1990), 5.

204   "I think that sisters who feel called": The questions from the survey and their peculiar similarity to the opinions expressed in *The Changing Sister* are explored in Carey, *Sisters in Crisis,* 113–21. The complete survey can be found in the Collection of the Leadership Conference of Women Religious in the archives of the University of Notre Dame.

208   "Father we can only attempt to assist": Sister Mary Regina Werntz, *Our Beloved Union: A History of the Sisters of Mercy of the Union* (Westminster, Md.: Christian Classics, 1989).

209   "The dissenters advocated pacifism": Maurice Isserman and Michael Kazin, *America Divided: The Civil War of the 1960s* (New York: Oxford University Press, 2000), 11.

209   "Parallel presence . . . apostolically ineffective": Werntz, op. cit., 299.

209   "In the course of analyzing data": Helen Rose Fuchs Ebough, *Becoming an Ex: The Process of Role Exit* (Chicago: University of Chicago Press, 1988), xv.

209   "Miracles can happen": Helen Rose Fuchs Ebough, *Women in the Vanishing Cloister* (New Brunswick, N.J.: Rutgers University Press, 1993), ix.

209   "They took kids out": Ware, op. cit., 299.

210   "Before the sessions ended": Ibid., 165.

210   "When we got to the roof": Ibid., 218–19.

211   "It was like being knocked off a horse": Ibid, 240.

212   "The short skirts, the drinking and smoking": The quotations are taken from letters to Mother Cunningham in the archives of the Sisters of Mercy, Silver Spring, Maryland.

212   "These are the years of change": Carol Garibaldi Rogers, *Poverty, Chastity and Change: Lives of Contemporary American Nuns* (New York: Twayne Publishers, 1996), 67.

212   "Where have all the sisters gone?": Neal, op. cit., 32.

18. COLLISION

214   "The stormiest decade since the Civil War": Maurice Isserman and Michael Kazin, *America Divided: The Civil War of the 1960s* (New York: Oxford University Press, 2000).

215   "Among the most precious adornments": Monsignor Francis J. Weber, *His Emi-*

nence of Los Angeles, James Francis Cardinal McIntyre, vol. II (Mission Hills, Calif.: Saint Francis Historical Society, 1997), 416.

216 "He has been to me all things that": Ibid., 71.

216 "An aging lion": Ibid., ii.

217 "A disciplined outfit": Jeanne Cordova, *Kicking the Habit: A Lesbian Nun Story,* (Hollywood, Calif.: Multiple Dimensions, 1990), 103.

217 "As the youngest members of the community": Ibid., 154.

218 "For weeks I endured": Ibid., 170.

218 "Walked around with a dazed look": Ibid., 204.

219 "Much too good to be true": William R. Coulson, *Groups, Gimmicks and Instant Gurus: An Examination of Encounter Groups and Their Distortions* (New York: Harper & Row, 1972), 104.

219 "This set off a period of sobbing": Ibid., 113.

219 "All in all, the group seemed": An "Interim Report" of the experiment, prepared by the Western Behavioral Sciences Institute, La Jolla, Calif., April 1968, 20.

220 "They felt compromised by the groups": Coulson, *Groups, Gimmicks,* 117.

221 McIntyre "paid scant if any attention": Weber, op. cit., vol. II, 436–37.

222 "The first time in America that nuns": Ibid., 416.

222 "Major breakthrough" . . . "we have many other sisters": Ibid., 423.

222 "Liberal light shining in the ultra-conservative": Ibid., 425.

223 "One of the greatest tragedies": Ibid., 431.

224 "We corrupted a whole raft": *The Latin Mass: Chronicle of a Catholic Reform,* edited by Jeffrey Rubin (Fort Collins, Colo.: Foundation for Catholic Reform, 1994), special edition, 13.

224 "Embodiment of the type of Priest and Bishop": Kevin Starr, "True Grit," *Los Angeles Times,* June 22, 1997, home edition, page 3.

19. BREAKDOWN

229 "A splendid kind of freedom": Mary Griffin, *The Courage to Choose: An American Nun's Story* (Boston and Toronto: Little, Brown, 1975), 98.

230 "I sign my name and it is over": Ibid., 202.

230 "Less able to respond to those needs": David J. Nygren and Miriam D. Ukeritis, *The Future of Religious Orders in the United States* (Westport, Conn.: Praeger, 1993), 238.

231 "They [members] seem to have lost": Ibid., 53.

231 "The experience of alienation of women in the Church": Ibid., 243.

232 "Anyone being elected at that time": Carol Garibaldi Rogers, *Poverty, Chastity and Change: Lives of Contemporary American Nuns* (New York: Twayne Publishers, 1996), 224.

234 "Good, I'm glad": Ibid., 225.

234 "Must respond by providing the possibility": Ibid., 230.

235 "I am very proud and grateful": The quotations from the letters of sisters to Theresa Kane and her letter to the Leadership Conference of Women Religious (LCWR), both in the aftermath of Pope John Paul II's visit, are taken from the archives of the Sisters of Mercy in Silver Spring, Maryland.

20. CLOSING

238   The order estimates that they have schooled: Sister Mary Augustine Roth, *Written in His Hands: The Sisters of Mercy of Cedar Rapids, Iowa, 1875–1975* (Cedar Rapids, Iowa: Laurance Press Co., 1976), 64.

242   "That was the hardest thing I ever did": Sisters of Mercy in Arkansas with Jane Ramos, *A History of the Sisters of Mercy in the Diocese of Little Rock* (Fort Smithy, Ark: St. Edward's Press, 1989). 195.

243   More than a thousand Catholic schools": The statistics are taken from a paper by Dr. John J. Convey, professor of education at Catholic University. The paper may be found in *Catholic Schools and American Cities: Signs of Hope,* edited by Frank Butler (Washington, D.C.: Foundations and Donors Interested in Catholic Activities, 1997), 5.

244   "Contribute less money to their churches": Charles E. Zech, *Why Catholics Don't Give . . . And What Can Be Done About It* (Huntington, Ind.: Our Sunday Visitor, 2000), 11.

244   If modern Catholics currently contributed: Ibid., 13.

245   "Most bishops have little understanding of religious": Ann Carey, *Sisters in Crisis: The Tragic Unraveling of Women's Religious Communities* (Huntington, Ind.: Our Sunday Visitor, 1997), 220.

245   " 'What the sisters did, they did in charity' ": John J. Fialka, "Sisters in Need," *Wall Street Journal,* May 19, 1986, 1.

246   "Across the board, our people were staggered": Ibid.

247   In the wake of the *Wall Street Journal:* SOAR! is located at 1400 Spring Street, Suite 320, Silver Spring, MD, 20910. Since its beginning, it has raised several million dollars and has made emergency grants to nearly every religious order in the United States. It has active chapters in Washington, New York, Los Angeles, San Francisco and Chicago.

248   "The issue cried out for resolution": "How the Diocese of Buffalo Raises $1 Million for the Retirement Fund for Religious: A Case Study and Guide," published by the U.S. Conference on Catholic Bishops in 2000, p. 7.

21. FIGHTING FOR LIFE

250   "Religious life also felt the pain": Sister Marion Duquette, *The Sisters of Mercy of Vermont* (Published privately, 1991), 85.

254   "Everything we have ever done has been a struggle": "Mercy Hospital History," an unpublished manuscript written in 1997 by Barbara Lockman, chapter 12, p. 28.

255   "I don't know how we ever lived through that": Ibid., 48.

255   "Some doctors called [Charlotte-Mecklenburg] Memorial a factory": *Charlotte Observer,* Jan. 12, 1974.

256   "We've done our share of crying": Lockman, op. cit., 26.

256   "Doctor Gerald Zimmerman . . .": Ibid., 30.

22. BECOMING HISTORY

263   At the altar the bishop celebrated high Mass: Sister Mary Loyola Fox, *Return of Love: The Story of the Sisters of Mercy in Tennessee, 1866–1966* (Nashville, Tenn.: Bruce Publishing Co., undated), 168.

263   "Miss Bell Baxter of West Nashville": Ibid., 46–47.

264   "The silence appalled them": Mother Frances Walsh, *The Annals of St. Cecilia Convent, 1860–1881* (Nashville, Tenn.: Published privately, 1969), 60.

264   "Use sulphur in your socks": *The WPA Guide to Tennessee*, Federal Writers' Project of the Work Projects Administration for the State of Tennessee (Knoxville: University of Tennessee Press, 1986), 184.

265   "Preachers mount boxcars and perch:" Ibid., 192.

267   "It is a leveler of men making indistinguishable": "Dominican Sisters of Saint Cecilia Congregation" (Nashville, Tenn.: Published privately, undated), 31.

267   "Where does the strength": Sister Rose Marie Masserano, *The Nashville Dominicans: A History of the Congregation of Saint Cecilia* (Roslyn Heights, N.Y.: Roth Publishing, 1985), 96.

268   "I beg you . . . to protect the balanced life": Ibid., 95.

268   Those years "were not easy ones": Ibid., 99.

268   "I am amazed and aghast": Ibid., 100.

270   "The very meaning of vowed religious life": Ann Carey, *Sisters in Crisis: The Tragic Unraveling of Women's Religious Communities* (Huntington, Ind.: Our Sunday Visitor, 1997), 281.

23. BLASTING OUT OF THE ROUGH

283   "Her standards, I assure you, are higher than those set by the MIAA": *Catholic Review*, April 15, 1999, 17.

24. GOD OF THE SMALL

289   "Still different from the rest of the world": An undated speech by Sister Helen Thomas, Archives of the Mercy Hospital System, Baltimore, Md., 13.

25. YEAST

301   "Failing to respect Catholic teaching": Arthur Jones, "Catholic Hospital Signs Accord with Union," *National Catholic Reporter*, April 20, 2001, 7.

302   About 16 percent of the nation's community hospital beds: Statistics compiled by the Catholic Health Association of the United States, St. Louis, Mo., April 2002.

302   Catholic hospitals are the fastest-growing: Deanna Bellandi, Barbara Kirchheimer and Ann Saphir, "Profitability a Matter of Ownership Status," *Modern Health Care*, published by Crain Communications Inc., Chicago, June 12, 2000, 42.

27. NO TIME FOR DANCING

326   "In a decline phase with many members": Sister Patricia Wittberg, *Creating a Culture for Religious Life: A Sociological Perspective* (New York/Mahway, N.J.: Paulist Press, 1991), 29.

326   "Extremely threatening": Ibid.

326   "More precipitious than any since the French Revolution": Ibid., 33.

327 He sees the decline of groups: To see a synopsis of the the full argument of
     Robert D. Putnam, consult his *Bowling Alone: The Collapse and Revival of Amer-*
     ican Community (New York: Simon & Schuster, 2000), 277.

329 A creative "tension" between religious orders: Roger Finke and Patricia Witt-
     berg, "Organizational Revival from Within: Explaining Revivalism and Reform in
     the Roman Catholic Church," *Journal for the Scientific Study of Religion*, June
     2000, 154.

329 Sister Mary J. Oates, a member: See Mary J. Oates, *The Catholic Philanthropic*
     Tradition in America (Bloomington and Indianapolis: Indiana University Press,
     1995), 167 and 170.

332 Has been to import priests: The statistics on America's growing shortage of
     Catholic priests and what the Church is doing about it are taken from *The Study*
     of the Impact of Fewer Priests on the Pastoral Ministry, Supplementary Document
     "D," which was published by the National Catholic Conference of Bishops in
     June 2000.

333 Fewer women marry now than: Taken from the "National Marriage Project," a
     study by Rutgers University, cited in the *Washington Post,* July 2, 1999, 1.

334 "The broadest possible inclusion of women": "Last Testament of John J. Egan,"
     National Catholic Reporter, June 1, 2001, 7.

INDEX

LaVergne, TN USA
06 August 2010
192329LV00001B/1/P